Mandaley Perkins
retraced her father's footsteps to Singapore, Malaysia and
the United Kingdom after working alongside him for seven
years at Perkins Shipping Pty Ltd. Born in Darwin and
educated in Perth, she completed postgraduate studies at
the Australian Maritime College in Tasmania. She lives with
her husband and two children. Tropic Tide is her first book.

In every age and situation there emerge people of outstanding character with a quality which we refer to as 'charisma' in an endeavour to encompass the force of personality. Bruce was such a one.

On the surface his swashbuckling exuberance, a man with whom one could spend hours in sparkling conversation and drink deep. He emerged as a man of major enterprise and imagination in the long stream of history going back to the Elizabethan age.

Bruce Perkins was one of the truly memorable people that I have encountered in a long life. His biography should prove a fascinating account of a life full of rich, colourful adventure.

He seemed to me the personification of Kipling's 'If'.

'A man of all seasons'.

EXTRACTS FROM THE LETTERS OF SIR EDWARD 'WEARY' DUNLOP

TROPIC TIDE

AN ADVENTURER'S LIFE

MANDALEY PERKINS

BANTAM BOOKS
SYDNEY • AUCKLAND • TORONTO • NEW YORK • LONDON

TROPIC TIDE
A BANTAM BOOK

First published in Australia and New Zealand in 1998 by Bantam

National Library of Australia
Cataloguing-in-Publication Entry

Perkins, Mandaley.
Tropic tide : an adventurer's life.

Includes index.
ISBN 0 7338 0204 4

1. Perkins, Bruce. 2. Adventure and adventurers -
Biography. 3. Explorers - Northern Territory - Arnhem Land
- Biography. I. Title.

920.71

Bantam books are published by

Transworld Publishers (Aust) Pty Limited
15–25 Helles Ave, Moorebank, NSW 2170

Transworld Publishers (NZ) Limited
3 William Pickering Drive, Albany, Auckland

Transworld Publishers (UK) Limited
61–63 Uxbridge Road, Ealing, London W5 5SA

Bantam Doubleday Dell Publishing Group Inc
1540 Broadway, New York, New York 10036

Edited by Belinda Yuille
Cover and text design by April Briscoe
Front cover photograph: 'VB' Perkins (Diana Calder). Back cover photographs, clockwise from top: Barbara, Joss, *Frances Bay*, VB.
Typeset in 13.5/15 pt Perpetua by Midland Typesetters, Maryborough, Victoria
Printed by McPherson's Printing Group, Maryborough, Victoria

10 9 8 7 6 5 4 3 2 1

Contents

To Dad,
with love.

And to Penelope,
because you
knew him
so young.

Acknowledgements

This book could not have been written as it is without the many people who had a favourite 'VB story' to tell. Among the old Singaporeans, thank you especially to VB's old friend Bill Steele, who so enthusiastically recounted his life with VB before the balloon went up and to Robert Edbrooke (Brooker) for his memories and photographs; among the old Malayans, to Patrick and Anita Bolshaw, Bill and Nan Humble, Ken and Marjorie Belton and Helen Wharton for their reminiscences; to Dr John Staargaard for photographs of the trip to Arnhemland with VB and many helpful comments; to Joss and to all the people from Perkins Shipping and from the Frances Bay community in general, past or present, who helped with material to complete the story.

Above everyone thank you to my mother, Barbara, for freely giving me access to her voluminous letters and diaries, for her valuable and experienced editorial advice and, in particular, for never losing faith in my ability as a writer or in the worthiness of the subject matter.

Last but by no means least, thank you to my family; to Paul, for his utmost support and useful suggestions, and to my children, Harriet and Edwina, for sometimes understanding that Mummy is very busy. I hope I have not neglected you.

Glossary

amah	house-servant/maid
atap	palm leaf thatch
baju	shirt/coat
barang	things; thus trade goods
berbaling	bamboo windmill
bunga laut	'flower of the sea', a delicacy
bungkus	a bundle, package
chi-chak	small house lizard like a gecko
chungs	bamboo slats
damar batu	hard resin
dhobi	clothes-washing
dhoti	a kind of sarong worn by Indian men
godown	warehouse
istana	palace
jelutong	a major ingredient in toffees and chewing gum
kampong	a village, settlement
kebun	gardener
kelong	large fish trap made of stakes
kolek	dugout canoe
kongkang	slow loris
lalang	a type of tall, coarse grass
mee	noodles
mem	European woman
merdeka	freedom
myall	an Aborigine living in a traditional tribal way outside European civilisation

naga	a type of loincloth passing between the legs and knotted at the hips, worn by some Australian Aboriginal boys and men on mission stations
padang	field, sports field
parang	large knife or machete
pasar	market
penghulu	headman
rakit	a raft of bamboo, timber or logs
ronggeng	Malay folk dance
sakai	the aboriginal people of Malaya;
samfu	loose trousers and jacket worn by some Chinese women
sarong	cloth worn around body or waist, a wrap
sola topee	pith helmet
songkok	a type of cap, usually of black velvet
stengah	½ measure of whisky—from the Malay sa-tengah (one half)
syce	chauffeur
tid'apa	not to worry, it doesn't matter
tikam tikam	a Malay game of chance
tikar	plaited mat on which to sit or sleep
tong	tub, water container in bathroom
tuan	Sir, respected (European) man
tuan besar	important (European) man
tukang ayer	person who prepares tea/drinks
tutup	button up
ulu	upriver or interior region, jungle country

Preface

'I was born at a very early age.'

He would say it with a perfectly straight face and only the hint of a twinkle in the eye, if someone asked him to tell them about his life. My father often replied to an earnest question with a ridiculous statement. He enjoyed the absurd. If told he was looking well he might state, in explanation, that he had got out of bed before he went anywhere this morning. If someone had a cold he might enquire whether they had been sleeping in a field with the gate open. In all my years of asking him what he wanted for his birthday he only ever came up with one of two things: a stick with a horse's head handle or a wigwam for a goose's bridle. If the person he was talking to was a stranger, it tickled his dry, rather offbeat sense of humour to note their momentary confusion at his reply. If they were perceptive they might notice the sparkle in his very blue eyes or the twitch of his handlebar whiskers, and relax and smile. But if the humour was lost on them they might walk away wondering whether this poor fellow was losing his marbles.

Victor Bruce Perkins, known as Vic only as a child and then variously as Perks, Bruce, or VB (as I will refer to him), was the sort of person whom people would meet, and remember. His charm could be disarming, a useful thing that sanctioned the sometimes unconventional approach he took to life, simply because he seemed able to get away with a lot. VB felt that life should always be exciting and was to be lived to the fullest, and it has been said of him that he packed more into his lifetime than many would have done in two.

Introducing one's own father in print is difficult. Weary Dunlop wrote to me that my father seemed to him to be the personification of Kipling's 'If'. I laughed when I read that, though I knew that the verse was a favourite of VB's and he was fond of quoting from it. It wasn't until some time later that I sought the poem again and, as I read, it dawned on me how much truth there was in what Weary had said. But all the same, daughters tend to know their fathers better than most and I would not be nearly as free with superlatives as those who looked at VB from a greater distance.

Maturing as I did in a generation twice removed from his own, it was sometimes difficult to appreciate my father's point of view. Out of my great affection and respect for him began a quest to discover more about him. I wanted to know what he had seen and lived through to make him what he was, to give him such definite opinions on things about which many of us are so wishy-washy. For example, why was he such a great moral supporter of the armed forces and defence spending? Why didn't he hate the Japanese after what they had done to him as a prisoner of war? Why did he disagree with the fashionable belief that Britain let Australia down in World War II? Why wasn't he bitter about his own war experiences? He always marched on Anzac Day, and marched proudly, his back straight, his head high. Yet his own war experience had been disastrous. The more I learned of his story the more understanding I became. Good times could turn sour all too quickly. And Anzac Day was not glorifying war. No-one knew better than VB that war was not a glorious business.

VB was a kind enough man and, to quote his one-time accountant, 'generous to the point of stupidity to people he doesn't even know' when they came to him in need. I knew he was not a bigot, neither mean nor narrow minded, but there was no denying the fact that he was right wing. He detested the Communist element so prevalent in Australia in the fifties and sixties, particularly on the waterfront, and engaged himself in a private war with certain party members and their ilk. He thoroughly disagreed with their philosophy. Something, somewhere along the line, had got up his nose when it came to lefties.

VB had firm views about the plight of Aboriginal Australians. While the media and many politicians seemed to plug the theory that what was required to help our indigenous population was more handouts, VB believed they had it all wrong. He was concerned about Aboriginal welfare. But he was also concerned for Aboriginal dignity, which he saw decline desperately in his thirty-five years in the north of Australia. What had he seen to be so convinced?

As I looked into his life, answers to some of my many questions began to surface. VB Perkins was fortunate to have been born with an independent spirit and a great exuberance for living. But his strength of character and personal resilience, although to some extent inherited, were also developed through his experiences. The way in which my father viewed the world was vastly influenced by his era.

This book evolved out of a daughter's fascination not only for her father, but also for the circumstances that steered the course of his life. Journeying back through the years I found myself delving into these events, for it seemed important that I should know what went on. Perhaps it wasn't so important. Perhaps it was just that I could not help myself, that from the immutable security of life as I have known it, I found the period all so incredibly interesting. It was there in the history books, but I would never otherwise have bothered to look into it. I suspect I am not alone in this. If that is so, I hope my efforts to set the background have been worthwhile. This book is not only about my father's life. Perhaps more importantly, it is also about his times.

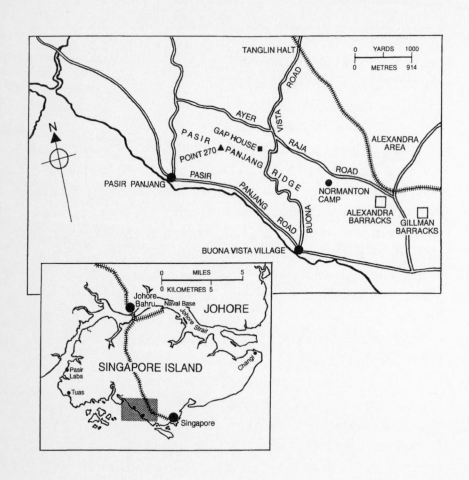

TANGLIN HALT

YARDS 1000
0
METRES 914
0

AYER

VISTA ROAD

PASIR
GAP HOUSE ■
POINT 270 ▲ PANJANG RIDGE
RAJA

ALEXANDRA
AREA

PASIR PANJANG
PASIR
ROAD

NORMANTON
CAMP

PANJANG ROAD
BUONA

ALEXANDRA
BARRACKS

GILLMAN
BARRACKS

N

BUONA VISTA VILLAGE

MILES 5
0
KILOMETRES 5
0

Johore
Bahru
Naval Base

JOHORE

Johore Strait

SINGAPORE ISLAND

Pasir
Laba

Changi

Tuas

Singapore

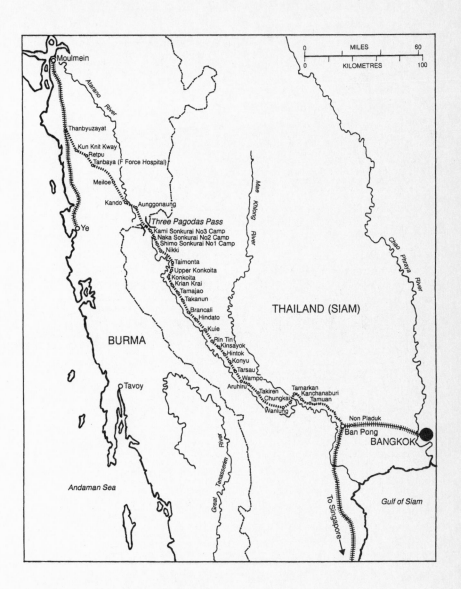

There is a tide in the affairs of men
Which taken at the flood leads on to fortune.
Omitted, all the voyage of their life
Is bound in shallows and in miseries.
On such a full sea are we now afloat,
And we must take the current when it serves,
Or lose our ventures.

WILLIAM SHAKESPEARE
Julius Caesar

ONE

Halcyon Days

W hat was it about ships? No woman had ever moved him in quite the same way, the knot of excitement in the chest, the lump in the throat, the thrill of the engineering triumph. This time he had all the symptoms of awe and wonder and reverence at once. The beautiful lines, the stately grace, the strength and sheer immensity of her. Now she was out of the water he could see her in all her glory. Painted in her grey wartime livery, as breathtaking as ever in all her nakedness, his eyes roamed appreciatively over her. They called her the ultimate ship. He'd seen drawings comparing her to the Eiffel Tower, the Empire State Building. She was the biggest ship in the world, a status symbol for Britain and the Empire.

VB Perkins stood on the deck of the King George VI Dry Dock at Singapore's Seletar Naval Base and gazed up at the new superliner, RMS *Queen Elizabeth*. The dry dock was the only one in the East capable of taking her, yet it was still too small to do the job comfortably and there were mere inches to spare. He'd been aboard to look her over, to take in her sweeping staircases, her state rooms and lounges, her ballrooms and swimming pool. Decreed an ocean-going palace, her fitting out was not even complete before her maiden voyage earlier in that year of 1940, a secret dash like a ghost ship across the Atlantic from the Clyde in Scotland to the

1

safety of New York, dodging Nazi submarines. Seeing the sumptuous, brand-new appointments he could scarcely believe his task now was to rip them out. They would be stripping the cabins and social rooms completely. *Queen Elizabeth* was built to accommodate around two thousand passengers in supreme style and comfort. By the time the conversion to troop carrier was completed in Sydney, she would carry many more thousands for the war effort.[1] But he could not stand and stare. There was much to be done.

Since the war had begun in Europe the days at the Naval Base just kept getting longer and longer. Singapore was a safe haven for ships and now they were working an around-the-clock repair service in the dockyard. As well as liners for conversion, a procession of shipping casualties limped continuously into Singapore. The first-hand reports of the bitter battles the crews had fought had brought the war in Europe a lot closer to VB.

The job on the *Queen Elizabeth* began. At first each piece of furniture was brought up onto the deck by means of the ship's lifts, in order to be carefully offloaded and stored. But this reverence could not last long. With not enough shore power to operate all the lifts at the same time, things were moving too slowly. There was a deadline to meet. Time was crucial and a quicker way of stripping the ship had to be found. Now teams of coolie workers swarmed over the liner, smashing the indulgent appointments into small pieces and poking them through the cabin portholes to drop onto the floor of the dry dock. Seeing this vandalism gave VB an uneasy feeling in the pit of his stomach. The gutting of *Queen Elizabeth*, a ship that represented so much that was solid about Britain, gave him a disturbing feeling that nothing was ever going to be quite the same again; that this war was going to change a lot of things. It was a feeling he was quick to repress. But it was a feeling that, could he have known its truth, would have chilled him to the core.

---

[1] *Her capacity was eventually increased to enable the carriage of a massive fifteen thousand troops.*

VB's love of ships was in his blood. Born in 1913 just on the Cornish side of the Devon–Cornwall border, he grew up in the tiny hamlet of Wilcove. From the upstairs bedroom window of Beach Cottage he could see some of the night-time lights of the Admiralty's great, grey Devonport Dockyard twinkling through the dusk across the Tamar River. His once-pretty face was maturing and his blond boyhood curls had begun to darken. His eyes were distant this summer evening in 1927, as he gazed across the water, for he was considering his future. The Admiralty Dockyard had been there since 1689 and, along with the Royal Navy, had provided careers for generations of his family. It was almost written that he, like his brothers, would find himself a career in the sphere of ships.

There was one thing he knew for certain. He'd known it since he was a lad listening to his grandmother read aloud the week's letters from any of her six sons, all serving overseas with the Royal Navy or Admiralty. He'd sat, fascinated, during the Sunday afternoon rituals, listening wide-eyed to the tales from colonial outposts. Wilcove was fine, but the world was a big place. He too wanted to get off his own dung hill and see something of the world.

His oldest brother, Roy, had joined the Admiralty; his brother Leslie would soon be with the Royal Navy. It seemed that undoubtedly the navy was the way to get around, but somehow the idea did not rest comfortably with him. It was the discipline that worried him. He just couldn't imagine himself shaking down well with it. Leslie, yes. But not he. He was very different. In character he took more after his father, Alfred, who was blessed with an ebullient nature and a real lust for life. His mother, Edith Amelia, the disciplinarian in the family, had always dealt with him using a firm hand. It hadn't seemed fair that while she'd chosen Hoe Grammar for the older boys, he'd been singled out for a different school. St Boniface's College in Plymouth was renowned for strict discipline. Discipline! He'd had enough discipline in his life already. Where had it got him? Kicked literally and repeatedly out of the classroom and all the way down the stairs by the senior master for inattention, but in academic terms not very far. Playing Rugby was his thing; apart from studying Shakespeare, which he enjoyed with a passion, schoolwork didn't interest him and he only ever did enough to scrape by.

VB Perkins had always had a bit of a lack of respect for authority and the masters of St Boniface's had done their utmost to beat it out of him, with limited success. At home his independent streak got him into perhaps more than his share of trouble, but as a child he'd learned by experience the merits of charm as a useful tool in a tight corner—though it was unreliable with his mother. His high-spirited antics had earned him a sort of working relationship with the local policeman, a kindly man who would say to him, 'Shall I deal with this or shall we leave it to your mother?' He had found the policeman's discipline far preferable.

For as long as he could remember VB and his two older brothers had been keeping loose tabs on the comings and goings of His Majesty's Naval Ships. At the bottom of the garden where the lawn turned into sandy mud and the salt water lapped the lawn at high tide, VB's wooden sailing dinghy was tethered. One of his greatest joys was to take the dinghy out for a closer inspection of the battleships and destroyers at anchor outside the dockyards, and to bet the vagaries of the wind on dodging the naval traffic. He'd take note of any new ships that he saw and then later, in the evening, sit down to pore over his father's books and find out what each had done. Every one had a history, for the Royal Navy had not long since fought the last battle of World War I, when all ships, including the Far East Fleet, had been called back in defence of the homeland.

VB had been weaned on tales of swashbuckling mariners, of Francis Drake circumnavigating the world, of the *Mayflower* sailing from Plymouth with the Pilgrim Fathers to settle in America, of smugglers and Cornish pirates preying off the Spanish merchant fleet and taking refuge in the sheltered creeks and covert anchorages of the local coast. He should never have been born in 1913. He was too late.

No, naval discipline was not for him. He would join the Admiralty, and become apprenticed to the Royal Dockyard Engineering School, Chief Constructor's Department. Britain's mighty empire was still intact and her colonies stretched to far-flung corners of the globe. With the Admiralty he would have an opportunity for a colonial posting in a civilian capacity, avoiding the rigours and regulation of the navy.

In a letter written from his ship, HMS *Terror*, during a stay in Singapore in 1934, Leslie Perkins wrote home, 'Out here Dock-yardies have a pinch. They automatically become chargemen and never work at tools—the coolies do that. Their pay is trebled and even a storeman gets more than twice my pay. They all run their own cars and have lovely bungalows with a couple of Chinese servants each, servants being very cheap. The boys ought to vol-unteer for it. It is a fine thing . . .' VB was already on the list.

It was in 1937 that VB, as a gregarious and carefree lad of twenty-four, left his native Cornwall for the East. On the day of his departure from home, when it came time to say goodbye on the busy Plymouth to Southampton rail platform, he barely gave his family a backward glance. As the train slowly pulled away from the station, had he realised the significance of the moment he might have turned just once more to wave again. For it was not to be three years, but nine, before his return. The next time he was to set foot on Cornish soil, he would be a different person. His ebullient nature was to survive relatively intact, but VB would return a man matured by the sort of worldly wisdom that cannot be learned except by experience; experience of the heights and absolute depths of what the world has to offer.

IT WAS THE FIRST TIME he had worn a pair of his new, starched, white Bombay bloomers, purchased at some expense at the colonial outfitters in London. The morning breeze wafted up the wide legs, gently ventilating. VB Perkins was feeling rather the part, standing on the deck of the P&O liner *Chitral*, as she steamed into Singapore through water the colour of milky jade. His face was fresh, almost boyish, not bad-looking under a crop of short sandy hair, and his deep set, clear blue eyes eagerly scanned the horizon. There was no great bay to shelter the harbour yet the water was calm, the outlying islands giving sanctuary to the ships anchored in the roads. This natural amenity, he knew, had been crucial to the development of the great port city, where the docks now lay sprawled along the foreshore. To the east of the port he saw a gentler facade, that of a shore lined with coconut palms, fish traps and a multitude of exotic, intriguing oriental craft.

For VB the days aboard *Chitral* had passed in a pleasant fog of leisurely luncheons and teas, deck sports, outdoor entertainment and relaxing afternoon snoozes. Each day as the sun descended he'd adjourned for a refreshing bathe and changed for cocktails, dinner and dancing, when single men such as he found partners among the frolicking 'fishing fleet ladies' travelling to Singapore in the hope of finding husbands among the city's excess of middle-class, eligible males.

At Keppel Harbour the *Chitral* joined a line of gleaming white passenger ships festooned with flags and alive with pomp and ceremony. The gangway touched the dock and a white-suited brass band launched into a lively welcome. VB joined the throng of disembarking passengers. He stepped onto the wharf and a blast of hot air hit him in the face. With all the activity on the dock, the cries of the hawkers, the chant of the coolies working further along and the razzamatazz of the ship's welcoming committee, he didn't notice the heat.

The wharf was a melee of people and luggage. VB was travelling light. He waved cheerfully to friends made en route and joined Bill and Nena Steele to drive by taxi to their destination, the Admiralty's Naval Base at Seletar. Away from the bustle around the quay and the waterfront, the streets of Singapore City were crowded with bicycles, rickshaws and their skinny wallahs, sedate Fords driven by Malay *syces*, their velvet *songkoks* perched at a jaunty angle on shining black hair, and yellow taxis hooting defiance. Everywhere it seemed the pedestrian traffic spilled out onto the roads: coolies laden with baskets; Chinese with all manner of push-carts; and people of every colour carrying babies, shopping and cane baskets from which peeped chickens and small pigs. Trying to look through every window of the taxi at once, VB was captivated by the new sights and smells. All too quickly they were into the rural area, where Malay *kampongs* dotted the countryside. There was little traffic on the road, save for a few bicycles tottering along with crates on the carriers at the back, and peasants trotting in time with the jig-jigging of the heavy loads on their carrying poles.

Almost due north of Singapore City the Naval Base sat on the opposite coast, facing the balmy Straits of Johore. At the large steel entrance gates of the base a turbaned Sikh stepped out of the guardhouse to check passes. Ahead was a pleasant-looking suburban area where red-roofed bungalows on stilts dotted the hillside. Further in, the concrete road led to another set of security gates and the dockyard proper. Having been dropped at his quarters VB dumped his luggage and unpacked in cursory fashion. He was itching to get on and see the dockyard.

The British government had stepped up construction of the new Naval Base only recently; though much publicised, the base had been very slow to develop. That afternoon on his first tour, VB was impressed by the large infrastructure taking shape: wharves for refuelling and revictualling ships, huge cranes and workshops, underground oil and armament depots, and a powerful Admiralty transmitting station. There were two floating docks, one of which could accommodate a 45,000-ton ship, and twenty-two miles of deep-sea anchorage—enough for the entire British and American navies at once. The Singapore Naval Base was regarded as the hallmark of Britain's naval superiority in the Pacific Ocean; the bastion of the future defence of the Far East.

A line of large, recently completed workshops was to be VB's first place of work. Here he would oversee the setting up of machinery and equipment for the new King George VI Dry Dock. VB stared in awe at the vast, concrete cavern of the not quite completed dry dock, at the huge, vulture-like steel cranes which overlooked it. He liked what he saw.

This was it. This was the place to be.

His brother had been right. The pay was good and conditions in

Singapore most agreeable. There seemed to be some degree of urgency about the construction of the new Naval Base, but the workload was certainly not unreasonable. Settling quickly into his new life, he had few thoughts of home. He had landed on a Singapore which had recovered from the depression of the late 1920s, a Singapore which was, in fact, booming, and had been since about the time Sir Shenton Thomas became governor in 1934. It was a Singapore in which life had never been so pleasant nor so prosperous for its European inhabitants, who lived a leisurely and often gracious existence. Business thrived but the atmosphere was genial and relaxed. There were a few rumblings of war and idle banter about the build-up of defence measures, but most residents remained complacent about any threat to their idyllic existence.

The time between the wars has often been referred to as the golden years of British rule in South East Asia. Among VB's circle the sentiment that the prewar years in Singapore were the happiest in their lives was almost universal. For VB the years were not only happy, they were the conception of a life-long love of the tropics. The allure of this lush and humid island, its dripping jungle foliage forever encroaching upon the outskirts of the city, was to prove the end of his days as a true Cornishman. Within a few weeks of arriving in Singapore he had discovered that whilst most newcomers became wilted and lethargic in the intense, almost liquid heat, he found it positively invigorating. He looked forward to the cracking lightning and black stormclouds which rumbled and hissed and let fly furious squalls almost predictably every afternoon. He learned to love the charge of ozone preceding each storm; the uncharacteristic hustle in the city as the first few drops of rain fell; the great scurrying for shelter and banging of painted wooden shutters; and the frenzied gurgling of the uncovered stormwater drains as they were transformed into raging torrents.

The climate was trying for most Europeans, but almost everyone of even modest means had help (including middle-class non-European households) so that, in general, life was very pleasant indeed. British citizens arriving in Singapore suddenly found themselves one of 'the ruling class', and as such were expected to observe high standards to uphold the reputation of the British, and to set an example. It was regrettable that this perceived superiority went to the heads of some British residents, incidents of which VB was to find abhorrent.

Young newcomers had to learn the ways of the East quickly. VB discovered that in colonial life there were things that were done and things that were not done. There were codes and there were prejudices. Those in business wore starched, white suits; evening wear took the form of black dinner jackets or short, white mess jackets. And there were traditions—curry tiffins on a Sunday, sola topees during the day, boaters worn at a slight angle in the late afternoon and whisky stengahs to revive the spirit. Cash was rarely used in European society—people just signed a 'chit' and received a bill at the end of the month.

From birth VB had always been an intensely social animal. He was happiest when surrounded by people whom he liked, and never tired of such company. In Singapore when the day's work was over and he had bathed and changed, it was his habit to go out and seek companionship. His gregarious nature and good humour led him to make friends quickly and firmly. In a society in which the way you spoke branded you absolutely, VB's accent was passable and there was but a small trace of the West Country lilt, discernible to a perceptive ear in the slightly but pleasantly rolled 'r's. His own background had been modest, but he found he could mingle easily with Singapore society, though he did not actively seek it. He disliked snobbery and tended to judge each person by his or her ability to amuse him. If a person's conversation didn't interest him, he would avoid them no matter who they were. His own social failing, and it was indeed a social failing, was that he was easily bored if the conversation was not to his taste; if, for example, it turned to domestic matters and he could not turn it again, his boredom showed.

Singapore's European community being the sociable turnout that it was suited VB admirably. He discovered the Raffles Hotel, the undisputed social centre of the city, where afternoon tea could be taken in the palm-filled gardens of the elegant, red-roofed, cream building. Or there was the Cricket Club standing majestically up one end of the *padang*, the city's main playing field and parade ground on the harbour's edge. To VB the rules in some clubs restricting membership to whites was one of the disagreeable aspects of life in the colony which he found, in so many other respects, idyllic.

Before long VB developed a fascination for the diversity of cultures in Singapore, many of which were represented among the men who worked for him in the dockyard. He discovered that to understand the eastern cultures you must not only learn the language, but you must think as an Oriental. Nowhere could these cultures be observed in such concentration as in Chinatown, a jumble of slate grey roofs housing half a million people, a myriad narrow streets and a moving sea of Chinese, Javanese, Indians, Arabs and Thais. For VB and his friends, an evening out might be a visit to Chinatown: a rickety seat at a table under which a dubious-looking spittoon invariably reposed, a plate of Peking duck, and a bottle of soft drink or Tiger Beer. For Chinatown was a cacophony of laughter, chatter and gossip, full of life and activity.

In the markets, food stalls crammed up against each other were piled high with the fascinating fruits of the East, heaps of steaming rice, slimy silver piles of fish, dried sea slugs, great basins of dried chicken's feet and flat red-glazed ducks hanging upside down by their legs. Here VB and his cronies from the Naval Base would come for a cheap *al fresco* meal, choosing a fish to be cooked on the spot amid the shouts of hawkers and that unique aroma which only the combination of durian, fish and open drains could possibly produce. The atmosphere was of great activity: frantic fanning of charcoal burners; bicycles, rickshaws, bullock carts and Timor ponies; Chinese women, in black trousers and white *tutup* jackets, clack, clacking along in a curious, short-stepped gait on their wooden sandals; Indians carrying straw baskets on their heads; shrouded Moslem girls and white-robed Arabs flowing their way between the stalls.

Of all the fascinations of 1930s Singapore, poking around the waterfront held most allure for VB. He loved nothing more than simply strolling the wharves and jetties past tangles of junk masts with old square sails loosely furled, sampans packed together and swarming with several generations of the same family, rusted coasters bustling with coolie labourers, stately passenger liners and cold, grey warships. He enjoyed walking the water's edge, where lines of *godowns* stored thousands of bales of rubber for export, past shipments of fragrant spices imported by junk from the islands of the south; or along the quiet beaches, past rickety houses standing out over the water on wooden stilts, a few yachts sitting quietly at anchor among the Malay fish traps, and sailing dinghies lying high and dry on the sand.

'Come on Rastus, out with you. Get her flat, she's got to be flat.' VB strained, leaning as far out as his stomach muscles could bear. It was a blustery day and there was obviously a storm brewing. He planned to finish this race before the fierce squalls knocked the dinghy fleet flat, before they all ended up sitting on their upturned hulls out in the Johore Strait waiting for the winds to quieten. Today he had Bill Steele with him, the quick-witted contract engineer whom he had befriended on the way out to Singapore. (They had taken to calling each other after two black comedians of the time, Rastus and Pussyfoot.) VB preferred to sail alone, but today the extra weight had come in handy on the 'pram', the carvel-built dinghy built for the fleet by Thornycrofts in Singapore. This was the sort of sailing he liked.

At first VB had joined the fashionable Royal Singapore Yacht Club, as racing crew on Magistrate Conrad Oldham's six-metre yacht. There he'd become intimate with the harbour, as courses were set through the busy roads, the sailors learning to dodge determined barges, junks and sampans unfamiliar with or unheeding of the maritime rule that power gives way to sail. Taking orders as crew was not VB's preference however, for he liked to be on the helm and when the chance came to start a sailing club at the Naval Base he'd jumped at it.

Regattas were now the centre of VB's social life. Competition was keen between the Royal Air Force (RAF) and the Changi

Garrison Clubs, which also sailed the same boat, and from the moment he got his own, much of VB's spare time was spent out on the water of the Strait, or else fondly tending his boat onshore. Bill Steele was amazed at the immaculate condition in which VB kept his boat, astonished that he put fourteen coats of varnish on the hull and was forever polishing it. 'That polishing seemed to work wonders, for Pussyfoot came in first in one race after another, winning all kinds of trophies. It was almost uncanny!'

At the day's end, after the boats were lovingly washed, packed up and stacked on the hard, the sailors gathered at the Rumah Merah for a glass of 'o'be joyful', to yarn about ships, shoes, sealing wax and the state of the wind of the day. VB loved the little clubhouse perched out over the water, the place of so many happy times. He was known for his propensity to burst into song, and he had a fine tenor voice. A favourite of his was 'Phil the Fluter's Ball', while beside him a gently spoken, fine-looking fellow sailor and West Countryman, Robert Edbrooke (Brooker), occasionally ground out 'Widdecomb Fair'.

Brooker, VB, Bill and his wife, Nena, on occasions slipped away for a weekend with friends Pip and Bunny Gardiner in their cruising yacht *Shangri-la*, sailing over to the Indonesian islands to the west or along the Malay Peninsula to the north. There they would anchor off an island, put on goggles and dive down to look at the coral and fish swimming indifferently around them, then pull up to a *kelong* and buy five pounds of *bunga laut* and have fried delicacies for breakfast. As Bill Steele wrote later, 'Those were the days . . . when we'd hang on to the shrouds while Pip gave us a bucketful of seawater as our morning douche, the sky was blue above, nary a care in the world. Sometimes Nena would say "Some day we're going to have to pay for this" . . . and I guess we did . . .'

For VB it was always good to see his brother Leslie when he visited from Hong Kong. The bond between them was strong though they were poles apart in nature. Leslie's smiling yet earnest disposition was unlike VB's more exuberant one, and his kind eyes were not tinged with mischief as were his brother's. Leslie was the middle son, and took after their mother. He'd done well at school and later topped the Naval Artificer examinations. He was studious, dedicated and hard working and VB could not help but be very fond of him. As VB's passion was for boats, Leslie's was for horses; point to pointing at Fan Ling in the Leased Territories and riding as an amateur for wealthy Chinese horseowners at the Happy Valley Racecourse. VB found horses unpredictable and uncomfortable, but was happy to indulge his brother's first wish when in Singapore: to inspect the local bloodstock.

As much as anything, the joy of a day at the races for VB was the spectacle of the turnout of, it seemed, the whole of Singapore: *tuan besars* in starched whites and sola topees; ladies in glorious hats clutching tickets in gloved hands; children jostling for a turn on the merry-go-round; *pisang goreng* men selling fried bananas; *tikam-tikam* players; Australian bookies doing a roaring trade; and revellers and hopefuls of all shades and persuasions. The racecourse at Bukit Timah was considered at the time to be the most beautiful in Asia. The winner's prizes were not enormous; the horseowners were men of substance who kept thoroughbreds either for the love of horseflesh or for the love of their wives, whose social status was much boosted in the members' area. VB was probably never going to be a betting man, but his experiences at Bukit Timah races cured him of it forever.

As a young man VB had a weakness for sporty motor cars; in Singapore he had a flaming red Vauxhall convertible, referred to by Bill Steele as 'the Tart-wagon'. In a city in which the competition to find young lady escorts was keen, VB did not do badly. Life was good, bachelorhood suited him and he was in no hurry to find himself a wife. There was no-one he would have called official, but unofficially he occasionally disappeared quietly in his dinghy to a remote beach somewhere, to spend the night alone with one friend in particular; a lady with stunning violet eyes he called 'Mrs Bridget'. The young VB learned in Singapore to appreciate the importance of discretion and the wisdom of the old Chinese adage that, 'If ever a woman shows you a great privilege, you must speak of it to no-one, not even your best friend. If you do, you will find his bicycle leaning against her gate, and she will never respect you again.'

VB began to love Singapore. He never viewed it as a typical colony, feeling that Britain's interest in South East Asia had always been driven by commercial rather than territorial ambitions. Rather he saw it as an accumulation of races drawn together by the lure of trade, opportunity and the promise of work, where people of different cultures could compete as rivals. After all, the island of Singapore had a sparse population of around 150 fishermen and a handful of Chinese when the colony was founded by Sir Stamford Raffles in 1819. Within two years the population was ten thousand; the trading post had flourished.

It was VB's own little brush with the British law that convinced him that the colonial administration of Singapore and Malaya was, on the whole, fair minded. In the years to follow, the story of his appearance in the faded dignity of the Havelock Road Police Court would remain one of his favourites.

The bench was hard and long, the room enormous. It was hot and crammed with people, mostly spectators, who variously chattered and whispered and ate peanuts throughout the whole of the proceedings. Magistrate Conrad Oldham entered and a large Sikh bashed a stave on the ground and yelled '*Diam*', silence. The hearings began. For hour after hour VB sat through the minor offences of the local people: the ladies caught soliciting for business the previous evening, the wayward rickshaw pullers, the reckless tricycle riders and finally a series of more serious traffic offences.

There were only three Europeans in court and their cases were the last to be heard. A young British RAF officer took the stand. He explained the circumstances of his case, and was then fined an amount five times higher than a Malay Singaporean had just been fined for the same offence. He was surprised at the decision, but accepted it and left the court without comment.

The second case was a Dutchman who worked for the Far East Asiatic Company, and Magistrate Oldham gave him the same treatment.

The Dutchman exploded. 'And you call this justice!' he barked. 'Why then is my fine so much more than the Malays received?'

'I take it you are a European, sir,' said the magistrate.

'I am a Hollander!' shouted the Dutchman, and VB watched as he loudly expounded his less than flattering opinion of the British judiciary.

The magistrate replied, 'One must assume that as a Hollander you will have had some sort of education. Singapore is a British colony, not Dutch. Here we expect Europeans to set an example as to standards of behaviour. I must inform you that it is within my power to fine you very much more than I have. Now have you anything further to say?'

Still grumbling, the Dutchman muttered, 'No, Sir.'

VB's turn came and he took the stand. His charge of driving through a red light was read out.

'Ah, Mr Perkins,' said the magistrate, looking over his spectacles at his crew member. 'And what do you have to say?'

VB looked up at Magistrate Oldham sitting behind a large table on a dais four feet above the rest of the court and, with his best choir-boy expression, said, 'Most guilty, Your Honour.'

The early years in Singapore were among VB's happiest. He worked hard but found life so agreeable that he barely gave a thought to home or the end of his posting. Before long his youthful face had grown a fine moustache and taken on the rather military look so fashionable in the colony. That moustache, handsome curls at either end, was there to stay. Over time he learned many of the ways of the East and the language of Singapore, some of which remained with him for the rest of his life. Years later he would still wear a sarong to bed, sign the chit, talk about *makan* for food, put his dirty clothes into the *dhobi*, put the company's chop onto documents, and call 'Boy!' with authority, at least when addressing his son!

As far as VB was concerned, his life was now in the East, and the times in chilly Cornwall began to seem *lama lama dahulu*—a long, long time ago . . .

TWO

Tid'apa

T he prewar years in Singapore were the twilight of the colonial
calm, the closing chapter of British rule in South East Asia.
But for the moment, nobody was aware of it. VB's civilian friends
were largely unperturbed by any talk of a threat from the Japanese.
They'd listen with interest to him talk of the activity at the Naval
Base, but the atmosphere was simply business as usual with all its
trappings: long lunches, extended social afternoons and cocktail
gatherings in the balmy, tropical evenings. Their attitude was more
than complacent; they held a conviction, fostered by the government, that Britain's much publicised 'fortress of Singapore' was
what they said it was—impregnable. The increases in military presence were most reassuring and, if appearances were anything to
go by, the country's defence requirements were very much in hand.
The perceptions of the civilians were correct in at least one respect:
there certainly was a great deal of attention being given to issues
of defence.

Though nobody shouted from the rooftops about it, all was not
well with the defence of the Empire.

So there really was no Far East Fleet. It had been a little hard to
fathom at first. Here they were, working to put the finishing touches
to a Naval Base capable of accommodating the biggest of the world's

battleships, but there were no battleships. Yes, the facilities were being used, but by visitors from other fleets, or from other countries passing through. VB had read of the heavy lobbying going on by Australia and New Zealand to have a fleet stationed in Singapore during peacetime, but it seemed they had to be content with promises that a fleet would be sent immediately to Singapore should Japan go to war.

VB felt he knew the Far East Fleet, the fleet that should have been in Singapore defending the lucrative trade routes upon which so much of the Empire was based. He'd watched the ships cruising up the Tamar as a boy, he'd seen them at Devonport Dockyard. They'd been at home since World War I, when the fleet had been called back to help out. Here in the East, the vacuum created in its wake had been filled by the Japanese and the Americans. It had been then that the first cracks in the foundations of the British Empire had appeared.

VB had vague childhood memories of the effect of World War I on the people around him. He remembered the grave faces huddling around the wireless, his worried grandmother waiting for news of her boys serving overseas, his family's shock at hearing the casualty statistics. His school years had spanned a period when the horrors of World War I were fresh in the memories of the British people, and most believed that lessons had been learned, that such an appalling thing could never happen again. Britain was experiencing a fundamental change in philosophy. No-one wanted to spend money on the military; they were more interested in welfare at home. There was little interest in creating alliances. People had had a gutful of war. The government had heeded the mood of the nation.

When VB arrived in Singapore in 1937, Britain's naval strength was so weak that no detachment could be sent to the East without compromising the defence of the home front. Britain had begun to rearm only in 1933, and by then the deficiencies in her defence had risen to the point where it was unlikely it could be remedied inside a decade. As both Germany and Japan began to look increasingly threatening, the government had few options but to use bluff as a tactic to gain time and dissuade the Japanese from taking advantage of Singapore's vulnerable situation. So began the campaign of widely promoting Singapore as 'impregnable' and the island itself as a 'fortress'.

As tension increased in Europe, Britain hurriedly prepared for war at home. Hitler invaded Poland in September 1939 and Britain declared war on Germany. France, New Zealand and Australia joined the Alliance soon after. World War II had begun sooner than the British government of a decade earlier could ever have imagined.

It was December 1939 and VB sat down to write a brief letter home, 'The war does not bother us at all here socially. We have plenty of food, the price of which has risen slightly . . . and a half pint of beer costs from 1/2 to 1/6 . . . I can honestly say I have never felt better in my life. Sunshine agrees with me.' He was not one to air his concerns but his mind had inevitably turned to how the folks back home would fare. He was only too aware of the close proximity of his home in Cornwall to the great naval dockyards in Devonport, surely a prime target for the German Luftwaffe. Still the war in Europe seemed a very long way away and for the moment he gave little thought to his own predicament. In the genial and gregarious atmosphere of Singapore it was easy to forget the threat of war and to adopt the *tid'apa*, 'not to worry' attitude for which Malay people were so famous.

VB watched from afar as Italy entered the war in June of 1940 and France fell. Britain had relied on the French Navy to maintain control of the Western Mediterranean to keep the sea lanes open. Her whole naval strategy was now altered. She had lost her only European ally and had the additional task of tackling the Italian fleet. Arms and equipment were required in the Middle East, which was now threatened by Italy, and Britain herself needed increased RAF protection from short-range air attack from France. Though nothing was advertised, resources looked very strained.

Still, he listened with enthusiasm to any talk around the bar at the RAF Sailing Club about the fifteen new airstrips just completed in Malaya, all ready to service the aircraft needed for the defence of Malaya and Singapore. However, the reality was that most Allied planes were required elsewhere. There were no modern fighter aircraft in Singapore and it was pretty obvious that few of the pilots around the place had any combat experience. Everybody knew that if Japan occupied the new airfields in northern Malaya she would have a good base from which to begin a southward advance, but the means to defend the land bases in Malaya were simply not available. For this reason nobody liked to talk about it very much.

The dispatch of a fleet strong enough to defend Singapore was already impossible. The likelihood of Britain being able to supply enough army and air reinforcements to Singapore also became increasingly remote. Although Australia, New Zealand and India were asked to help, the military strength mustered was still far from adequate.

The coastal steamer *Valaya* slipped easily through the protected waters of the Malacca Strait. VB was on leave, the sun was low, he had a *stengah* in one hand, a bowl of olives close by, and the last of the afternoon seabreeze was washing over him. He had done this jaunt up the west coast of Malaya with Bill and Nena Steele before, and it was a fine thing. Beside him in a deckchair Lieutenant Colonel Toby Andre of the Malay Regiment relaxed in long whites; even without his uniform he radiated 'army officer'. VB found Andre a charming fellow. 'You must come up to Port Dickson,' Andre said. 'The regiment has a fleet of dinghies and we'd love to have a bit of new blood to sail with. You can stay with Grace and myself.' VB made a note to do just that.

The Malay Regiment's smart headquarters was four and a half miles from the town. The barracks sat on a stretch of laterite ridge overlooking the shimmering Straits of Malacca and from the officers' mess there was a breathtaking view right across to the Indonesian island of Sumatra.

VB was surprised to hear that the regiment had officially come into existence only in 1935. Most of the officers of the Malay Regiment were British, although the regiment was now in the process of expansion and more Malay officers were being trained. The regiment's reputation for strict discipline and superlative standard of drill was well known and, watching the soldiers parade, VB had to agree that it was indeed a spruce turnout. 'The regiment was founded on the principles of discipline tempered with respect for Malay customs and sensibilities and due care for the welfare of the men,' Andre explained. 'Where the Malay soldiers like and respect their superiors, excellent results are being achieved.' VB was no military man but he now knew something of the Malay character, and it sounded good to him. Later at a regimental *ronggeng* the men were equally impressive, resplendent in their walking-out dress. It seemed dancing was second nature to the Malays, but when VB was invited to take to the floor he found he didn't have the free-swinging backside and didn't know the steps, so to an orchestra of gongs, guitars and a fiddle, he broke into a Charleston and the Malays in the audience applauded hugely.

The weekend was the beginning of a solid friendship with Lieutenant Colonel Andre. VB was flattered when Andre told him he was 'good officer material' and suggested he join the Malay Regiment. But the discipline of peacetime army life didn't much appeal to him and besides, he was fully committed to the Admiralty. The offer, however, he did not forget.

VB liked the spirit in the Volunteer Battalions. They existed in every state in Malaya and he saw them as a bit of fun for rubber planters or anyone else who wanted to 'do their bit'; everybody who was anybody and not already enlisted was expected to join. The Volunteers cut across the barriers of race and class and in this respect provided members with a unique forum for socialising outside their own crowd. They were staffed by officers seconded from the British Army and, in general, training was none too rigorous. VB had been along to watch various friends from upcountry don their full kit and march on their local *padang* to wave the flag at the King's Birthday Parade. Besides that they met about once a week or for the occasional weekend, with an annual fortnight's camp. Training sessions were seen as a bit of a lark and few of them ever took their role very seriously. For years they had never envisaged they'd have to deal with anything more alarming than perhaps a picket line or some civil labour disturbance. But as 1940 turned uneasily into 1941, they found their training sessions suddenly becoming more frequent and more intense.

In the same year the trickle of troops arriving in Singapore began to turn into a flood, but as VB couldn't help but notice, they looked very young and very green. As new contingents arrived the population of the Naval Base boomed, providing the sailing club with fresh blood. There was a prevailing attitude in VB's circle that if war was coming then all the more reason to have fun now. But occasionally something would happen to remind them that all was not as well as they would have it.

It was a balmy evening and VB was at the bar of the Rumah Merah after an afternoon race out on the Strait dodging wooden sampans and Catalina flyingboats. A chorus of singing had begun and a fellow from the RAF was bellowing a tuneless 'It's a lovely day tomorrow!', when the sound of a Vickers-Vildebeeste roared overhead. Nicknamed the 'Flying Coffin' and declared obsolete in 1940, the Vildebeeste was nevertheless the only type of torpedo bomber possessed by the RAF in Malaya. The Naval Base searchlight flicked on and scoured the darkness to pick up the obviously stricken aircraft. The singing stopped and outside the sailors watched in silence, horrified, as the ancient aircraft with its old-fashioned cockpit swung wildly one way then another, before going completely out of control and diving, engines roaring, right into the Strait of Johore opposite the Sailing Club. VB joined the united scurry to launch boats to go to the rescue. When they got there they found no survivors, nothing but the wreckage of a very, very old RAF aircraft. It was sobering to think that it hadn't even been shot at.

The notification came impersonally and in writing; that was the way they did things in the Admiralty. VB had already applied for and received an extension to his tour of duty in Singapore; now he couldn't help but stare bleakly at the official missive in his hand.

Why should they post him back to the UK now, and to the Rosyth Dockyard in Scotland of all places? Weren't they keeping up in London with events on this side of the world? They were scraping the bottom of the barrel in India and Australia to get personnel to Singapore—so why on earth send him home now? He didn't want to return to the UK. Goddammit, he was needed right here.

His application to remain in Singapore was refused and he was instructed to take passage to the UK when his replacement arrived. The next news was that the ship carrying his replacement had been torpedoed by a German submarine; he should carry on until he heard further.

In the meantime he watched developments in the region closely. By the end of July 1941 Japan had occupied the whole of South Indochina and now had bases from which she could attack the Philippines, Borneo and Malaya far more effectively. The US froze all Japanese assets, ending all commercial transactions between the two countries. Britain cancelled existing trade treaties with Japan and the Dutch followed suit. Japan was now forced to draw upon her reserve supplies of oil, so essential to her expansionist policies.

As war clouds gathered over Singapore the news arrived that the ship carrying VB's second relief had also been torpedoed. In his mind his fate had been sealed. It was now September 1941 and it seemed highly unlikely that bluff could continue to keep Japan out of the war. The Naval Base was complete but in the last two years he'd seen all the naval vessels from the China and Indian Ocean fleets heading west to the Atlantic and the Mediterranean. The many Japanese spies in Singapore had no doubt seen them go as well. The RAF was in a dismal state and the Japanese must surely take advantage of the fact that Singapore and Malaya were so vulnerable.

VB was convinced he could better serve Britain by remaining in Singapore than by returning home to a reserved occupation in an Admiralty dockyard in Scotland. He went over it again and again in his mind. The defence of Singapore depended upon the mustering of enough manpower and equipment, and he was sure this was not a time for an able-bodied man to be leaving. His conviction to remain in Singapore was passionate; and if staying meant ending his career with the Admiralty, then so be it.

The conversation sparkled and the silver glistened. Nothing much had changed in VB's social life, except that now dinner parties began to vibrate to the sound of far-off explosions of military and naval night exercises. Tonight there was discussion of just how awful it was to see the beautiful pavilions built on pillars over the water around Pasir Panjang blown up to give a clear line of fire to the guns on shore. It was a favourite swimming spot for everyone and VB too had found the thought of it jarring. An earsplitting blast shattered the ambience and the house boy jumped, spilling a drop of red wine on the white damask linen. What the hell were they doing tonight? VB looked up at the boy. '*Ada baik*,' he said, smiling. Don't worry.

He couldn't help but notice that the locals found all this build-up of defence a bit bewildering. To them, war seemed incomprehensible. For the last hundred years the British had been doing all they could to promote peace among the once hostile factions in Malaya, and had led by example. Apart from a small garrison of soldiers based in Singapore there had never been a real military presence in Malaya. There was never a military governor and order was kept by the civil service in the form of a modestly sized police force. How times had suddenly changed.

To the civilians the air-raid drills and practice blackouts had an air of unreality. Pamphlets advised them to construct air-raid shelters, and provided full instructions on how to build the various types. Some heeded the warnings while others scoffed. After all, Singapore was impregnable. Everybody said so.

In Japan tension was building. Japanese diplomatic discussions failed to secure any further supplies of oil and the Japanese Army and Navy pushed for a decision to go to war. The Japanese Prime Minister resigned in mid October 1941 and was replaced by General Hideki Tojo, who had also retained his position as Minister for War. Japan was now in the total control of the military.

Crowds gathered on the northern shores of Singapore island on 2 December 1941 to witness the arrival of the pride of the Royal Navy as she cruised slowly up the Strait of Johore. VB joined the throng on the wharf at the Naval Base, in an atmosphere charged with suppressed excitement. As the mighty 35,000-ton fighting ship appeared and cruised imposingly to her berth, the large contingent of admiring bystanders hummed with enthusiasm about her power and armament, her 35-knot speed and her ten 14-inch guns. This was the HMS *Prince of Wales*, the newest and most powerful battleship in the British fleet.

Prime Minister Churchill, unconvinced of an imminent attack on Malaya, had sent *Prince of Wales* along with the battlecruiser HMS *Repulse* to Singapore as a show of strength. The Admiralty had advised that a larger fleet of older battleships would be preferable but Churchill had disagreed, believing that the political effect of sending such a modern ship would be tremendous. (Fatefully the aircraft carrier earmarked to provide air cover for the ships went aground off Jamaica and had to be docked for repairs. By the time the carrier was recommissioned, it was too late to join them.) Now, as the *Prince of Wales* approached the wharf, VB looked up at the main deck to the white uniforms lining the rails and scanned the faces. He was looking for his Uncle Arthur.

Arthur Squance was a shipwright, 1st Class. Having already served his time he'd been recalled and by January 1941 had joined *Prince of Wales*. He had always been a favourite of VB. Arthur was VB's mother's brother, and was a quiet but physically strong man. He considered loyalty and the performance of one's duty highly important, and had an air of being utterly dependable as well as possessing a great natural dignity, something VB admired. VB was looking forward to showing him the stuff of Singapore.

The arrival of the two warships in Singapore heralded a huge fanfare, and for a few short days her crews were able to relax and enjoy their welcome. VB was keen to see every inch of Britain's latest battleship and there was no-one better than Arthur to give him a full and intimate tour. In return VB swept his uncle into his hectic social whirl such that later Arthur was to report home that he had been 'entertained royally' by his nephew, who had 'good social connections and friends in influential places'.

As a newcomer Arthur Squance could not help but be surprised at the apparent lack of tension on the island. From what he could see people seemed to be going out of their way to enjoy themselves, and Singapore did not appear to be a city on the brink of war. In the city area crowds thronged to the entertainment centres, and packed theatres and cinemas. The dances, films and cabarets seemed to provide an excellent diversion from reality, as did the publicity surrounding the strength and armament of *Prince of Wales* and *Repulse* and the impenetrable defences of Singapore.

THREE

Battleship with No Bottom

The night of 7 December 1941 was clear and still over Singapore. The Naval Base was under blackout orders and the windows in Nena and Bill Steele's bungalow were heavily shrouded. Still the muffled sound of laughter and spirited conversation floated out through the dining-room shutters into the cool night air. The Steeles' smiling Chinese cook, Tan Peck Gee, had a reputation for his *mee hoon* and tonight *Tuan* Perkins, a regular guest, was in for dinner. Commander Ross McLean and his wife, the *mem* they called Spinnaker Maggie, were also there. All were in typically good form with, as VB would say, everybody talking and nobody listening.

Later that night, the hillside bungalows at the Naval Base were quiet and VB slept soundly. Occasionally a frog croaked outside his window or a little *chi-chak* scampered across the wall of his room, chicking comfortingly. Somewhere, way off in the distance, came the low-pitched, purposeful droning of seventeen Japanese bombers on course for Singapore. At 4.15am the sound of explosions ripped through the nearby Sembawang and Seletar Airfields. VB awoke with a start. There was no air-raid warning and for an instant, in his confusion, he wondered if it was some sort of exercise.

Then he realised. 'My God it's started.' After fumbling to get out of his sarong and into his clothes he bolted from his room and made for the nearest air-raid shelter. Running blindly in the dark, he ducked instinctively as the high-angle guns aboard the *Prince of Wales* in dock nearby blasted into the night sky above. Over the top of all this an air-raid warning sounded belatedly.

Singapore city was ablaze with lights and presented the bombers with a perfect target. Unlike the Naval Base the city was not under blackout orders, and the first bombs dropped on a sleeping population unaware it was at war. In the central city area casualties among the Asian population were heavy. Had there been an early air-raid warning many of these people would have had nowhere to go in any case, for there was a dearth of civic air-raid shelters in Singapore and many people had not heeded the advice to prepare their own.

Dawn saw the residents of Singapore wandering around and surveying the damage in dazed fashion, mulling over the fact that they seemed to be at war and yet there had been no declaration of war; there had been no warning and no counterattack by the RAF. VB later heard that three old Buffaloes of the Royal Australian Air Force (RAAF) had been warmed up, but permission to take off was refused at the last minute because the gunners were still 'green'.

Discounting local time zones, Japan attacked Malaya, Pearl Harbour in Hawaii, Singora in Siam and Hong Kong all within a few hours of each other. At Pearl Harbour the surprise air attack was cleverly timed so that there were no American aircraft carriers in port. The US Pacific Fleet, which might otherwise have come to the aid of Singapore, was masterfully disabled.

Later on the day of 8 December 1941, Great Britain and the United States declared war on Japan. Australia and New Zealand, themselves part of the grand scheme of the Japanese to create a new order in Asia, followed.

In Japan the decision to go to war was justified to the people by reason of 'stabilising' the region and saving Asia from the threats of both Western imperialism and Communism. The vision was to make Japan, Korea and Manchukuo the centres of industry, technology and finance. To supply the raw materials for the massive industrial appetites of these countries the Japanese planned to control China, India, South East Asia, Siberia, Australia and New Zealand. These were real and very serious ambitions.

VB would have liked to wish his uncle good luck, but there was no time. On the first day of the war in the Pacific *Prince of Wales*, *Repulse* and four destroyers slipped quietly out of the Naval Base for the east coast of Malaya, where it was believed the Japanese would attempt a landing. There was still no aircraft carrier to accompany them, but Admiral Tom Phillips, sailing aboard *Prince of Wales*, expected shore-based fighter cover would be available. Using the element of surprise he intended to foil the Japanese landing before the enemy had a chance to establish itself. He knew it was a risky move but found the idea of the navy remaining inactive during such a grave emergency unacceptable.

The situation quickly turned ominous. The next day Admiral Phillips received the disturbing news that there would be no fighter cover. The fleet was shadowed by enemy aircraft during the day, and the element of surprise was also gone. The risk of continuing was now unacceptably high and the mission was abandoned. The fleet turned south, and that night set course at high speed for Singapore. At around midnight Phillips detoured to investigate a report of an enemy landing at Kuantan. The report proved to be false and the diversion would cost Britain heavily.

At 10.20am on the morning of 10 December 1941, enemy aircraft were sighted and the crew of *Prince of Wales* were ordered to assume first degree of readiness. As a shipwright, 1st Class, Chief Petty Officer Arthur Squance was in charge of a damage-control party of six. For the next uneasy hour he waited at his battle station below decks in the ship's bow. At 11.13am he heard the guns open fire—a high-level bombing force of nine Japanese aircraft were attacking the fleet in formation. From below decks it was difficult to know what was happening, that the brunt of that first attack was being taken by *Repulse*. *Prince of Wales* was escaping undamaged.

In the skies above there was suddenly nothing for some twenty minutes and all guns were quiet. Then a squadron of nine torpedo bombers appeared over the horizon, and attacked from the port bow. *Prince of Wales* manoeuvred sharply to port. The evasion tactic failed. Stationed in the bow Arthur heard a gut-wrenching explosion echo forward from the stern and felt the huge bulk of the vessel's for'ard lift out of the water a little. The flagship rapidly slowed and began to list gently to port, settling after a few minutes at about thirteen degrees. She had been hit by two torpedoes in the port quarter. They had found their mark: both port propeller shafts were rendered inoperable and the steering gear was severely damaged. The speed of the ship was reduced from twenty-five to fifteen knots, and from that moment *Prince of Wales* was never under real control.

Below decks in the bow there was nothing to be done and Arthur took two of his team aft to the scene of the greatest damage. His responsibility was to try to stop seawater from entering the ship and to maintain the integrity of the hull in general. Today it was a tall order. Bulkheads had to be shored up to stop the flooding through the ship and he quickly organised repair parties to do anything possible. Then he ventured further into the depths of the ship to see what could be done in the engineroom, descending with one other into the inky darkness of the unlit companionways. Moving along by the light of their torches Arthur sensed his colleague from Devonport was close to panic. At the door to the engineroom he left his offsider standing by and plunged inside alone. The room was deserted and the sound of screaming engines and sea water pouring in resounded deafeningly around the bulkheads. The situation was obviously beyond salvation. He had to get out quickly. The *Prince of Wales* lurched suddenly. Clinging to a piece of plumbing he held his breath as the ship listed a little further, then thankfully settled once more. He was now waist-deep in warm water. Struggling, he made his way back up to the door of the engineroom to find that no-one was standing by to let him out. For a few brief moments he imagined his end, entombed in the hot, howling blackness of the bowels of a sinking ship.

The next squadron to attack found an easy target: a disabled battleship unable to manoeuvre and with all guns except one out of action. When the next torpedo found its mark, the quarter deck on *Prince of Wales* was already awash. Meanwhile Arthur Squance had been let out of the engineroom and made his way forward to the cinema flat, an open area above which lay the protection of the ship's main armoured plating. Hundreds of crew-members were already assembled there, many soaking wet and wounded, waiting for instructions. There was little sign of panic.

Overhead enemy aircraft prepared to deliver the final blow. With lethal accuracy a bomb landed on the deck above, killing all those in the vicinity. The force of the blast ripped through an open hatch and Arthur was momentarily knocked unconscious, his hair burnt off, his face scorched. When he regained his senses water was pouring into the cinema flat and he knew there was no hope. *Prince of Wales* would succumb, and earlier rather than later. The captain gave the order to abandon ship. Arthur joined the orderly dash to crawl out of the hatches onto the main deck and found the sea already lapping at the gunnel. He inflated his lifebelt and stepped off Britain's greatest battleship into a thick film of black oil.

Ten minutes passed. Then suddenly *Prince of Wales* heeled, capsized and sank into a seething, swirling, inky sea. The pride of the Royal Navy had been lost on only the third day of the war against Japan. With her was Admiral Tom Phillips, her captain, and 325 of her crew. As he watched, horrified, Arthur tried not to think of those still on board, their bodies now being smashed down flooding companionways or worse, trapped hopelessly in hellish air pockets. Clinging to a piece of wreckage he looked around to see the destroyers cruising through the filthy water and picking up survivors. He could not see the battlecruiser *Repulse*. In the distance what he hoped were the last of the Japanese bombers disappeared over the horizon, having jettisoned their bombs into the sea. Rescue could be some time off and he set his mind to lifting the morale of those around him. Circling overhead were eleven friendly Buffaloes which had arrived too late from Singapore. The pilot of the first aircraft on the scene later reported that 'during that hour I had seen many men in dire danger waving, cheering and joking as if they were holiday makers at Brighton waving at a low-flying aircraft. It shook me, for here was something above human nature'.

It wasn't until rescue came in the form of the destroyer HMS *Express* that Uncle Arthur had confirmed what was almost unthinkable, that *Repulse* too had gone down. In terms of loss of life this was an even greater disaster, for she took with her five hundred and thirteen good men.

In Singapore an impersonal voice announced over the radio that *Prince of Wales* and *Repulse* had been sunk. The city struggled to take in news of the losses. People everywhere were stunned into a disbelieving silence, none more so than VB. Churchill later wrote:

> *In all the war I never received such a direct shock . . . the full horror of the news sank upon me. There were no British or American capital ships in the Indian Ocean or the Pacific except the survivors of Pearl Harbor, who were hastening back to California. Over all this vast expanse of waters Japan was supreme, and we everywhere were weak and naked.* (W.S. Churchill, *The Second World War*, Vol. III, Cassel & Co Ltd, London, 1950, p. 551)

At the Naval Base the remainder of the fleet slipped quietly into port. This time there was no fanfare to greet them, just a crowd of grave-faced figures. Among them was VB. Detailed to assist in the identification and organisation of survivors, he was faced with the pitiful sight of their return. The magnitude of the loss was chilling. Most crew were in a terrible state: some burnt, many half drowned, others still covered in diesel oil. Some walked ashore but many were carried. The injured were laid out in bedraggled lines on the wharf while VB and others recorded names, grouping the men for dispatch to the already hopelessly overcrowded hospital. Those unable to speak he identified using the 'dead meat tickets' they wore around their necks. Some were unrecognisable and one figure had bandages swathed around his head. As VB bent over to peer at the tag he spoke to the man in his unmistakable voice. A muffled 'Is that you, Vic?' told him it was his uncle.

Beneath the *Straits Times* headline 'Britain Loses Two Capital Ships off Malayan Coast' was another, 'We Have Other Battleships', on which it didn't elaborate. Reports of the losses covered only the number of survivors, not the number killed, and also the number of enemy planes shot down. The reports were peppered with spirited talk such as, 'This is not the first time in our long history of glory that we have met with disaster and have surmounted it.' Censors allowed only carefully chosen words and euphemisms to be used by the media. The real situation was known only to a few.

VB was shocked to learn that the Japanese had already made their first landing in northern Malaya. In the early hours of 8 December three transports anchored off the east coast at Kota Bharu and landingcraft overcame treacherous surf, artillery and air attack to get to the shore. The Japanese established themselves quickly on the airfields in southern Siam, and from there attacked and occupied the new airforce bases in northern Malaya. The bases had limited anti-aircraft protection and inadequate warning systems, while the Japanese had a numerical superiority of four to one aircraft. They were now in a position to begin a southward advance down the Malay Peninsula.

Each and every day air raids on the city of Singapore terrified the civilian population and the death toll began to mount horribly. From the Naval Base VB heard the daily attacks on the nearby RAF airfields where the enemy force efficiently targeted individual planes on the ground, losses the RAF could ill afford. It was discomfiting to know from his airforce cronies that the RAF in Malaya possessed only some one hundred and forty serviceable planes, while the men on the spot had asked for five hundred and sixty. The Japanese Air Force had on tap around seven hundred modern aircraft. The Zero fighters were superior to the British Hurricanes at lower altitudes and severely outnumbered them. The news he heard was all bad, and by 10 December the RAF had been reduced to a force of only fifty operating planes. Within a few days the Japanese had achieved both command of the sea and overwhelming air superiority in northern Malaya.

British defence plans depended upon preventing a major landing on the Malay Peninsula and maintaining control of the air until the main fleet arrived. These plans were already in tatters. The Naval Base was almost empty and the brunt of Malaya's defence was now with the army, who were left to fight every inch of the Peninsula almost alone.

For the most part the Europeans in Singapore put on a good show of 'business as usual' and life went on as normally as possible. There was a feeling that morale should not only be high, but for the sake of the local population it should also be seen to be high. In mid December the air raids abruptly ceased and the almost unreal calm brought residents a false sense of security. There were some comforting signs. The fifteen-inch guns, which were Singapore's main defence, could frequently be heard practising firing their shells miles out to sea. The planes that now droned overhead were all friendly—indeed there hardly seemed to be a time when the RAF were not patrolling above, and the streets and entertainment centres thronged with splendid uniforms; shoulders of flashing brass, scrambled egg and smart wings, tartan kilts and khaki Bombay bloomers.

Socially not much had changed for VB. They were now at war but there was little food rationing; meat and butter allowances were three to four times higher than in England and there were no restrictions on sugar and milk. There was plenty to drink and though restaurants were supposed to observe two non-meat days per week, poultry and game was not rationed so the restrictions were barely noticeable.

After his discharge from hospital Arthur Squance moved in with VB. To him the apparent calm and confidence that 'surely the Japanese will be stopped' seemed misplaced. Having had an unsettling experience at the receiving end of the Japanese war machine, he couldn't feel the optimism that he saw in others. At a dinner party at a bungalow in Johore, Arthur pressed home his view. The atmosphere was convivial and festive and for the moment even VB seemed to have forgotten about the war. Yet there had been another air raid that weekend and the situation, he knew, was deadly serious. At the risk of putting a dampener on the evening, he told the party in no uncertain terms that Malaya and Singapore were in for a tough time and that those with families *must* send their wives and children to safety in Australia or India as soon as possible. To the other guests it all seemed so unreal.

It may have been that VB's uncle was aware of a few facts which those present that night were not. Few of the soldiers fighting in Malaya were jungle trained. The Japanese were well seasoned in jungle warfare and were moving not only through the jungle but also, by using bicycles, very rapidly through the rubber plantations and narrow back roads, employing enveloping tactics to get behind the Allied lines. Often they wore little more than shorts and a singlet, making it difficult for the Allied troops to even tell them apart from the locals. The Allies had to face tanks, but had no tanks themselves. Their positions were poorly prepared and the pressure from the Japanese was unrelenting. While the Japanese rested troops and sent fresh men to the front line, the exhausted British, Australian and Indian troops had no respite. Communication broke down and confusion reigned.

The Admiralty selected Arthur Squance, among others, to be sent back to London to give evidence at the Court of Enquiry into how and why Britain had lost its greatest battleship. Later he was awarded a Mention in Despatches for distinguished conduct. For now however, he was happy to be going home, and perhaps had a premonition that his nephew would not be following him for some time, at least not with all his worldly belongings intact. Packing up the pitifully few things he had acquired over the last fortnight, he asked VB whether there was anything he'd like taken back to England. Blithely VB rustled around his bedroom, picking up a few photographs and nine pewter mugs from among his sailing trophies. As Uncle Arthur walked out the door on 21 December 1941, he put the photos in his pocket and threaded a piece of rope through the handles of the mugs.

Those few things were to prove to be the only physical remnants of VB's life in prewar Singapore.

At a time when the Malaya Campaign desperately needed more manpower, VB was ordered to leave Singapore. It was December 1941 and the Japanese were bearing swiftly down the Peninsula. VB's orders were to sail for the UK aboard CPR *Andes* and take up the position at Rosyth. But to VB, leaving now seemed like abandoning the people of Malaya and Singapore in their hour of need. He had already decided he would do no such thing.

At a pleasant, rambling bungalow set up high on the Pasir Panjang Ridge in the west of the island, VB met Ronald Bertie (Perky) Perkins, Hugo Hughes and Norman Bewick for dinner. Weekend jaunts upcountry to the rubber estates in Malaya had been a feature of VB's life in Singapore, and Perky and Hugo were two of his many friends in the planting fraternity. Hugo Hughes was a solidly built, modest and gentle man who took on giant proportions on the rugby field in the afternoons after work. Perky Perkins was a character of seemingly tireless good humour, sharpish features and a twinkle in the eye to rival VB's. He and VB referred to each other always as 'my fellow Perkins', and occasionally chortled together about Perky's theory that had not the great Perkin-Warbeck been decapitated at the hands of Henry VII in 1499, one of them would have been on the throne. Tonight however, the conversation was of war.

Gap House was an enchanting place and one of VB's favourite haunts. In the daylight one could see the tiny islands dotting the Singapore Strait and the western approaches to Singapore harbour. This evening they dined in the courtyard, where the tables were set with globes of water in which tiny candles winked among a pool of floating flowers, as if to reassure guests that this life in Singapore really could go on forever. But already it seemed the writing was on the wall.

Five months earlier Norman Bewick had been Private Secretary to the Sultan of Pahang and a member of the Federated Malay States Volunteers; now he was a full-time soldier with the Malay Regiment. Perky had left Bahau Estate to join the Officers Cadet Training Unit in Singapore and enlisted in the Malay Regiment three days after the first Japanese attack on Singapore. Both were serving in the fledgling 2nd Battalion, which was formed only on 1 December and was now seeking new recruits; 1 December was also the day the Volunteer Forces were mobilised and their civilian members suddenly found themselves full-time soldiers. VB was very much aware that most of his friends outside of the Admiralty had joined the forces and were doing their bit. And he was more than ever determined that he would do his.

Nena Steele had been working in the Admiralty office at the Naval Base since the war in Europe began, and was now in a position in which she was privy to classified information. Throughout she had maintained a strict code of silence but in late December she came out of a meeting severely shaken. All of the Chiefs of Staff had been present and the topic under discussion had been the inevitability of defeat. Nena decided to tell her closest friends the truth. VB was left with few illusions.

VB was not a great writer of letters. While his parents at home were regularly delighted by his brother Leslie's long and detailed epistles, they waited anxiously for the letters that only too rarely came from their youngest son. When the letters did come they were usually brief. But as VB's scheduled departure day loomed he sat down to write, and this time put in a bit more effort than usual. The letter was to prove to be his last for three and a half years. It was dated 29 December 1941. He knew well his family would be unhappy with his decision to stay, and he tried to offer them some comfort through his words. He hoped they did not read between the lines:

'. . . *Malaya seems to be the centre of attention these days—I am sure the world is worrying much more about things than we are here . . .*' Indeed, thanks to the strict censorship imposed upon the local media, most in Singapore remained blissfully ignorant of the gravity of their predicament. When the news of the front line in Malaya was all bad, there was often no mention of it at all in the newspapers and the war front still seemed a long way from Singapore. Yet still the Japanese tide of killing and pillage swept relentlessly down the length of the Malay Peninsula towards them.

'. . . *We had our usual race on Sunday morning. I sailed with Bill Steele and we won . . .*' Indeed they did have their usual race on Sunday morning. He and his friends had sailed off the beach facing Johore, to where the enemy was advancing daily, unhindered by even a single strand of barbed wire. The likely landing places on the beaches on the western, southern and eastern sides of the island had been fortified, but there were no beach defences at all along the entire north coast.

'. . . *Leslie must have been having a pretty warm time of it lately but I am confident he is alright. To me, no news is good news. Try not to worry about it too much . . .*' In fact his brother was at that moment experiencing his first few days as a guest of the Imperial Japanese Army. Hong Kong had fallen on Christmas Day after a bitter seventeen-day struggle with an overwhelmingly superior opponent. At the time VB was writing, Japanese troops were rampaging wildly across the surrendered island, drunk on victory and any hard liquor they could find. They were raping, they were looting and, if it took their fancy, they were murdering.

'. . . *I start my four months training next week. It will do me a lot of good—I have a little corporation I want to get rid of . . .*' The reference to four months must have sounded comforting to his mother. Regrettably it was not to be.

'. . . *Now I must do some more packing. You wouldn't like a clock that won't go would you? It's a really old specimen of a Beach Cottage timepiece. I have many such articles. I think the answer is a jumble sale tomorrow at high noon . . .*' In fact the market for second-hand goods was a little flat. A steady stream of Europeans had tickets to leave and were packing the little they could take with them and leaving the rest behind. Just the day before VB had driven to Singapore to pay a visit to the 'Honkers and Shankers' to settle a few affairs and transfer some money to an account at Lloyds in

London. In the great hall of the Hong Kong and Shanghai Banking Corporation he joined a crowd of people queuing patiently, clutching their bankbooks. There were not many depositors among them.

In December Lady Diana Duff Cooper, the wife of Churchill's Special Envoy, broadcast an appeal to all European women with children, being 'useless mouths' (an expression she had borrowed from Churchill himself) to depart Singapore as soon as possible. Childless women in VB's circle found the decision to go more difficult. Wives such as Nena Steele were reluctant to leave their husbands, most of whom were required to stay on to do war work. Some felt that their presence had a calming influence on the Asian population, and lent an air of normality to the situation. These women lingered, waiting for an official order to leave. Concerned that an evacuation order given to European women would leave the Asians feeling they had been deserted, the Governor vowed that no racial discrimination would take place in Singapore. As a result no evacuation order was given to any civilians and many left it until too late.

The New Year started badly: on 1 January 1942 Singapore was attacked, marking the beginning of a solid month of bombing. From that day there was little respite for anyone and hardly a day passed when Singapore was not assaulted from the air. Day after day the raids came, in formations of twenty-seven, fifty-four or eighty-one planes. The RAF had been rendered so ineffectual that the Japanese bomber squadrons often didn't bother with a fighter escort, and they dropped their bombs all at once, virtually unchallenged.

In the city the effect was devastating. There could never be any accurate statistics because so many bodies in Chinatown and surrounds were never dug out. Mass burial grounds were organised in an attempt to dispose of the bodies quickly and stem the danger of typhus. The hospitals were hopelessly overcrowded with injury cases.

The dock area was a prime target for the bombs; chaos reigned supreme. Air-raid shelters were few and understandably the coolies had become bomb-shy and fled, leaving troops with the work of unloading the ships. On 3 January VB heard that a shipment of fifty-one Hurricane fighters in crates had arrived at last. There were however, only twenty-one pilots to fly them and they had little experience of the region and conditions.

As the Japanese swept down the Malay Peninsula, thousands of bewildered evacuees from upcountry converged on the city and a steady stream of civilians lined up at the P&O office. Finally the day came for VB to leave. The ship was waiting and he had his instructions. With his bag packed, he said his farewells to friends at the Naval Base. Few knew of his real intention. When he drove out of the great steel gates of the base for the last time, he didn't look back. Instead of heading for Keppel Harbour he headed west, in the direction of Gap House.

Out past the coconut and rubber plantations of the Buona Vista Road, the traffic was thick with military trucks and staff cars. At the top of Pasir Panjang Ridge he parked his car and glanced around at the once well-tended gardens surrounding the old bungalow, to see frangipanis and the remains of gardenia bushes lying withering in haphazard piles of fresh earth. The trenches were still being dug. Gap House was now the Headquarters of the 1st Battalion of the Malay Regiment and under the Command of Lieutenant Colonel Toby Andre.

On 5 January 1942 VB was appointed to an Emergency Commission in the General List, awaiting secondment to the Malay Regiment. By his own admission remaining in Singapore was not the best decision he ever made, but it was a decision that had been well considered and he felt it was the right thing to do. The Admiralty believed him more valuable in other theatres of war, but VB was in Singapore and Singapore was in trouble. The Malay Regiment was desperate for men to bolster the six-week-old 2nd Battalion. VB now spoke Malay quite fluently and felt certain he could make a worthwhile contribution.

Some time previously Toby Andre had confided to him that

he considered the Naval Base a 'dead horse' and that the Admiralty would have little role in the battle for Malaya and Singapore. As the last of the naval vessels quietly slipped away from Singapore in the early weeks of January VB was left mulling over how right Andre had been. Soon after, the rumours began about the evacuation of Admiralty staff from the base. VB found the idea distinctly disturbing. The *raison d'être* of the Naval Base was war, and now war had come. The base had been hailed as the bastion of Britain's supremacy in the East, to be defended at all costs. He had spent four years of his life dedicated to helping build the facility into one of the most impressive in the world and now all was prepared for the arrival of the main fleet. It had everything: docks, cranes, a dry dock, a floating dock, workshops, facilities for thousands of men. But there was no main fleet. The idea that it might be abandoned seemed unbelievable.

By the middle of January the battle for northern Johore had begun and the war front moved uncomfortably close to Singapore. The official war communiqués continued to be ridiculously optimistic but there were some in the community who were not fooled. VB got a rude shock one day when he was refused credit at a local Chinese store. Nobody had ever paid cash in Singapore. The chit system had always worked admirably but now, except in the clubs, it was cash on the nose—a sign as sure as any that the Chinese community considered the Europeans done for.

On 19 January 1942, VB was commissioned as a Lieutenant in the 2nd Battalion of the Malay Regiment, under the command of Lieutenant Colonel Walter Young. Around one third of the under-strength 2nd Battalion was made up of young recruits who had done but six months' training. VB was not the only officer who joined so late in the piece: the following week two more of his planter friends, Donald Webber and Hugo Hughes, joined up. Donald, Hugo and the few other officers who joined at the last minute at least had the benefit of their training with the Volunteer Forces. Lieutenant VB Perkins knew little of the army, but was destined to find out soon enough.

He had under two weeks to learn.

To the background of droning bombers and fierce explosions over Singapore, VB threw himself into a week's crash-course at the regiment's Normanton Camp. The only reading material provided about the type of warfare to be expected was a small and, under the circumstances, rather obsolete green booklet entitled *Tactical Notes on Malaya*. At the week's end he packed his kit bag, put the book in his pocket and with his head crammed with the essentials of weaponry, battle practice and the duties of an officer, he reported to B Company, 2nd Battalion, where he would serve alongside his friend Lieutenant Norman Bewick. The company of about one hundred and thirty men was stationed at the Six-inch Coastal Defence Battery at Pasir Laba, at the western entrance to the Johore Strait. There he was shocked to find that between Pasir Laba and Changi, at the eastern entrance to the Strait, there was still not a single permanent fixed defence. The north coast of the island of Singapore, to where the enemy was advancing daily, remained unfortified. It was unsettling to know that Singapore's main defence, the fifteen-inch guns, were designed to repel an attack on the Naval Base from seaward. The guns were all sited out to sea and not all of them could be brought to bear to the north. Most of the fixed defences were equipped with ammunition designed for piercing the armour of ships and were unsuitable for land defence. Only the 9.2-inch guns had suitable high-explosive ammunition, but there was a very limited supply.

The myth that Singapore was a 'fortress' caused confusion among even the topmost echelons of the military and the Government. Churchill himself was not made fully aware of the real situation in Singapore until 16 January 1942. On being informed he was horrified. He later wrote:

I ought to have known. My advisers ought to have known and I ought to have been told and I ought to have asked. The reason I did not ask was that the possibility of Singapore having no landward defences no more entered into my mind

than that of a battleship being launched without a bottom.[1]
(W.S. Churchill, *The Second World War*, Vol. IV, Cassel
& Co Ltd, London, 1951, p. 43)

A new Commander-in-Chief, Far East, had been appointed just
before Christmas. During his first visit to Singapore on 9 January
Field-Marshal Sir Archibald Wavell was seriously alarmed to discover the situation on the north shore. On demanding an explanation of Lieutenant General A.E. Percival, General Officer
Commanding, Malaya, as to why no landward defences had been
prepared, Percival replied that he had been concerned about the
effect on morale of doing so. Wavell immediately pressed to have
something done and although the Malay Regiment was detailed to
reconnoitring the area, incredibly little more happened until the
last week of January. By that time the supply of civil labour had
dried up.

And so VB found the first task of his military career to be the
belated construction of shore defences against an enemy which was
almost on Singapore's doorstep. His company, along with many
other units, scrambled to land-mine the beaches, obstruct landing
places with underwater obstacles, wire and booby-trap mangrove
areas and build concrete pill boxes. Time was all too much against
them.

Towards the end of the month all but a handful of fighter aircraft
had left Singapore for Sumatra from where it was planned they
would mount long-range attacks and provide protection in the
shipping lanes. The battle in Malaya moved into Southern Johore
and the Allied troops retreated steadily down the trunk road to
Johore Bahru and the causeway to Singapore. From the north-coast
beaches VB could hear the sound of explosions drifting down across
the Strait. With every day they came a little closer.

---

[1] *Defences to protect the Naval Base from a land-based attack from the north had
begun in 1938 with the construction of defences in Johore. However when Japan
invaded Indochina in 1940 the defence of the Naval Base became reliant upon the
holding of the whole Malay Peninsula, and construction of those defences ceased.*

Then the rumours about the evacuation of the Naval Base were confirmed. The Admiralty wanted the evacuation of all skilled and trained naval and dockyard personnel to take place in a timely fashion. To this end all European and civilian staff were moved to Singapore City on 28 January. While VB joined the panic to construct defences on the north coast, most of his old sailing friends and contemporaries from the Naval Base were preparing to leave Singapore for Ceylon.

The city of Singapore was a smoking ruin. In the last days of January men worked desperately to control the fires, especially round the docks where many godowns were ablaze. The smell of burning rubber hung heavily on the air. The city was crammed with evacuees from Malaya and many roads were blocked by bomb debris or jammed by civilian vehicles heading for the docks or army trucks trying to get supplies and men away.

On 29 January four large troopships nosed their way into Singapore, bringing with them the 18th British Division as reinforcements for the retreating army. Overnight the *West Point*, *Wakefield*, *Duchess of Bedford* and *Empress of Japan* were discharged of troops and military equipment. The civilian labour had disappeared and troops worked under constant threat as the dock area was systematically pattern-bombed. The ships, which waited like sitting ducks at the docks, represented what could be the last chance for many women and children, to say nothing of the evacuees from the Naval Base, to escape from Singapore. The result was chaos.

Diana Carey, a nurse and sailing friend of VB in the good old days at the Naval Base, had married and moved to Christmas Island. Recently she had been evacuated to Singapore under express orders from Sir Shenton Thomas, and had arrived just in time to learn what life in the fortress was really like. Now she had a ticket for the *West Point*. She had been 'shilly-shallying' all month: should she go or shouldn't she? The only direction the nurses were given from the authorities was for them to make up their minds so that those remaining could get on with their job. Disorganisation was rife. All around her people had begun to panic and many who had been dithering suddenly realised they really had better leave. 'Even the matron herself left the day after. We simply had to go,' Diana said.

Bill Steele had stayed on with the Johore Volunteer Engineers, not envisaging that at the crucial moment he would contract dengue fever and be whisked into hospital. On a day late in January he phoned VB from the hospital and said, 'For Christ's sake, will you get Nena onto a ship!' Determined not to leave Singapore, Nena had used her work for the Admiralty as a reason to remain. Now that the Naval Base had been evacuated she had no more work and was torn between staying on to do whatever else she could to help, or leaving. Stories about Japanese outrages on women in Malaya convinced Bill she must go. From his hospital bed he told VB he was counting on him. His voice had a despairing note.

On both the civilian and the military front sympathetic superiors were handing out leave passes for men to see their wives and children to the docks, and VB procured a half-day pass. Nena's ticket was for the *Duchess of Bedford*, but getting her there wasn't easy. The roads around the harbour area were bomb cratered and congested and the eastern approach to Empire Dock was completely impassable. The previous day the air raids were unrelenting and hundreds of civilians had been killed around the wharf area. Now, as he got closer, VB could see smoke billowing up from the godowns lining the docks and chose a different route. Approaching from the opposite direction yet another road was blocked by debris and he cursed the fact that his vehicle had no solid cover. He did a U-turn and tried again. The police and the army had given up trying to direct traffic and the roads were at a standstill. Within a mile of the wharf he stopped and parked close to the burnt-out shell of a building, for he could go no further. They hopped out of the car and VB, carrying Nena's suitcase, picked a path through the rubble the rest of the way to the dock.

At the marshalling area an incredible melee of luggage and tearful women and children jostled for a position in seemingly never-ending queues, while grave-faced husbands and fathers hovered around them. It was a hot, humid evening and the queues moved agonisingly slowly. Just a trickle of passengers seemed to be leaving the desks of the officials to walk up the gangways. VB and Nena joined the scrum and prepared for a long wait. Having been in a panic all day about getting to the ship, Nena now had a chance to look around at what was to be her last image of Singapore. Along the six-mile stretch of dock area, past the outline of the huge ships, rubble had been bulldozed up into heaps or lay strewn around where it had fallen. The dying embers of fires glowed through the hazy night air and further along, opposite burning godowns, the reflection of fierce orange flames danced upon the water. There were no Asians to be seen anywhere, just a sea of anxious European faces reflecting the heartbreak and uncertainty of separation from family whom they wondered if they'd ever see again.

Perhaps it was a blessing that they didn't know the Causeway had already been blown and that Singapore was now a lone and desperate island.

FOUR

Disagreeable Types

As the *Duchess of Bedford* slipped out of port in the early hours of 1 February 1942 the local newspaper was printing some disturbing news, news which had been censored for the last twenty-four hours. Thirty thousand Allied troops had withdrawn to the island. Singapore was now under siege.

The General Officer Commanding, Malaya, Lieutenant General Percival, had a Naval Base with no navy and airfields with only a token air force remaining. The enemy had two hundred tanks. Percival had none. He had eighty-five thousand military men on the island, of which fifteen thousand were non-fighting, unarmed troops. Most battalions were either soft after weeks at sea, battle weary from fighting on the Malay Peninsula or 'made up' with untrained or semi-trained troops. Such was the state of the ground forces which, in the original defence plans for Malaya, were supposed to have played only an auxiliary role to the navy and air force.

For the first few days after the withdrawal to Singapore all was quiet across the Strait in Johore, as the Japanese prepared to launch their assault.

VB's company, laying defences along the north shore, were now joined on the beaches by soldiers who'd been fighting in Malaya. VB didn't like the look of them. They were exhausted and demoralised. They had straggled over to Singapore the previous night thinking they were retiring to a fortress, thinking that at last they could put the nightmare of the past weeks behind them and get some real rest and recuperation. When they learned that so little had been done they were horrified.

Back at his station at the Pasir Laba battery in a jungle clearing on a hill at the western end of Johore Strait, VB could look out to a typical stretch of the north-west coast of the island; to low-lying mangrove swamps laced with muddy creeks and rivers flowing out into the Strait, where he and friends had once explored in their dinghies, never dreaming it would all too soon become the site of a bloody, bloody battle. The defence in the area was thin, for General Percival expected that an attack from the mainland would be combined with a seaborne attack, and had stretched the defence around the entire coastline of the island. He also expected that the land-based assault would be concentrated to the east of the Causeway, and the right flank of the Pasir Laba position was left with only a thin defence in terms of both infantry and artillery. This was to prove disastrous.

It began on 4 February. The guns across the Strait let loose, and VB had his first taste of artillery fire. Here was something different to the aerial bombing, something far more sinister. In an air raid the position of the planes at least gave one some indication of where the bombs might land. Now the only warning was a low whine in the distance which quickly worked up into a piercing scream as the shell approached. The scream only stopped when the shell hit something and it was almost impossible to tell what that would be. One was forced to adopt a fatalistic attitude.

Columns of thick black smoke billowed high into the north-east sky, laying a dark and heavy shroud across the horizon. There was talk among the troops about what could cause such a blaze, but VB, a sick sort of gut-feeling sitting heavily in the pit of his stomach, said nothing. When news finally filtered through his suspicions were confirmed. The fires were from the Naval Base. Worse, they were not the work of the Japanese, but of the British. They called it 'scorched earth', tactics of denial.

That day, as VB looked across at the smoke from what may as well have been the funeral pyres of Britain's eastern empire, he was more than a little shaken. Sixty-three million pounds worth of investment in the defence of the Empire was being decimated before the enemy had so much as set foot on the island. Everything on the Naval Base for which he had worked since he had been in Singapore was now being stripped, smashed, set alight and destroyed. The thought of it was appalling.

Now he had the task of explaining it to his platoon. They had everything to lose in the event of a British defeat and from where they stood it seemed as if the navy and air force had given up the fight. The destruction of the Naval Base looked like retreating from behind and left an unfortunate impression on their minds. What could he say? Only what General Percival said at the latest press conference: 'Today we stand beleaguered in our island fortress. Our task is to hold this fortress until help can come—as assuredly it will come. This we are determined to do.'

The air raids to the west of the Causeway were unusually heavy on 8 February. By nightfall the bombing raids had cut the lines of communication to the defending troops and the area was left isolated.

From Pasir Laba VB could see the night sky to the north-east light up in a fierce bombardment of artillery and mortar fire. At the time he was not aware that enemy landings had begun along a five-mile front to the west of the Causeway, that wave after wave of Japanese troops in collapsible outboard dinghies and small land-ingcraft were descending upon the naked island of Singapore. The Australians defending the area were fighting bravely, inflicting heavy losses on the Japanese, but the invaders just kept coming and coming, appearing as if from nowhere, out of the blackness. The defenders could get no signals to the searchlight operators, who could have flooded the Strait with light. They could get no signals, other than a belated SOS, to the artillery who could have let the heavy guns fly immediately. They were defending blind and had little backup. Before they knew it they were fighting hand to hand in the mangroves and jungles, while the Japanese sought out the gaps and moved quickly to outflank them.

By dawn twenty-three thousand Japanese troops had landed, and were moving quickly south using compasses through the cover of mangroves, jungle and rubber. To the west the exposed Pasir Laba position became the focus of attention from the guns across the Strait. The air was heavy with acrid smoke and the smell of cordite, and each time it began to clear low-flying Japanese aircraft appeared out of the haze to strafe the battery with fire. Before the day was over the six-inch guns were put out of action and VB stared in disbelief at the mangled wreckage of what was the only fixed defence for miles. It was a severe shock to his system.

Pasir Laba was now in danger of being cut off behind Japanese lines and had to be abandoned. The garrison withdrew under orders along the Jurong Road and B Company of the Malay Regiment marched intact throughout the long night. As he marched VB felt stunned, hollow, disturbed. It was one thing retreating down the Malay Peninsula but now they were retreating in Singapore. When they ran out of island there was nowhere else to go. Christ, and the assault had only begun last night. What the hell was going on? He'd thought they'd put up a better show than this. He ducked instinctively as a mortar flew overhead. A few seconds later he was prostrate in a ditch, taking cover as the ground erupted in an explosion nearby.

As VB's company fled from the remote corner of Singapore island, events were occurring to the east which had grave consequences. Holding the Jurong Line, a natural line of defence stretching through uncleared jungle and swamp between the headwaters of two rivers, was crucial if Singapore was to hold out against the Japanese for any length of time. But a series of debacles occurred, through lack of communication and misinterpretation, and the Jurong line gave way before the Japanese had even seriously assaulted it.

By the time VB's company was re-deployed on 11 February, any sort of coherent plan for the defence of Singapore was in tatters. A quiet twenty-four hours after reaching the Regiment's Norman-ton Camp in the south-west corner of the island, his company

joined the First Malaya Infantry Brigade (made up of the two battalions of the Malay Regiment and the 2nd Loyal Regiment) just
north of the west-coast fishing village of Pasir Panjang. There, as
VB waited with his troops at the southern end of the line, all was
quiet but for the sounds of battle to the north. All indications were
that things were not going well. While VB tried not to notice the
leaderless and panic-stricken soldiers, alone or in groups of two or
three, scuttling through the Malay Regiment line, making for the
nearby coast and a chance to escape, the battle for Singapore moved
quickly. The Japanese troops were trained to pick off officers first
in order to create confusion. Lines of communication were broken
by shelling and many troops were cut off and left to their own
devices. The Japanese found themselves at one moment unable to
advance, the next, marching unchallenged, the defence having
melted away. Morale was already low from the constant withdrawals in Malaya and in many cases now began to crack completely.
Some of the men VB saw making for the coast were deserters.
Others had seen their own company decimated and had no ambition
to join another.

That afternoon Japanese tanks advanced to within a few miles
of the city along the main Bukit Timah Road and a close perimeter
defence around the city was organised. The 2nd Battalion of the
Malay Regiment was still in position at the western end of a line
of defence stretching from Pasir Panjang, encircling the city at a
radius of eight to ten miles.

As the noose tightened on Singapore, the streets bulged with
people. The population had doubled and over one million people
now choked the city, making the job of the military all the more
difficult and putting enormous strain on the civil service to supply
basic needs such as food and water. Armed deserters, mostly from
recently arrived and barely trained troops, mooched around in
greater numbers than the military police could deal with. The
governor gave orders for the civil denial scheme to be put into
effect, and everything that could be of any possible use to the
Japanese military was ordered destroyed, including stocks of rubber
and other raw materials as well as manufacturing plants, factories

and garages. As a result many people were witness to the heart-breaking spectacle of watching what amounted to their life's work destroyed in front of them. Wary of a repeat of the Japanese atrocities in Hong Kong, the governor ordered that every bottle of strong drink on the island be smashed. All State money also had to be destroyed and a stock of some five million Straits dollars (600,000 pounds) held in the Treasury was thrown into a furnace and burnt.

On the evening of 12 February, VB's company was ordered to retreat to form a new line conforming with withdrawals further north. Overnight VB found himself retreating yet again to a new position along the top of Pasir Panjang Ridge, not far north of Gap House. As he walked he could not help but feel that so far in this war he had been a part of a battle in which he had not joined, against an enemy which he had not seen.

The dawning of Friday the 13th was to change all that.

According to the official British war history, *War Against Japan*, by the morning of 13 February the battle for Singapore was irretrievably lost and it was only a question of time before capitulation would occur. The men who made up the 1st Malaya Brigade, however, were not aware of this. Many had seen the courteously worded message from General Yamashita which had fluttered down from the sky in an airdrop, calling for the surrender of Singapore. No doubt there was a proportion of exhausted troops on the island whose morale had flagged to the extent that they were ready to agree to it, but the men of the 1st Malaya Brigade were not among them.

Whatever General Percival might have felt about the situation, he could not ignore Prime Minister Churchill's view, cabled in no uncertain terms to General Wavell on 10 February:

> *There must at this stage be no thought of saving the troops or sparing the population. The battle must be fought to the bitter end at all costs . . . Commanders and senior officers should die with their troops. The honour of the British Empire and of the British Army is at stake. I rely on you to show no mercy to*

weakness in any form . . . the whole reputation of our country and our race is involved.

And so as the pre-dawn light of 13 February 1942 filtered on to the flanks of Pasir Panjang Ridge, the already hopeless battle for Singapore continued. VB aroused himself from a short, fitful sleep; the Japanese had been active enough over the past two nights to ensure that nobody got much rest. Suddenly, out of the smoky rose hue of the north-west sky, the hideous screams of shelling began again. The Malay Regiment line was the prime target this morning, for behind them lay the vital Alexandra area and the island's largest ammunition dump. Behind also was the big Alexandra Military Hospital and the 1st Malaya Brigade had orders to defend these sites at all costs.

All that morning and into the afternoon, the sun hardly seemed able to break through the pall of smog over the ridge to lift the day out of an ominous twilight. VB was dug into the side of a ridge and the atmosphere around him was eerie and unreal. A shroud of thick black smoke had drifted north from burning oil tanks at the Normanton Depot a few miles away and hung heavily in the air. Through it the onslaught of artillery and mortar fire continued, shells landing unpredictably, taking toll of both men and equipment. Occasionally the barrage ceased, but only to allow the Japanese Air Force to dispense its own brand of pleasantries. At one such moment VB looked up for a split second as a Japanese bomber approached unusually low from behind. Moments before its machine guns opened up he glimpsed the dim outline of the pilot. It was the first time he had sighted the enemy in person. A few yards away Lieutenant Norman Bewick was hit. They were within half a mile of the Gap Headquarters and through the mayhem of noise and smoke VB half carried his friend to the old Gap House where they had dined so often. There he heard that Hugo Hughes had had his right leg almost severed by a mortar. VB left Gap House, shaken to think of the fate of the giant rugby forward. A short time after he left the headquarters received a direct hit and was completely wrecked.

Back on the front line senior commanders occasionally appeared like apparitions out of the smoke, their headquarters gone, telephone communications cut. Around mid-afternoon the order was given for the 2nd Battalion to readjust positions and in the middle of the move the Japanese launched their real attack. The Imperial Army unleashed the might of its 18th Division, which pushed forward in mass formation with cover from tanks, aircraft and mortar fire. B Company rapidly dug into a hollow behind the highest point on the ridge, Point 270, and from there VB put his short army training into very real practice.

The history states that for the next few hours the 2nd Battalion 'took heavy toll of the enemy with grenades, rifle and automatic fire'. But like most of his fellows VB never had a clear recollection of the events of that day. The shrieks of the Japanese as they charged up the hill with bayonets fixed was nothing short of blood-curdling and would always be sharply etched on his mind. The rest was a blurred reflection: of firing into a mass of advancing humanity, half obscured by smoke from burning undergrowth, with a rifle that soon became almost too hot to hold; of turfing grenades; of at times not being able to see what the hell was happening; and of the distressing business of dealing with the dead and wounded in a battle zone.

By twilight it was all over. The battle had been lost. In the semi-darkness of Friday 13 the remnants of the 2nd Battalion of the Malay Regiment fell back through the Gap Ridge and past the wreckage of Gap House. Captain Monks and VB were the only British officers in B Company who walked back that night. As darkness set in, the bedraggled, filthy, exhausted men retreated through the Normanton area, the fires from the oil depot reflecting off their blackened faces. At the Alexandra Brickworks area they stopped and collapsed wherever they could find a place to lay their heads, drifting off into an uneasy sleep, their minds still churning with the ugly images of the day.

To the north-east of Pasir Panjang Ridge, the Allied soldiers of the city perimeter defence had a quieter day, but many had already had enough. Some of them had been fighting for weeks down the

Malay Peninsula and their morale was at rock-bottom. In the city administration was breaking down and the water mains were badly damaged. Thousands of soldiers with no fight left in them congregated on the Esplanade to form a mass-slaughter target for machine gunners in low-flying aircraft. The city was incessantly bombed and shelled and dead victims lay uncollected and unburied. Evacuees from Malaya had nowhere to flee and they ran confused in the streets, turning this way and that, not knowing where to go to find shelter from the bombs and debris crashing down around them.

On 14 February General Percival reported the situation in full to General Wavell and received the reply by cable:

> *You must continue to inflict maximum damage on enemy for as long as possible by house-to-house fighting if necessary. Your action in tying down enemy and inflicting casualties may have vital influence in other theatres. Fully appreciate your situation but continued action essential.*

While the battle for the Alexandra area continued, Hugo Hughes had his leg amputated. The military hospital was packed with patients on the morning of 14 February, and a queue of desperately injured men waited in the corridor for operations. In a small room adjacent to the theatre Hugo opened his eyes. His first thought was for his leg. He could have sworn it was still there; he could still feel it on the bed. He reached down to touch it. There was nothing there. He closed his eyes again for a while. Still groggy from the operation, at first he thought the screams were a dream. Then he realised that something was terribly, terribly wrong.

On the front porch of the hospital a young lieutenant lay dying. Beside him lay the large white flag he had been holding unflinchingly as the enemy approached. The first soldier up the stairs had bayoneted him deep in the ribcage. The Japanese had been fighting ruthlessly to get through the lines and were in an angry, murderous state. Now they stormed through the hospital indiscriminately bayoneting defenceless patients as well as staff. The Red Cross emblems worn by the staff did nothing to help their cause. The Japanese troops deliberately thrashed already broken limbs and used their rifle butts to smash plasters. One party entered the operating theatre where a hapless patient lay awaiting his operation. He too was bayoneted to death, along with the anaesthetist and all the theatre staff. Only the surgeon, who feigned death, survived. In the next room Hugo Hughes lay listening, horrified, waiting for the door to open. It didn't open, but the sound of the screams was to remain with him for the rest of his life. Around three hundred were massacred at the Alexandra Military Hospital that day.

As Hugo lay on his bed, appalled, another 2nd lieutenant from his company, C Company of the 1st Battalion, was hanging upside down in a tree, dead, strung up by the Japanese. Most of the rest of his company were also dead, having fought in a bitter clash in the defence of 'Opium Hill', standing their ground until they were fighting hand to hand.

Elsewhere on that grim day, General Yamashita again demanded an unconditional surrender and General Percival again refused. The refusal was answered in full. The bombardment of both the city and the military installations was intensified and civilian deaths rose to horrific levels.

Since their last retreat VB's company had been patrolling the high ground around the Mount Faber area just north of Keppel Harbour, watching for Japanese landings from Blakang Mati Island. That night, as he looked across the water, the harbour seemed dark, lifeless. The shimmering lights of the usual plethora of junks, sampans and ships had long since disappeared. The day had passed in a sort of dazed, slow-motion nightmare and the air drifting across from the city was thick with smoke and the stench of death. His uniform was dirty and sweat stained, for he'd been wearing it for days. He'd been accustomed to bathing at least twice a day in Singapore, and now there was not enough water to wash in. Most of the little water still being pumped was running to waste through damaged pipelines, and because most of the water supply was in the hands of the Japs, a complete failure was imminent. Even when the rain fell it was heavy with soot, which left clothes stained and faces black. He was a bit hungry, for they'd been on short rations. The military food depots at Bukit Timah had been taken and supply was down to seven days.

So here they were, trapped in the south-west corner of the island, with the Japanese fleet standing between Singapore and the safety of the Dutch East Indies. The only bright spot in the day was news that the enemy push down Pasir Panjang Road had been stopped by a company of the 1st Battalion, dug in around the Alexandra brick-works. The Japs had retreated for the moment and the rest of the Malay Regiment was having a quieter time of it.

In the besieged city, streets were blocked by the wreckage of buildings, burnt-out vehicles, broken telegraph poles and entangled wires. It was overcrowded with desperate people. Beneath the grime on their faces was a mixture of despondency, despair, humil-iation, bitterness and anger. Hospitals had long since overflowed and hotels were being used where possible to bed the wounded. The Singapore General Hospital was crammed with patients, many lying on the floor and under beds. Outside in the once lovingly tended gardens great pits had been dug and were quickly filled with bodies. A sprinkling of lime did little to prevent the stench. Public services had ceased and civil labour was virtually non-existent. Looting became uncontrollable. By now it was clear to even the most wildly optimistic that the end was near.

The next morning Percival held a conference at Fort Canning. Of major concern was the state of the water supply, the shortage of military food stocks and the consequences to the civil population when the Japanese broke through into the crowded city. The only alternative to capitulation was an immediate counterattack to regain possession of the water resources and the military food depots in the Bukit Timah area. The unanimous opinion of the formation commanders present was that a counterattack was impracticable. The decision was made to surrender.

At 6.10pm on 15 February 1942 Percival signed the terms of the surrender and at 8.30pm that evening all hostilities ceased. History immortalised the event in Churchill's own words as 'the worst disaster and largest capitulation in British history'.

As for the Malay Regiment's part in the ordeal, VB had little to say. His own experience was limited and he did not consider himself a judge. He was unaware that the official war history mentions the defence of the Pasir Panjang Ridge as one of the three most courageous stands in the battle for Singapore Island, only that without air support or tanks they were severely outclassed in terms of cover, as well as ammunition and weight of numbers, and that the troops were utterly exhausted.

General Percival wrote of the Malay Regiment that 'these young and untried soldiers acquitted themselves in a way which bore comparison with the very best troops in Malaya' and that 'The Malay Brigade showed what esprit de corps and discipline can achieve. Garrisons of posts held their ground and many of them were wiped out almost to a man.' VB later reflected that the Malay Regiment troops had not arrived in a ship from a distant land, as had most of the troops in Singapore. They were not fighting a battle on somebody else's ground; they were fighting for their country and they had a lot to lose. He had to wonder later at the policy which had delayed the raising of local forces for such a long period of time and at why the Chinese, who made up most of the population of Singapore and who had every reason to hate the Japanese, were not drafted to the cause.[1]

Looking back many years later, VB did not feel bitter, as so many do, about what happened in Singapore. Whilst military bungles and bad decisions characterised the battle for the island, he felt the stage was set for defeat much earlier. He remembered his school years, when the people of Britain were rallying for peace and turning a blind eye to the possibility of another war. Nobody wanted to spend money on defence; they wanted it spent on welfare at home. The government had responded to these calls and in the years since World War I Britain had let her guard down to the extent that when the time came she was

---

[1] *Fear of Communism was the official reason given. Whilst most of the Chinese in Malaya were dedicated (and often highly successful) capitalists, a minority group of Chinese Communists had been agitating to throw the British out since the 1930s, so that there was some distrust of the Chinese community in Government circles.*

simply unable to defend the western and eastern fronts at the same time.

As VB pointed out, Churchill took the blame for the fall of Singapore upon himself and avoided looking for fault in the high-ranking men on the spot, many of whom later died as prisoners of war. In VB's eyes the Far East could only be last on Churchill's list of priorities, for the indisputable fact was that if Britain lost the war with Germany there was nothing she could do for her empire in the East. A Britain occupied by Germany would have been of little comfort to her colonies.

Percival himself admitted, 'The choice was made and Singapore had to suffer . . . this decision, however painful and regrettable, was inevitable and right.'

FIVE

Guest of the Emperor

Singapore fell into a disquieting silence. After a week of continuous artillery barrage, bombing and general pandemonium it was suddenly so quiet it seemed not even the crickets were chirping. For days VB had been shouting over the top of the war to make himself heard. Now he found himself speaking startlingly loud in the uncanny hush and switched to talking in quiet tones.

All over Singapore people were asking each other 'What has happened? Surely we haven't given in. What does it mean?' VB knew the situation was grim, but when he officially heard of the surrender it still came as a stunning blow. Over the last tumultuous week he had tried not to think about the outcome of capitulation. Now the realisation that they would probably all become prisoners of war hit home.

The Malay Regiment was ordered to assemble in the Keppel Harbour Golf Course area. During the night and through the morning of 16 February the remnants of the debilitated 1st Battalion trudged the last couple of miles to join those of the 2nd on the pock-marked turf of the first hole. The spectacle of the rabble of dirty, battle-weary men was a far cry from the usually splendid turnout for which the regiment had been known. Tired, stunned and anxious, they sought out friends in other companies to see how each had fared. VB felt a hand on his shoulder, and smiled as he heard the voice, 'Ah, my fellow Perkins! I see you are still with us.' The irrepressible Perky Perkins was intact in all respects, having come through unscathed the bombing of 2nd Battalion headquarters where he'd been stationed as an intelligence officer. News of the massacre at the Alexandra Hospital had reached the regiment. Of the fate of Hugo Hughes and his fellow officers in B Company, Norman Bewick and Frank Smith of the Malayan Civil Service, VB knew nothing.

The men had little idea of what was to become of them and when, yet many realised that now might be their only chance to do the things they had to do. One who had a matter of great importance to attend to was a good-looking young lieutenant named Alastair Mackenzie who had joined the regiment with VB at the last minute. Attached to 1st Battalion headquarters, Mackenzie managed to get leave enough to slip away into the city for a few hours, and some time later he was standing in the matron's office at the General Hospital; at his side was a tired, pretty, volunteer nurse in a blood-spattered uniform. Archdeacon Graham White of St Andrew's Cathedral was there, and with little to-do he delivered the familiar recitals, concluding 'I now pronounce you man and wife.' The couple kissed. It was not the customary brief, wedding kiss but the passionate, desperate kiss of two people in love who wondered if they would ever see each other again. Within a few minutes Mackenzie had gone. He returned to the regiment beaming, the proud bearer of a document. It was handed around and as VB looked at the piece of hospital paper headed 'Certificate of Marriage' he felt a brief moment of happiness. There were few to come.

Arms were collected and British officers ordered to separate from Malay officers and troops. Though he knew it was for the best VB was surprised at the wrench he felt at the idea. He had been with these men but a few short weeks, yet already he felt a bond with them. Most knew so much more than he of the army, yet they had served with him respectfully without baulking at his inexperience. In particular the young Lieutenant Ibrahim bin Sidek had been a solid and honest performer beside him, and now VB found himself arguing with him. Lieutenant Colonel Andre had given permission for the Malays of the 1st Battalion to go in search of their wives and families, and though it seems no such permission was given by Lieutenant Colonel Young of the 2nd Battalion, VB encouraged his men to do the same. The idea rested unhappily with some, but VB was sure that under the circumstances getting rid of their uniforms and into civilian clothing was the only sensible thing to do. There would be no joy from here on as a soldier. Those who did decide to go changed quickly into their regimental mufti and, heartfelt goodbyes said, slipped quietly away into the smoking ruins of Singapore. There was nothing VB could say to convince Ibrahim bin Sidek to get away. Looking into the earnest brown eyes of the young officer as he said goodbye, he wondered what on earth would become of him.

VB now turned his thoughts to the chance of escape. With two others he slipped away for a reconnaissance of the region. Three Malay Regiment officers from 1st Battalion headquarters had successfully got away overnight on 15 February but now, twenty-four hours later, it seemed it was too late. At the nearby Royal Singapore Yacht Club VB looked in dismay at the scene before him. The place was deserted, just a sea of lonely, bobbing moorings, an abandoned jetty and a hard stand from which every single boat of any description had disappeared. The rest of the Keppel Harbour shoreline was the same; not a junk or a sampan was to be seen anywhere.

Of those who had already gone many did not make it, their fate sealed by a sprawling net of enemy planes and warships patrolling the desperate waters around Singapore. Those captured on other islands were either incarcerated under tormenting conditions or executed immediately. Many were never heard of again.

The morning of Tuesday 17 was stinking hot. On the Cricket Club *padang* the British civilians of Singapore assembled as they had been ordered, the men at one end and the women and children at the other. Across the road the dignified buildings of the Supreme Court, the symbol of British law and order in Singapore, overlooked the pathetic scene of sweating, humiliated men in soiled, crumpled whites or torn khakis sitting or standing by their luggage and waiting for further instructions. No longer were they the masters. Some looked longingly towards the opposite end of the *padang* where their wives and girlfriends, dresses limp with perspiration, waited in an anxious array, variously intent on shielding their children from the burning sun, sitting on their suitcases in tearful despondency or putting on the bravest of faces in an effort to cheer up others. Unknown to them then lay three and a half long years within the cheerless, grey walls of Singapore's Changi Prison.

The remains of the Malay Regiment moved to the Raffles Place area. VB looked around at the thousands of soldiers gathered there, some sitting, smoking, lost in their thoughts, others joking and playing impromptu games almost as if the gravity of their predicament had not yet struck them. In the streets there was hardly a non-European face to be seen. The Asian shops were boarded up and most stayed locked up in their houses waiting with trepidation to see what would happen next. It was hard not to sneer at the sight of the Japanese in commandeered cars driving around looking at them, the defeated men. The Japanese smiled, laughed, savoured their victory.

The march began, nine hot miles along the road, to the area that would become the main military prison camp in Singapore—Changi Garrison, on the eastern tip of the island. The Malay Regiment officers joined the line upon line of Allied troops, 68,000 men being shunted along by Japanese soldiers barking orders in an unfamiliar language. The spectacle of it brought home the enormity of the defeat, not only to VB and his fellow soldiers, but to the civilians watching in bewildered silence. Occasionally VB noticed intrepid individuals dash out onto the road with offerings of food and water. On their faces was a mixture of shock, sympathy and confusion. That the British forces, much respected Protectors of the Empire, could have suffered such a humiliating defeat at the hands of Nippon was still difficult to conceive.

While the prisoners struggled to come to terms with their new situation, so too did everyone else on the island. The Chinese were especially nervous, and with justification, for the Japanese considered them sworn enemies. There were many massacres. One that occurred on 28 February was at an isolated place near the village of Pasir Panjang. A group of men were ordered to stand in front of a large trench. The staccato blast of machine-guns ruptured the scene and a line of bodies slumped into the pit. Hours later, as darkness fell over the macabre site, some of the boards covering the pit began to move. From among the dead a solitary Chinese survivor, wounded only in his leg, crawled out to tell the story. Among the bodies were four officers of the Malay Regiment. They had refused either to join the Japanese forces or accept release, declining even to remove their badges of rank. One of them was VB's mate, Ibrahim bin Sidek.

In the final analysis half of all the Malay officers who survived the fighting were subsequently executed by the Japanese. Such was their welcome to the Japanese Co-Prosperity Sphere.

VB had been to Changi Garrison as a guest often enough, but never as a guest of the Emperor of Japan. It was a pleasant sort of place, where cream-coloured barracks and large, red-roofed bungalows sat among hibiscus gardens and palm trees, where undulating coastal ridges offered excellent views to the sea. But the complex was designed to accommodate two thousand people. Now there were over thirty men for each bed. There was no room even for the beds and VB, along with most, found himself sleeping on the floor, using his kitbag as a pillow. Most of the buildings still serviceable after the bombing were already filled to overflowing with troops and their possessions and the Malay Regiment were allotted part of the top floor of the Gillman Barracks, uncomfortably close to around fifty Japanese who slept on the floor below.

At first there was little semblance of order in the camp. A system had to be quickly established to provide for the basic requirements of around sixty-eight thousand men. There was little food provided. VB still had a few rations left in his kit, but when these ran out he was introduced to what was to become his staple diet for the duration of the war—rice. There was nothing to supplement it and the sudden change of diet led to a quick weight loss. Soon he was

experiencing his first bout of dysentery, an unpleasant malady characterised by acute looseness of the bowels, which was to plague
all the prisoners, as well as the latrine-pit diggers.

Being now part of a relatively small party of just over forty
officers with no troops, VB was in a different situation to most.
Both the Malay Regiment remnants and the Volunteers had a natural
advantage over the bewildered soldiers who had recently arrived
from overseas. They were acclimatised, they knew the country and
they could all speak Malay. Many spoke Tamil or even Chinese.
VB had a happy reunion with Bill Steele, safe and well after an
unsuccessful escape bid in which he ran out of petrol in a dinghy.

On contemplating his new situation VB was less inclined to
bitterness than some. While accepting after the event that remaining
in Singapore was perhaps not the best decision he had ever made,
it was, nonetheless, his own decision. He had entered into it with
his eyes open and he did not have a need to find someone to blame
for the military disaster which had led him to his predicament.
Others who had been more disillusioned found their situation more
difficult to interpret, and during the first few weeks despondency,
rumours and recriminations were common.

Almost daily men were being sent out of camp on working parties
around Singapore. These were popular as a diversion from dull
routine, for although the work was usually hard, rations were better
and there were occasional opportunities to scrounge something
extra to eat or some useful item to be smuggled back into camp.
VB was not unduly displeased when his name came up. But his
spirits sagged when he learned the nature of his group's work:
finding and defusing anti-personnel mines around the coast of the
island. The anti-personnel mine was a nasty bit of work in the form
of a cylindrical grenade about nine by three inches, buried in the
ground and fixed to a staked trip wire. The mines on the east and
west coasts had been laid for months and the trip wires, entangled
in the *lalang*, were rarely visible. As VB discovered to his regret,
this made the task of locating first the wires and then the mine
very hazardous.

VB had thought time passed slowly in camp, but now each long day seemed a never-ending agony of tension, working in a grid pattern, walking slowly and deliberately, peering for all his life was worth into the foreboding tangle of grass. The Japanese appeared to have no regard for the fact that they were not expertly trained for the task, and casualties were inevitable. During the four weeks VB worked at it two of the party had limbs blown off. They were lucky they survived at all.

He had never imagined that the gates of the Changi Garrison camp would hold much appeal, but now he was thankful to be walking back through them. Over the month of his absence there had been many changes for the better in camp and the system at Changi was now being run with full military discipline. Work units kept prisoners gainfully occupied performing tasks for the common good. Vegetable gardens flourished and whereas food was still insufficient in quantity and variety it was adequate for subsistence. There was a hospital at the nearby Roberts Barracks where the wounded and the continual stream of sick were accommodated in what, by later standards, were reasonable conditions. To relieve boredom, recreational activities were organised; one of the most successful was 'Changi University', which provided lecturers from among the prisoners. There were bands and a theatre, and the concerts that resulted did wonders for morale.

Encouraging rumours abounded about the progress of the war and the imminence of release. Such rumours were eventually dubbed 'boreholes' because it was whilst visiting the latrines (forty-foot holes dug side by side) that one tended to hear them. Had the prisoners known that their incarceration was to last three and a half years, their morale would most certainly have been shattered. Maintaining morale was vital, and VB was to see the result of the lack of it many times over the next few years, as men lost interest and began to let themselves slip. The first signs were a loss of self esteem and interest in social interaction, closely followed by a lack of attention to personal appearance and hygiene. Before long the victims had fallen foul of disease and the downhill slide continued to its inevitable conclusion. In Changi Garrison everything possible was conceived of to prevent this from happening. Still there was a limit to what could be done about problems such as avitaminosis, manifesting itself almost universally in the symptoms of a raw tongue, a raw scrotum and sores that would not heal.

But despite the discomforts of living with this and dysentery and almost constant hunger, there were moments of pleasure to be found in this new life in Changi Garrison camp. Having always derived great amusement through the company of his fellows, VB found plenty of time for good conversation. The highlight of his day was a regular stroll with one or two companions in the cool of the twilight. Occasionally he would wander over to the road above the beach, where the hushed murmur of the sea breeze in the palm trees was so peaceful that one could almost look through the barbed-wire fence without seeing it. There he would stop and gaze out at the Strait of Johore and remember the good times at the Rumah Merah and humming across the water in his dinghy, and wonder where on earth all this was going to lead.

The weeks passed and VB started to become acquainted with his host, the Imperial Japanese Army. In the early days the guards were made up largely of fighting troops, whom VB felt had at least some sort of grudging respect for their fellow fighting men. This was not apparent at the time but his later experience with the uneducated peasants who were not of front-line calibre served to firmly convince him of it. Stubbornness and insistence about seemingly trivial matters seemed to be characteristic of all the Japanese, both of officers and guards, but VB would never have guessed just how far this trait could be taken.

It started on a morning near the end of August 1942, when all POWs were marshalled and told that the Japanese Commander wished them to sign a declaration that they would not attempt to escape. Despite the threat of retribution, senior officers advised the prisoners not to sign it, to which agreement was general. The response from the Japanese Commander was to order all prisoners to assemble in the Selarang Barracks Square. There would be no exceptions. On his way to the square VB helped some orderlies struggling across from the hospital with bed-ridden patients and medical equipment. Even the very sick had to be moved from the hospital to front up.

VB's spirits were high enough. It all seemed so ridiculous as to be almost amusing. But standing there in the sun, the sweat running down his face in the intense heat and close confinement, his sense of humour began to pale. What on earth could be going through the minds of these people? There was nowhere to go to the toilet. Teams were digging trenches through concrete for latrines. Within hours they were filling with the liquid excreta of thousands of men with dysentery. His water bottle was empty and he queued for hours to refill it; the Japanese had cut off supplies except for two taps in the square. There was nothing to eat. When night fell it was so crowded it was difficult to find space enough to lie down comfortably.

The second day was long and there was an issue of gluey rice, but nothing else. The next morning several senior Allied officers were taken out of the camp to Changi Beach to witness the execution of four prisoners who had tried to escape. Morale in the square plummeted, and that night a concert was organised in an effort to revive spirits. At the end of it VB joined the biggest choir he had ever known, to sing 'God Save the King'. As he sang he looked around him at the many thin men, weak from illness and exposure, holding their heads high and mustering what little strength they had to join the gesture of heartfelt unity and defiance. He sang a little louder. Rarely had he been so moved.

For all their spirit the prisoners were in a no-win situation. Across the square they were dropping like flies, and senior officers finally advised them to sign. They were now clearly signing under duress, and the signatures would be worthless. VB joined a long queue to a table set up near the clock tower at one end of the square. When his turn came to sign he looked the Japanese officer straight in the eye, then bent down and signed 'Bill Shakespeare'.

Life as a prisoner at Changi Garrison was an unpleasant existence, though tolerable, VB found, if one was of a mind to make it so. Nevertheless most were happy to be chosen to move somewhere else, imagining that, as had happened when they'd left the camp on work parties around Singapore, their lot might again improve. Their willingness to leave was fostered by the Japanese, who promised better food and environment and minimal work. In July Bill Steele was chosen for a working party draft for Japan. Mas' Rastus, with his clever mind and wit, had been a sure tonic to revive a flagging spirit and VB would miss him greatly. On the morning he left VB slipped a copy of a much-loved sailing photograph of the two of them into Bill's top pocket. On the back were the words, 'Till we meet again under happier circumstances. Don't forget New York 1945. Good luck.'

Two months later VB too was drafted to the second group of prisoners to be sent to the north, 'somewhere in northern Malaya or possibly Siam—to greener pastures'. The word from the Japanese was that conditions would be far better, but as he packed his belongings, he had mixed feelings. Later at the Singapore Railway Station the guards were heavy and they were forbidden to speak to anyone, but when VB noticed the crowds of Malays chatting to each other and waiting for their trains on the platforms, he began to feel good about the move. Everything looked so refreshing and normal after the confinement of Changi Garrison and it was obvious they were going upcountry, where fresh fruit and vegetables would surely be more easy to find. The train pulled in and with much unnecessary shouting from the Japanese guards he was herded with about thirty others into a steel box-type freight car. Inside it was incredibly hot and they couldn't even all sit down at the same time, let alone lie down. Sleep was going to be virtually impossible.

The trip north began. Out over the Causeway and past the scattered reminders of war, burnt-out vehicles and bomb craters, and on into the jungle and rubber country, mile after incredibly hot, airless mile, bumping and jolting against each other and dripping with sweat. The only ventilation was the open door and soon the steel sides of the car were almost too hot to touch. All day and all night they travelled, a jumble of bodies, boots and baggage, men standing, curled up, or sitting with legs stretched out in a pile of other legs, falling heavily against each other as they dozed fitfully.

Into the next day and then the next, up through the rice *padi* country of northern Malaya. The train stopped infrequently and food was scarce, just the occasional bit of watery stew or sour rice, or fruit thrown into the trucks by sympathetic locals as the train moved along. There was no provision for hygiene and no water in which to wash. After a couple of days dysentery added to the general discomfort. This seemed the bitter end. Any last vestiges of modesty were dispensed with as VB jostled for a position to relieve himself in the only possible place: out of the door.

Over the border into Siam (now Thailand) and into the fourth day, glimpses of huge outcrops of rock, tangled jungle, an enormous triple pagoda on a hillside and the extraordinary sight of lumbering elephants ploughing fields. The nights were colder here and condensation dripped down the steel walls of the freight cars, chilling those in contact with them. By the time they reached their destination, Banpong, to the west of Bangkok, the prisoners were dirty, smelly and bleary-eyed. They had lost what little condition they had and were exhausted. The journey had lasted four days and four nights.

VB tumbled stiffly out of the train, grateful that at last the journey was over. After a short march from the station he looked around at the squalor of the POW camp at Banpong and began to get an inkling that the nightmare was only just beginning. His fears were well founded, for this was to be a nightmare of barbarous reality which he, along with many thousands of others, would endure for three very long years. It was a nightmare from which some thirteen thousand British, Australian, Dutch and American POWs were never to emerge, but were to die of starvation, disease and sheer brutality. With them, between seventy thousand and ninety thousand civilian labourers would perish; Malays, Tamils, Chinese, Javanese and Indians, their bodies left to rot in the depths of Siam and Burma, or to be buried in shallow, unmarked graves, their deaths never to be recorded, their families never to know of their fate.

SIX

The Line to Three Pagodas

The Imperial Japanese Army did not kowtow to International Conventions. Japan had never ratified the Geneva Convention and had no qualms about drawing labour from its ample stock of prisoners of war to fuel its war machine. That war machine demanded a rail link between Burma and Siam so that its large army stationed in Burma could be supplied securely from Singapore, instead of via the submarine-infested sea routes, now being hit hard by the Allies. The Burma–Siam railway would link an existing Singapore–Bangkok line to another linking Rangoon to Ye in Burma and would cover a distance of 263 miles (421 kilometres) through country largely rugged, mountainous and matted in dense jungle.

The Emperor's forces enjoyed free passage through Siam, thanks to a cleverly conceived non-aggression pact between Japan and Siam. Japanese engineers first estimated the completion time of the project as five or six years, but as the supply situation in Burma became more urgent the target time for completion was cut to eighteen months. Scheduled to start in June 1942 the project didn't really begin until almost November, yet the target date for completion remained the same: October 1943—only twelve months away.

70

By the time VB's party arrived in Banpong there had been a handful of advance parties through the southern area, clearing ground and building a few hut camps to accommodate the labourers to come. The building of the railway linking Siam to Burma was about to get under way in force.

Banpong camp was dismal. It didn't take long to discover that the only facilities were a few flimsy bamboo huts thatched with *atap* and latrines only three feet deep, stinking, totally inadequate and teeming with flies and blue-bottles. VB was filthy with four days' sweat and grime but washing was out of the question; the one well was some 300–400 yards outside of camp and they were forbidden to go in search of it. They'd been told to prepare themselves for a march that night, and it was clear there would be little time to recover from the exhausting journey. A feeling of dread began to creep over VB but he quashed it quickly and allowed his ready optimism a free rein; this was obviously just a staging camp and it seemed likely that things would get better further north. There appeared to be plenty of food about. He could see fruit trees, banana palms and sugar palms to the west of the camp and the wet, black, sticky soil looked nothing if not fertile.

The prisoners rested. It was nice at last to be able to lie stretched out in the shade of a tree and get a real snooze. All too soon it was over; the heat of the day began to ease and they were mustered for the move. Fortified by a few hours' rest, a couple of balls of issued rice, and fruit bought from Siamese traders at the railway station, they trudged away from the uninspiring Banpong. Packing their bags back in Changi no-one had imagined having to walk. Now they found the luggage they'd brought quickly became heavy and uncomfortable on their ill-padded backs. Bare essentials turned to granite hunks and bedrolls into marble columns. Within a few hours it was clear that much of the provisions and equipment would have to be abandoned, and there began the heart-breaking business of choosing what to leave behind.

For mile after exhausting mile they marched, until VB was mesmerised by the pack on the back of the man in front, plodding one step at a time along the dark, dirt roads. They walked all night with just a few short breaks, and in the morning stopped and collapsed onto the ground near a small village. VB's eyes lit up as traders appeared, some equipped with yokes across their shoulders, a wok and brazier swinging beneath. He gave one a few coins and the fellow squatted down on the spot to cook *mah-mee*, a delicious fried concoction which filled VB's belly for probably the last time in many months.

That night the second part of the march turned to sheer hell and men began to stagger and fall behind. Every time the group stopped for a rest VB found it harder to get up until the process became an absolute agony of protesting feet and muscles. Eventually the marching formation became a straggling line and some of the sick had to be supported by others already loaded down with their own luggage. When the sick could go no further they dropped onto the road where, if a few swift kicks or thumps with the rifle butts from the guards failed to produce the desired results, they were left behind to be collected the next morning by local bus.

Their destination was the prison camp outside the small town of Kanchanaburi, or Kanburi, near the junction of the Kwai Noi and Mae Kong rivers. The town itself, at least partly enclosed by an old, dilapidated battlement brick wall, gave the impression it had once been fortified. On the outskirts buildings were scattered haphazardly in a general scene of overgrown disarray. The camp, three or four kilometres upriver from the town, was overlooked by limestone hills falling sharply to the bamboo-lined river bank a little past the camp's landing jetty. The area had been cleared out of thick native vegetation and banana palms, and now consisted of nothing more than two primitive bamboo and *atap* huts already overflowing with men. There were still no latrines and no cookhouses. The Japanese were not allowing work parties to work on the camp, instead pushing every available man out each day to clear a trace for the railway line.

At Kanburi the men were regrouped and told their specific tasks.

VB was to remain with a group made up of officers only, whose task it was to build the bridges ahead of those who built the embankments and excavated the cuttings. Past the *padi* plains of Kanburi and surrounds, along the river flats winding through small teak and bamboo jungle and steep, jagged limestone mountains, the route of the railway ascended the valley of the Kwai Noi. From that point, about a third of the way to the Burmese border, countless bridges had to be cut into the mountain sides and across the valley floors.

For VB's group Kanburi was just another staging post. The camp with its nearby town represented what was to prove the last place of civilisation before the formidable jungle country to the north. By the time they left, VB had gleaned enough information from the local Siamese and other prisoners in camp to know for certain: the jungle country to the north was hell on earth.

There would be no convalescent camps, no greener pastures.[1]

If ever there was a year from hell, it was 1943 for the prisoners on the Burma–Siam Railway. The campaign in Burma was going badly for the Japanese and many of their supply ships were being sunk by the Allies—good news for the Allied cause but disastrous for those toiling to build an alternative route. From about December 1942 pressure from the Japanese Command to push the railway through mounted, and the attitude of the taskmasters became increasingly more offensive and violent.

There hadn't been much for breakfast, just the usual sort of gluey rice porridge. Standing in the line-up of the dawn parade the barking of the Japs at roll call echoed to the background of screeching birds and early-morning hooting of gibbons cavorting in nearby valleys. Ahead was another long working day, a day VB knew would not

---

[1] *'Of the period that followed, enough has been written.'* VB had no desire to have his experiences during the next dreadful three years become a feature of any manuscript written about his life. *'It was an unfortunate episode, but so be it.'* For me, however, the story of his life could not hope to be complete without describing something of the experience that made him so much what he was.

end until the chorus of jungle night sounds was underway. A day working under the Japanese engineers who designed the bridges, 'vicious, puttee-legged little bastards' determined to prove their designs could be quickly and efficiently constructed; a day in the jungle felling teak and rosewood with axes and cross-cut saws, and hauling the logs out using only manpower. He'd heard that some parties had the use of elephants for hauling, but he'd never seen it himself. Tools were few and far between—holes were drilled mostly with hand drills and piles were driven using a pulley system with a rope. Then there was rock to be blasted and cut, earth to be hauled with poles and slings, and pick and shovel work that never ended. Thoughts of sabotage were never far away, but it wasn't easy and those caught trying it were dealt with severely. He'd learned to be content with small things, such as stuffing holes in the main bearers with white-ant nests. It wasn't much but it was something.

They'd just moved up the line to a new site and the camp was but bamboo benches and ragged tents and tent flies. As well as work on the railway there was jungle to be cleared, tracks to be made and buildings, first for the Japs, to be constructed. Their own huts would have to wait—they'd struggle to knock something together after working hours, in the dark. Doing battle with jungle bamboo was a difficult business. The stuff grew in mammoth, tightly knit clumps designed specifically not to be chopped down. The men's arms and legs were covered in small cuts that quickly turned septic if not nurtured carefully.

At least being in an advance party the ground was unfouled and hygiene better than in the large camps to the south. He'd already discovered the dismaying intimacies inherent in living in heavily populated areas. The roll call went on. One by one VB heard the names of the men with whom he would stick during this ordeal: Perky Perkins, Max and Donald Webber, Louis Denholm, Frank Smith. All good solid types. These men were mostly older, but not too much older, and a little wiser of the capricious ways of the world than some of the naive youngsters he'd met on the line, some of whom it seemed had barely left the arms of their mothers before joining up. It was the youngest prisoners, he'd noticed, who most often broke down first. He knew he was in good company. He knew he had a head start.

It hadn't been so bad at first. In the early months the river Kwai had been a life line. Traders in barges brought with them the few additional calories and vitamins that kept them going. They'd all had a little money with which to buy something extra, perhaps the odd egg or banana, to supplement the staple diet of rice. Occasionally there'd been vegetables. Meat was a rarity. If any had ever arrived with the supplies it was usually flyblown and full of maggots, having been transported from Singapore for days without refrigeration. But the cooks always made something of it, even if they had to boil it for days.

The grim reality was that the further north they went the less likely it was that supplies would reach them safely. Thousands upon thousands of men were flooding the camps to the south and supplies destined for the north were often looted or commandeered before they arrived. Now they were out of reach of traders. Now there was no way they could supplement what the Japanese provided.

To one side of the clearing the sick parade was bigger than usual. There would be no rations issued to those not strong enough to work since, in Japanese eyes, they did not deserve it. Food for the sick would be taken out of the rations of those who worked, leading to further malnutrition in the well and more sickness generally. It was a mediaeval logic.

VB was faring all right but he'd had his share. Dysentery and the interminable diarrhoea which accompanied it made life a misery on and off for everyone. Sleep was all too difficult lying on uncomfortable benches of split bamboo, but when the nights were broken by griping pains, fever and almost hourly visits to the wretched latrines they took on nightmarish proportions. Out of reach of the vital egg supply, the raw and ulcerated mouths and 'strawberry balls' of avitaminosis added to the misery. Scabies was another discomfort. He treated himself by painfully scrubbing the nasty scabs and sores back to raw flesh with teased bamboo brushes and hot water. Recurring bouts of benign tertian malaria plagued him.

At first small amounts of quinine had been irregularly available in the camps in the south, but now there were stocks only for the Japanese. The faintness and nausea was all too familiar and each time it swept over him his spirits plunged, for he well knew the chance of convalescing was remote. Three or four days toiling in the sun with a splitting headache, aching bones and attacks of cold sweats and shivering was a cheerless prospect. Still, it was probably better than a beating.

He shuddered at the thought of the last time. It was a familiar scene, the Jap engineer faced him, screaming unintelligible abuse, fists clenched, narrow eyes bulging, face contorted with rage. The sun beat down on VB's bare back, sweat and dirt trickling over each protruding rib. He had wondered what the devil the engineer was on about, but did not have a bloody clue, and knew instinctively that he was about to pay for this lack of understanding. The spare pick handle had lain just a few metres away. Suddenly it was in the little man's hand and he was flying at him, swinging wildly. Running was out of the question; that would only lead to more beatings. There'd been nothing for it but for VB to take the punishment, and hope like hell that a couple of good hits would be enough to appease the Jap's rage, and that he would escape only bruised, not broken.

VB was lucky enough never to be broken. But he saw others, already frail and weak, beaten to death. If they did not die immediately then they died later, the bashings having proved the final assault on their suffering bodies. Lack of communication and language difficulties led to misunderstandings and frustration on both sides. Though being in an officers-only party had its advantages, VB couldn't help but feel that the Japanese, and particularly the engineers, felt even more need to beat and humiliate them for the simple fact that they were officers. He decided early on that the civilisation of the Japanese was but a thin veneer. By experience he learned that men who were capable of civility one minute could exhibit the savagery born of a mediaeval culture the next. The sheer brutality of many Japanese, some of whom held respectable positions in civilian life, convinced him that their behaviour was not normal. It was bred by a system of codes indoctrinated by the military to further its own ends. Codes such as *bushido* taught that the Emperor was divine, that Japan was divine and that the Japanese had a divine mission to rule the world. The *Senjinkun* (Combatants Code) instructed that to be taken prisoner was a soldier's greatest shame, and it was spiritually binding on Japanese soldiers. The code dictated that death should come before the dishonour of capture, offering the comforting assurance that they should 'expect death to be lighter than goose down'. In view of this the Japanese soldiery, particularly those who had never been in the front line to witness the fierce defence put up by so many of their wards, looked upon the prisoners with absolute contempt. They believed that the POWs should have died in battle and this, along with the notion that the railway was to be completed no matter the cost in human lives, was a disastrous recipe for the unfortunate prisoners on the spot.

The Imperial Japanese Army required absolute discipline and there was little scope for either guards or junior officers to act individually. Soldiers were taught to regard the command of a superior officer as a command from the Emperor. Junior officers who failed to achieve their allotted work target experienced severe penalties, even bashings. In reciprocation junior officers bashed the guards, usually Korean, and the guards bashed the prisoners, who sat on the bottom rung of the ladder.

The jungle was never quiet. Even at 2am it seemed to teem with life. VB put the drum down beside him at the latrine and took a leak, the official reason for his nocturnal wandering. As he dealt with the business of looking legitimate he glanced around him. There was no-one about. The guards liked to steer clear of the reeking latrines, one reason why the Dickybird was buried nearby in the jungle fringe. This was a dangerous lurk, but one that gave him great satisfaction. Having a sense of purpose other than that of slave to the Japanese was vital for morale. Putting one over the Japs at the same time was even better. He finished. Holding his breath slightly he walked boldly on. A few more steps and he was there. He scrabbled at the leaves and dug the freshly turned earth quickly, just an inch or two, for he was the third of their party to visit that night. He opened the steel container. They couldn't be too careful. Just a piece at a time, each piece fitting neatly underneath the false bottom of something, in this case the drum which, he would explain if challenged, was being used as a chamber pot into which the bedpans of the sick were being emptied. The dysentery in their hut was so severe that the drum had not lasted the night, having to be urgently emptied and rinsed. That should be enough to put them off. The guards had a horror of disease, and it was unlikely that any would wish to take the matter further.

Tomorrow they were moving on, and the large and unwieldy wireless set known more usually as 'the Bird' had to be dismantled and hidden in the false-bottomed tins and boxes they used for transport. For the team of six men who looked after it, it was a restless night. Penalties for being found out were severe. He'd heard on the grapevine that six wireless operators caught in the act at Kanburi were beheaded for their efforts. Being a part of it was a huge risk, but each of them was convinced that news of the outside world was vital; it was all too easy for men wallowing deeply in their own misery to forget that there was an outside world, that there was hope, that one day the nightmare really would come to an end.

Max and Donald Webber were ice cool. They operated the wireless, an enormous thing some 18 inches by 8 inches and devilishly difficult to hide.[2] It happened almost always at night, while VB and other members of the team kept guard. Often it was impossible to operate it at all, but for the most part the Bird had been a reliable if irregular source of news, passed to senior officers by word of mouth directly from the BBC Far Eastern Service broadcast from New Delhi.

Not the least dangerous part of the operation was liaising with the Siamese Resistance Movement which kept the Webbers' radio supplied with a bulky collection of torch batteries. As they had

---

[2] *Max Webber was later awarded the OBE for his role in operating the radio, for his courage and devotion to duty.*

pushed north contact had become more and more difficult and the small quantity of desperately needed drugs the agents brought along with them became almost impossible to get. The agents had disguised themselves as local traders and operated at enormous risk to themselves; any who were found out were executed without ceremony. VB had pondered over why the local Siamese villagers, who were used to grow crops to help feed the Japanese Army, were treated cruelly. These were people who were theoretically part of the 'Co-Prosperity Sphere' and neither they nor the civilian labourers should have been indicted under any military code. He concluded that they were simply innocent victims of the ruthlessness, desperation and reality of war. Japan saw the Burma–Siam Railway as a military necessity, and the Japanese war machine sacrificed their own men to the cause. Others were far more expendable.

On a more personal level the war had bred hate. Hate had bred brutality. Brutality had became the norm. And there was worse to come.

The period dubbed 'speedo' began in February 1943 after a decision from the Japanese High Command in Tokyo to bring forward the deadline for completion yet again. The Works Unit of the Railway Section, with the backing of the Imperial General Headquarters, made extreme demands on the camp commanders. With the increased pressure from the top, the men on the spot were spurred on to unsurpassed brutality in their efforts to follow orders.

By the time VB's group reached an area around Takunun camp, three-quarters of the way to the Burmese border, they were working all day on a small amount of rice and a dried substance something like seaweed. Desperate, gnawing hunger was a permanent state. Now at dawn sick-parades wretchedly ill men, some struggling even to stand on their leprous-looking, matchstick legs, were forced outside to line up, even in the rain. If the sick parade was too big the engineers flew into hysterical rage and the gaunt, wasted skeletons of men could only watch with glazed, despairing eyes as they were declared fit for work, or 'light duties'. Light duties was supposedly half a day's work but was often extended. Men who could sit but not walk were forced to work sitting. Shifts for everyone got longer, sometimes well into the night. In VB's group few, if any, fit men were allowed to remain behind in camp to carry out essential sanitation work, so that latrines could not be dug or maintained, and conditions in camp became appalling. Proper huts were not built and they slept on the ground under leaky tents or on hastily put together bamboo platforms. As if things were not bad enough already, the monsoon came early.

The rain deluged the camps. The river became a swollen, swirling torrent of muddy yellow, drowning the bushes overhanging the bank and carrying with it great entangled rafts of jungle trees and bamboo. With the almost incessant rain came mosquitoes, fever and disease. Being constantly wet and working in deep bog made everything twice as difficult. It took everyone longer to complete their daily quota of work and the slower rate of work meant increased pressure and more beatings. As the roads became impassable and rivers unnavigable, supplies were cut off and some died of starvation. Cases of dysentery, cerebral malaria and cholera increased alarmingly. Few precautions against the disease were taken in the civilian labour camps, and waterways quickly became infected. Within a short time cholera took thousands upon thousands of lives. In most prisoner of war camps strict measures were taken to prevent the spread of the disease. In VB's camp all crockery and cooking equipment had to be sterilised in boiling water before each use. A ration of boiled drinking water was given daily to each man with instructions that no unboiled water was to come in contact with the face. Since there was barely enough boiled water to drink, this meant that faces could not be washed, teeth could not be cleaned and shaving was out of the question. Still the epidemic worsened, for open, flyblown latrines were another source of infection.

In the remoter camps victims were kept isolated in tents, if tents were available. There would be rows of men who had suffered such acute diarrhoea that they had been reduced to dehydrated, shrivelled skeletons, their faces wizened, their features pinched, their eyes sunken and their blood thick and gluey. There they lay awaiting their only relief: almost certain death. Funeral pyres were kept alight to cremate the victims and these became sentinels of the stricken camps. In the main camps cholera hospitals were set up and in some cases doctors were able to improvise equipment to administer intravenous saline solution. For once the Japanese did what they could to contain the spread of the disease, even finding vaccinations for the prisoners of war in some camps. Cholera terrified them, for they too were vulnerable.

Such concern was rare in the civilian camps, where cholera was rampant. Civilian labourers, brought up to Siam either on false promises or forcibly, numbered some two hundred thousand. Since Siam was not Japan's enemy it was difficult to extract labour locally, so instead the Japanese military looked to Malaya where they recruited sixty to seventy per cent of their requirements. Most of the remainder came from the Dutch East Indies and Indochina. At first the Japanese used ruse to attract labour, but when that failed to provide the quotas they resorted to force. VB was acutely aware that his own party made up no pretty sight, but what he saw in the few glimpses he had of conditions in civilian labour camps made him feel sick to the core. The wretched, stricken people, kept separate from either the Japanese or the POWs, were being knocked around brutally and treated as entirely expendable. They were largely uneducated and had no hierarchical system in place to organise themselves. They therefore lacked discipline and their camps quickly fell into filthy disarray. Latrines were rarely dug and sickness and disease became uncontrollable. During the cholera epidemic the death rate was sometimes so high that there was no-one to bury the dead properly; bodies either lay where they fell, stinking with liquid vomit and faeces, or were buried in shallow graves which were soon washed out by the rains so as to expose the rotting corpses. A grim and dreaded fate for POWs was to be detailed to a burial party to go into a civilian camp to bury the dead or rebury the deader. The whole business was so ghastly that the only way to deal with it was to block it out of the mind. VB did his best, but the despairing faces of the Malays, a people he knew and loved, he could not forget. The images gnawed at him.

The monsoon saw the end of VB's cherished boots, which disintegrated in the constantly wet, sodden conditions. Once they were gone there were no others. He tried boots made out of palm leaves and vines and so forth, but they were never very successful. Now, walking on muddy, rocky tracks in constantly wet conditions the skin on the underside of his feet rotted and they became raw, swollen and ulcerated. If anything during his prisoner of war years inspired his disgust, it was going without boots, walking around in filthy, revolting, disease-ridden muck in the camps. Lack of clothing fortunately did not arouse the same revulsion, for his wardrobe was reduced to one pair of dilapidated shorts and the remains of a shirt which he left in his kit for special occasions. Everyday wear was now a somewhat abridged garment known as a 'Jap Happy'— a type of loin cloth tied round the waist and made out of whatever scraps one could find. Most in his group were in the same predicament and makeshift hats and Jap Happies were the standard workwear in the north. (Much later, in 1944, the Red Cross did manage to get a couple of shipments of blankets and clothes through, but to VB's great chagrin, there were never any boots.)

Time ceased to have any meaning. Day in, day out, VB fought a private battle with himself to muster the mental strength and determination to carry on. Once the battle was lost and the spirit broken the chances of survival plunged. Friendship was vital. Friends depended upon each other for care when they were sick or injured and for general assistance whenever they were in need. When VB felt his nerves were at breaking point he depended upon his friends to somehow lift his spirits enough to get him through the worst of it. And they depended on him.

With experience he found a formula which, through sheer dogged determination, seemed to work for him. He took each dreadful day as it came without dwelling on the bleakness of the future. In the worst times he concentrated on getting through each grim moment without giving a thought to how he was going to get through the rest of the day. He found defiance and purpose and comradeship in working as a team, particularly in relation to the wireless. And he was still able to find humour when his situation was anything but funny. Unexpected amusement at a time when from all indications there was none was a tonic for failing mental strength and morale. Humour at the expense of the Japanese was very satisfying and his dry cheeky sense of humour was well appreciated by those around him. He was not one to laugh long and loud, usually just a short guffaw and a series of chortles from beneath his moustache. But his eyes laughed a lot. Another with a particularly robust sense of humour was Perky Perkins, a good performer who rarely lost his cool even under the most difficult of circumstances.

The monsoon had well and truly set in up towards the Burma border, and once again VB's group had just moved camp. It had been raining for days, there was no proper shelter and they'd had very little sleep. Some of the party were out in the jungle that morning cutting bamboo and making bark ties for lashing the framework of the Japanese engineers' house together. VB, Perky and two others were erecting the frame, at the stage of fastening the ridge poles over the trusses, and lashing the purlins. Perky sat astride the ridge pole at one end, about sixteen feet up, and VB was astride at the other. Dawn had hardly broken and the rain ran off their noses and down their bare backs. It was very cold, they had nothing in their bellies and there was nothing to be happy about. There had been no conversation—not even the birds seemed to be singing—and the only sound was the miserably incessant drip, drip, dripping of the steady rain through the trees. Then suddenly and without warning Perky let forth with a stentorian burst of song:

> Oh dear, what can the matter be,
> Three old ladies stuck in the lavatory
> They were there from Monday to Saturday
> Nobody knew they were there.

He continued with a further three verses VB had never heard before and which are quite unprintable. VB did not often roar with laughter, but by the last verse of Perky's rendition he was doing it so hard that he lost his balance and began falling off his perch. He tried to grip the wet bamboo with his skinny shanks, but only tipped over so that he landed awkwardly but without injury in a cushion of soft, deep, squelching mud. The fall was not something he needed that morning, but the warm glow within him from having had such a good laugh lasted well into an otherwise bleak day.

On 22 October 1943, VB turned his gaunt face to the south to listen. The sound of laboured puffing, grinding and screeching was unmistakable. The first steam engine was on its way up the line to the border where, at Three Pagodas Pass, the railway through Siam had met the railway south through Burma. That day they were put to a new task: the building of high screens of bamboo between the camp and the railway line. Two days later another engine passed by. This one pulled a string of open goods carriages, or flats, with *atap* roofs attached to specially built frames. In the shade of the *atap* Japanese men of high office sat on chairs. They were making the journey north to take part in a great ceremony to witness the laying of the final rails linking Burma with Siam. The bamboo screens ensured that the exalted officers were spared the wretched sight of the civilian labour camps and the worst of the POW camps. The railway, at an inestimable cost in human lives and suffering, had been completed. As if in compensation, VB's party had their very first day off.

The work of construction was now over but, for most, the nightmare was not. In Siam and Burma there remained the arduous task of maintaining the embankments and the line, and repairing the none too substantial bridges being damaged by Allied bombers, which had been making occasional air raids since June 1943.

Some prisoners were returned to incarceration in Singapore. Others returned only to be shipped to Japan to begin work in mines and factories. Many were sent back to base camps in southern Siam, to Chungkai, Kanburi, Tamuan, Nakom Patong and Nom Pladuk, from where they carried out maintenance and repair duties.

VB's party remained upcountry in Siam. At the end of 1943 they were back at the base camp at Takunun, about 230 kilometres from Banpong, engaged in line maintenance. These smaller parties, which had separated for work further north, now rejoined their original groups. VB found Takunun a hive of rumours and information;

there was bad news about friends who had perished and happy reunions with others. Some were hardly recognisable, reduced to shrunken, sallow skin and bone. It was shocking to see the change in people, yet it was an unwritten rule that nobody ever mentioned to another that he looked like death itself. VB's weight had dropped by half: from his usual 190 pounds (86 kilograms) to 95 pounds (43 kilograms). Repulsed by his appearance, he went out of his way to avoid his own reflection.

At Takunun VB met Dr Hugh (Ginger) de Wardener,[3] a young doctor who had been sent out to Singapore with the British 18th Division. Despite VB's wasted appearance, de Wardener gained an 'indelible impression' of him as 'straight backed, solid, reliable, always cheerful and ready to help—the sort of person you'd want to be with in a tight spot. If one divided people into drains and radiators, he stood out as a sturdy and reliable radiator'.

When VB fell seriously ill, the realisation filled him with dread, despite de Wardener's being close at hand, for he had seen enough of conditions in the hospital tents. Just the day before, he'd spent a full day working with a burning fever and a sore throat. Twenty-four hours later he was so debilitated that he could scarcely move. Hugh de Wardener looked him over and made his diagnosis—diphtheria. VB would be evacuated to the so-called 'hospital camp' at Chungkai, further south. His kitbag had long since perished and when the time came, Hugh wrapped up his pitiful belongings in a little swag. With several of his closest friends he helped VB onto a flat-topped carriage of a train. There was no certainty that the train would stop in Chungkai but VB had instructions to roll off anyway. He would probably be picked up.

Nineteen hellish hours later, the train did stop in Chungkai. Stretcher bearers unloaded those too ill to walk, including the fragile, soot-covered bundle that was VB Perkins. On a sacking stretcher he was carried to a long bamboo and *atap* hut. The 'ward' was the usual style: walls open to about two feet from the ground,

---

[3] *Later awarded an MBE for his devotion to duty in the treatment of cholera cases.*

a walkway down the centre, and the beds simply one, long, raised bench of *chungs* (bamboo slats) along each side, on which patients lay. VB was too ill to notice the wretched scene before him: the rows of desperately thin, sick men lying with only a few inches between them on their uncomfortable benches. A place was found for him and he was laid with several other diphtheria patients on the blood and mucus stained bamboo near the end of one row.

Hugh de Wardener had sent VB to Chungkai with some valuable advice: not to sit up for a period of two weeks, no matter the circumstances. Hugh had worked previously with diphtheria patients in Chungkai and noticed the association between movement and paralysis. He had told VB of seeing people die immediately after sitting up and VB was determined to follow his instructions.

The stench in the ward was overpowering. The hut was crowded and there was a dire lack of both bedpans and people to empty them. Desperately ill men had no choice but to lie in their own mess, or that of a neighbour, until help came, as it eventually did in the form of overworked orderlies who themselves laboured under appalling conditions. For immobilised diphtheria patients there was no question of visiting the latrines. Now VB's will to survive was tested to the very limit. The horror of the place, the agony of the situation, threatened to push him over the edge. The urge to move, to help oneself was almost overpowering. The days seemed never ending. Lying in filth and squalor, feeling a vile specimen of human-ity, he drifted in and out of miserable consciousness trying to sleep away the time. The nights were hellish—men crying out restlessly and despairingly during the long, dark hours, and weak voices calling for help which rarely came. One morning he awoke from a fitful sleep to find the man at his side dead, his wizened face having found peace at last. One claw-like hand had fallen against VB's arm and he pushed it back under its ragged, filthy blanket. It seemed all too long before someone came to take the corpse away.

A day or two later his other neighbour was dead. But still VB did not move. For two long weeks he lay there, the last of his numbed senses blocking his mind to his loathsome plight. During the day he tried to concentrate on the play of light made by the sun through the *atap*, for the view from above was the only visual relief from the squalid surrounds. As day after sordid day passed, his condition began to gradually improve, and it became all the more difficult to remain unmoving. Eventually the long fortnight passed. The worst was at last over and a doctor advised him that he could slowly and gently begin to mobilise his body. He had made it. This time.

It was a pleasant surprise to venture out of the hut the first time. Chungkai was a great improvement on the camps in the north. Hygiene was typically lacking but food rations were far better. The camp, west of Kanburi, housed around two thousand sick at its hospital. But such was the shortage of doctors and orderlies that in many cases patients looked after each other. As soon as he was well enough VB helped out in his ward and did what he could to clean up the hut a little. At the same time he was donating blood from which a serum could be made to treat other diphtheria patients. (After the war a doctor from Chungkai visited VB's family in Cornwall and remarked at his generosity in giving blood, not only for serum but for transfusions, at a time when he could hardly spare it himself.) Later, to keep himself busy he worked in the tropical ulcer ward, where one had to have a particularly tough constitution. The smell was indescribable, rows of skeletal men lying helplessly watching their fetid flesh being eaten agonisingly away until bones and tendons were exposed. Holding down patients having their legs sawn off with little or no anaesthetic was one of the most difficult things VB ever had to do.

In mid January 1944 Colonel Edward (Weary) Dunlop took over as Officer in Charge at Chungkai Hospital, and began a drive to improve hygiene and conditions generally. His work in this respect was recognised as outstanding and his efforts have been well documented. VB met Weary several times in Chungkai, but he was one of thousands of men to pass through his hands. It wasn't until well after the war that they met again, discovered a great liking and mutual admiration for each other, and became firm friends.

In early March 1944 the rest of the Officer's Battalion from

Takunun were sent down to Chungkai. VB joined them in the fit
men's camp where they were packed into a single large hut; it was
hot, uncomfortable, crowded and teeming with insects. He was
very happy to be back with them again.

Life in Chungkai was altogether more peaceful and agreeable
than in the camps upcountry. VB began to gain a little condition,
for here extra rations could be purchased from the canteen run by
men from the Volunteer Forces; there were omelettes, soups, even
toffee fudge. Another plus was the entertainment and recreation
scheme in place; in particular the 'Chungkai Theatre', which
boasted its own band and orchestra. The camp strength at that time
of some four thousand five hundred supplied a surprising number
of professional artists. Others made up for their lack of experience
with sheer enthusiasm. VB had performed Shakespeare at school
and throughout his life was prone to quoting the bard at the most
unexpected moments—perhaps in a lull in the conversation a misty-
eyed rendition of 'On such a night as this the sweet wind kissed
the trees' etc., or a wizened Shylock delivered convincingly. In
Chungkai he took to the stage once more in Dr Dudley Gotla's
production of *Thai Diddle Diddle*, a rollicking burlesque extrava-
ganza. The cast included Perky Perkins, and over the period of
preparation and rehearsal RB and VB earned themselves the titles
'Bullshit Perkins' and 'More Bullshit Perkins' respectively. (The
names, I am assured by Dudley Gotla, carried 'no hint of disrespect
for either of them—they were both very popular and valued
members of the community . . . rather one should put it down to
the peculiar habits of the rude soldiery.')

Unfortunately *Thai Diddle Diddle* had a shorter than scheduled
season. After only one performance Dudley Gotla was called before
the Japanese commandant to explain what was meant by the title
of the production. In fact there was nothing in the show about the
Thais, nor indeed about diddling, but the producer found this
impossible to explain. The interpreter couldn't convey to the
humourless commandant that the title was a totally innocent parody
on a nursery rhyme. On looking up the word 'diddle' in a dictionary,
he discovered that it meant to swindle or cheat, and the show was

banned. Just for good measure the Chungkai Theatre, which had done such a lot to revive the tortured spirits of so many, was ordered to be shut down for a period of three weeks. Dudley Gotla thought they got off lightly. (Later when it was clear that Japan was losing the war the theatre was pulled down, since it was deemed inappropriate for the prisoners to be singing and enjoying themselves whilst Japan was in difficulties.)

Standing wet through on the parade ground ankle deep in mud, VB could not believe they were going to go through with it. The monsoon was heavy and high up in the mountains it had been raining for days. It was late July 1944, and torrents of muddy water gushed down the river, threatening to break its banks. Still the Japanese insisted the move to Tamarkan go ahead on schedule. A large group of them were destined for the camp near the junction of the Kwai Noi and Kwai Yai rivers. It should have been an easy move, for the country was flat for miles, but the rain just went on and on.

The river did break its banks. Within hours of them leaving Chungkai, the water was creeping quickly across the rice *padis*. The road flooded and suddenly there was nothing but a sheet of water in every direction. It was obvious to all of the sodden contingent except the guards that they should turn and go back, that it was madness to continue, but they were forced on, wading through the brown water which kept getting deeper until it was waist high and still rising. Eventually the only dry land to be seen was an area about the size of a tennis court, enough for only a third of the men. There they eventually halted, caught like stranded cattle in the monsoonal flood. For the next two or three miserable days they kept up a system of shifts; two hours sitting down on the drier area, two hours standing in water over a metre deep and two hours sitting in water a third to half a metre deep. Sleep was impossible, their equipment was soaked, their food rations sodden. There was nothing they could do to help themselves but to do the British thing, and sing. So they sang, and sang, until no-one wanted to sing any more.

At last the flood level began to drop and they waded on, arriving at their new camp exhausted, hungry. Tamarkan, another large camp, was originally built for prisoners involved in the construction of what has since been immortalised as the 'Bridge over the River Kwai'. Rows of well-built huts, the likes of which they had never seen up the line, were laced by roads, and real gravel paths led to the cookhouses and latrines.

The ten-span Kwai River bridge was a vital link in the Japanese supply line. A hundred yards downstream from the main concrete and steel bridge a smaller wooden bridge provided a backup crossing. From about April 1944 VB had noticed from Chungkai some occasional high-level aerial activity in the region, and the ack-acking of the anti-aircraft guns stationed at the big bridge. So far it seemed the bridges had suffered little.

It was an evening in late November 1944, and the last rays of the sun were filtering through the tops of the feathery bamboo. VB heard the sound of a large approaching squadron and felt a ripple of tension and excitement sweep through the camp and he rushed outside to look. Twenty-one large, four-engined American Liberators were heading towards them in the first major high-level air raid on the bridge. There was no warning of this and VB's excitement at seeing the aircraft turned to horror and disbelief as he watched the first bombs sail down to land on the Tamarkan camp itself. He and other fit men flew to take cover where they could amongst a confusion of black smoke and the glare of incendiaries. The sick and maimed had no choice but to lie where they were and let fate do its damnedest. It was all over in minutes. As the drone of the bombers receded into the light of dusk and the smoke began to clear, VB joined the scramble to tend the dead and wounded. The bridge had suffered no damage in the raid but official figures listed eighteen prisoners of war killed that day and a further sixty-eight wounded. As he knelt trying to stem the blood loss of a sobbing man who had just had an arm almost severed, VB struggled to maintain his own composure. After all they had been through, after all they had suffered and endured in the hands of the Japanese, this really hurt. It hurt badly.

Morale at Tamarkan plummeted as they realised their situation.

This was not to be the last inaccurate, high-level raid; competition became keen to be transferred to other camps. The raids continued. At both the River Kwai and further up the line, bridges and railway lines were damaged and the supply line to the north disrupted. Now little or no food or medicine was getting through to the prisoners repairing the line upcountry, and once more they began to starve. Occasionally parties of sick and emaciated prisoners were sent down to Tamarkan and it was obvious to VB that conditions had regressed to something akin to the worst seen in 1943. Death and injury through the air raids added to their misery.

After a time the Royal Air Force took over the raids, using aircraft capable of lower-level attacks. They'd appear over the horizon at Tamarkan in twos or threes, then one would peel off and make a pass over the bridge, with its machine-guns firing up in the air as a warning to the prisoners to get off. Then the attack proper would begin, one aircraft at a time approaching at low level and dropping a bomb on each run with devastating effect. The physical danger from the attacks had reduced, but spirits still plunged at the sound of the bombers, for brutal reprisals followed every raid and prisoners had to work day and night with little rest until the bridges were repaired. Then in order to test the wooden bridge, now barely able to take the strain, VB and others were forced to push box-cars gingerly across it, wondering when the hell the whole lot would crumple like a pack of cards. And every time the bridge was repaired the air force returned to demolish it.

By late February 1945 two complete spans of the main steel bridge had been blown off completely and fallen into the swirling yellow waters of the River Kwai. To VB's great relief, further repairs were now impossible. Soon after, a large-scale move from Tamarkan was ordered. Officers were separated from their men and moved to nearby Kanburi; troops went a little further to Tamuan. The Kanburi camp now covered a large area and VB's group was detailed to the task of digging a moat three metres deep and five metres wide around the entire perimeter. The explanation from the Japanese was that it would lessen the prisoners' chances of escape.

The latest news from the Dickybird was that Allied bombing had rendered the railway inoperable from Moulmein in Burma as far as the Kwai River bridge, and that the Japanese were in retreat from Burma and north-west Siam. Allied planes dropped pamphlets on Kanburi showing the Allied fronts in both the air and sea, pushing steadily towards Japan. Now the relationship between the prisoners and the Japanese began to change. Knowing that the war was not going well, the Japanese, and particularly the Korean guards, began to show signs of being a little easier on the men. For VB it was a thrill to receive his very own tin of beans and packet of high-protein biscuits, the first issue of Red Cross food allowed. Suddenly the administration became more lenient about them purchasing food from Siamese traders. Searches of personal possessions became more frequent, as if the Japanese were looking for diaries or anything else that might later incriminate them.

At the same time VB became uneasy. Why had the other officers been separated from their men? Why had they been forced to build a moat around the camp, and why had the machine-gun wielding guards been so heavily increased? Rumours were circulating that should southern Siam be invaded they'd all be executed *en masse*.

In July 1945 the officers' camp heard of a further move, this time via Bangkok to a camp to the north. The officers were divided into ten groups, the movement to be carried out progressively by rail. VB was among a number of reasonably fit prisoners detailed to Group 9 to assist with the movement of the sick and dying. In mid August their turn came.

Loading the stretcher cases into the steel box cars was heavy work. There were not enough box cars and there was little choice other than to put the walking sick on the flats, where they sat or lay, pitifully holding their blankets over themselves as protection from the searing sun. VB did his best for those assigned to him, rigging shelter out of blankets and piles of kitbags for those too weak to help themselves. It was barely enough. The journey was difficult and trying, for there were many delays due to the damaged bridges. Some were incapable of supporting the weight of a loco-motive and he spent hours with a shoulder to the box cars and flats, physically pushing them across. Then there were more delays waiting for an engine to meet them on the eastern side while they all cooked in the broiling heat. The box cars were like furnaces when standing still, and each time they stopped patients had to be physically unloaded from both these and the flats, and moved into shade, if there was any. It was exhausting work but despite the difficulties VB was in good spirits, for the last radio news he had heard before leaving camp indicated that the Japanese could not hold out much longer.

The Japanese NCOs were in an extremely dangerous frame of mind and strictly forbade contact outside of the group. But at one stage, while they were waiting for an engine, a villager slipped out of the undergrowth to whisper something to a patient. His words swept through the men like a shot: 'The war has ended.' Many of the bedraggled assortment of prisoners were reluctant to accept the news. VB received it with only a subdued excitement, not daring to fully believe in case it wasn't true. But later there were other signs; local people smiled and cheered and some held up their fingers in the V for victory sign.

Around midnight the train screeched slowly to a final halt at Bangkok Noi. There the bridge across the river had been demolished completely and the train could go no further. Once more the sick were unloaded and made as comfortable as possible in the scrub at the side of the railway. VB rested, waiting for transport across the river. From the other side of the water, a few lights winked comfortingly. It felt good to be getting close to a city again, to real civilisation after so long in the *ulu*. What would the next few days bring? A small boat putted up to the bank and several Japanese officers got out and summoned the guards. The senior Allied officers were called over and shortly after they returned and called an assembly of prisoners. As they waited in the moonlight there was an uncanny quiet. Four hundred sets of bleary eyes turned to their commanding officer and heard him utter the words they had only dreamed of for what seemed an eternity: 'Gentlemen, the war is over.'

A raucous cheer shattered the stillness as the first wave of elation swept through the group. Some burst into song, others into tears.

Men who had bottled up their emotions for three and a half long years wept unashamedly in relief, in joy, in immense sorrow for those who had not made it. VB, having blocked his mind to the outside world for so long, had an overwhelming feeling of unreality about the war having finally ended, along with a sudden peace of mind. But his exhilaration was repressed by emotions he had deliberately kept anaesthetised for so long: bitterness about the futility of the unnecessary suffering and death and a sense of 'well I've made it . . . but what about Malet and Bellingham Smith and all the others'. He looked down at one of his charges, a frail, shrunken figure critically ill with amoebic dysentery, and wondered if the lad would survive long enough to see freedom. The tragedy of watching a man die now would be almost too much to bear.

The men grappled to take in the news that the war had ended, while their senior officers were engaged in a battle of wills with the Japanese about whether to continue the journey to the camp in the north. After a great deal of unpleasantness it was finally agreed. They would remain in Bangkok.

In the small hours of the morning, as VB waited with the other men for a vehicle ferry across the river, his tired mind was swamped by questions to which he soon realised there were no answers. Trying to find answers could only invite further distress, and once more he made a conscious decision to put those thoughts firmly to the back of his mind—to keep them there *indefinitely*—and to apply his mind to more immediate and practical matters.

SEVEN
Bangkok (& Boots)

V B sat on a stack of old rice sacks nursing his raw and bleeding feet. His eyes were open but where there was despair he tried not to see. A few men were reduced to hysteria that day, and the sight of them sitting with knees drawn up and sobbing inconsolably unsettled him profoundly. It was the morning after the end of the war and he felt he should be in a party mood, but all around him emotions were fragile. They'd marched all night carrying the sick on the metalled roads and had hobbled into the godown at the Christiani Neilsen Docks in a musty Bangkok dawn. He glanced up to see one of the patients crying quietly, and began to feel his own emotions cracking.

Word had got around that it had been a single nuclear explosion that had ended the war. For many this only served to make each man's personal agony seem all the more futile; in the end the nuclear bomb turned every battle, every maiming, every death, every tragedy into a vain, meaningless sacrifice, for this powerful weapon of mass destruction could have ended the war before it started. It would take a little time, a few days, to come to terms with freedom.

Feeling his control waver VB was almost overwhelmed by a sense that now it was all over it was all right to let go, to let the guard down. But he didn't, he couldn't. He got up to look for something constructive to do, and set his mind to pinching some boilers and cooking pots from the Japs and getting the cookhouse in some sort of order. Along the docks he could hear shooting and wondered which side was letting off steam. The roughly forty thousand Japanese in and around Bangkok were still armed and, understandably, unwilling to take orders from their ex-prisoners. Things were not destined to happen quickly.

The reoccupying forces and relief teams assembled by Mountbatten couldn't land until the Japanese formally signed the surrender document in Tokyo, which would not occur until 2 September. During the next two and a half weeks a group of commandoes known as 'E Group', who had parachuted into the jungles of Siam weeks before, undertook the recovery of some sixty thousand Allied POWs and internees. They became known as RAPWI (Repatriation of Allied Prisoners of War and Internees), commanded by Lieutenant Colonel Douglas Clague.

Supply aircraft were flying in, and those in the Bangkok area were first in line to receive a new issue of clothes and toiletries, including their own towel, soap and razor. For VB it was the highlight of those first few days. When he was given his brand new, black, shining boots he held them for a moment, and couldn't help but run his fingers along the grain and breathe in the smell of polished leather. He put them down and pulled a pair of thick cotton socks luxuriously over his clean feet, then slipped them on. Savouring the experience, he tied the laces, slowly, lovingly. This was better even than his first square meal in years. His stomach had objected to the halfway decent quantity of food and the whole thing had been a bit of a disappointment. But the boots . . . For two and a half years he had been barefooted and the horror of walking around with unspeakable filth oozing up between his toes was to have an enduring effect on him; he would rarely go without shoes or something on his feet again, even in his own house.

It was not the only thing to stay with him forever. The whole war experience had given him a new set of values. Waste became something which would always appal him. Having survived on so little for so long, eking an existence out of nothing, he was to find life back in a western society an extravagance. Never again could he throw out an apple, no matter how far gone it was. He could always find a little bit that was still good, more or less, and would eat it on principle. Having eaten meat that arrived at the cookhouse green and maggot ridden, a piece of steak a few days past the use by date was never of much consequence. And it wasn't just food. Anything that could possibly be recycled, used again, rejuvenated, adapted, he would set about doing it rather than buy something new. It was to be a source of annoyance to some people around him in later life.

While some came out of the war with their nerves shot, VB emerged with a calm that would prove itself particularly in times of adversity. Somehow the experience served to put his life into perspective, to give him a sort of hierarchy of what was important. The day-to-day tribulations of living in normal society would hence-forth seem trifling after what he had been through. He'd always had a spirit of optimism about him, but this was to become an almost ridiculous capacity not to worry about things; it would not always serve him well. Then there was the comradeship thing. VB had always enjoyed the conversation of men, but now the bond with his fellow man was stronger than ever. He was surprised at the intensity of his feeling that morning, 25 August, when he was awoken at 5am to be told that he'd been given early evacuation, that he was to be ready to leave Bangkok within the hour. He and the other members of Max Webber's team were given priority as a reward for their efforts in operating the radio. He should have been relieved and delighted. It really was all over and now he could go home. But he knew there was no way he was leaving first after what he'd been through with these men. Besides he was fit enough, both physically and emotionally, while others were desperately in need of attention. He gave up his place to someone in greater need. Max and Donald Webber did likewise.

All the same, the next night as darkness closed in he began to wonder about the merits of his decision. RAPWI had swung into action and Lieutenant Colonel Clague plucked him from the godown at the dock to become part of 'Operation Swansong Siam'. VB was detailed to take the first convoy of supply trucks out of Bangkok heading for the POW camps north of the city, at Nakon Nyok and Prachai. Until the Japanese surrender was officially signed and the Allied military authorities and occupation forces arrived, still at least a week away, the Japanese were to remain armed, to maintain order. And now here he was, a lone, dilapidated, unarmed British soldier sitting in the front seat of the lead truck clutching a tin box containing 100,000 tikals, trying to impose his will on about twenty truculent Japs, all armed to the teeth.

He had set out cheerfully enough in the late afternoon, but as Bangkok disappeared behind and night fell his confidence evaporated. Nobody at Allied Headquarters in Bangkok had been able to tell him where these camps were, just that they were located in the middle of Japanese defensive positions in northern Siam, away from the route of the Burma–Siam railway, and that they were possibly difficult to reach from the south. He'd since discovered that the Japanese had little clue either. Or were they just playing dumb? The idea was playing on his mind when the Japanese NCO barked something to the driver and the truck stopped. VB felt the prickle of sweating palms. This was bizarre. He was the only European on this trip for Christ's sake, and he was at the absolute mercy of these Japs, who were in no good humour. As he waited to see what would happen next he felt more than vulnerable and an image of his bleeding body crumpled on the side of the road flashed across his mind. But then the Jap NCO finished his pee and got back into the truck. It was all right, for the moment.

An hour later the truck stopped again and the driver began a heated debate with the NCO. The driver was all for turning back, arguing that he didn't have enough fuel for a trip of indefinite length. VB ventured to suggest they might be able to refuel at one of the camps but the NCO, furious, clearly resented the advice. They drove on, now along tracks barely discernible in places and every so often the whole convoy ground to a halt again and another altercation ensued. VB was tense, acutely conscious of his position and, around him, tempers strained close to breaking point.

It was after midnight when, with a stroke of good luck, they spotted the dim lights of Prachai POW camp. VB breathed a sigh of relief. He couldn't help but reflect upon the discipline of the Japanese, and wonder whether had he been in the same position alone in a truck with armed but defeated German soldiers, he would have made it to his destination at all. The sound of the trucks roused the whole camp from sleep and having reported to the Japanese guards on duty, VB was surrounded by expectant faces bombarding him with questions. Everyone wanted to know the procedure for evacuation but there was little VB could tell them at the time except to say their location was known and things would begin to happen.

As the trucks were unloaded many prisoners scuttled back to their huts to scrawl letters to loved ones, pressing them into VB's hands before he left. By first light the convoy was on its way to No. 5 camp and Nakon Nyok. In the daylight and with directions from the Japanese CO at Prachai, they had no difficulty in finding them. At every camp VB witnessed the uplifting sight of Allied flags, some the tattered remains of flags carried and hidden for three and a half years, others simply pieces of canvas or sacking lovingly patched with an assortment of material scraps—anything that could be found in the right colours to make up something akin to the Union Jack, the Southern Cross or the Stars and Stripes. At each camp VB fielded more questions, often about missing mates, men who had gone upcountry on work parties and hadn't been heard of since. Occasionally he could help, but most often not, and he recorded the names of those to be tracked down, promising to pass the inquiries on. Despite the lack of news on the evacuation front and the intense company between camps, it was an uplifting experience to be the bearer of supplies so desperately needed.

It had been eighty miles back to Bangkok and having barely slept for forty-eight hours VB walked through the door at Headquarters. It was 10pm. Lieutenant Colonel Clague was still at his desk and he, too, looked tired. He looked up as VB entered. 'How did it go?'

'Not badly sir,' VB replied, dropping the maps on Clague's desk and unclipping his reports. 'I think we found all the camps in the area.'

'Good man,' Clague said. 'I was rather counting on that, for I've got another convoy waiting for you. I want you to go back up to Prachai to bring in the first load of prisoners. Can you be ready to leave within the hour?'

For VB it was to be the second of many, many trips out of Bangkok collecting ex-prisoners. He had got himself deeply involved. The evacuation continued, although not as fast as some would have liked. The airstrips in Singapore were in poor repair and monsoonal weather delayed flights. There was a shortage of transport ships to move ex-prisoners out of Bangkok in large numbers. The harbour was full of mines and until these were cleared ships had to anchor offshore and men had to transfer by motorboat. RAPWI became cynically known as 'Retain All Prisoners of War Indefinitely'.

Back at Headquarters after an early mission VB was astounded to find a message waiting for him—Flying Officer Robert Edbrooke of the RAF had inquired after him. VB was delighted; the last he had heard from Brooker was from the UK, where he had been posted back from Singapore in 1941. What on earth then was he doing here?

From the UK, Brooker had watched the disastrous chain of events unfold in Singapore. Thoughts of Perks (as he called VB) and others as prisoners of war under the Japanese were never far from his mind. The Navy was not recruiting at the time so Brooker joined the RAF and trained as a navigator. Now, at the end of the war, he found himself on one of the first Dakotas into Bangkok from Rangoon, in Burma, the clearing centre for prisoners evacuated by air. Years later Brooker recalled:

We set out from Rangoon on that first flight with great trepidation and excitement. No-one seemed to be certain if, in fact, the Japanese had thrown in at that time, as communications were still very inadequate. As soon as I arrived at the Don Muang airfield I asked a few people if they knew if Perks was alive. Luckily I found an MO who said, yes, Captain Perkins was alive and evidently reasonably well, as he had gone up country to

bring back more POWs. I left a message and imagine my delight
when on my very next flight in, there he was on the airstrip
waiting for me, as large as life. He'd come through . . . it was
a truly great moment for us both.

There was work to be done, however, and the real reunion had
to wait until some time later when VB was finally granted a couple
of days' leave. Brooker arranged leave to coincide and they spent
much of it together. The city abounded in high spirits and it was
the first time VB had been free to really kick up his heels for almost
four years. It felt good, very good. A day at the Bangkok races
with his old friend brought back all the happy times in Singapore.
The bustle of the crowds and the calling of the hawkers—it all
looked so normal that for a short time one could almost forget that
the war had ever happened. Even Brooker's having his wallet stolen
could not dampen the realisation that, after all the suffering, life
went on. And life, Godammit, was good.

Over the weeks VB became aware of the current plight of the
Malayan indentured labourers who had worked in slavery on the
Burma–Siam railway. At the time of the surrender there were some
thirty thousand Malayans still in Siam and Burma, the remnants of
a huge labour force the size of which was impossible to accurately
assess. They had no organisational structure of their own and there
were few records giving the location and population of the hundreds
of camps scattered throughout Siam and southern Burma. VB shuddered at the memories of how they had been treated, at memories
of the Japs trying to get the Allied prisoners to bury the cholera
cases before they were even dead, at stories in some camps of men
being forced at the point of a bayonet to bash them with a hammer,
at how dying men were taken out into the jungle and dumped there
to perish, at how he'd heard of tents full of sick and helpless coolies
having their shelter removed to be left behind in monsoonal rain.
Each time he had seen these things or heard of them, he'd felt a
stab of pain. He had worked with the Malays and he'd fought with
them, and they had been treated by the Japanese even worse than
he had. He had an uneasy feeling that the British had let them down.

The British were supposed to have protected the people of Malaya and Singapore. Though he felt no direct blame could be put on anyone in particular, the fact was that the people had trusted them. Now he felt some sort of personal debt.

In early October he refused evacuation again and joined the small party of selfless Malay or Tamil speaking ex-POW officers[1] who had been collecting, housing, feeding and providing what medical help they could to the civilian labourers.

Back into the jungle he went, collecting coolies up the main north–south line and along a branch railway north of Bangkok, concentrating them in the Kanburi area to be transferred to a transit camp in Bangkok when they were well enough. Immediately after the war ended the labour force in the north of Siam were still in an appalling state: sick, suffering from malnutrition and many without clothes or shelter. By now they were becoming scattered. Those who were anywhere near other human settlements had left their stinking camps and wandered into Siamese villages, where they lived as fringe dwellers on the outskirts of town, or off handouts from kindly locals. Many were simple, uneducated people with no money or means to get themselves back to Bangkok. The arrival of VB or another member of the repatriation party, with food, a little money and the promise of a ticket home must have seemed like manna from heaven to the shocked, broken people who had suffered so appallingly for so long.

There were some moving moments, particularly on the few occasions he located members of his own regiment. Those who had sensibly evaded being taken prisoner when Malaya and Singapore fell found they were the first to be tracked down by the Japanese for use as forced labour. He hadn't recognised the two soldiers from his own platoon. They were just skin and bone. But they recognised him. They'd been at a staging camp some way up the railway, waiting for something to happen. Though he'd been with them but a short time before the war, he couldn't help but

---

[1] *Including Lt. Col. W.M. James, Capt. Tom Carey, Major Chamier, Capt. Du Boulay, Capt. A.N. Ross and 2nd Lt. Richard Middleton Smith.*

feel responsible and was charged all over again with a desire to do what he could. Next time he was at Headquarters he put their case, as well as that of Malayan members of the regular army, the various Volunteer Forces and the Civil Police Force who needed to be identified, separated, re-equipped and paid at the scale. The outcome of the meeting was that VB was given responsibility for doing the job, and for co-ordinating the evacuation of all Malayan members of military or quasi-military units.

The memory of the telegram was fresh in his mind. The agony of its contents was just another reason VB threw himself into this work and kept going. For him it was a tried and true formula. When mental anguish threatened he applied his mind and body to something else. VB had ripped open the telegram from home happily, supremely confident that everything and everyone were all right. Skipping over the words, he returned to reread them more slowly, then slumped into a chair, his face ashen. The news that his brother had been missing since 1942, presumed drowned at sea, was a stunning shock. How could this have happened? If anybody deserved to come through this war it was Leslie Perkins; warm-hearted, studious, gentle, incapable of a mean act and far more thoughtful than he himself had ever been. For a few moments VB had felt dazed, almost apart from himself, as images of his brother flooded over him; most recently, sitting at a table at the Satay Club in Singapore, his amiable face smiling, telling amusing stories of the Hong Kong racing fraternity; as a boy, standing beside him singing in the choir at Maryfield Church; the look on his face when he put his arms around his first horse; as a youth, stopping in at the florist in Torpoint to buy flowers for his mother.

In the days that followed his thoughts inevitably turned to home. It wasn't the first time. Over his years as a POW VB had thought more of his family than he ever had in the halcyon days of prewar Singapore, for the memories of happy times at home in Cornwall had been a tonic for misery. He had thought about his father, Alfred Perkins, a handsome man with large, blue eyes and a curly black handlebar moustache. He had thought about Alfred's love of the

country, his vast store of knowledge of local flora and fauna and
the joy it gave him to take his family on long rambling walks through
the local woods of the Antony Estate, bordering Wilcove, or the
rolling, green countryside and wild, rugged cliffs of the Cornish
coast. VB remembered watching, fascinated, as his father followed
minute traces of wild animals, it seemed to him with the sense of
a prize beagle, fossicking around to find a burrow or a nest. Alfred
had taught his sons how to wait quietly on a cold, frosty winter's
morning, to see the fine wisps of a hare's breath floating up through
the long grass, to take note of its direction and to creep up on the
animal from downwind. He was familiar with the habits and migra-
tory patterns of the birds of the area and enjoyed being challenged
by his children. They'd return from a romp in the woods with
barked shins and muddied boots, bursting to tell him of a new bird
they had seen, or clutching a bird's egg in small hands, supremely
confident that their father would know what it was.

VB had thought about St John's Lake, a favourite of his father's
for wildfowling, where Alfred had frequently taken him to venture
quietly out on the flat, brackish water in his little duck-punt. A
small shot cannon mounted on the front of the punt, fired by pulling
a string, was the means by which many a Sunday roast dinner graced
the table at Beach Cottage. Occasionally the family would wake
up in the morning to find a plump pheasant hanging in the kitchen.
Alfred well knew that when a stiff, cold breeze blew at night, the
pheasants from Antony Estate came down from their high roosts
to the steadier lower branches of the trees, and when conditions
were right he would occasionally slip quietly out of the house.
Pheasants were always referred to as 'canaries' at Beach Cottage
and, as Alfred would tell his boys, some of these canaries were
foolish enough to roost in the trees just outside the boundaries of
Antony. VB had known better than to ask too many questions about
canaries.

He'd thought about the way Leslie had inherited his father's love
for horses. Alfred was known in the district as an authority on
equine ailments and it was said he knew better than any what brought
a shine to a horse's coat. He'd joined the Admiralty not long after

the turn of the century, at first in charge of the horses of the Dockyard Fire Brigade and later, after serving an apprenticeship, in a technical capacity. Alfred Perkins loved life. He was happy, affable and had a dry, cheeky sense of humour. He was a good father to his children but preferred to leave the task of disciplining the family to his wife, who was made of sterner stuff.

VB had pondered over the idea that the strength he'd found in himself at the worst of times as a POW he had inherited from his mother's side. His grandmother, Ambrosine Power, had brought up her six sons and two daughters alone after her husband, a tenant of Antony Estate, had died when her children were young. VB had always admired the way she had conducted her affairs under the most difficult of circumstances, and had kept the farm working. He had happy memories of Yonderberry Farm, on the opposite side of the same inlet of the Tamar River to Beach Cottage, and a particular fondness and respect for his grandmother, whom he always referred to in conversation as Ambrosine Maria. He seemed proud that she was one of the 'Powers of Cork', whatever that meant, and saw her as a strong and interesting character.

Her daughter, VB's mother (whom VB referred to in later years as Edith Amelia), was also strong in character. She was intelligent and capable, not given to displays of emotion, and shunned weakness in any form. VB remembered how much she disliked impoliteness and how she kept his father, who was inclined to frivolity, firmly in line. She did not suffer fools gladly and had a strict moral code. Some outside the family saw her as hard, and VB could forgive anyone who had been on the receiving end of her disapproving look for holding that impression. She didn't smile readily as did his father, and when annoyed her pale blue eyes steeled and her lips became thin and drawn. But VB knew her as essentially kind and the Perkins household was noted for its hospitality and the fact that the best of everything was always brought out for visitors. Like his father, she was a strict Conservative and they both attended the local meetings in Torpoint religiously.

VB had never fathomed how it was that his mother had been able to look into his eyes when he was a boy, and see just exactly

what he was trying desperately to conceal. Yes, perhaps he was
the least disciplined in the family, but his mother's standards were,
he felt, unreasonably high. At night, at the dinner table, how was
it that she had picked that he had been up to something just as he
was busy reflecting with satisfaction on the likely outcome of the
afternoon's escapades? When word went round the village that
somebody had climbed onto the roof of the house belonging to the
irascible old man up the street and had stuffed a carefully measured
clod of turf down the stack, she seemed to know immediately it
was him. His explanation that the old boy had swiped at him with
his walking stick for cutting through his garden had done nothing
to lessen the crime in her eyes. Was there something so obvious
about his expression? Perhaps she had recognised it as the same
one he was wearing when he decorated Alfred's pigs with stripes
of black tar; or when he trussed up the family dog and brought it
to church in a sort of nappy to ensure it would not disgrace itself;
or when he climbed up the china cabinet to get at an apple tea-
cake for the afternoon's visitors which his mother had put, she
thought, out of reach of small hands. She had caught him just in
time to witness him, the china cabinet, the china and the apple tea-
cake all come crashing to the floor. In each case the result was a
thrashing.

Despite vivid memories of her disciplinary tactics, above all else,
when VB thought of his mother he remembered her principles
about hard work. That his images of her were of efficiency and
industry above tenderness and nurturing was not surprising, he'd
decided, given her determination to provide all of her four children
with a good education. Alfred's modest salary fell far short of
providing for good schools and she had made up her mind to fund
the children's education herself. VB remembered the business of
converting one of the front rooms of the house into a small shop,
hanging a bell on the front door and opening the family home for
business. From that time he felt they had almost lost her as a mother,
for she threw herself into the enterprise with such resolve that
there was little time for anything but work. Wilcove itself didn't
provide enormous custom but the little lane past the house led

down to a stretch of the Tamar where two anchored and obsolete warships provided a training base known as HMS *Defiance* for naval personnel. The custom of the servicemen who passed by on their way to do a stint on torpedoes and naval mines made a solid success of Edith's enterprise, for Beach Cottage was the only shop within three miles and she kept it open for long hours. All the money that she earned she put into a school fund for her children.

Now, as VB thought about his family in Cornwall from his billet in postwar Siam, tiny twinges of guilt made their presence uncomfortably felt. He began to appreciate for perhaps the first time the enormous sacrifices she had made for her children, that it was only her dedication that had given him his education, the education that had been vital to his ability to mix with people from different strata of society, that had led him away from the path to becoming a parochial villager to another which set him towards becoming a man of the world. That he was at ease in any company was a social asset he held extremely valuable, and for that he had a lot to thank her. Yet what had he given her in return? Like his brother Roy, a lot of trouble probably. Had he neglected her? The contrast between Leslie and himself was stark.

VB was always the one his mother had to constantly reprimand for sailing his little boat too far out into the Tamar, and for playing chicken with the naval vessels. It was he who seemed to have least time for his younger sister Lyn; he was always rushing from one adventure to another and wherever at all possible leaving her behind, despite constant requests that he look after her. And while he and his eldest brother, Roy, were devising methods to escape from her, it was Leslie who had the patience to wait for her, to look after her and include her in what he was doing. VB had a great affection for his grandmother, but it was Leslie who spent the most time with her, who sensed the old lady's loneliness at having all her sons away, and who even eventually moved in with her to keep her company. VB's social life as a young man was full and hectic and would barely have allowed him time even to notice her plight, let alone do something about it. Since Leslie and he had been in the Far East his mother had written to him of the long and detailed letters she'd had from Leslie. But while VB had always had good intentions himself, he only ever managed to scrawl a few token lines together to send home. For the most part he was too busy with his own life and his mother had waited in vain for letters from her youngest son that came all too rarely.

Leslie had never neglected his mother, but now Leslie was dead. How devastated she would be at losing the son she never had to worry about. He pushed the thought from his mind, for dwelling on it was almost too much to bear. Yes, perhaps he could have done more for his mother. But it wasn't too late. He resolved to make up for it when he went home to England. In the meantime he had to control his grief for his brother. There was much to be done.

For part of the war Alfred and Edith Perkins had been faced with the probability that both of their sons in the Far East were dead. The first notification arrived some time after the fall of Singapore in 1942, informing them that Lieutenant V.B. Perkins was missing, presumed dead. When, some six months later a similar envelope arrived, Edith Perkins felt sick to the core. Reluctant to open it, yet tormented by not knowing, she sat down with a heavy heart and slit the envelope. The format was all too familiar. The authorities regretfully informed her that Chief Engine Room Artificer Leslie George Perkins had been reported missing, presumed drowned at sea whilst a prisoner of war of the Japanese, aboard the Japanese freighter *Lisbon Maru*, in the region of the Chekiang Province, China.

The family was shattered. This was Lyn's favourite brother, the one who never seemed too busy for his little sister. This was the loving son who had done his best to try and fill the void felt in his family when he left for the East. This was the son whose future had always seemed so assured. There was no other information, in many ways a blessing for the family as Leslie had died in tragic circumstances. Not knowing the detail gave them time to grieve for their son, without the added distress of dwelling upon the horror of his last hours. Later they learned more, for the story was eventually told.

'2000 British Battened in Sinking Ship'; 'Left to Drown By the Japanese'; 'Machine-gunned in Water'. It wasn't easy for the Perkins family to learn more about what happened to their son by reading about it in the newspaper. The *Daily Telegraph* of 23 December 1942 carried the story of how the Japanese freighter *Lisbon Maru*, against the Geneva Convention, displayed no sign that it carried a cargo of POWs. As a result it was torpedoed by an American submarine and abandoned by the Japanese, damaged and sinking. Before the Japanese left they battened down all the hatches, leaving the prisoners to go down with the ship in the pitch black, airless holds. There had been a last-minute breakout from one of the holds but many of the prisoners who got out in time were shot in the water or left to drown. Three survivors who made it ashore were successfully hidden by islanders, and later found their way to Chungking, China, in territory still held by General Chiang Kai-shek. Knowing then that there had been survivors, Edith Amelia was filled with hope that her second son was still alive. Throughout the war years she cherished the belief that Leslie had made it to an island somewhere and was living among the natives awaiting discovery. Indeed many survivors were picked up by sampans off the Sing Pang Islands in the Chusan Archipelago, near the coast of the Chekiang Province. Others were later plucked from the water by the Japanese, who apparently had a change of heart when it was realised that some had got to land and that the story would be told.

It wasn't until the war ended and a survivor turned up on the doorstep that VB's mother lost all hope. The man had been with Leslie, who was weak and ill, on the bow of the *Lisbon Maru* just before she went down. They had jumped off together. As the ship lurched into the depths she sucked powerfully, plucking the weakest from the surface, pulling the flailing bodies down and down to eventually come to eternal rest with her on the bottom of the Yellow Sea. Leslie Perkins was one who did not have the strength to fight her, and his companion saw his sandy-haired head go under. He was one of eight hundred and forty-three men who were either killed or drowned on 2 October 1942. A further two hundred and forty-four of those who survived the sinking eventually died in prison camps in Japan, in the custody of the Imperial Japanese Army.

On hearing of the tragedy the British government tried to instigate a full investigation and report on the trial and due punishment of the responsible Japanese officers and men, pointing out that:

The torpedoing was followed by behaviour on the part of the captain, the crew and guard which was so callous as to be a disgrace to the naval and military traditions of any civilised country . . . His Majesty's Government appreciate that the Geneva Convention has never been ratified by the Japanese Government. Nevertheless they expect Japanese naval and military authorities to respect the principles embodied in the Convention and to treat prisoners of war in a manner befitting a civilised power.

Report on British Protest re sinking of *Lisbon Maru*, Public Record Office, Kew, U.K. (P.R.O. C0980/67)

The Japanese Minister of Foreign Affairs refused to recognise the necessity for a Court of Enquiry. As the men of Whitehall had perhaps not yet fathomed, and as VB and many like him had discovered through bitter experience, Japan, with its mediaeval codes and prejudices, was not a civilised power.

The Malayan Refugee Camp at Bangkok's Mitsui Dockyard was a large, rambling shambles of a transit camp housing thousands of ragged civilians in godowns on the wharf. VB was Commanding Officer of the camp during most of November and December 1945. During that time he installed a few ex-Malay Regiment and Civil Police Force members as guards, and fancied that when he'd finished there was a bit more military organisation among his undisciplined charges. He was finally relieved on 20 December 1945, but still he did not leave. He'd thought about it, but there were few people around capable of carrying on the work with the Malayan coolies and he'd made a commitment to himself to finish the job. So he packed up his kit and headed upcountry again. He'd been at it for well over four months after the last of the Allied POWs went home, and one of the few breaks he'd had was ten days in the Chulalongkorn

Hospital recovering from a severely infected pi dog bite.

Now at last he was leaving Bangkok. The refugee camps lay empty. He was satisfied there were no Malayan labour camps unaccounted for, and no Malayans uncollected. He boarded HMS *Empire Beauty* on 26 February 1946 with the last thousand civilians to be repatriated to Singapore. With the exception of Captain William Bangs, who did not return to the UK, VB was the last of the ex-POW officers to leave Siam. It was over six months after the war ended.

A month later, on 26 March 1946, he sailed from Singapore for home. As HMS *Winchester Castle* slowly made her way out into the roads and beyond, VB watched the war-scarred city for which he had grown such an attachment gradually fade into the distance. He was leaving the Far East with mixed feelings. The good times in prewar Singapore evoked in him enormous fondness and warmth. The bad times, the sheer agony and wretchedness of his experiences as a POW, he wanted to block completely from his mind. Yet through them he had found in himself spirit, strength, compassion, willpower, and the kind of comradeship with his fellow man that he was unlikely to ever experience again. Whatever happened in the future, these sentiments and the friends who remained behind, buried in jungle graves, would tie him intangibly to the East, for ever.

EIGHT

Blown Home Again

The icy cold of the English winter of 1946 had thawed. The crisp spring day was clear and chilly as *Winchester Castle* pulled into the wharf at Southampton. There VB heard that the dockers had recently been striking for higher wages, and it came as a sharp reminder to him that he was now back in the Western world. How different it seemed to the one he had inhabited for the last few years. For the first time he felt a little ill at ease about returning home. How would he fit in now? The plight of the striking docker was a world apart from that of the war-hardened soldier who had been through hell and back, and it dawned upon him that the next few months were not going to be easy. Nine years and a world war had passed since he left his native Cornwall for a three-year tour of duty in the East. He was not a youthful and naive 24-year-old any more. He was 33 years old and he had learned a lot about life.

VB planned to surprise his kinfolk and had not announced his impending arrival. But a friend of the family spotted him on the train, his frail figure huddled in a thin coat. Fearing that the shock of seeing him might be too much for his mother, she rushed ahead to warn her. Now, as VB turned into the road, his kitbag slung over his shoulder, his mother and sister Lyn were waiting for him outside the house. From a distance he was unmistakable, for his walk was just the same, his head held high, his back straight and the characteristic spring in his step still there. But when he reached them the sight of his worn features and yellow complexion took them aback and his mother was so overcome by his changed appearance that for a full minute, as she hugged his thin frame and struggled with the tears her upbringing told her must not be shed, she could not say a word.

Things were different at home now. VB's mother and father seemed to have aged more than nine years. There were lines of worry in his mother's brow and she had far more grey hair than he remembered. His parents had bought another waterfront house, on Alexander Terrace, Torpoint. It overlooked the approaches to the Admiralty Dockyard and his father could live out his retirement years with a view of the marine traffic of the Tamar, in all its forms, just as he had always wanted. His eldest brother, Roy, had married a local farmer's daughter and was living in Beach Cottage. Lyn was also married, having attached herself to the local school master, Charles Cardew, on his return from wartime service in Egypt.

The war had not been easy on the Perkins family, even discounting that it had taken from them their much loved and admired son, the son whose future always seemed so assured. Their new house in Torpoint, a small town across the Tamar River from the Naval Base at Plymouth, was a casualty of the blitz by the German Luftwaffe. The enterprising Edith Amelia had opened another shop on Alexander Terrace, only to see it destroyed the day the enemy bombers appeared over the horizon of the Mt Edgecumbe estate to deliver their deadly consignment to the naval families and citizens of Torpoint.

The war had left indelible scars, but still the people remained fundamentally the same. When VB returned home after so long he found he couldn't settle into life as he'd known it nine years before. He realised, not for the first time, that he was a different person. His family desperately wanted to know everything that had happened to him, to share it with him, to understand what he had been through and the changes they saw in him. But VB could not open up to anyone about his wartime experience. He just didn't want to talk about it. How could they understand? How could anyone understand except those who had been through it; and he had no particular desire to talk to those who had been through it about it either. It was all in the past now. He wanted to forget, to bury it completely.

As the days passed he found he couldn't stand being cooped up in the house with the family and their regular routines. Instead of relaxing and convalescing as was his mother's wish, he found himself unable to keep still or remain inside for long. Not long after his return he had another attack of benign tertian malaria. The family hovered around him, unnerved by the apparent severity of his symptoms, mopping his brow and piling blankets on his shivering, sweating form. When he had barely recovered, he was out of bed despite his mother's protests. He loathed doing nothing and set about busying himself wherever he could. Before long the Perkins household had been renovated and had new hot-water pipes laid in. Then he left for London.

Most ex-POWs had been back many months by the time Captain VB Perkins turned up on the doorstep of the War Office in London. Perhaps it was because of his apparent tardiness that he was received so curtly by the officious young clerk at the desk, who made it clear he'd seen enough of ex-POWs. VB had a problem. When Headquarters in Bangkok closed down and he'd finished work evacuating Allied POWs, he was no longer employed by the Ministry of Defence. Working in the rescue team to evacuate indentured labourers he'd received no pay, assuming that he was a Colonial Office responsibility as were the other members of the party. For a period of some four months he'd been bereft of funds, supposing things would sort themselves out and that eventually he would receive some form of pay for his efforts.

Now at the War Office the clerk went in search of his file, to return with the discouraging report that there wasn't one. According to his records VB Perkins did not exist. VB was stunned, almost lost for words. This was not at all what he had expected in recognition for his efforts in Siam. The clerk was quick to retort, 'You know, stragglers like you really can't expect us to be able to deal with you efficiently when we've all but closed the files on this business. Everybody else has already been through and been paid. Since we don't have a file on you I'm afraid there is nothing I can do. All I can suggest is that you pay a visit to our archives and see if they have something on you.'

The least VB had expected out of his trip to London was that he'd receive a ration book like every other citizen. But until he could somehow get himself resurrected he didn't have even that small recognition of being. It wasn't until he'd put in a great deal of effort that his file was eventually found—in the Archives of the Dead. There it had been laid to rest with those of the deceased, apparently when he had been reported dead in Singapore, and had somehow never been retrieved. There followed a protracted period of communication with the War Office, wherein VB had to write further reports on what he'd been doing since the end of the war, pointing out with respect to his work with Malayan RAPWI that 'During the whole of this period I did not receive any communication from the Colonial Office or any other authority whatsoever regarding posting or pay . . . I was not in receipt of any subsistence allowance and for long periods in my travels, collecting Malayan troops, I had to provide my own food and lodging.' The reason why this came about, one suspects, though VB was vague about it, was that at the time he was more interested in getting on with the job at hand than doing the paperwork. VB was never very interested in paperwork. It was a low point in his life. He felt flat, empty and, as friends noticed, a little lost. At the War Office nothing happened quickly. He still had no ration book and he hadn't been paid; it was to take years to sort out his case. This sort of treatment did nothing to make him feel any happier about being back in England.

VB had learned to ignore the swimming feeling in his head, but then came the sudden nausea and hot flush that warned him of collapse. He'd lived with his malaria long enough and was accustomed during the war to soldiering on regardless. But one day

his disrespect caught him short, and he crumpled into an undig-
nified heap on the cold, concrete footpath of Charing Cross Road.
For a moment or two he lay there, disoriented and dispirited,
before a kindly lady appeared through the blur to help him to
her car and deliver him to the nearest Military Hospital in
London. Now he received the first full medical examination he'd
had since his release from the tender care of the Japanese. On
top of the malaria he was found to have a gut full of distinctly
unsociable amoebae, which explained why his appetite had not
been what it once was, why he hadn't put on as much weight as
he would have liked. Unsettling also was the news that his heart
was not where it should have been; it was three inches further
to the right. The quack's theory was that the strains imposed
upon him whilst labouring in a weak condition as a prisoner had
literally displaced his heart. But at least now he'd have something
to live on. A disability pension. He didn't much like the idea of
it, but considering his lack of funds and the fact that His Majesty's
Government was showing no inclination towards paying him what
he was owed, he went along with it.

It was a difficult time. He found he missed the close companionship of other men, for he had spent three and a half years in
their exclusive company. Yet he was not interested in organised
reunions with other POWs, nor in becoming a member of the
many ex-POW associations which sprang into being during the
postwar years. He had closed the door on that chapter of his life.
Trying to find a place back in the material world was not easy,
and he became irritated by the pettiness he saw around him in
civilian life: meaningless disputes between people of all walks of
life who really believed they were hard done by, people who
were bitter towards others through little jealousies or rivalries,
people he judged would probably never know what doing it hard
really was. If anybody had reason to be bitter he did, but he and
many others who had been through the same experience had
overcome bitterness, had overcome hatred, and learned some
profound truths about what really mattered in life.

Upon his release from hospital VB scouted about trying to find something he could fit himself into. The feeling of displacement was acute. He constantly sought company, for having spent the war years living in such close proximity he did not like to be alone. Bill Steele had come through the war relatively unscathed, and he and Nena now lived in a house in London, where VB spent much of his time. As well he oscillated between family in Cornwall, Brooker's place in Buckinghamshire, or sailing on the Clyde in Scotland with Ross and Maggie McLean. In his heart he knew that Cornwall was not for him. He didn't try to resume his career with the Admiralty; it all seemed too predictable now and he had lost interest. That phase of his life was well and truly over. He pined for the East and thought about returning to the Malay Regiment, now in the process of reforming, after six months compulsory home leave. He still had the telegram informing him he'd been posted to South-East Asia Guides for absorption back into the regiment. But a career in the armed forces was not for him either. He knew well that the discipline of the army in peacetime would not suit him. He had done his bit, for what it was worth, and the idea of all that spit and polish and parading did not appeal.

VB had a dream. It was a dream he'd had since he was a little boy. He wanted to be a shipowner, to run small ships to interesting, out of the way places, places that were perhaps difficult to get to, remote places. In the month after he left Bangkok and before he left Singapore, he'd had a good sniff around to see what he could find of interest. Pip and Bunny Gardiner were already back in Singapore, and Pip was also looking for something to do. The seed of an idea was sown in their heads. VB and Pip would somehow set up a shipping business in Singapore after VB's return from leave. They would operate around the islands and up the remote east coast of Malaya. VB's capital base was a bit lacking, but he had plenty of enthusiasm to invest. Between the two of them they chipped in to buy an old and rather unseaworthy Chinese double-ended barge. It wasn't much, but VB saw it as just the beginning.

Since then all had gone awry. Pip had found a very good job

with the Port Authority in Malaya and the barge had sunk at its mooring. Prospects for VB Perkins & Co, Singapore, were looking only fair to middling.

During the latter part of the war Nena Steele had lived in Earls Court, on the first floor of a large Victorian house belonging to two elderly and wealthy Jewish sisters. Rose and Nellie Isaacs were not partial to taking in boarders, but there was a war on and they'd felt they should do their bit and had taken Nena in while her husband was a guest of the Japanese. On Bill's return Nena had moved out and the ladies had since left the first floor free.

Nena told VB about the apartment. She was convinced that between them they could woo Rose and Nellie into opening their door to VB. She knew full well of Pussyfoot's capacity to charm ladies of all vintage, and she arranged afternoon tea. A week later VB was ensconced in a very pleasant, spacious, well-appointed and (most importantly, as he was suffering terribly from the cold) well-heated house.

Rose and Nellie Isaacs were spinsters, both well into their seventies, and still lived very much in the Victorian era. Always beautifully attired in long skirts and high-collared shirts fastened with a piece of jewellery at the neck, they were never seen in public without gloves and hat, the latter about which they were most particular. An invitation to afternoon tea would be received weeks in advance to allow time for hats to be retrimmed, for it wouldn't do to be seen in the same hat twice. They were attended by a maid, in a black and white uniform and mob-cap, who lived in the basement flat usually with an enormous and odoriferous cod. Rose and Nellie adored cats and kept several; they insisted the animals be fed only on fresh fish, which were hung in the basement pantry by the tail.

Rose and Nellie's days were filled in the Victorian way with painting, embroidering, reading or playing the piano. When the 'nice young man' moved in on the first floor they welcomed his visits, which became more regular until they found themselves greatly looking forward to the friendly 'What-ho' of his daily greeting.

Rose, though the more outspoken of the sisters, was the frailer of health. Not long after VB moved in she suffered a heart attack, collapsing in her wing chair over a side-plate of sticky bun. VB was in at the time and, alarmed by the shrieks from Nellie, flew downstairs to her aid like Austen's Willoughby to Marianne and, by delivering mouth-to-mouth resuscitation and heart massage (a useful thing learned during the war) he was able to revive her. Rose and Nellie's fondness for their new boarder was much affirmed by the incident and in the ensuing weeks his good works continued, as he ministered to Rose small doses of champagne and good humour which saw her on the way to a full recovery. As VB admitted with all due modesty, from then on he was their blue-eyed boy and they looked after him exceedingly well.

To keep himself in funds whilst keeping an eye open for a chance to return to the East, VB busied himself with odd hands-on jobs, the last of which was the renovation of a friend's London cafe. Rose and Nellie disapproved. They considered this beneath him, and had grander ideas. They decided that he, being so personable, might do very well in the art world in which they themselves had a great interest, and suggested to VB that they provide him with a small loan to begin with, as well as good advice and excellent contacts. So it was that VB Perkins, Engineer, Sailor, Soldier, Prisoner, Builder, became VB Perkins, Dealer in Fine Arts.

Under the gently guiding hands of Rose and Nellie, VB began buying and selling paintings and antiques. He rented a small garage which he used as storage but for the most part he operated straight out of Rose and Nellie's house. He had a gentlemanly and con- genial manner which, as Rose and Nellie had predicted, quickly led him to develop a network of friends and acquaintances. They soon realised, however, that the venture was never going to lead to fortune because VB preferred to deal only with people he liked. As he had always done, he avoided people who did not appeal to him, though they were potential customers with possibly greater means. The problem further manifested itself in that, because he liked the people he dealt with, he could not take anything but a very small profit. Despite this handicap and to the astonishment of his oldest friends, he succeeded in making a living out of it, the modest size of which was more than adequately compensated, he felt, by the agreeable social nature of the business.

Dabbling in the business of Art was never going to be a long-term prospect in VB's eyes, and he intended doing it only as long as it took him to find something else. But for some time finding something else took a back seat, for he was so happily situated with Rose and Nellie that he remained at it far longer than he had originally intended. At the back of his mind he was concerned about the effect that the venture would have on his curriculum vitae, which up until now had a maritime bent and which he still hoped would be his ticket back to the Far East. To resolve the problem he undertook a part-time course on radiography as applied to ship construction and a Lloyd's Surveyor's Course in Gamma Radiographic Interpretation. Still he was acutely aware that he was really only fumbling about, and the years were slipping away.

Twice VB made a short sojourn into Europe with his fifty pounds, the maximum the British government allowed to be taken out of England during the postwar period. His main memory of his travels was an incident in a French *pissoir*. Besides a horror of going without shoes and of wasting food, another hangover from his prisoner days was that he was very particular about cleanliness and private about his toilet. If caught short he preferred to drive out of his way to get home to attend to nature's call rather than use a public lavatory. Travelling Europe his options were limited and he became particularly dismayed by the public conveniences provided in France. His dismay was by no means ameliorated by the fact that one had to pay for the privilege of having a pee. Having just visited one particularly nauseating *pissoir* in Paris, he felt compelled to say something. Effecting payment he pointed out to the male attendant that his establishment was distinctly smelly. 'But monsieur,' remonstrated the attendant with an exasperated gesture, 'this is a smelly business!' The reply tickled VB's ability to find humour in the obvious. One couldn't argue with that.

VB had a way with ladies and many female friends. But while his basic domestic requirements were taken care of—as they were, thanks to Rose and Nellie's generosity—the idea of settling down and marrying had never been high on his agenda. He was by now quite set in his ways, and in any case he had never met anyone who had made him consider a change. In January 1952 the situation changed dramatically.

It was not uncommon that his friends played cupid, for they all considered his time had come. So far their plots had met with no success, and this particular blind date all sounded like the same old ho-hum. He didn't want to be in it on this night, particularly as the woman was called Smith, but he had to humour the affable Australian who arranged it, and he'd agreed. At the appointed time he joined his friend and drove round to the Holland Park apartment to pick up Barbara and Pat Smith.

Though unrelated Pat and Barbara were close friends and had left Australia together to do the Australian thing. They'd been abroad together for nine months with never a cross word and had just returned from a hilarious fortnight in Europe. Pat was blonde, elegant, vivacious and garrulous. VB noted that her friend seemed quiet and a little shy at first. But she was dark-haired and attractive and tonight she looked a picture in a green organdie evening gown. VB's interest was agreeably aroused. During the course of the evening he began to probe her at a pitch that interested him and she met him with spirited and very definite opinions of her own. He was impressed. This Smith person was intelligent, well-read and perceptive. She was also imbued with an unusually high quota of common sense. Later, as he took her in his arms to dance, something felt unnervingly right.

Well after midnight the evening was drawing to a close. VB was very aware that in those few short hours he had been moved as he had never been moved before. In the subdued light of a smart Piccadilly nightclub, he leaned over the table towards Barbara, fixing her hazel eyes with his very blue ones. Licking his index finger, he pressed it onto her bare shoulder. 'Sold,' he said firmly.

Barbara was the only child of Nancy and Arthur Smith, he a bookman and publisher. She was born in Dunedin, New Zealand, of English parents, and during World War II her family had moved to Melbourne, where Arthur took up the management of the Book Depot in Little Collins Street. Later, when her father became a director of the publishing company Angus and Robertson, they lived in Sydney. She had grown up in a quiet, book-lined household where reading was very much the done thing. Being an only child she'd had a pleasant, if lonely, childhood, and had longed for the day when she could leave home and travel abroad. Intent on experiencing something of the world, she was not particularly interested in men. All the same she found Bruce Perkins, though sixteen years older than she, charming, interesting and amusing. He had an engaging twinkle in his eye and there was something, she felt, rather special about him.

VB pursued solidly the young woman who was to become my mother. She found a job as secretary to Mrs Cecil Chesterton at what VB soon dubbed 'Mrs Cecil Chesterton's Homes for Fallen Women'. He would arrive to collect her in his battered old Austin and they'd roam London, seeking out the lively spots of the lovely old city which he now knew intimately.

It seemed to Barbara that VB knew everybody. He was ever on the move and there always seemed to be another gathering at which he had to 'show the flag'. Barbara found his company entertaining and his driving unnerving. VB had a habit, when stopped at a traffic light, of chatting to anyone stopped alongside, then sweeping off around a corner as the lights changed while still finishing his conversation with the occupants of the other car, hitting gutters and narrowly missing lamp posts.

VB's income was modest, but money was never a worry. He was unmindful of the concept of carrying cash in his pocket, for he had lived without it for ten years. The clientele of his art and antique business was solid enough but he played little heed to the financial side. Under his bed he kept a suitcase containing receipts for things he had bought, but rarely did he send out invoices for things he had sold. Sending invoices, he considered, was a vulgar formality. In business a gentleman's word was enough. Regrettably, however, a gentleman's word frequently took a long time and often VB was in dire need of funds. There were occasions he wasn't paid at all, one of the most unfortunate instances of which was the sale of a valuable painting to a member of a family who owned a chain of up-market Australian department stores. Barbara entreated him to send an invoice but VB flatly refused. 'Certainly not,' he replied. 'You don't send a chap like that a bill—he'll pay up.' But that particular chap never did.

In the summer of 1952 Barbara, determined to do what she had set out to do, set off once again for Europe. After a few weeks she'd found a happy situation on Sandham, a beautiful island off Stockholm, working at the Royal Swedish Yacht Club in the mornings and sailing with newly found Swedish friends in the long, golden afternoons. The Olympics were being held in Helsinki and the hospitality shown to Australians seemed warm and heartfelt. Barbara was having a ball, and it came as a shock when VB arrived, suddenly, unexpectedly and unannounced, declaring he had come to take her back to England. Europe had been there a long time, he said, and was not likely to run away. There would be plenty of time to see it again, and he wanted her help now. Something very important had come up.

By now VB was very much the man in Rose and Nellie Isaacs's lives. The old ladies took great interest in his comings and goings and it appeared to Barbara, who felt rather like the competition, that they believed the very sun shone from him. He still visited them regularly in the early evenings, to pour them a sherry, to tell them of his day, of people he had met and pieces he had bought or sold. His amusing stories delighted them and they giggled like schoolgirls at his tales, dabbing at their eyes with their lace-bound lawn handkerchiefs. Occasionally he would squire them to the theatre or a concert, and when they entertained he was usually on hand to amuse their guests and pour the drinks. His attentions brought light into their staid Victorian lives.

But it could not last forever, and of this Rose and Nellie were well aware. VB's newfound interest in another woman was apparent and they sensed the business of Art would not keep him in London much longer. They had thought about something else for him and eventually had hit upon the idea of buying him a farm. They would buy the property and he would manage it until he was in a position to acquire it from them. It would be a property of substance with a house big enough to accommodate them all in privacy, for Rose and Nellie had always fancied a weekend place in the country.

VB had never imagined farming as his lot in life but had to admit that the more Rose and Nellie talked about it the better it sounded. Rose and Nellie were childless, had substantial means at their disposal and the whole idea had animated them to the extent that they talked of little else. After several excursions into the country to look at some splendid prospective properties, the price of which did not appear to bat a lightly powdered eyelid, VB began to think that perhaps he could see himself as Lord of the Manor after all.

To Barbara this all sounded like the stuff of which dreams were made. She had become totally charmed by Bruce Perkins and had quite fallen in love with England. When VB asked her to marry him she accepted, her head full of visions of settling into life in an ivy-covered Georgian house in the country, with a snug and rambling barn full of animals, gently rolling pastures of green and an avenue of hundred-year-old oak trees.

The snag was that though VB wished to marry right away, Barbara could not, for she had a promise to fulfil. An only child, she had consoled her mother on leaving Australia by promising faithfully that she would return from England unmarried. The wedding would have to wait until she had made a trip home.

VB took matters into his own hands. He bought a ticket for a passage to Australia on the *Moultan*, due to sail in two days' time. He was surprised at Barbara's reaction when he presented it to her; she was less than happy at leaving at such short notice. She'd complained that nothing had really been settled, that there was no time to say goodbye to her aunts who'd been so very good to her during her stay. She'd pointed out that although they'd been all over the countryside meeting the English contingent of her family, she hadn't yet met his, for he'd put off the event on several occasions. Yes, he had put it off. He hadn't seen much of his parents of late. He felt a twinge of guilt. Was it because they were just a bit parochial that he hadn't rushed Barbara down to meet them? Was it because they didn't fit the image he now had of himself? Reflections of his tired mother working long hours to fund the good schools she was so adamant they attend flicked across his mind. He blotted them out. It was not something he was comfortable with. He would make it up to her soon.

Barbara very much wanted to attend the coronation of Elizabeth II in June 1953, and VB told her that was all the more reason to go now. 'If you leave immediately,' he said, 'you can spend six weeks in Australia and still be back in England in time for the coronation.' With that he packed her off.

Barbara was never to see the coronation. In fact she was never to see England again for many, many years.

NINE

Trouble with Bandits

'**D**ON'T COME STOP GOING TO MALAYA STOP'
Barbara gazed at the cable in amazement, and reread the few brief words. What on earth had happened? She had no inkling of any change of plan. Everything was packed for a permanent move to England and she was to sail in ten days. Did this mean the wedding was off?

It seemed an eternity before further news arrived, in the form of a brief, scrawled letter from her husband to be. From it she gathered that VB had caught up with a fellow named Windsor who ran a little place out in Malaya and wanted a partner. He was going out by sea to have a look at the job, and if he decided to stay then she should come out and they would be married in Singapore. That was all.

Malaya! This was not quite what she had imagined. She knew little of the country except that it was hot, that it produced much of the world's rubber and tin and that it was having a lot of trouble with Communist bandits. Or something. Later she went to the library to find a book on the subject and as she read, her dreams of a rambling, ivy-covered farmhouse in the English country rapidly faded.

VB had met CJ Windsor socially in Malaya before the war and the chance reacquaintance in London had seemed fortuitous indeed.

He hadn't mentioned the Far East to Barbara, but he was confident she was the type to take to it well. Rose and Nellie? Well, that was more difficult. He couldn't pretend that his leaving would not leave a gap in their lives. They had almost settled upon that very nice place in Sussex when he'd had his sudden attack of cold feet. They had taken the news very well, as one would expect of two great Victorian ladies. One couldn't show too much emotion. He had tried not to notice their eyes damp and glistening behind their spectacles. He knew they would cope.

Imagine his spending a lifetime feeding cattle and sheep! He shuddered. What had he been thinking? This was more the thing. This was what he wanted to do. Operating small ships in remote places. Windsor had lived for years in Kuantan on the central east coast of Malaya and knew the country and its people well. It all sounded perfect. At the back of his mind he wondered how the Communist Emergency would affect their lives, how the country had shaken down after the war, how things had changed. He was to find out soon enough.

In 1953 Malaya was in many ways the same country VB had known and loved in the late 1930s. The barbarism and austerity that its people had suffered at the hands of the Japanese could not affect the natural beauty of the Malay Peninsula, hanging like a teardrop on the map of mainland Asia. Around four-fifths of the country was covered in thick, luxurious jungle that stretched tentacles into the outskirts of almost every town and village. Beneath the towering trees, in the patches of sunlit understorey, hundreds of varieties of butterflies fluttered round the giant ferns and ground orchids, and colourful tropical birds sang after every rain storm, darting among eight thousand species of flowering plants.

A mountain range rising to a maximum of 7,000 feet split Malaya down the centre for much of its length. The perspiring British could escape the heat by going to the comfortable colonial retreats of Fraser's Hill or the Cameron Highlands up in the cold high country, where temperatures reached as low as 38 degrees Fahrenheit. From the mountains heavy rainfall formed streams that plunged into water-falls, then turned to turbulent rapids, which gradually eased into the muddy brown rivers lacing the whole country. The mountains formed a physical divide between the developed west side of Malaya, with its large towns, its roads and railways, its tin mines and miles of rubber plantations, and the quiet undeveloped east side to which VB was going. On the eastern side, where Kuantan lay, in the state of Pahang, there were few roads and vast tracts of jungle lay undisturbed. There the population was small and the long and lazy rivers were the high roads for the local people. Near the coast the river banks were dotted with little Malay *kampongs* and occasional green *padi*-fields, and the rivers poured into the South China Sea along sandy, white, palm-fringed beaches. Close to the river mouths sampans, *koleks*, junks and fishing boats plied to and fro, laden with people, chickens, ducks, rattan and fishing pots.

Malaya was peopled largely by those with the same cultures and religions as Singapore, although in different proportions. Along with the industrious Chinese, the languid Indians and the British, the well-mannered, easy-going Malays made up almost half the population. Their lives were based around their *kampongs* and their families, in a land where nature provided all they required. Crops and fruit trees flourished: rice, tapioca, breadfruit, pawpaw, durian and an abundance of other exotic tropical fruits. Most villages had a Chinatown, where the saunter of the Malays gave way to the bustle of the Chinese as they went about their business. Whilst the Mohammedan Malays did not work on Fridays, fasted at Ramadan and did not eat pork, the Chinese often worked every day, celebrated traditional occasions by having huge feasts and loved eating pigs. They were two totally different cultures living separate lives, yet tolerating each other in an unusually congenial atmosphere.

Well away from the *kampongs* and towns were a lesser known group of Malayans who lived a mostly separate existence, a group of Malayans of whom VB was to learn a great deal. They were the *sakai*, the original people of Malaya; jungle-dwelling aborigines who were, in their natural state, long-haired, shy and usually naked but for a loin-cloth or sarong of bark. They kept to themselves, preferring to live traditionally away from development or society, letting mainstream Malaya pass them by.

Over the years since the Japanese invasion VB had thought long and hard about the effects of the initial defeat of the British on the people of Malaya and Singapore, about the indelible impression it must have left on them. He'd heard that when the British returned in 1945 to begin the rehabilitation process they were greeted by most with relief and welcome. But he knew that their image as the all-powerful rulers and protectors would have been shattered. He knew that the process of restoring government and rebuilding the country from the shambles in which the Japanese left it had been destabilised by the Communists, that the country had eventually been thrown back into a state of war. In mid 1953 when he arrived in Kuantan he discovered that 'the Emergency' was still very real.

A small, square-sailed fishing boat glided across the bow of the coaster from Singapore, as it gently navigated around a sandbank at the mouth of the Kuantan River. VB looked ahead eagerly. On the southern side of the river he saw a tract of swampy jungle lying undisturbed by the settlement opposite. Lazily dangling vines dipped hesitant tendrils into water the colour of *café au lait* along muddy banks held together by exposed, knotted roots. On the north side, just visible through the trees, were a few Malay houses, wooden dwellings on stilts, with big unglazed windows and verandahs looking onto palmy gardens. One or two modest brick houses behind high fences came into view, and further along the ship gently berthed alongside a small, quiet wharf. Among the few people waiting he recognised the smallish figure of Jay Windsor.

VB immediately liked the place. This east coast of Pahang had a real feeling of remoteness, the town was flanked by jungle on all sides. With around twenty thousand residents, Kuantan had a large dispersed population of Malays and a small Chinese community. Its town centre was typical of those he remembered; a pleasant green *padang* fringed by modest government buildings:

the Court House, the District Office, the Public Works Department and the Government Rest House. Across the grassy expanse
of playing fields was the main shopping area—a couple of lines
of dusty Chinese shop houses and the all important Cold Storage,
known locally as the Colesitoley. At the western end of the *padang*
and a few doors up from the open air picture theatre was the
Windsors' bungalow, a darkly timbered two-storey house set in
a well-tended garden.

The Windsors had been in Kuantan for years before the war and
were both very much of the old school. Jay Windsor, wiry and
energetic with a tall pinkish forehead on top of which sparse white
hair sprouted enthusiastically, spoke excellent Malay as did his wife
Edna. He ran the business, a diverse operation consisting of a small
shipping and engineering service, with interests among other things
in *jelutong* (a major ingredient in toffees and chewing gum) and
damar batu (resin). Edna Windsor was considered the doyenne of
European society in the town. Intelligent, slim, small with unusually
gold hair, she was always impeccably dressed despite the climate
and never went out without putting on a brooch and a brown felt
hat. With a low speaking voice she was everything of the archetypal
old-fashioned, colonial *mem*. A very useful member of the Town
Board, she was the centre of most things in Kuantan and ruled the
other *mems* with great efficiency. ('You're looking tired, my dear.
You know, husbands must understand that once a week is quite
enough in this climate.')

VB relaxed into the deep-seated rattan chair. It felt good to be
back in the East. A ceiling fan whirred gently overhead in the sitting
room of the Windsor bungalow, and a Malay boy in a checked
sarong and clean white jacket brought an icy *stengah*. '*Terima kasih*',
VB said in thanks, and smiled at the boy. He savoured the first
mouthful. Why was it that whisky and soda tasted so much better
in this part of the world? Jay Windsor was already talking about
the position. He listened.

The job description was Operations Manager of CJ Windsor &
Co, with responsibility for all sea and river transport. The salary
was modest but the position came with accommodation, a vehicle

and a share in the profits of the *jelutong* business. *Jelutong* was a major part of the business and Windsor had a contract to supply Mac-Robertson's in the UK. The *jelutong* tree, *Dyera costulata*, was one of the largest and most impressive of jungle trees, but each tree grew individually, scattered and rarely in the vicinity of another. Difficult or impossible to grow in plantations, the only way to obtain *jelutong* was by finding the trees and tapping them. There were a few trees in the jungle around Kuantan and VB would be responsible for supervising the tappers who lived in the lines (employer-provided accommodation) with the rubber tappers at Atbara estate. Most of the *jelutong*, however, came from far further afield.

This all sounded very interesting. VB liked the idea of taking the small coaster *Kelana II* along the coast to the south and up the rivers of Pahang, then transferring to smaller craft to get far upstream where tribes of aborigines lived in the remote jungle of the head-waters. Through trade they could be encouraged to collect *jelutong* from the trees in their area, prepare it and store it ready to be picked up. His task was to arrange just that, at the same time delivering rice provided for them by the government administration.

There would, of course, be an element of danger. The situation with the Communist terrorists, or CTs as they were known, had improved over the last year but nasty incidents were still occurring. The Communists were well established in the jungle and a major food-denial operation had just been launched in Pahang in an effort to starve them out. It was proving very effective and the protection of the cargoes carried up the rivers was of utmost importance. He would be carrying more rice and dried fish than the CTs could get in one haul from just about anywhere else. The capture of only one shipment of twenty tons would prolong the Emergency in the area for months, so he and the crew would be armed. Because of the danger of organised ambush, the destination of each trip would remain secret, only high-ranking police officials being informed of the details.

The state of Johore, to the south of Pahang, was one of the worst areas for CT activity. There was a particularly nasty group operating not far from the Rompin River in southern Pahang, and the Endau River on the border. On these rivers he'd be provided with a heavily armed escort to be picked up at the river mouths. The Rompin River in particular was shallow and convoluted and some way up the river the cargo would have to be transferred from *Kelana* to an open, slow-moving, flat-bottomed barge. The risks were there. As Windsor talked, VB reflected that he had returned to a very different Malaya. The casual observer may have noticed little change, but this was not the tranquil, unruffled country that he remembered from earlier days.

The trouble had begun at the time the Japanese surrendered at the end of the war. It was not the British who were first into the streets to claim victory; they were still on their way by sea. Out of the jungle emerged the Communist guerillas, parading in the streets waving red hammer and sickle flags. They had fought during the war under the banner of the MPAJA, the Malayan People's Anti-Japanese Army, and were received as heroes. During the war they had worked in co-operation with Force 136, a group of about four hundred British Army personnel who fought as guerillas in the jungle throughout the war. The Communists had been provided with weapons and training in jungle warfare and at the time of the Japanese surrender the presence and comradeship of Force 136 was a restraining influence on them.

When later the main British and Allied Forces arrived, Malaya was reoccupied in a peaceful manner. But over the next year the Malayan Communist Party regrouped and began a period of political agitation against the British, infiltrating unions and creating labour unrest. As the British administration gradually gathered strength, the country began to return to normal. That was until 1948, when the Central Committee of the Communist Party, unhappy with the progress of their campaign, turned to terrorism.

Three thousand ex-members of the Malayan People's Anti-Japanese Army took to the jungle to mobilise, train and organise a military structure under the new title of the Malayan People's Anti-British Army. They were led by Chin Peng, a dedicated

Chinese Communist, and their objective was to conquer the nation by following Mao Tse Tung's method of rural revolution. By concentrating their terrorist activities on the country areas, they relied upon getting support from and recruiting the simple, rural people until such time as their army was able to take on the large urban areas. Chin Peng envisaged that, if necessary, the might of China could be enlisted to assist in the final takeover. The Chinese method of revolution was a protracted technique and Malaya's was to be a long campaign.

The State of Emergency in the Federation of Malaya was declared in June 1948. In reality it was a war that was to last twelve years. The fact that it was never officially called a 'war' has been attributed to the effect of doing so on the London insurance market, on which the economy of Malaya relied for cover. The protection of Malaya's rubber and tin industries was of vital international interest. Losses through riot and civil commotion were covered, war losses were not. People were very careful to avoid using the word 'war' and indeed the real situation was played down because, as in Singapore before it fell, the newspapers were censored. This time it was to keep the CTs guessing. It also kept the civilians guessing and many of the civil servants in the cities were quite ignorant of the real gravity of the situation. Another reason it was called an 'Emergency' was so that the civilian authorities would have control over the war rather than the military. The concern was that if the armed forces were given their head, innocent civilians would be caught up in the violence and bombing. Political stability was considered fundamental to winning a guerilla war, and in the Malayan Emergency the war was largely fought by the police, with armed support from the military, rather than the reverse.

By 1949 there were between ten thousand and eleven thousand communist guerillas mobilised throughout Malaya, either full or part time. They worked in groups of around fifty, terrorising villagers who would not submit or conform, slashing rubber trees and disrupting production, wrecking mine machinery, ambushing road, rail and river traffic and murdering civilians. In Pahang one in five British rubber-plantation managers were murdered. Over the entire country the figure was one in ten killed. VB had kept in contact with Perky Perkins since leaving the East, keeping a toe in the door and in case anything interesting came up. Perky, being a great writer of letters (unlike VB), had filled him in fully. It sounded like rubber planting was not the recommended career for the present. Alone on their isolated rubber estates, with or without families, the planters were easy meat for the terrorists. So were the villagers and the estate labourers, some of whom it would be VB's responsibility to look after. The terrorists had been walking into *kampongs* and labourers' quarters and assembling the frightened people at gunpoint, demanding food and what they liked to call 'subscriptions'. Any man who defied them was shot. As an example to others, his wife and children often suffered an even worse fate. The police force was in no position to patrol all the isolated plantations and lonely villages, and the unfortunate victims were very much on their own.

For the first few years the war had gone badly for the British but fortunately for VB the tide had begun to turn by 1953, when he landed in Kuantan, and the campaign against the Communists had moved from the defensive to the offensive. The CTs had changed their tack. Now called the Malayan Races' Liberation Army (MRLA), they'd realised they were not gaining the support of the masses by terrorising them, and the number of incidents against the innocent villagers and essential public services such as power supplies and post offices began to decrease. Violence continued against 'traitors', British and Gurkha troops, senior civil servants and police officers. The new policy stated that British officers and managers of production centres and rubber estates could be killed, but British health officers and engineers were to be left alone.

VB was impressed by the grip which Jay Windsor appeared to have on the current state of affairs in Pahang. For the protection of his employees Jay needed to be informed, and was one of only a few key civilians who occasionally attended District War Executive Committee (DWEC) meetings. In Kuantan, as elsewhere, local operations were planned and controlled by the DWEC, which met every morning at what was known as 'Morning Prayers'. It was chaired by the District Officer (the DO), the senior civil servant responsible for the overall administration of the district, who did his best to restrain the natural antagonism between the police and the army.

'The DOs have the chair so that both parties have someone to shoot down in flames,' said Kuantan's DO, Patrick Bolshaw. 'We have our war map with the latest positions on it and listen to what the police think is happening and what might be done, then listen to what the army think is happening and might be done, and then say okay, we'll do this. Then if it goes well the police and the army can feel chuffed and if it goes badly they can say well we didn't think it was the right thing to do but the DO made the decision. Frequently we don't get it right. It's very difficult because we're just looking at the jungle and wondering what on earth is going on inside it. We can only make best guesses from the information on hand.'

VB was quick to fathom then that the critical factor for the DWEC was police intelligence, basic information about the tactics and location of the terrorists and their suppliers. In this Jay Windsor had apparently proved himself quite useful, for he'd developed a network with the *sakai*, who could often, if they would, provide information about the Communists. They could also be of service as guides. Jay had thus become an important part of the intelligence-gathering function and appeared to VB a great enthusiast for it.

Since VB would now be the man on the ground as far as the *sakai* were concerned, he too would be involved. As part of his briefing he went along to the local Special Branch office to check in with Bill Wall. Special Branch of the Federal Police was instituted the previous year by General Templer, the new High Commissioner and Director of Operations. Its charter was tactical intelligence and counter-subversion work. Over a cup of thick black coffee, Bill Wall, a tough-looking man with a sleepy expression and a quiet drawl, who didn't miss a thing, briefed VB on the situation in Pahang as it was then.

He explained that up until 1953 security forces in the area had carried out many successful 'elimination' operations on the CTs. These operations had been carried out in a random fashion, concentrating on trouble spots as they occurred. The problem was that as one group was dealt with, another emerged somewhere else, so this year they had embarked upon a series of 'flushing out' operations in Pahang, concentrated in adjoining areas moving from east to west. Long-term food-denial operations were being instituted so that the CTs were being forced either to surrender or to take big risks to obtain food. Other measures, such as curfews and restrictions on the sale of certain items, had also been enforced.

Then he talked about the Min Yuen, another group of Communists who worked less visibly. They were ostensibly perfectly ordinary citizens: cooks, waiters, clerks, rubber tappers and school teachers. They formed a backup for the CTs, providing them with food, supplies, information and money. They were essential to the Communist cause and had infiltrated many facets of Malayan society. Good intelligence was vital to crack down on them. Since VB would be visiting *sakai* communities he was required to gather as much information as he could. Anything at all concerned with the whereabouts and movements of CTs was valuable. Wall also briefed VB to be aware that the *sakai* themselves could be supplying CTs, and to keep an eye open for evidence of this. So along with 'Operations Manager' for CJ Windsor & Co, VB was given another hat: that of honorary Special Branch Inspector.

The briefings were lengthier than VB had imagined, but he'd made up his mind long before. This was an interesting place, these were exciting times. He was to be a partner in a business operating a small ship, and he had quiet ideas of his own for expanding that side of the enterprise. Who knew where it would all lead?

Besides, for the ordinary citizen, Kuantan seemed an idyllic place to live. He'd have to get on to Barbara to get herself out here ASAP.

TEN

Hitched

J ust as he remembered it, the port of Singapore teemed with craft of every sort: ships anchored in the roads, square-sailed Chinese junks and fishing boats, industrious-looking dredges and tugs towing huge wooden barges with enormous rudders pivoting off the stern, creaking from the exertions of sweating, sarong-clad tillermen. The stopover enroute to Kuantan had been necessarily brief, but this time he allowed himself a few extra days before he was to be married, to go for a cruise around the harbour in an old, wooden sampan and to revisit his old haunts.

Out at the old Naval Base the thought troubled him that it was the British who had destroyed this place which was once so much a part of his life. He drove around the narrow streets, among the red-tiled, black and white Tudor-style painted bungalows and barracks that looked so British it was almost like being back in England. At the Cricket Club he joined his old friend Perky, one of the guests invited down from Malaya for the wedding, and it seemed nothing at all had changed. The domed clock tower and terracotta-tiled roofs of the building had escaped unscathed by the Japanese. A tall, dig-nified, immaculately dressed Sikh met them at the top of the stairs, as though the war had never happened. At lunch the silver still glistened, the enormous linen napkins were still perfectly starched and the view down the lush, green *padang* was much the same.

The day of the wedding came, and the only person missing was the bride.

There had been complications. The arrival time of Barbara's ship, *Chakrata*, was being kept quiet, for it was carrying a cargo of bombs and ammunition for the troops in Malaya. Over the next few days VB rearranged the wedding several times, but still his bride did not arrive. The guests partied well in any event, but eventually had to go home to their respective jobs, leaving VB anxiously reviewing his dwindling leave.

It wasn't until the early morning of 10 February 1954, under a beautiful pink and grey pearl sky, that *Chakrata* steamed quietly up the roads, almost a week later than scheduled. Barbara was on deck early that morning, watching the flying fish disturbing the glassy calm of the sea, trying to quieten her nerves and perhaps a few doubts in the back of her mind. What was she coming to? For security reasons the six passengers had not been told about the cargo until after they had left the departure terminal when the ship moved to an explosives anchorage. It had brought a certain realism to the fact that where she was headed was into the middle of a terrorist insurrection. She was a little unsettled by it. And how well did she know this man? She hadn't seen him for almost ten months and the ship's kindly, rounded captain, aptly named Bunn, was dubious of the whole arrangement. 'Besides that,' he'd said, 'the fellow sounds far too old for you. And have you considered the possibility that he could be something in the way of a white-slave trader? These things happen, my dear, in the East.'

Feeling not quite as cheerful as she thought she should have, she went down below to put curlers in before breakfast; she knew her hair was not going to behave well in this climate. Behind her the cabin door opened gently and she looked around. There stood VB, looking frightfully pukka in starched white shorts and checked shirt, brown as a berry and with his marvellous blue eyes laughing and almost spitting golden sparks at having caught her in curlers. Melting into his arms, any doubts she had went straight out of the porthole.

'I came out on the pilot boat!' he said, grinning widely. Then, fishing for something in his pocket for a moment, and dusting off the tobacco shreds, he produced a delicate, elegant diamond ring. 'Bought it from George—his girlfriend changed her mind. Better make the engagement official.' It fitted perfectly.

Ecstatically they twirled around the cabin, locked together, until reminded by a bemused steward that breakfast was waiting. The officers and five elderly lady passengers were already assembled at table. VB sat down in an atmosphere of a retinue of uncles and maiden aunts ready to censure; but in no time he had charmed them into approval, everyone was relaxed and laughing, and they had all accepted invitations to the wedding.

Later that morning, sitting in the office of Archdeacon Whitfield-Dorkes, VB noticed Barbara fanning herself. 'I feel as though someone has pulled a plastic bag over my head and tied it at the bottom,' she said quietly. The heat and humidity had come as quite a shock.

'You'll get used to it,' VB assured her firmly. 'In time you'll even love it.' He never found the heat tiresome and had every confidence that his wife would feel the same.

The Archdeacon arrived, by now a little dubious of their intentions, and fixed a time to marry them that very afternoon. Wonderfully happy, they dashed up to Orchard Road to buy a wedding ring and arrange a bouquet for Barbara to carry, and by 4.30 had assembled with a small party under the cooling rain trees in the gardens of St Andrew's Cathedral. The Anglican Cathedral stood like a tall, many spired, wedding cake in the centre of vast and manicured grounds. The guests, by now, were few; not even the officers from the ship were able to come, since *Chakrata* was being moved to the explosives wharf that afternoon. The wedding dress made for the occasion was still in the hold of the ship, not to be unloaded until the following day. Instead the bride wore her old, white cotton dress with black squiggles and a white straw hat, and felt radiant all the same. VB was happy and proud. It had seemed an eternity before Barbara arrived and he held her hand tightly, as if he was never going to let her go again. As she stood at the altar rail she looked at him and her cup truly ran over. All doubts were dispelled, all would be well. Bathed in the afternoon light filtering through the stained-glass windows, and under the low pitched whirr of the fans suspended from the high nave walls, they were quietly married. The Archdeacon conducted the service beautifully, in a well-modulated, full-toned English voice, and because it was such a quiet wedding neither VB nor Barbara was nervous, just proud and very glad to be together at last.

The wedding had not gone according to plan, but it didn't seem to matter. Later in their room at the elegant, high-ceilinged Goodwood Park Hotel, Barbara, hoping to impress, donned the first piece of really luxurious nightwear she had ever owned, bought at David Jones especially for the occasion. But VB, ever the romantic, gave it short shrift. 'You can't wear that thing out here,' he said, and tossed her a sort of check cotton tablecloth sewn up the side. 'Here, put this on. You'll have to learn to wear a sarong in this climate. It's more comfortable.' Barbara found he was right and from then on wore a sarong to bed, just as VB always did.

Two days and several parties later, they crossed the Causeway to Malaya, setting off in the afternoon in great comfort in Jay Windsor's new car just arrived off a ship from England. Heading north up the Malay Peninsula row upon geometric row of seemingly endless rubber trees flickered past, the awkward crowns perched atop leggy, scarred trunks which wept into earthenware cups. Occasionally a palm-oil estate or pineapple field abruptly broke the pattern. Here and there a Malay *kampong* nestled among the trees; clusters of *atap*-thatched houses on stilts, shaded by storm-bent coconut palms, among neat little gardens and washing lines strung with chequered or flowered sarongs.

Barbara couldn't help but notice the signs: 'Communist terrorists are active and dangerous in this area. Motorists are *strictly* forbidden to stop on the roads.' They were written in bold print in three different languages, depicting a skull and crossbones as a warning. 'Don't worry, Charlie,' VB said (he had a habit of calling people he liked 'Charlie'). 'It's just that North Johore is a particularly dangerous area.'

The afternoon drew on and black clouds gathered and suddenly opened, sending down torrents of monsoonal rain, hard and fast, reducing the car to a crawl. At the safety of a small village they stopped and got out, slopping through roadside mud into a dilapidated Chinese shop. '*Ada-kah minum sedjoh?*' VB asked, and was handed two bottles of the locally produced soft drink, Green Spot, which was all that the proprietor had. It was bright green, warm, fizzy, and sickly sweet with little other flavour. 'It's known as Green Spit in European circles,' VB said, as Barbara regarded the bottle dubiously. 'Very popular with the locals. About all they stock in these little places. You'll get used to it.' Barbara doubted it.

The sun reappeared and VB was keen to be on his way. Damp and clammy with perspiration, and thirstier than ever, Barbara felt like a wrung-out dish rag. The shadows lengthened as they drove, through more rubber country, occasionally past a latex-gathering station where greyish white latex was fed through iron rollers and the sheets hung out to dry. The country reverted to jungle, a hundred shades of rampant green broken only by the brown, bedraggled, dead lower branches of palm trees. VB had been quiet for a while. He was not feeling at all happy and there was an unusual line of worry in his brow. Of all the absolute twits . . . Barbara noticed nothing and began to nod off. Suddenly VB pulled the car up abruptly on the side of the road and leaped out.

Barbara snapped out of her doze. 'I thought you weren't allowed to stop the car!' There was no reply. She leaned across the driver's seat to inquire out of the window as to whether they had a flat tyre, and a bus rumbled past. Looking up she saw, to her amazement, her new husband waving from the back step.

For a moment her mind spun in confusion. It couldn't possibly have been VB on the back of the bus. She got out of the car to look for him and sure enough he wasn't there. Now totally befuddled and very uncomfortable she began to wonder whether it was happening at all. Then she began to think about all the things the people on the ship had said. How well did she know this man? Her imagination began to take over. All around her was jungle and the one thing she knew about this strange country was that it was dangerous to stop on the side of the road. And here she was, stopped on the side of the road, alone.

Exhausted from the heat and the parties and the situation, she tried to calm down and think about things rationally. Back in the car she thought some more, and finally concluded she was not dreaming. He really had gone. She began thinking about the terrorists, and resolved that she was not going to sit there and be shot. She got out of the car again, walking into the jungle on the side of the road. Under the cover of the undergrowth she continued for about a quarter of a mile back the way they had come. Then she lay down under a bush to contemplate her position. She had been ashore for less than three days and now, from her hiding place, she began recalling the conversations she had heard in Singapore about such-and-such an estate being attacked and so-and-so was killed, or poor old Joe was ambushed in his car and had his throat cut.

A wiry, brown man wearing a sarong and a dirty white singlet appeared, jogging along the opposite side of the road. The pole across his shoulders was tied with a bundle at each end. She peered at him through the undergrowth, trying to tell whether he was Chinese, Malay or Indian, but she couldn't yet tell them apart. He didn't appear to be armed and he didn't look like a terrorist. But then she had no idea what a terrorist looked like. He passed and she followed him for a while, stumbling through the jungle, keeping out of sight. Ever present in her mind were VB's words, 'Europeans are much fairer game than the local people.'

Eventually she came across a small, thatched, bamboo house on stilts. A couple of women sat on the verandah, a few children played on the grass outside. She stayed hidden, watching. A young boy came up to the house and gave the women some fruit. They were all sitting talking. There appeared to be nothing sinister going on, and with the thought that sitting in hiding was not going to get her far, she materialised out of the bush. The Malays were very surprised, but friendly enough, and waved at her to come over to their house. No-one spoke English, and a small boy was sent off, returning shortly after with an older boy who spoke a little. Barbara explained that her car was up the road, and the boy said that his father had seen the car, but there was nobody in it. For a minute the conversation stopped, and nobody seemed to know what to do, and neither did Barbara. She was taken inside so as not to be sitting in view on the verandah, and eventually one of the boys went off, apparently to take a message to someone.

Wondering what would happen next, Barbara ate some fruit that was kindly offered, and for the next long hour, smiled at her Malay hosts. It was twilight before a car pulled up on the dirt road outside the house.

'Hey, Charlie, are you there?' a voice called.

'Where the hell have you been?' she retorted, with mixed relief and fury.

'Forgot to check the fuel tank before we left Singapore and we were running short. Sorry about that.' VB had seen the bus in the rear-vision mirror at the last minute, and knowing the bus would not have stopped for him he had dived at it as it went past. The idea to take it to go and get some fuel had occurred to him so late that he didn't have time to fill Barbara in. 'Thought you'd find somewhere,' he said casually. He hadn't been at all perturbed to find she wasn't with the car, and had every confidence in his wife's ability to look after herself. Barbara was beginning to learn that communication was not VB's forte.

By comparison the rest of the journey to Kuala Lumpur was uneventful. On the last leg herds of fat bullocks and flocks of geese roamed the coarse grass, and limestone boulders lay whalelike among acres of tattered banana palms, more rubber and more jungle. When at last they reached the capital of Malaya in the late afternoon of the next day, VB was feeling as cool as a cucumber while his wife felt like someone had locked her in a sauna and thrown away the key.

In the hotel they showered and Barbara, deliciously refreshed, opened her suitcase to get some clean clothes, only to be overcome by an appalling smell—something between a rotting Singapore drain and a pineapple, with a few off prawns thrown in. The smell was from a durian, a fruit VB described as the most delicious in the East, which he had purchased from a market *en route* and deposited on top of her suitcase in the boot of the car. It had permeated everything. Calmly VB assured her that most people in Malaya liked the smell of durian, but in any event Barbara had no choice but to put on her malodorous dress, and face the world.

The smell stayed with them all the way to Kuantan.

With his natural optimism VB had always been confident that Barbara would take well to Malaya. But the heat seemed to have knocked her a bit and at the back of his mind he feared that she had not been overly enthusiastic about her experiences to date. He was keen to get on, to leave KL and show Barbara what he called the real Malaya. There was only one road to Kuantan and they took it. It was narrow and long and wound its way up through the high country of the central mountain range and down the other side. Jungle reigned supreme for most of the way, growing undisturbed to the very edge of the road. Immense, vine-covered trees towered above and everywhere was vivid green. Occasional sprays of brilliant colour high up in the canopy gave a tantalising glimpse of the magnificence of the jungle in flower. Through the open window of the car the air smelt warm and mushroomy, with a hint of perfume from the flowers wafting in now and then. VB looked across at Barbara, and he could see she was warming to the experience. At one point she was excited at seeing a huge pile of steaming manure in the middle of the road, and wanted to stop and look for the owner of the ordure. VB was quick to quash her enthusiasm, pointing out that in the present political climate it wasn't an awfully good idea to stop and go thrashing about in the jungle after elephants.

The sealed road gave way to graded dirt for a short time, and the feeling of remoteness grew. At the tiny township of Temerloh, a small, flat-bottomed barge ferried them across a tributary of the Pahang River and a little further on another barge took them across the Kuantan River. By the time they reached Kuantan VB was satisfied that Barbara's sense of adventure had been

VB (centre) with his brothers, 1915.

The Perkins family in Cornwall. Back row, from left: *Roy, VB, Leslie.*
Front row, from left: *Alfred, Evelyn, Edith Amelia.*

Leslie Perkins, RN.

Picnicking upcountry in VB's Vauxhall, Malaya, 1940. From left: *Nena Steele, Frida Jensen, Bill Steele, VB and Rolf Jensen.* PHOTO COURTESY OF BROOKER

'Some day we're going to have to pay for this…' Homeward-bound on the Johore Strait: VB (foreground) with the Jensens and the Steeles, 1941.
PHOTO COURTESY OF BROOKER

Singapore, 1942. An elevated view looking over the city where smoke can be seen rising from burning buildings, after the Japanese air raids.
AUSTRALIAN WAR MEMORIAL 011529/03

Burma–Thailand Railway, c. 1943. POWs laying railway track. A. SEARY,
AUSTRALIAN WAR MEMORIAL P0406/40/17

Captain 'VB' Perkins, postwar Bangkok, 1945.

''Til we meet again in happier times...' The sailing photo VB gave Bill Steele in Changi POW camp, 1942.

Wedding day, 1954.

Aboard Kelana, *wet through after clearing the propeller, Pahang, 1954.*

stirred, and that she had begun to understand why he was so taken with this country.

Two impressive flights of stone stairs lent an air of dignity to the otherwise small, two-storey whitewashed brick house with deep sloping eaves and leaded windows that was Bruce and Barbara Perkins' first home. At the landing where the stairs met VB picked up his bride and carried her up the last few steps to the double stable door. As he crossed the threshold he tripped over the sill and they both fell in a laughing heap at the feet of the Chinese cook, who eyed them disapprovingly, unamused.

The house belonged to the Windsors and lay on the bank of the Kuantan River, where it caught the best of the cool sea breezes. Next door, a path from the Windsors' godown ran down to a small wharf at which *Kelana* was berthed. The ground floor of the house was used to store cargo for *Kelana*; the living quarters were spartan, with the distinct air of a bachelor's pad. The house also had a somewhat dark past, but VB had already decided that Barbara need not know about that. The servants, who always refused to sleep in the house, held no such protective sentiments and over the next few days the gruesome details about what had gone on in it during World War II began to come out. It was not exactly butter on her paws.

The house had been used as an interrogation centre by the Japanese *kempeitai* during the occupation, and had become a place of fear and loathing for the town residents. In each of the two bathrooms opening off the bedrooms at either end of the house was a large, square, waist-high concrete *tong* (or vat). The *tongs* were designed for bathing, the customary practice in Malaya being to stand beside them and ladle water over the head. But the Japanese had found them useful for holding the heads of interrogation victims under water until they talked. If they didn't talk, or perhaps if they did but were of no further use, the job of finishing them off was completed and their bodies taken down the front steps and disposed of in the river. Barbara listened wide-eyed to the *dhobi amah*'s enthusiastic explanation as to why the crocodiles in the river were so large. And some were very large.

VB had words to say to Woh for her lack of tact, for he didn't want his wife completely unnerved already. But it seemed that over the first few weeks, with a little determination, Barbara put unpleasant thoughts out of her mind and did her best with the resources available to make their house into a home. 'Take your cue from the people around you,' VB advised, 'and you'll soon find that the Emergency doesn't encroach very far into anyone's social life.' Around the town most people who were not involved in any way were fairly at ease with the situation. As Helen Wharton, the wife of an Australian entomologist working for the Institute of Medical Research, told Barbara, 'The Communists are not trigger happy. They don't just have a pot at anyone, you know—you have to be a target. Tin miners and rubber planters are fair game, but it never really worries Harry and me too much.'

VB could not be as unconcerned, since the safety of his local *jelutong* tappers living in the lines at Atbara rubber estate was his responsibility. These people were even more vulnerable than rubber tappers, as their work involved venturing into the jungle adjacent to the estate. There was still plenty of CT activity in the area and in his first few months on the job VB had had to evacuate the tappers several times, while army troops were sent in to conduct clearing operations.

He was already well settled into Kuantan, and thoroughly enjoying it. This was the life for him; this beat starting the day in the dark in the depths of a London winter. Here, because of the heat, the working day started early, at what he referred to as sparrow fart, when he'd take a starched Aertex cotton shirt from the stack in his wardrobe, one of several he'd wear throughout the day, and pull on khaki Bombay bloomers and a khaki cap. The cookie, Ah Ling, would have his bacon and eggs ready, and his lunch when he returned by twelve. After lunch he'd have a short camp (siesta), and disappear again until four when it was time for tea and sticky bun, after which the day's social activities would begin.

The theatre, the movies, or reading fiction never interested VB. He had no requirement for escapism or fantasy, for his own life was always full. His recreation was people, and as well as the local population of Malays, Chinese and Indians there were some one hundred other Europeans living in Kuantan. Life was so much more sociable out here and it suited him perfectly. His thoughts flitted back to London, where Rose and Nellie prepared for days, even weeks, to receive visitors. Here everything was easy, one just arranged dinner parties on the spur of the moment, popped in on people whenever it suited, or dropped into the Kuantan Club. This was the way life should be lived. Then there were the regular events: Sunday curry tiffin at Jabor Valley Estate, to which everyone was ferried in armoured vehicles, and Scottish Country Dancing at the Kuantan Club on Thursday nights, of which VB partook with great gusto, priding himself on his neat and twinkling feet. The Kuantan Club, a convivial establishment run by a comfortable Chinese known as Gin Lime, was the focal point of European social life in Kuantan. When VB first joined the rules were 'Europeans only', but times were changing. General Templer had been talking of 'Malayanising' the country and breaking down prejudices, and except for a few of the older generation, general opinion was that the Club couldn't go on like this for much longer. And it didn't, in fact. Very soon afterwards the rules were changed and people from other races were allowed to become members. But as VB was quick to point out, since the other races all had their own clubs, it was some time before anyone seemed interested.

Because everyone in the European community had help, dinner parties were easy. In the Perkins household, as well as the live-in cook there was an *amah*, Gayah, who came in every day to sweep, dust and make the beds, and Woh, the *dhobi amah*, who did the washing in a large galvanised tub on the back lawn. Twice a week Jappah, the *kebun*, arrived to cut the grass with a long-handled sickle, a laborious business in which the sickle was swung around in the manner of a golf club, giving the impression that only one blade of grass at a time was ever cut.

VB related well to the servants, as he did to most Malays. In general he was fond of the local people, regarding them as equals. There were some Europeans who were a little superior with the Malays, but VB had no such pretensions. He was not afraid to get his hands dirty and worked alongside them in his job. His Malay was good and he enjoyed nothing more than joking with them and teasing them until he had them in fits of laughter. Barbara could not help but notice that the boys at the Kuantan Club and other people's servants did something a bit special if they knew 'Tuan Perking' was coming, simply because they liked him.

Occasionally the Sultan of Pahang, His Highness Sultan Abu Bakar, gave parties at his *istana* at Pekan, a coastal town some twenty miles south and the centre of the Malay community in Pahang. Parties at his palace, an attractive two-storey cream stone house with wide lawns and lines of standard hibiscus pruned to look like rose bushes, were formal affairs to which ladies wore long gowns and gloves. The formality, however, did not extend to the plumbing. Mrs Windsor was well acquainted with the facilities for the ladies: a small enamel chamber pot barely large enough for the average-sized European bottom. Dilatory callers were very likely to find it full, whereupon the form was that one had to empty it out of the window. By all accounts it was a difficult business. So it was that on one occasion, having found the pot full Mrs Windsor, with several other ladies, slipped quietly out into the garden. There they found an apparently secluded spot behind a thick row of cannas, not realising that they were quite close to the car park in which several *syces* were waiting with their vehicles. Upon hearing the disturbance in the garden one alert individual turned on his car headlights, thus illuminating the ladies in a less than dignified atti-tude. For Mrs Windsor this was the last straw. Shortly afterwards she approached the Public Works Department and from then on the Sultan was provided with portable loos for his parties. Thanks to Mrs Windsor's good work the situation had vastly improved by the time VB and Barbara arrived.

Mrs Windsor's good works were well known and, as VB became aware, in some areas she had to have a particularly tough constitution to keep at it. He approved of the government policy in Malaya where it was each employer's responsibility to look after the health and welfare of their Malay workers. At the same time the law of the country forbade any interference with Malay religious or other customs. Malays could not be forced to go to hospital if they believed, as they often did, that their affliction was the will of Allah and that they should not do anything about it. Regularly Mrs Windsor inspected the quarters of the Malays living in the lines, to ensure they were clean and that the drains were clear of debris. She disliked these inspections and often called upon VB or Barbara to accompany her. Though it had to be done to ensure that the employees were living to the standard required by the government, to them it felt a little like interfering. They developed a great admiration for the way Mrs Windsor kept hammering away at the health affairs of the people in the face of their resentment. One little boy had a crooked leg and Mrs Windsor wanted to send him away for orthopaedic treatment, at her expense. His parents refused, saying that his crooked leg was the will of Allah. The child was destined to remain a cripple and Mrs Windsor almost wore herself out with worry. She was similarly distressed over two children who lived with their TB-infected grandmother. The parents would not allow the children to be inoculated and the grandmother wouldn't go to hospital. When she finally consented to do so, it was too late, and she died. The hospital was then seen as being responsible for her death.

As in most colonies, sport was a big part of life in Malaya. VB had found Kuantan not well suited to sailing; the river was too narrow and the sea too rough. Unlike the west coast of Malaya, protected by the land mass of Sumatra, the east coast lay open and unsheltered, exposed to the great expanse of the South China Sea. On a clear day, he had noticed, the wrecks of the *Prince of Wales* and *Repulse* could be seen lying in the water off Kuantan. The first time he had seen them he'd shuddered.

Sailing, then, was off the agenda and though he was a rugby man at heart, cricket was the game in Kuantan and, for what it was worth, he joined the Kuantan Club team. The Indian Club provided good opposition, and the town of Pekan also fielded a team. When the nearby Sungei Lembing area was cleared of CTs their team bolstered the competition. It was during a weekend's play at the

Sungei Lembing Tin Mine that VB particularly distinguished himself, becoming the toast of the Kuantan Club. That day, he had doubled his batting average. He had scored two.

Sadly the Kuantan Club cricket team could not always count on VB to boost their tail-end score. His schedules were uncertain and because of security he could never be sure when *Kelana* was sailing until the last minute. Often he would arrive back from one trip and have time only to reload and sail again.

ELEVEN
Beads and Baubles

N estled among coconut palms at the mouth of the river a small Malay *kampong* of bamboo and *atap* houses lay high and dry on spindly stilts. Banana palms with long, splitting leaves bent over with the burden of their fruit, and gentle, soft-eyed water buffalo grazed close by. Naked children frolicked in the river shallows whilst their mothers stood knee-deep, plunging and scrubbing the daily *dhobi*. VB left *Kelana*'s skipper, Karim, at the wheel and wandered outside the wheelhouse to pay his respects. The women in the river stood up to look as the boat passed, smiling shyly. VB doffed his cap and bowed ever so slightly, his usual way with the ladies.

He'd done this trip up the Merchong and Bebar rivers a few times now, but this was the first time he'd taken Barbara with him. Mrs Windsor had been furious. 'Certainly not!' she'd said when Barbara broached the subject. 'It's far too dangerous on the rivers and no place for a woman.' But Barbara knew her own mind. It was hot in the house and Cookie was objectionable. She'd decided to come anyway. VB was confident she'd be all right. These particular rivers were so remote and far from anywhere of interest to the CTs that it was very unlikely they'd run into trouble. In the lower reaches ahead were the coastal plains of unpopulated swamplands, in places infested with mosquitoes carrying filariasis, a crippling disease leading in the later stages to elephantiasis. Much higher up the river, where the *sakai* lived, it was even more remote. In any event the security surrounding his movements was so tight that anything he did run into would have to be unprepared, like that one attack on the Rompin River. It had come out of nowhere, launched from the cover of bamboo thickets on the bank. They'd been on an open barge at the time, which made it a bit awkward, but as it happened it was swiftly dealt with by the escort, courtesy of Her Majesty's Armed Forces.[1] No, he wouldn't allow Barbara on the other rivers, but here was fine.

Kelana continued west, alone on the river. Since the Communist threat she was the only vessel to venture far from the coast, and to provide a service of any kind to the *sakai* communities in the headwaters. Navigation was often difficult. The approaches to the smaller river mouths were shallow and the lower reaches long and sinuous. In the monsoon the rivers flooded, and torrents of water brought with them sunken timber and debris. Sand bars shifted unpredictably. But VB had a good Malay crew of four, and they knew these rivers well.

Away from the coast the river began to wind through the tropical rainforest that covered most of the state of Pahang. It was typical of the dense jungle in Malaya that grew to a thousand feet in elevation and was almost impenetrable along the river banks, where the sunlight reached the ground vegetation. In places a continuous canopy of foliage created an eerie, cathedral-like atmosphere. VB made his way up onto the bowsprit. It was a favourite sitting spot of his when the river was littered with fallen trees and roots, and he could give

---

[1] *In the opinion of the Officer in Charge of the Police District, Ken Belton, 'Bruce took tremendous risks, in fact everyone involved in that operation was constantly at risk. In the case of a serious ambush the situation would have been pretty hopeless. A few chaps with rifles sitting on an open boat when you are being shot at with a Bren gun from the banks of the river wouldn't have done much good at all. The only real thing protecting them was the high security surrounding the movements of the boat, ensuring that the CTs never knew when it was coming. Communications were, fortunately for Bruce and his crew, pretty non-existent in those days.'*

Karim due warning to steer clear. Alongside vines hung down into the water in great loops and festoons. Overhead epiphytes clung to the trunks and branches among determined climbers winding their way up to the roof of the jungle. Away from the river banks shrubs and palms struggled for their share of sunlight, while on the dark forest floor saplings, herbaceous plants, ferns and gingers competed for room with enormous buttressed tree trunks. They were getting into the sort of jungle where the *sakai* lived.

Few people seemed to know much about the *sakai*. For the most part the British government had always left them to their own way of life. Up until 1952 when it was realised that the CTs in the jungle were being assisted by the *sakai*, there had been little contact besides a few excursions by anthropologists and health workers. The government didn't even have an accurate estimate of their numbers. The state of Pahang was home to the largest population of *sakai* in Malaya, and VB found some of the tribes he visited had had little contact with the outside world since the arrival of the Japanese in 1942.

The aboriginal tribes of Malaya were highly interrelated both culturally and linguistically, so that even ethnologists had never come up with an entirely satisfactory classification. The general term *sakai* was used among Europeans in Malaya, and to distinguish between them VB tended to use the Windsor classification: *orang dalam* (people of the interior), *orang sungei* (river people) and *orang bukit* (hill people). Another very small tribe of around twenty or thirty people living totally traditionally who were rarely seen but whom Mrs Windsor had been carefully documenting, she called the *orang liar* (wild people).

The *lingua franca* of the jungle was Malay. Many tribal languages consisted of some words the same or similar to Malay, so that even where Malay was not spoken VB was usually able to get his message across. The easiest tribes to locate lived along or close to the rivers. Their settlements were not permanent, for they practised a form of shifting cultivation, a semi-nomadic existence enabling them to crop the infertile jungle soil. A group of between twenty and one hundred people settled in an area for two or three seasons, building houses and clearing an area known as a *ladang*, to plant tapioca, hill *padi*, maize, banana, sugar cane, and other crops. When the fertility of the soil was exhausted they moved on to a new *ladang*.

VB had quickly found that the location of each tribe had a bearing on their degree of economic and cultural development. Those in the swampy lower-lying areas were always on the move because the fertility of the soil was exhausted quickly. Their houses therefore were less substantial, and the villages gave a less settled impression. These people were keen to trade, as it was easier for them to collect jungle produce in exchange for food than to grow it themselves. For VB the most productive tribes were those living near the headwaters of the rivers, in the preferred habitat of the *jelutong* trees. These were also the most difficult to reach, which was why he spent so much time away from Kuantan. There was a limit to how far upriver *Kelana* could go. Sometimes it was as far as 130 miles before she'd have to be anchored under guard. Cargo was then manhandled into a shallow draft vessel, in the upper reaches usually just an open boat with an outboard motor.

Tomorrow they'd be leaving *Kelana*, for VB wanted to explore a small tributary of the Merchong where he'd never before ventured. He'd leave Dola and Kadia behind to keep watch, take the dinghy and see how far they could get. Quietly he wondered how Barbara would cope when the going got tough.

Alone in Kuantan Barbara had missed VB terribly, for she was deeply in love. Never knowing quite when he would return she'd found herself forever listening for the deep throb of *Kelana*'s engines that sent her heart thumping wildly. As she greeted him each time, he brown and fit, tugging at his moustache and with blue Cornish eyes sparkling, she saw him as a cross between Clark Gable and Humphrey Bogart, a real swashbuckler. She felt there was nothing she wouldn't do for him, nowhere she wouldn't go for him; she would have walked on water had he asked her to. She ached to be with him. She was also very interested in what he was doing. Having worked for Professor AP Elkin in the Anthropology Department of Sydney University, she was interested in the subject, and had been tantalised by what VB told her.

Now she had the chance to see for herself. She had bought her portable typewriter along on this trip and, back aboard *Kelana* in the quiet of the evening, she was catching up on her diary. She felt a hand on her shoulder and stopped typing for a moment to put her own hand on VB's. 'May I?' he asked, and picked up a few sheets of paper. To the rhythmic sound of *Kelana*'s engines heading back to the main branch of the river, he settled onto his bunk to read Barbara's impressions of the past few days.

> *We are in the dinghy and Mahomet takes the controls at the stern. In front of me sits Bruce, looking relaxed in his white shirt and khaki cap, a carbine resting across his knees, and Karim, in brief, once-white shorts and flowing head draperies, squats cross-legged in the bow, sun and shadow rippling on his mahogany satin back. The river at this point is narrow and particularly beautiful. In places the trees arch themselves almost right across the water, looking top-heavy and faintly threatening with their thick growths of fern and creepers straining up to reach the sun. The water is black and clear, mirroring the green finery along its banks so perfectly that one wonders where reality ends and reflection begins. A flash of brilliant scarlet and blue across the water, and a kingfisher or a parakeet darts into the cover of the trees. Wave upon heady wave of perfume, some delicate, some almost suffocating in intensity, intoxicating, then so fragile. It seems that the leaves must exude the scent, for of flowers one sees none.*

Further up the river had narrowed to become a jungle stream, too shallow and littered with debris to allow even motoring in a dinghy, so Karim raised the outboard and they poled their way through the fallen trees, roots and vines. When this became impossible the journey continued in borrowed transport, a *kolek* (dugout canoe) belonging to the locals. The headwaters of the rivers, almost always beautiful, were not always pleasant, for it could be stiflingly hot and humid. VB read on.

Paddling in a kolek, high up in the Merchong, four of us sitting cross-legged on the floor with about an inch of freeboard. It is a tiny narrow stream full of snags and logs fallen across the water. No air seems to penetrate the tall trees, but the sun, high overhead, shines down mercilessly reflecting off the water. I am wearing sunglasses, am wet with perspiration and have a towel wrapped round my head like a turban, but the heat still seems to penetrate and the glare is blinding. I look behind me at Bruce, and his cotton shirt is cool and dry and not even clinging to him. The air around him is insect free whilst around my ankles and in front of my face the vicious little jungle sandflies hover and circle. I look at Karim, paddling at the front, and he is hardly sweating. My head feels hazy and I try to concentrate on the jungle trees and the heavy vines weighing them down, seemingly trying to drag them into the thick undergrowth around their broad roots. Then I concentrate on the Penghulu [a headman they had picked up], sitting impassively in the bow ahead of me, fending off the vines, his near black skin with its peach-bloom finish, his crinkly, dusty hair flecked now with grey, his warm, brown smell, pleasant and sweet, his shorts painstakingly patched in a variety of materials. Though I feel I will expire of heat exhaustion at any moment, I dare not comment. I've heard enough about it being no place for a woman and I am not going to give anybody any satisfaction in that department.

No, she hadn't complained, VB thought. He'd had no idea she had found it so hot. He'd thought she was doing admirably. Later that day, returning in the outboard dinghy, an enormous, newly fallen tree had blocked their path. The understorey of the jungle was thick with bamboo and matted vines and the river bank high and slippery. VB smiled as he read Barbara's account of watching unhappily as he stripped to the waist and slipped into the muddy, orange water. 'Would you mind shooting any crocs that come along,' he'd asked casually, before joining the others diving and hacking at the branches under the water.

Barbara had quizzed him throughout this trip with a seemingly insatiable thirst to know more of the culture of the people, and between them he and Karim had done their best to fill her in. Cultures differed from area to area, but hereditary tribal areas were respected by the *sakai* and rights of hunting, cultivation and gathering jungle produce were strictly observed. While some communities had a dwelling for each family, others were just a single communal longhouse accommodating twenty or thirty people. Designed to last only as long as the fertility of the surrounding soil, the bamboo and *atap* houses were furnished simply with *tikars*, mats on which the people both slept and sat, and in the cooler high country stone hearths kept them warm. Festivities were held in a large, open, social area in the centre. The longhouse, ruled by an elder who chaired a council of all adult males, was the basis of the social organisation. If there was more than one longhouse, the whole group was ruled by a headman, the *Penghulu*.

Some smaller communities preferred to live over the river in a single-room house built on a large bamboo raft, or *rakit*, where they had a constant supply of running water for fishing, drinking, washing, rubbish and sewage disposal. When a *ladang* onshore was exhausted they poled the *rakit* along the river to a new position. Barbara had noted with interest that the domestic arrangements appeared based upon simplicity and tolerance.

At Pah Adam's rakit *some thirty people—men, women and children—live communally, sleeping on the floor with nothing to give privacy from their fellows. The younger children are slung up to sleep in long pieces of rag, doubled over like a hammock and attached to the roof with rattan strings. The older children sleep on the floor near their parents. In one corner is the communal stove and cooking pot, with the fire on one large piece of stone which has been hollowed out in the middle, providing a surrounding hob on which sleep two very thin native dogs. A tiny, grey, long-tailed monkey is tethered on one wall, with two young hornbills as companions. A small child busily crams a plateful of rice down her own and the birds' throats with complete impartiality, while the monkey helps itself with grubby little paws.*

One woman and the baby at her breast look vaguely reminiscent of old potatoes; their skin is flaking off their faces, body and limbs in peculiar circular patterns. The monkey, having finished with the rice, scampers over to the woman and suckles from her other breast.

Within a longhouse community the women and children of individual families planted their own small gardens with chilli bushes and vegetables, but for the major crops like hill rice and tapioca the men of a longhouse worked together, sharing the harvest. The same principle applied to the gathering of *jelutong*, with each longhouse sharing the proceeds of what was collected.

VB was amused at the degree to which Barbara, like most women, was interested in how major events were celebrated. He could tell her that death greatly disturbed the *sakai*, particularly the death of a *Penghulu*. One group he knew of believed butterflies were the spirits of the dead, to be treated with great respect, and he'd had to remember that one shouldn't laugh in the presence of a butterfly. Marriage, on the other hand, seemed a casual affair. Paying due deference to some spirit or other, perhaps the spirit of the river or the rain, and announcing simply that one was taking so and so to wife was sufficient, with perhaps a *ronggeng* and an extra feed of rice to celebrate. In some of the tribes when a man married, he was allowed to sleep with any of his wife's younger sisters or cousins, as long as they agreed. Barbara had raised an eyebrow at this, but VB assured her that affairs of love and lust were of such great interest to the general community, that all such liaisons were known and discussed at great length and in an open fashion. Gossip, therefore, acted as a natural check on overly promiscuous activity.

They'd had a good run in the last twenty-four hours and VB was looking forward to introducing Barbara to Pah Din. He was one of the more reliable suppliers of *jelutong* on the Merchong River, and he was jovial into the bargain. There was nothing better after a long, often difficult trip than to pull up alongside a *rakit* and glimpse a decent line of *bungkus*, or *jelutong* parcels waiting for them under the water. Pah Din knew his area thoroughly, and had scouted out every *jelutong* tree in the vicinity. His boys were adept at tapping the trees in the morning when the sap was fast flowing, and coagulating the *jelutong* into the large balls they kept immersed in the river to prevent them spoiling. The current system of collection did have its failings. For security the communities could never know when VB was coming, so sometimes the *jelutong* wasn't ready when he arrived. Some, if they didn't particularly want or need anything, just didn't bother to collect any, so that VB would have made a long journey for nothing. But Pah Din had never let him down.

Then there was the excitement created by their visits to look forward to, something the whole crew enjoyed. It was, VB realised, something Barbara too delighted in.

> *It's always great fun unpacking the* barang *[trade goods] at each little village we come to. Everyone comes aboard* Kelana *and mills happily around. For us privacy is non-existent for the time we are moored alongside. Faces black, brown and brindle muscle for position at the cabin windows, stricken into alarmed silence by the crackling of the radio, and chattering excitedly at the sight of the* tuan *and* mem *sitting down to eat with a knife and fork.*
>
> *Karim,* Kelana's *skipper, is a most attractive ladies' man. His headgear takes a turn for the piratical and exotic and he is a sight to behold as he strides through the village, muscles knotting and rippling under satiny skin, tossing off a light jest here and a casual appraisal of the younger belles there, pipe clenched nonchalantly between the teeth. Bruce is wonderful with the people and always seems to have them laughing in a very short time. He and Karim tease them and joke with them so that soon everyone is in high good humour and I think they enjoy our visits even more than we do.*

Pah Din's *rakit* came into view and the sound of *Kelana's* engines brought the whole community out onto the banks of the river, smiling, laughing and cheering as the men scrambled to be the first to catch the line thrown ashore. Pah Din's craggy, brown face was beaming. He knew VB would be pleased by the stock of *jelutong* they had to trade, and the thought of the haul awaiting them aboard *Kelana* pleased him no end.

The *sakai* of the jungle were more interested in trading for goods than money. They had nowhere to spend money, for not only was it difficult to get to any town, they didn't want to go to town. They were basically self sufficient and had few needs. The goods they preferred to trade were small things to make their life easier such as *parangs* (knives), medicines, food vessels, matches, kerosene lamps and the kerosene to run them. While VB dealt largely with the *Penghulu*, the whole community always turned out to witness the proceedings. Today was no exception and after the major negotiations for the important things were over, people crowded around making enthusiastic suggestions about what else they fancied from the *barang*. The men were particularly fond of a highly scented hair oil, whilst the women were very taken by the cloth he'd brought, giggling and laughing as they held the different sarongs up against themselves. Some went straight for the box of adornments, shrieking with delight as they tried on strings of beads and baubles, the brighter the better. To Barbara it all looked like chaos, but VB was as ever totally cool and thoroughly enjoying himself.

A bit of knowledge about local customs never went astray in this business. He'd amused Barbara with his tale of a tribe on the Endau River to whom he always took a good stock of Chinese crockery. There the *Penghulu*, who acted as a kind of magistrate, enforced the law by imposing fines to be paid in plates in accordance with the gravity of the wrongdoing. Half of the fine was paid to the person who had been wronged, and half to the *Penghulu* himself. As such the *Penghulu* was a wealthy man indeed.

Good old Karim. He'd been a Godsend in building a relationship with these people. He was VB's right-hand man, an old hand with the *sakai*, and somehow he managed to ensure VB knew of any community taboos so that he didn't put his foot in it. To Barbara VB seemed in his element with the *sakai*. As she watched him squatting down with a group of men, heels on the ground just like them, talking, laughing, totally at ease, she felt a surge of pride. What was it about him that enabled him to get on so well with people from all walks of life, of different classes, different races, different sexes? It had its drawbacks of course, for it meant he was always in demand and there was often little time for her, but when she was with him there was no doubt about it. It was sheer bliss.

That night, after finally slipping quietly away to their cabin after the evening's festivities, Barbara was feeling excited, inspired about what they had seen. She wanted to write of it straight away, and though VB would have preferred her company in his bunk he didn't object, and for the next half hour she spilled forth their experience onto the paper. It was something about her that he liked, the way she took such an intelligent interest in other people.

It is a dark night, but clear and cold, the moon rising late and the stars brilliant, reflected in the black mirror of the river. Sitting in the warm cabin we can hear the ronggeng *drum boom out its sonorous strokes over the water and far into the jungle. The drums are joined by laughter and high-toned singing and handclapping as a girl goes through the motions and words of one of their stylised dances. Sleep is impossible, we are too near; so we steal softly into the rowing boat, and let the drift of the tide take us out and down to the* rakit, *into the path of the one oil lamp, where we sit quietly and watch, as couple after couple go through the ancient rhythm of the dance, the girls leading and singing the words, and the men following the movements of their feet.* Ronggeng *is more a singular self expression than a dance as we know it. The man and the woman dance separately, two or three feet apart, but the man must follow the woman as she moves backwards and forwards, and should keep the same step as she does. He should immerse himself in the rhythm, and he usually does, however badly he follows it. The arms swing loosely and the shoulders sway, the hips gradually take on an undulating motion and the head is thrown back, eyes unseeing, until the dancer loses himself in the ecstasy of the movement he is creating himself. Then the drums stop, abruptly, and the man, self-conscious now, shuffles back out of the lamplight to make room for another to take his place.*

We are not unobserved. Pah Din steps out for a puff of Siam, a particularly noxious tobacco they love, and asks us to come aboard. We bend our heads to enter and make our way out of the lamplight to a stack of rice sacks over against the hearth, where in a short time we are forgotten. The hut is warm and cosy, its dirt hidden by the dim light. Its inhabitants sit around the walls on their tikars or on tins of kerosene which we have just brought them. The children, despite the lateness of the hour, are still wide awake, though a few of the younger ones lie curled up like puppies on the floor.

The small children are dancing now, two girls, two boys, the girls exact replicas of their older sisters, betel-red lips, earrings dangling almost to their shoulders. They are giggling— they suddenly remember we are there, and in an overpowering excess of shyness they scuttle off the dancing mat and dive behind their mothers. One small boy keeps doggedly on—he is Pah Din's son and feels he has some face to save. His head sways on his neck and his eyes, not far away as the others had been, watch from under his lowered lids to see the effect he is having on his audience. He dances on and on, exerting himself to greater efforts until his movements are so exaggerated as to be almost frenzied, signalling to the musicians to keep playing, until finally his father gets up and takes him, kicking, off the floor. He knows he is good, and he wants to show off before a new audience, before the white man. The dancing goes on for hours. We finally leave and retire to our cabin, to fall asleep to the rhythm of the drum.

VB knew the symptoms well. He'd seen it before on the Burma–Siam Railway and though it wasn't nearly as bad here, it was still pretty obvious to him that some of the tribes were malnourished due to a lack of protein from meat and fish. Along with the government-issued rice he always carried a stock of dried fish to the upriver communities, to give them a little extra in their diet.

Part of the problem, he thought, was that the men preferred to hunt with their blowpipes, impressive weapons of elaborately decorated bamboo. He could understand that a man proficient with his blowpipe would be much admired. The darts, small and featherless and notched at the end to prevent them falling out, were laced with poison from the gum of the Ipoh tree, the strychnos vine or a concoction of delights such as toadskin and snake venom. Possession of a blowpipe was considered a sign of maturity for young men, who were proud of their weapons and kept them beautifully maintained and polished. But blowpipes were difficult to use against an animal sheltering in dense undergrowth. Clearings were not always in the right place at the right time and though more success was often found hunting with traps, men still preferred their blowpipes.

Lack of meat was not the only problem. VB had found whole communities of people whose skin looked like potato peelings, as though they were suffering from a lack of vitamin C, where the season had been poor and vegetable crops failed. Others who didn't rely on crops had the same condition. He and Barbara had been concerned for a small group they'd discovered in a tributary of the Merchong.

We finally come across a kolek *moored against the bank and Karim gives a hoy. A strange man, thin and angular, and with the old, potato peeling look to his skin that so many of the people of the river have, appears on the bank. We draw up to the landing, two thin, narrow pieces of bark jutting out from the bank, and the* Penghulu *steps out with the rope and holds the boat steady. We walk up to this strange 'village', which is only a bark and* atap *wall leaning against a tree, a lean-to in fact, and Bruce squats down to talk. There are two women there, and seven children, and one other old man with a nose quill, one eye and no teeth and a mouth stained with betel. A thin, red stream trickles from one corner. I notice that all have the potato skin, even the three month old child that is being suckled. Their two dogs, on thin, rickety legs, skin stretched tight across*

their ribs and moulding into the hollows that were their stomachs,
hang back, lips drawn tight over their teeth in a silent, suspicious
snarl.

There was little VB could do for these people in the long term.
He gave them enough rice and dried fish to see them through a
month or two and they were delighted with their windfall. But
they were hunters and gatherers, constantly on the move, and had
little wish for material possessions since anything they had would
have to be carried with them. They were not interested in trade.
If they spent too much time in any one area they risked going
hungry, and couldn't stay around to tap *jelutong*. VB had a good
look at them before he left, noting their clothes made of a type of
bark cloth and their adornments of coloured seeds, and wondered
whether they were among Mrs Windsor's *orang liar*, the wild
people.

Before the Emergency tribes in the more accessible areas had
received visits from 'dressers', paramedics who attended to their
medical needs as they could. With the CT threat the government
stopped providing this service and now at most *ladangs* some
people were in need of attention. *Kelana* carried a few simple
medical supplies, things such as bottles of Dettol, dressings and
enormous boxes of quinine tablets for malaria. VB was no medico
but he did what he could. His time in the jungle as a POW came
in useful, for he well knew how to treat tropical ulcers and dress
small injuries. Some old boys would whisper to him that they
hadn't *pergi sungei* (gone to the river) for a few days, and he'd
give them something to fix that. The demand for quinine tablets
was great, VB believed, because the pills gave people such a good
headache they felt they were getting something worthwhile. Police
orders regarding the supply of medicines to the *sakai* were clear.
Under the CT denial scheme only small amounts of medicine
could be left with the jungle people in case it fell into the wrong
hands. So those in need of serious medical attention he took aboard
Kelana, if they would come, to be taken to hospital. Most often,
however, they wouldn't and it wasn't uncommon for VB to arrive

at a community to find that someone had died since his last visit.

Out on the Merchong and Bebar rivers VB felt so isolated and remote from anywhere that it was easy to forget about the Emergency. But it wasn't always like that. The rivers in southern Pahang near the Johore border were particularly dangerous, and in the inland area around Lake Tasek Bera, it was impossible to forget the Communist threat.

Lake Tasek Bera, where the Semelai people lived, was a difficult place to get to. It was reached by taking an open boat from the village of Temerloh and following the Pahang River to where the Bera River emptied into it. It was a ghostly feeling, stopping in the upper reaches of the river where the jungle gave way to an open swamp of twisted, stunted trees, listening for the eerie sound of a *berbaling*. Every Semelai village had one, a bamboo windmill with no other purpose than to produce a loud, haunting sound that could be heard miles away. The swampland offered few distinguishing geographical features, but following the hum on the breeze led you through the reeds to the open expanse of tranquil, deep, dark water that was Tasek Bera.

The Semelai were not new to trading with the outside world. Before the Emergency they'd received occasional visits from Chinese traders who had travelled upriver from Temerloh, but now these visits had ceased, as no ethnic Chinese were allowed out of the towns. At Tasek Bera the atmosphere was quite different to the more remote settlements VB visited. A band of CTs were active in the region and now the police force had set up a jungle post. Fort Iskandar was one of a number throughout Malaya built since 1952, when the government recognised the extent of the control CTs had over the *sakai*. Here in western Pahang the problem had been worsened by the food-denial operation forcing CTs deeper into the jungle. For them, the assistance of the *sakai* became critical. It was easy to see why dealing with the *sakai* was such a difficult issue, for the concept of government or politics meant little or nothing to most of them and they lived an existence entirely separate from the rest of Malayan society.

The relationship between the CTs and the *sakai* had begun during the Japanese occupation when the CTs had developed friendships and mutual co-operation as a matter of course. So isolated were the *sakai* that for some time after 1948 a few believed they were still helping the guerillas against the Japanese. When they discovered it was the British that the guerillas were fighting they cared little, as long as their life was not disrupted.

As VB well knew, if you won over the friendship of a *Penghulu* you had the whole tribe won over. The CTs then grew food in *sakai ladangs* without attracting attention from the air, and in return the CTs assisted them to improve their own cultivation methods, providing them with new types of seed. The *sakai* acted as guides, porters and spies for them. They provided information as to the presence and movement of any security patrols and were trained to identify different types of aircraft and note their direction.

VB had originally been briefed that the CTs dominated up to thirty thousand *sakai* in the jungle throughout Malaya. With little contact from the outside world, they were easy meat for CT propaganda and were fed a lot of bad information about how the war was progressing. In most cases they were shrewd enough to realise that for their own sake they should back whichever side was winning, and when they thought it was the Communists, they continued helping them.

The 'forts' such as the one VB visited at Tasek Bera were established in areas around CT-dominated *sakai* settlements. They were the result of a new and concerted effort to win over the jungle people, begun towards the end of 1953. The new policy called for a better organised and more permanent presence in the jungle, as opposed to the unsuccessful jungle-bashing operations carried out in previous years. The forts were manned by Malay police jungle-squads under British lieutenants, plus a few Department of Aborigines liaison officers and medical orderlies. No attempts were made to interfere with the way of life of the *sakai*; the aim was to extend the hand of friendship and trade, and to win over their confidence.

When the *sakai* found that these officials could do a lot more for them than the CTs could, they changed their allegiances.

Visiting the fort at Tasek Bera was the highlight of VB's journey, for he was welcomed warmly by these men who lived an isolated and spartan existence and who may have spent periods in excess of six months at a time at their post. Their dwellings were basic, built largely out of jungle material, and continuity between the *sakai* and the fort commanders had to be maintained. As VB tramped in as if from nowhere they were delighted to see him; he was a new face, and they knew the night ahead would be a long one, discussing the affairs of the outside world by the dim light of a kerosene lamp.

In his own efforts to collect intelligence at other more isolated communities, VB met with some limited success. It was more difficult to build up a relationship of trust and confidence with *sakai* in contact with CTs, and often they were not eager to tell what they knew. They had an aversion to violence and if the CTs had threatened them they wouldn't talk. They were also very loyal to each other, and if providing information about CT movements could endanger any others of their kin they simply wouldn't do it. VB knew he could offer them many things, but he couldn't offer them what they really needed in order to provide information: protection. It was an awkward business and the *sakai* under the direct control of the CTs in these more isolated areas were at great risk. *Penghulus* were convinced that the British were losing the war. They had heard that troops from China had bolstered the Communist forces and taken control of the country. When outsiders tried to tell them that a thing called a government existed and that the British were running it, it was little wonder they were sceptical.

Word of the problem got back to General Templer and he agreed something had to be done. An extraordinary meeting was called. One hundred and fifty *sakai Penghulus* from all over Pahang, Perak and Kelantan were collected and brought by river, road and helicopter to Kuala Lumpur. The group of small, brown, wide-eyed men were greeted at King's House by Templer himself. Over the next ten days they met senior officers of the army and police force and were taken to various depots to be treated to an impressive display of armoury. From all reports there were great choruses of oohs and ahs when the two-pounder guns, mortars and automatic weapons were demonstrated. They were given a tour of the Kuala Lumpur Air Base and shown how and why 'voice aircraft' were used. They were asked to speak into tape recorders and then later gasped in amazement as they heard their own voices coming from the aircraft flying low overhead. Some who were still not convinced were asked to walk alone in the streets of the city to talk to people themselves.

The meeting was a great success. The *Pengulus* returned to their *ladangs* with stories of how they had been tricked and lied to by the Communists. The next time VB visited the tribes in southern Pahang, their attitude had changed. Slowly the *sakai* were being won over.

TWELVE

The Power of a Tiger

Mrs Windsor *had* warned them. 'Meenah is very keen,' she'd said in her clipped accent, 'but she will need a bit of polishing up.' VB had agreed with Barbara to let the surly Chinese cook go, for he'd always made it perfectly clear he considered himself a bachelor's cook. Now Meenah had joined the household and though efficiency was not her forte, her smiling Malay face was a delight to have around. VB saw her as a nice old girl, broad across the beam and amiable, and got on very well with her, forever reducing her to a heap of giggles. He called her Meenah *binti chulas*, which meant 'Meenah daughter of idleness', which she thought hilarious. A great sufferer of cold feet, she'd potter around the house wearing his old socks with her brightly coloured sarong and *baju*. Having come straight from the *padi* fields she had to be taught how to do everything, several times over. Barbara persevered because she liked Meenah, and knew she'd have to go back to labouring in the fields at half the wage if she lost her job. Besides, what Meenah lacked in experience she made up for in enthusiasm, and her philosophy— which she applied to most things, including floor polish—was that if a little was good, a lot more must be even better, sticky or not sticky.

Meenah didn't cook, at least Barbara didn't let her cook, and neither did she shop, but at her first dinner party she proved her real worth. Emerging from her room to serve the drinks she was an immediate hit with the guests. Determined to make a good impression she had gone to great effort to look her best for the occasion, and her normally brown Malay face was white, covered in a thick layer of face powder. Her lips were bright and shiny with inexpertly applied red lipstick and her eyelids glossed with purple eyeshadow. The whole effect was finished with her betelnut-stained, gaptoothed and hugely cheerful smile and an enormous red hibiscus behind each ear. Everybody loved her. Barbara had cooked a cheese soufflé for the first course and as VB seated the guests she checked the oven to find it rising splendidly. A little later Meenah brought it to the table and Barbara gasped in dismay, for the soufflé seemed to have disappeared. 'Meenah! What has happened to the soufflé?' she asked.

Meenah grinned widely and proudly proclaimed in Malay, 'Oh *Mem*! I watched it like you said and it was getting bigger and bigger and climbing out of the dish so I beat it down with a spoon.'

The house on the river had become a pleasant home. Redecorated, it was now difficult to imagine some of the ghastly scenes it had accommodated during the Japanese occupation. While Meenah could usually be found drinking coffee with her friends on the back steps, another new addition to the family was more often than not sleeping soundly under the new chintz cushions of the settee or hanging upside down under a lampshade. Little Jo had been in residence since Barbara fell in love with him on a trip to the Temerloh area. She'd accompanied VB, who had been looking for *jelutong* trees. Calling into a *kampong* to check with the workers, they saw a man with a baby *kongkang*, or slow loris, a tiny, almost bare little thing no bigger than his hand. Barbara, who was never completely happy unless surrounded by animals, asked if she could buy it. Since then it had been waxing fat, furry and contented.

There were times when the main bedroom in the house became VB's refuge from the world, people—even light—for his malaria was still giving him hell. Every couple of months the familiar headaches, sweating and high temperatures hit him with all the subtlety of a steamtrain. If it happened while he was away upcountry it was particularly unpleasant and he realised something had to be done. Dr Edeson, an expert in malaria and who was working with a new form of quinine at the Kuantan Institute of Medical Research, had been determined to rid VB of malaria permanently. He'd prescribed a course of quinine in such high doses that VB spent four miserable days in bed nursing one of the fattest heads he'd ever had. It seemed to do the trick, however, and it was several years before he had another bout.

Somerset Maugham wrote of the colonial *mem*, 'They played tennis if there were people to play with, went to the club at sundown if there was a club in the vicinity, drank in moderation, and played bridge.' Except that it was usually mahjong instead of bridge, one could be forgiven for thinking that life in Kuantan really was so relaxed, at least from what Barbara wrote of it.

Riding around on my bicycle, slower than a car, and never in too much of a hurry, I have time to see and wave to so many people, Chinese, Malay and English, and to stop and pass the time of day with them, even if I don't speak the same language. There's Tony from the Cold Storage, looking like an Indian but very conscious of his Eurasian stock; the little Chinese lad from the market, with his English limited to 'oh yes' when you meet him, be you buying carrots in the pasar or riding past him in the street; Hock Bee, the wealthy Chinese businessman, waving and nodding like a broadly beaming sunflower from behind the wheel of his huge, green Ford; Lt. Derry Livingstone peddling past on his towering bicycle that looks something like a penny farthing with its seat and handlebars up as high as they will go; nearly running down the old Tamil wise-man who wanders the town, his feet like black sticks protruding from his ancient shorts, his chin sunk into his chest in deep thought, or perhaps because of the immense weight of the magical bullock-dung plastered into his long hair; Tamil women who sweep the roads, in long bright cotton gowns, their sarongs thrown around to form a pocket hanging like a sporran in front of them, their headcloths pushed (not folded) into square shape and balanced precariously above their tight, dusty buns (so different from the shining, smooth, black hair of the Malay women), bright jewels glinting in their nostrils, gold bracelets dusty around their ankles.

I walk into the bank, the door held open with a sober, friendly nod from the one-eyed Sikh guard with his green turban, tightly rolled beard and bandolier around his shoulders and across his chest. Inside there is a large crowd and I feel guilty as my Indian friend with the quiet manner and the huge white-toothed smile comes over to give me a little personal attention. One of the Lancer officers who has been waiting half an hour complains with a cheerful joke about the pull some people have around this town; my Indian friend asks me if I enjoyed the cricket match on Sunday—he is a keen cricketer—and we launch into a discussion about the merits of the local bats. I congratulate him on a fine catch.

Off again on my bicycle, waving to Colonel Blackie churning past in a Bren gun carrier; on again towards home, then a loud hail from the rear—it's Towkay who runs the Resthouse— 'Mem Wharton and the Kidmans are looking for you to have coffee with them—they're at the Resthouse now.' So we ride off together and that's the end of anything constructive being done for the morning.

While the police and the army fought a war in Malaya, those not directly involved could go about their business happily cocooned in a blanket of strict censorship. But Barbara's leisurely prose, written to stop her parents worrying, belied the fact that the more she learned of the Emergency, the more she felt she should be contributing. Some of her women friends were very busy indeed.

VB had told her of General Templer's visit to Kuantan before she arrived, of how he'd galvanised the community, particularly Europeans. He'd worked hard to draw everyone into the fight against the Communists, emotionally if not physically, and insisted that anyone who had qualifications, including wives, must do what they could. He'd also made it clear that everyone must be involved in 'Malayanising' the country, breaking down old racial prejudices and traditions such that all races could look towards the Federation of Malay States as their real home. These morale-boosting measures also encouraged loyalty from the people and renewed determination to defeat the Communists.

In Kuantan it was the habit of some of the *mems* who were at leisure during the day to hold mahjong mornings, loquacious affairs punctuated by clacking tiles and tinkling coffee cups. VB was amused to hear that during the Templers' visit all mahjong playing among the European women had actually stopped. Lady Templer thoroughly disapproved of ladies sitting around socialising. There was a war on and she considered every woman should be doing her bit; there was a lot to be done to win over the Malayan people.

Though he never said so directly, Barbara sensed VB would have been happy to know his wife was also doing what she could. Colonel Blackie of the Kings African Rifles had organised tuition in shooting for women, declaring that it was 'the duty of every thinking woman in this country to learn to defend themselves', and Barbara had completed the course with enthusiasm. To keep herself busy she'd taken over the library at the Kuantan Club and been assisting Mrs Windsor in her good works. But as the months passed she began to feel it was not enough.

VB was very busy, having acquired another responsibility now that Windsor had won a contract to build several new barges. There were no bridges over the rivers of Pahang and flat-bottomed barges were used to ferry cargo, cars and passengers from one side to the other. VB had regarded them dubiously when he first saw them, for many were reaching the end of their useful life. Matters had come to a head when the Pekan ferry sank with the Sultan's favourite car aboard. (The Sultan was visiting Kuala Lumpur that day and his vehicle should have been in its garage at the Istana. A rumour circulated that somebody left Pahang in rather a hurry.)

While VB threw himself into the building project with great energy, Barbara was looking for something else to do. When the new Special Branch Chief, Bill Humble, began casting about for a European assistant, she jumped at the opportunity. By the end of the week she had the job.

Whap . . . whap . . . whap . . . whap . . . It was unmistakable, the sound of her boss walking down the long corridor of the building, opening the dividing swing doors with his chest. Bill Humble was strong and nuggetty and a little larger than life. He had been a Commando during World War II and seen active service parachuting behind the lines in Sicily, Yugoslavia, Albania and Greece. Having been one himself he had a good idea of the way guerillas thought and acted, and since then had earned the Colonial Police Medal for Gallantry, been badly wounded by a grenade in an operation south of Kuala Lumpur and had earned a reputation for getting his man. He had not been in Kuantan long but already he had the bit between his teeth.

Barbara soon learned of her boss's firm belief that the police alone could handle the Communists, and that he liked to do things his own way. He'd specially chosen and trained his mixed-race team himself. He had four platoons, sections of about ten or twelve strong. 'I don't need the army,' he complained to Barbara on one occasion, after a muffed operation. 'They just blunder their way through things. The army can't move a lot of men through the jungle because the CTs always hear them. My men are thoroughly trained and work on agents' information. They only go out for a specific job, never on spec. There's no point in that.'

The job was exciting and stimulating. Barbara worked alone in Bill Humble's office, away from other people, for it was all top-secret stuff. As Bill admitted when he hired her, paperwork was not his forte and her main job was to look after that. Often he'd just give her a verbal draft of what he wanted to report and say, 'Now you just pad it out for me.' The wall in the office was plastered in large black and white photographs of the faces of CTs known to be in the jungle around Kuantan. Every so often Barbara would walk into the office in the morning to find a big cross over one or more of those faces—a red cross for a kill, blue for a capture or yellow for a surrender—and she'd know the operation of the night before had been successful.

On occasions Bill would take her into the field with him to take notes while he questioned an informant or visited another town to interrogate newly captured or surrendered CTs. 1954 was a lively time for Special Branch, and what became known as 'the Battle for Pahang' was in full swing. The first operation had been launched the previous year, an operation which was considered afterwards as having brought about the beginning of the end of the military war. Operation Ibex was the tight control of food, medical and other essential supplies, relentless ambushes and constant military pressure in the jungle.

The food-denial program was all-encompassing, and in some way or another it touched the lives of everyone in the community. Shopkeepers were compelled by law to punch a hole in every tin before it was taken away. This even applied to Heinz baby food. It didn't matter who you were. Rice, sugar, tea, flour and cooking oils all had to be bought on ration cards and each time anyone bought any of these items they'd have their cards punched at the shop. People were only allowed to keep enough food to eat almost immediately. Carrying food in vehicles outside a town or village was strictly prohibited; even taking a single sandwich on a day trip out of town was forbidden.

VB was happy to see Barbara so animated about her employment. He knew that having taken him on as a husband she'd need a fair degree of self reliance to be really content. He'd been impressed at the way she'd dealt recently with a first-hand experience of the effect of the food-denial operation. He was away upriver at the time, and she'd been awoken at around 2am to the sound of movement in the garden. Peering cautiously out of the bedroom window, she'd seen two men below her working at the padlock on the door of the rice store, a gun on the ground beside them. It was obvious that, as *Kelana* was not moored at the jetty, they thought no-one was in the house. There was no phone to call for help and the shame of reporting the loss of the rice stores to her boss the next day loomed large in her mind. VB had taken the guns with him and the only weapon left in the house was a tiny Beretta pistol for which there was no ammunition. Armed with a knife from the kitchen and the empty handgun she'd crept to the top of the steps and launched herself down them with the wildest shriek she could muster. So startled were the intruders, they abandoned their mission and bolted off into the darkness along the river. Hazy with shock, she'd sat down heavily on the bottom step, terrified at what she'd done, and it was some few minutes before she'd stopped shaking enough to get herself back upstairs. On reporting the incident at the office next morning Bill Humble had warned her sternly to keep her head down unless she wanted it shot off. VB had given her no such reprimand. 'Well done, Charlie!' he'd said, and slapped her on the back. 'Well done indeed.' From VB this was high praise. Barbara had already learned that VB did not waste superlatives and had high expectations of those close to him. Her performance, apparently, had passed muster.

VB looked up from his mahjong tiles to see his wife wince again. It was almost three in the morning, the shutters were all fastened and outside they were still at it. Dining with the Rooths at their rubber estate outside Kuantan, the din outside had been incredible. Along with the police and the army, the air forces of Britain and Australia had been making a significant contribution to defeating the Communists. Tonight a harassing campaign was being waged in the jungle nearby, and Paul and Shirley had begged them to stay and play mahjong all night, for sleep was impossible. So they played, to the sound of bang, crack, whump, crack, the unsettling backdrop of shelling and bombing from both the army and the air force. VB couldn't help but compare the concept of playing mahjong while there was a war going on to the unreal period in Singapore before the Japs invaded. Only this time he really did have nothing to worry about. He felt sorry for the poor devils in the jungle, whoever they were, particularly as he'd been caught in a monsoon storm himself at Atbara coolie lines earlier in the evening, and realised how wild and cold it was out there. All hell had been let loose on the CTs this week. What it was like to be out there hungry, cold, hunted and perhaps wounded and with nowhere to go, was not difficult for VB to imagine.

He recalled a conversation he'd had with police chief Ken Belton, who'd been 'out there' and had a good idea of what it was like.

'One is not afraid of these people,' he'd said, 'but one respects them as soldiers of another army, the enemy. Yet when I come across them in the jungle, either surrendered or dead, and see these miserable, pathetic little underfed people, I never quite get over the fact that we are being chased about by them. They seem ruled by fear more than anything else. But of course they are totally at home in the jungle and we are not.'

VB glanced again at Barbara. She looked miles away. He imagined she was thinking something similar, only it was a bit closer to home for her, since she often saw the end results of these operations lugged back into the police station. It was an unpopular job, bringing the bodies back in from the jungle for identification. The usual method after a patrol was to sling them under a bamboo pole to which the hands and feet were lashed, and it was hot, heavy work. She'd come home a bit shaken the first time a small military patrol had decided they'd had enough of toiling miles through the jungle with their burden, and brought only the heads back to present to Bill for identification. The practice had not been popular with the top brass in Kuala Lumpur and Bill was told it wasn't to happen again. He'd passed on the order but the next time there were a couple of kills, in came another two heads. Bill was a bit unhappy about it, but got around the official photographs by padding out the place where the body should have been on the table, and laying each head at the top tucked in with a sheet under the chin. They'd looked very effective in the pictures.

The *kampongs* where VB's workers lived were secured by clearing undergrowth, installing barbed wire fences and lights; the people couldn't be expected to refuse to supply CTs unless they were protected. He knew that the real success of the operation was measured not by successful captures or kills, but by the numbers of surrenders. As Kuantan's DO, Patrick Bolshaw, commented, 'We're not trying to achieve an all out war to blast the Communists off the face of the earth. What we really want to do is demoralise them, to get them to surrender themselves and then turn them into decent citizens. Sometimes the methods are rather odd, rewards for CTs who give themselves up and so forth.'

Initially there had been a lot of uncertainty in government circles as to what to do with surrendered and captured enemy personnel. As Emergency measures were being directed by the civil police, the obvious thing was that all terrorists, surrendered or not, should be brought to trial. However, this procedure offered little incentive to surrender, as many terrorists had committed serious crimes which under the normal system of justice carried sentences of death. Another option was treating surrendered enemy personnel as POWs for the duration of the Emergency, but likewise this did not make surrender an attractive proposition. In view of this it was eventually decided that as an inducement, surrendered CTs would not be tried or punished. Any who were willing to co-operate with the police were given cash rewards for their assistance and many joined the Special Operational Volunteer Force to return to the jungle to eliminate their former comrades. Others were put through lengthy 'rehabilitation programs'.

The value of psychological warfare was well recognised and widely used. In western Pahang *sakai* had shown VB leaflets dropped from the air. They showed the faces of dead CTs and gave the names of those who had surrendered. He'd seen 'voice aircraft' fly low over the jungle broadcasting the same message that could also be heard on Radio Malaya in twelve dialects. The message was, 'We know that what you have done was in the name of the Revolution. But you are still human. Surrender and all will be forgiven.'

The policy of forgiveness did not extend by any means to those who were captured. As Bill Humble made clear, 'If there are special circumstances which make them useful, such as in the case of top party members or someone who has contact with a top boy, they might be spared. Otherwise they are almost always hanged.'

Barbara walked out of the office of Special Branch, clutching her handbag tightly. In it was the key to Bill Humble's safe. His behaviour had been unusual that afternoon and he had never asked her to take the key home before. She'd noticed how quiet and reflective he was at his desk, apparently writing a letter. When it was finished he'd put it in the safe. 'If I don't come into the office tomorrow morning,' he'd told her, 'I want you to open the safe, remove that letter and take it to Nan.' Barbara knew of the strength of the bond between Bill, his wife Nan and the children. He had been on many a dangerous mission but had never before shown doubts about his own safety. Knowing that if he wanted her to know more he would have told her, she'd asked no questions.

That night Barbara was restless, lying in bed going through in her mind the missions her boss might be undertaking tonight. She was thankful VB was beside her while she had Bill's key. As ever he was a calming influence. 'Don't worry,' he said. 'Bill's a tough cookie and he knows exactly what he's doing. He'll be all right, you'll see.'

But Barbara was not so sure. The office safe contained a great deal of money used to pay surrenders. The higher a CT was in the hierarchy, the larger was the reward after surrender. The funds were also used to pay informers, who made contact with Bill Humble at night, in a special informant's room at the back of his house. Part of Bill's charter was to seek to identify and understand the minds of leading CTs in the area. She knew the head State Committee member of the MRLA in Pahang was a dedicated Communist named Foo Tin who, despite suffering from diabetes and tuberculosis, had steadfastly held out in the jungle. His second in command was a man named Ah Tan. Bill Humble had recently taken the unusual step of writing personal letters to leading CTs, urging them to surrender. The letters promised good treatment, understanding and, if they co-operated, liberty. They had been delivered by agents, left on jungle tracks or given to tappers to pass on. Bill was always a bit of a risk taker, but whatever it was he was doing that night, there was something very important at stake. She wondered if it was one of the big boys.

In the morning she went to work early, slightly bleary eyed from an almost sleepless night. She walked around the corner into the office and breathed a sigh of relief. There was Bill, sitting at his desk as large as life. 'What happened?' she asked.

He nodded, grinning, towards the wall. She looked across to see a large yellow cross over the face of Ah Tan. No wonder Bill was grinning. There had been a letter passed on by a tapper through the manager of the Atbara Rubber Estate. It had been from Ah Tan himself, stating he was ready to come out of the jungle. But there'd been a condition: he would surrender only to Bill Humble himself. Ah Tan had demanded Bill present himself alone and unarmed at a certain location on the border of the estate at 6pm and toot the horn of his vehicle five times. The chance that this was a trap was high and Bill had gone into it knowing that he would be a perfect target, that there was a very real possibility that he would be killed. Now Barbara handed him back the key to the safe, and he took it. 'This time,' he told her a trifle sheepishly, 'taking such a risk, all I could think of was Nan and the children. I guess I was overcome by a sense of guilt. Thankfully you can throw my letter in the bin.'

The surrender of Ah Tan was a coup for Kuantan Special Branch, indeed for the state of Pahang. Ah Tan agreed to write letters to his previous comrades and these were copied and dropped from the air. The next to surrender was District Committee member Wong Kow and he also wrote letters. This type of psychological pressure combined with the food denial and military offensives really began to pay dividends.

Chest-deep in water, John Dickie was holding Barbara's attention in conversation. It was a humid Sunday morning and the three of them were having a quick dip at Sixteen-Mile Beach before returning to Jabor Valley estate for lunch. The open jeep in which they'd come lay parked in the shade where the jungle met the sand, and two Malay guards sat on the bonnet. Some distance behind, the undergrowth was thick over a slight rise, and through it the barrel of a .303 calibre rifle was aimed at Barbara's head.

Back from a swim VB saw his chance. Holding his breath he dipped under the water and swam silently up behind to deliver his wife a surprise dunking. Up in the jungle a finger, tight on the trigger, loosened off.

Two days later, a CT was brought into the Special Branch office. He had been responsible for the horrible death of one of the local Tamil tapper women. The woman had been unable or unwilling to smuggle food to him, and he had tied her to a tree, disembowelled her with a *parang* and left her to die. She was seven months pregnant. Barbara had seen the sickening photographs of her mutilated body against the tree. Now the man responsible had surrendered and was sitting in the office, left alone with her for a while. He was not nervous, haggard and dirty as so many were; he wore khaki trousers, a fairly clean white shirt and a conceited expression. In view of what she knew of him, and appalled by the fact that as a 'surrender' he'd go free, Barbara felt she could not be civil and decided not to speak at all. Silently she put a cup of coffee and a plate of Chinese dumplings in front of him and returned to work at her desk, her skin crawling.

'You were lucky on Sunday,' he said suddenly. His English was good. 'You and your husband were out with *Tuan* Dickie at Sixteen-Mile Beach at about eleven o' clock.' He was right. 'I knew you were *Mem* Special Branch and I had you in the sights of my gun. I would have killed you but I was on my way to a meeting to get rice, and decided that if I did I wouldn't have got it. You were lucky I was hungry.'

It was quite usual for Bill to leave CTs in his office to settle down a little. When they were brought into the Kuantan police compound from the jungle they were often wet and dirty, tired, hungry and sometimes very frightened. They were pale from lack of sun, sometimes sick, and covered in insect and leech bites. After they'd been given fresh clothes and had their wounds dressed, they'd wait with Barbara and she would order them something to eat and some coffee. Occasionally, if they spoke English or Malay, they were keen to talk. Most who had surrendered were worried and suspicious and wanted to sound her out about whether there really was a noose at the end of the road, despite all the promises. Sometimes they would relax and begin to talk about themselves; what made them surrender or even what made them turn to Communism in the first place.

Most of the men and women who came through the office as surrenders were part of the middle order in the spectrum of human characters that made up the Communism movement in Malaya.

The people who had been disillusioned with life were the first to be attracted by the Party's well-oiled propaganda machine, by the excitement and adventure of joining an army, by the chance to become someone, to work their way up and later be offered a good position in the new Communist government. Then there were people who had been offside of the British system of justice and saw Communism as a way to lie low, and others who were black-mailed into it after having become involved with smuggling to the CTs. For some, Chinese nationalism was a driving factor. Then there were those who joined the MRLA because they truly believed that the ordinary person would live a better life under a Communist government. They saw in Communism a new kind of humanitar-ianism and were sincerely moved towards its ideals. The young Chinese girl brought into Kuantan Special Branch one day was such a one.

Captured by the police, she was brought into the office tired and frightened, dressed in a baggy khaki uniform. Well educated and idealistic, she had been a local school teacher and had joined the Communists because she believed in what they were doing, that Malaya really would be better under Communism. When she found it was not as she had imagined, she couldn't get out. To Barbara she looked anything but a terrorist. As she tried to calm her Barbara churned inside, for she was well aware that as a capture this CT was destined to be hanged. The girl's dark brown, frightened eyes seemed to search her own in desperation, looking for some-thing, some small hope to cling to. They were hard to meet. Later, as the thin, almost childlike figure climbed into the truck bound for headquarters in Kuala Lipis, Barbara had to fight to maintain her composure. As usual, she was to arrange to have the girl's jungle clothes burned, and as she bundled up the shabby uniform tears welled up uncontrollably. How was it that the CT who had mutilated and murdered the tapper woman could be spared his life while this girl was to lose hers? The girl had acted upon ideological beliefs and had committed no such atrocity. She was to be executed simply because she was captured rather than surrendered. Before handing over the pathetic bundle of clothes, Barbara took her little hand made cap, dirty khaki with the red star of the Communists stitched to the front, to keep always as a reminder of the girl.

That night in the middle of dinner Barbara burst into tears. 'What's upsetting you?' VB asked, and it all spilled out. 'I'm afraid that's war, Charlie,' he said. 'War is a dirty business and there is very little justice about it.' To VB it was a tragedy. He felt a deep resentment at the way in which young, impressionable people had been sucked in by Communist propaganda. It was also, he knew, hard on their families who tried to carry on a normal life, worrying about their sons and daughters and torn in a no-win situation between trying to help them or not.

The girl was one of many CTs who, having committed themselves, realised that Communism was not all they had imagined and wanted to get out. It was as though they had climbed on the back of a tiger. It was very exciting and they had the power of a tiger; they moved as it moved. But then when they wanted to get off, it was more dangerous than staying on its back.[1] CTs suspected of considering surrender would be killed by their comrades. It was a capital offence even to pick up a leaflet dropped by the British.

And then there were the best youth from other countries dragged into the fight. Among these were two young Lancer officers on national service, lively, intelligent lads whom VB had had to dinner often when they were in town, and whom he saw go out into the jungle, never to return. He was not one to show emotion, but when he heard news of their death he was quiet for an unusually long time. And he kicked the front door, very hard.

The general situation in Malaya was improving vastly. The incessant military and police operations were taking their toll and the Communists were losing strength rapidly. Operation Ibex achieved its objective: to cut off the CTs in the Kuantan area from the main Communist body in the state. It was part of a plan to clear a line right across the centre of the country, through the neighbouring

---

[1] *From L. Pye,* Guerilla Communism in Malaya, *Princeton University Press, New Jersey, 1956.*

states of Negri Sembilan and Selangor. The other operations in Pahang had also begun in 1953, and were proceeding well.

By April 1955 the CT numbers around Kuantan were reduced to the point where they could be controlled by the normal District Police Force and the Home Guard. East Pahang was declared 'White' (free of Emergency restrictions) two years earlier than originally expected. In Kuantan all spot checks and night curfews ceased. Food was no longer rationed and permits were no longer required to take medicine out of the town. Rubber tappers were allowed to take their midday meal out with them instead of having to go hungry, and the Europeans could stock up their pantries and take a picnic to the beach. The government knew that when an area was declared white the villagers were so relieved that they would work towards keeping the area clear of Communists. By the end of that year the whole of Pahang, except for two small areas in the south, were declared 'White'.

A lot of people had worked at clearing the Kuantan area of CTs but, according to the District Officer, Patrick Bolshaw, Bill Humble was the star turn. 'In my years in the district, if one man could be singled out for what he achieved it would have to be Bill Humble. The defeat of the terrorists in Pahang was the main aim of Bill's existence at that time, and he did it in his own way. He was unconventional in some respects, but clear headed and cool. He was also a good chap to have on hand in a nasty corner . . . a very good chap.'

Jay Windsor had never been an easy man to work for. He'd been running his business his own way for many years and VB found his own independent streak constantly thwarted. VB enjoyed the work but the situation was stifling, and there was little outlet for his own ideas and aspirations. He had found, to his disappointment, that Jay Windsor did not have the same vision as he, to begin a shipping service in the South China Sea, specialising in moving difficult cargo to difficult places. VB still had that dream. His current position was not particularly rewarding financially and his share of the profits never seemed to amount to much. Since the 'partnership' arrangement had never extended to VB being given access to the books, there was little means of determining what his prospects might be. The arrangement, he suddenly decided, was less than satisfactory.

Barbara was having a cup of tea with Anita Bolshaw when, in general conversation, Anita remarked, 'When Bruce leaves you can come and stay with us until you both find somewhere.' Barbara replied that it was very kind of her, but was wondering what on earth she was talking about. Was VB going somewhere? It was the first she'd heard of it. When she got home she asked him about it.

'Oh yes,' he said. 'I must tell you about that. I've given Pa Windsor the push and I'm going to KL to look for another job. I'm leaving at the end of the month.'

They had to be out of the house in a fortnight.

THIRTEEN

Kippers and Toast

V B eyed the mosquito net draped limply around him and wondered whether it had ever been washed. He turned over and
flung his leg across a Dutch wife, a long, tubular cushion traditionally
used in the colony to keep the limbs from sticking to each other
in the heat. The Government Resthouse in Kuala Lumpur was, as
always, a convenient stopover point. This was a far more down-
market establishment than the one in Kuantan, and was not going
to be a long term option. On the bedside table yesterday's cigarette
stubs still floated in the ashtray, which had been half filled with
water by the room boy, the usual practice to prevent ash blowing
about. He turned on the fan and the mosquito net began to wiffle
around him. He felt certain that it wouldn't be long before something came up.

It was good to be in KL, for the place abounded with prewar
friends and acquaintances. The familiar capital city of Malaya was
a conglomerate of old and new, British and Malay, Chinese and
Indian. Standing out amongst the hotchpotch of buildings was the
highly ornate railway station and a great mosque with three lemon-
yellow domes. The government buildings with their air of British
dignity stood haphazardly alongside more hastily erected structures
with little attraction, and colourful, often luridly painted Chinese
shops. The first place VB headed was the sprawling Selangor Club,

a bastion of European conservatism which took up almost one side of the city *padang*. Its mock Tudor facade stood across the green expanse of turf from the grandeur of the Secretariat building, with its pink brick minarets and arches. 'The Spotted Dog' or 'the Dog', as the Selangor Club was known, was a good place to start tracking down old friends and sniffing out the prospects of a job. He remembered the prewar days, and the rumour then that the name originated when a well-known society lady took up the habit of tying her Dalmatian dogs outside the club while visiting, as a warning to her husband not to barge in with his mistress. Idly he wondered whether it was still the accepted explanation.

It was not a good time for a European to be looking for employment in Malaya, for the country was in the throes of a major upheaval. Inside the club VB caught up with Dick Lee, an engineer with Harrisons and Crossfield. Dick was less than optimistic about VB's chances. 'I'll put in a good word for you at H&C,' he said, 'but the fact is the directors are a trifle wary of the prospects for the company over the next few years. With Independence looming they're being pretty cautious about taking on new staff. I'm afraid the old days are leaving us.'

H&C was not the only company contemplating the future. Pip Gardiner, VB's old sailing friend from the Naval Base days in Singapore, was in town from Port Swettenham, where he still worked for the Port Authority. 'There's a chance you might find some work repairing the floating dock at the port,' Pip said encouragingly. 'I have to admit, though, the long-term outlook is not good for shipbuilding jobs.'

'What about the Colonial Office?' asked VB.

'Give it a try,' said Pip, 'but the Colonial Office is already cutting back on the employment of Europeans. Times are changing. The process of Malayanising this country has well and truly begun.'

The people of Malaya had been promised self-government as soon as the country was prepared for it, that is as soon as the Communist threat was over. However, military planners realised the war was not going to end quickly, for despite the massive food denial operations there were still many areas where the CTs were well dug in and being kept adequately supplied. There still existed all over the country pockets of local people who were not whole-heartedly behind the government in their efforts to defeat the Communists. To encourage a more positive attitude, five community and political leaders were invited to sit on the Federal War Executive Committee, while other leading Chinese, Malays, and Indians were given seats on the State War Committees. The move changed the face of the war. No longer was it a war between the British and the Communists; now it was between the Malayan people and the Communists.

The first national elections were due to be held in July 1955. In KL VB found the subject a topic of great discussion among his friends, particularly those who stood to be displaced or dispossessed by Malayanisation. But there was also a general concern about the balance of power between the three main races in the country; that after Independence tension could develop between the Malays and the Chinese for the top jobs, with the Indians and the Anglo-Indians in particular coming a very poor last. Strict guidelines were issued to the European community not to get involved, and to abstain from discussing the political or electoral situation with the locals at all.

In the lead-up to the election in Kuantan there had been great debate among the local male population, and one day a Malay headman with the Windsor organisation had come to see VB at the house. He had arrived with such an air of gravity that VB thought he must have fallen foul of some terrible deed. In fact he had come only to ask VB's advice about the elections. He was afraid that the Chinese, with their business acumen and political know-how, would take over completely; and yet he did not trust or like the Malay candidate who'd been proposed to stand for his area and for whom he had been instructed to vote by the local *Imam* (priest officiating at the Mosque). VB heard him out but had to tell him that Europeans were not allowed to interfere. All VB could offer were words of comfort, that this democracy was a good thing and, though it might take a little time, all would be well in the end.

Discussion of the coming election was not limited to the men-folk. The *amahs*, Meenah and Woh, had tried to sound him out in a roundabout fashion as they sat in the shade on the back steps drinking their morning coffee. They said the men had been talking a lot about *Merdeka*—freedom—and that they didn't really under-stand what 'freedom' was about. 'We are already free, except those with husbands!' chimed Meenah, who didn't have one.

VB tried to explain voting and elections and that soon most of the British would be leaving and that they would have an admin-istration of their own.

'*Ada Sultan, Tuan, dan Imam*' ('We have the Sultan and the Imam'), said Woh, who was a good mosque-goer. 'And *Mem* DO tells us good ways to make cakes and about what the children should eat. Who else do we want to tell us what to do?'

Then Meenah broke in. 'Where will I work if you leave? My friend works for the wife of Ah Chee and doesn't have any day off like me and has to work very long hours. No coffee either.'

'Perhaps you could get a job with——' VB said, and mentioned a wealthy Malay lady in town.

There were shrieks of laughter. 'Oh no! I'd rather go back and work in the *padi* fields,' said Meenah, and sadly, that is what she later had to do.

District Officer Patrick Bolshaw presided over the election period in Kuantan. Of this period, he said:

> *The Malays were cheerful enough about it, although many did not really understand what was going on. They were given the war cry of* Merdeka. *I think it was some African politician who said, 'If I have one man who says he wants freedom, then I have a national movement towards independence.' The election came and a local Malay was elected. When the result was acknowledged he turned towards me and said, 'Do you mind if we say* Merdeka?' *I said, 'You can say anything you like. It's a free country.' They were great days and on our side of course nobody took it too seriously. We all knew it had to come. One senior state official, whenever a Malay shouted*

Merdeka, *would jokingly shout back* Mendurhaka!, *a similar sounding word which means 'to turn traitor'.*

After the elections Malaya had internal self-government for the first time and Independence was only a step away. It was a bitter blow for the CTs. In the rural areas the events had great significance to the villagers who had listened to so much propaganda from both sides. Action was far more convincing than words.

As Malaya moved steadily towards Independence, Europeans all over the country were pondering their future. VB, however, was not fazed. With typical optimism he applied to sit a series of Public Service examinations in case something turned up. The exams were held in Singapore every six months and the next lot were scheduled for October. He had several months up his sleeve to do a bit of study and scout about for something else.

In the meantime he'd bought himself a pale fawn Austin 90 sportscar; it was fast and had curves in all the right places. He found accommodation in a shared house with a very decent chap named Johnny, who needed a bit of cheering up since his wife had left him and returned to England. Barbara joined him and they settled into KL in a typical old-style Malayan bungalow. In the centre were a formal dining room and sitting room, around which the walls went only to waist height. Windows were unglazed so that even the smallest breeze blew right through the house, and *chiks* (wooden blinds) were let down when it rained. Johnny lived at one end of the house and the Perkins at the other, they shared the expenses of a cook, an *amah* and a gardener, and it was all very pleasant.

Barbara was quickly offered employment with Special Branch, KL, and accepted happily. VB wasn't sure he was impressed with this new arrangement. It was bad enough having his wife working while he wasn't. Now she wanted to take the car. This all had whiskers on it. He'd have to find something soon. And he hoped she didn't bend the Austin. It was just as well he wasn't there on her first morning.

The hill leading up to Special Branch Headquarters was short and sharp. On that first day she gamely joined the queue, moving slowly, one car length at a time. Having only just learned to drive in the Windsors' jeep in Kuantan, where it was flat, she fancied she was doing quite well. That was until, to her horror, she noticed in the rear-vision mirror a large black car driven by a Malay *syce*. The car had a flag on its bonnet and the passenger in the back wore a lot of gold braid. Completely unnerved, she muffed the next take-off and bumped back into the car behind, jiggling its flag in the process. A short session of horn blowing followed before the *syce* got out and came to her window. 'Lieutenant General Bourne sends you his compliments and says would you care to have me drive you up the hill because he thinks it might be safer for his vehicle.' Having had a brush on her first day with the new Director of Operations, Malaya, Barbara resolved to avoid the eight o'clock crush in the future.

The Thai Border Section of Special Branch, for whom Barbara now worked, was concerned with CTs coming and going over the Thailand–Malaya border in the far north of the country. Chin Peng had moved his headquarters from Pahang to southern Thailand, and the Thai border proved an excellent sanctuary for himself, his Central Committee and four hundred of his hard-core guerillas. There was little the police could do to stop the movement of men and supplies across the border, largely rugged, mountainous jungle except for three frontier posts on cultivated areas. There were simply not enough resources to patrol such a vast area. The police knew that, as with the *sakai*, the key to getting the people of such a remote area on side was to help them. Economic development became the key to defeating the CTs.

In an office in a long row of hot, tin-roofed buildings around which all the trees had been cleared for security, Barbara began work with the taciturn but pleasant Superintendent Bunnings and a Chinese inspector. She found the most fascinating part of the job to be piecing together reports from informers, trying to fit the CTs concerned into a picture of the Communist framework on the other side of the border: who were the active party members, who were their supporters, what the level of support was like and so forth. The missives came in on all manner of bits of paper and some were immensely useful and enlightening. Others were so lightweight it was difficult to decipher just who was who, particularly when one or two or even three separate reports came in at the same time advising that a fellow named Chang/Cheng/Chen had been seen talking to Ah Lim/Ah Ling in a small *kedai* (coffee shop) in a village with an unpronounceable Siamese name.

Sitting in the heat of the office all day could be trying, but occasionally a fun job came her way. One was being sent out as 'quarry' for a small group of Cambodian policemen in KL for a training course, part of which was learning how to shadow people. For once she could discuss her day with VB and over dinner she told him of her afternoon dodging around the city. 'The thing was,' she laughed, 'that the Cambodians, with their round faces and bright blue shirts, stood out in the crowd and were not at all difficult to spot. I wasn't allowed to lose them altogether of course, and tested their ingenuity and cooled us all down by leading them into the department store. They did quite well in toys, immersing them-selves in trying out cuddly teddy-bears and small tricycles, but the ladies' underwear department completely threw them. It wasn't really fair.'

To VB this was all very well. But the thing was, he didn't have a blasted job.

VB sat at the breakfast table, listening to Johnny and Barbara discuss the working day ahead. He now thoroughly disliked breakfast time. He took another mouthful and wondered if they'd do it to him again. How he hated it when they did that. Perhaps if he finished his meal first and left the table early. . . The cook had a habit of coming in when breakfast was almost over to ask what to cook for the rest of the day. None of them liked making that decision. He began to eat a little faster. He was almost finished when, suddenly, Cookie appeared as if from nowhere, standing behind his chair.

'Must run, got a meeting at eight,' said Johnny, as if on cue.

'Me too,' Barbara chimed. 'Big day today.'

Before he knew it they had leapt from their chairs and beaten a hasty retreat, leaving VB to decide whether it was to be kippers and toast again for breakfast tomorrow, or something else. Close on Cookie's heels the *kebun* would show up, then the *amah* would want instructions, and VB, being the man on the spot, was left to arrange the domestics. The goddamn domestics, of all things. He wasn't interested in domestics. That was women's work. Where the hell was Barbara when he needed her?

The only saving grace in his current situation were his friends. These few months in KL had been socially very busy. Johnny had a couple of polo ponies and VB had found catching a late-afternoon match to be an agreeable and sociable lark. He'd made a point of catching up on people he'd known before the war, such as Hugo Hughes, formerly of the Malay Regiment. Having lost his leg in the battle for Singapore and survived the massacre at the Alexandra Military Hospital, Hugo had spent the rest of the war years in Changi Garrison POW Camp. He was now working for Guthries, the rubber company. He was managing well on his artificial leg, and once again VB admired Hugo's capacity to stay cheerful.

Then, of course, there was Perky. Ronald Bertie 'Perky' Perkins had, after his release in 1945, returned to rubber planting with Dunlops at the Kota Tinggi Estate. Now he'd bought his own estate at Port Dickson, and built a magnificent bungalow on a promontory overlooking the Malacca Straits. He called it 'Bukit Tersenyum' (Smiling Hill). When VB introduced Barbara to his old friend for the first time, Perky was lazing on his back in the crystal clear sea of his own white sand beach, squirting a fountain of water from a sea slug up from his nether regions, giving the clear impression that he was relieving himself. Barbara hadn't quite known what to think, but had eventually concluded he was trying her out. He was, and soon proved truly delightful company with his mischievous sense of humour.

VB was finding people very relaxed about the Emergency in KL, now that it was winding down in the area. However, one evening as he stopped by at the Dog he found it full of talk about the outcome of a paper chase organised on the outskirts of the city. Apparently the hares got off to a flying start and were doing very well indeed, until in the jungle flanking the city they ran into a

camp with six or eight CTs in residence. The CTs were so flab-
bergasted at the sight of two athletic types in bright red shorts and
faces to match, scattering bits of paper as they went, that they all
turned tail and fled. The hares kept running in the other direction
towards the nearest police station and in the follow-up five CTs
were killed.

FOURTEEN

Twilight of Empire

*D*riving around KL there is always something new to be seen, and in between the new things are the old sights one sees every day: the beautiful girl in traditional Chinese working dress, with plaits down almost to her knees; the old Indian men in our street who by day are very sedate and proper, sitting in their cool, tiled money-lending shops, cross-legged in front of their legless desks, but who in the sweet air of early morning wander across the road and call and chat to each other with their dhotis tucked up around their thighs and their faces white with ash and a gleaming red spot, as a sign that they have performed their routine morning prayers; the pathetic little beggar boy, black shining shoulders hunched into terrible deformity, calling to his friends as they pass by and exchanging his latest little witticism as they stop beside him, leaning on the parapet of the bridge; the washing, hanging limp on long poles from the first floor windows; the women labourers on their bicycles, with black dusty samfus and brightly coloured headscarfs that so completely blinker their faces until you meet them head on and you notice their young fresh complexions, the bright smiles and shining eyes; the chillies and dried fish spread out on the paving stone around the traffic sign in the centre of the road, drying in the sun, *absorbing the flavour of the streets; the Indian chapati seller, moving his 'shop' to a new site, his table and its wares balanced on his head as he threads his way through the crowded pavement; the trishaw boy pedalling furiously through the traffic with a fat old Chinese on board, bald head gleaming like polished brass; the Pasha women, tall and plump in their graceful, long, fine trousers, caught at the ankle, their heads covered with filmy scarves. A Chinese funeral; the road almost completely blocked by the hired mourners, twenty women in white (the Chinese colour for mourning) with white sacks pulled over their heads, squatting in the middle of the road, rocking backwards and forwards on their heels wailing hideously, surrounded by an admiring band of onlookers. The coffin, sitting on its gaily decorated coffin stand, with pink and yellow painted flowers and streamers massed on the canopy and trailing onto the roadway; piles of paper money, a paper car, a paper house, a paper refrigerator and other luxury items to be consumed by flame as they accompany the deceased on his journey into the hereafter; great jarring clashes of cymbals. A feast is laid out on two push-carts; and stilt walkers, two women and a man, garbed in exotic tradition, walk at least six feet above the crowds ... but it is just another day in K.L.*

This was Malaya, the way of life and its people as seen through Barbara's light-hearted notes on KL. But as destiny would have it, they were not to be in the capital for many months. In September 1955 VB, now thoroughly disgusted with the domestics of life, jumped at a job as operations manager at a bauxite mine at Ramunia in Johore, on the south-eastern tip of Malaya. His employer was a small outfit which contracted to the mining licence holders Alcan, and the work included organising the shipping of the ore and its lightering to bulk carriers waiting at anchor in deep water in the Strait of Johore.

VB brimmed with optimism about the job, though Barbara did not, for there was a very real snag. The mine area wasn't considered safe for women and Barbara was not, for the time being, allowed to live with VB on site. The southern-most state of Johore was one of the few remaining black spots in Malaya. The CTs in the region, cut off from their counterparts in the north of the country, were still active and dangerous, largely because of the ease of smuggling men and supplies directly from Singapore across the Strait into the jungles.

The core of Communist control in Johore was the central town of Kluang, a sullen township of thirty-five thousand people gripped like a vice by the Communist machine. A general amnesty to all Communists had just been announced. The terms of the amnesty were that in return for surrendering and abandoning Communism, the CTs would, after a period of detention, be either freed or repatriated to China. Over most of Malaya the CTs waited for instructions from the Central Committee but in Johore the Regional Commander, Hor Lung, demonstrated his contempt for the amnesty by sending his forces out on a paroxysm of terrorism and murder.

On the shore of the Strait of Johore, the Ramunia mine complex was a prime target. Thirty police were stationed at barracks on site and a small platoon of field force patrolled twenty-four hours a day. The area was floodlit at night and surrounded by a high security fence with a barbed-wire entanglement. The jungle, cleared to a hundred yards from the fence, lay untouched beyond, and on the seaward side security could not be total.

VB did not allow the situation with the terrorists to deter him. Anything to be working again. He moved into the mine manager's house at Ramunia, which he shared with two other Europeans, one of whom was his superior, a man of Germanic extraction who was large, a bit explosive of temper, but pleasant enough. It was an isolated existence but with the heavy police and army presence there was no end of people coming through the place and VB did not want for company. The pit area, raw and red, was at the back of the complex and on the shore huge, red stockpiles of bauxite lay waiting to be loaded onto lighters tied up at a long, concrete and wood jetty. Along the coast silver green *lalang* stretched down to the beach while sand swept up to rocky headlands to the east.

A few hundreds yards from the water's edge, small, craggy islands jutted out of the pale jade sea.

Six miles down the open beach to the west was the nearest village, Sungei Ringgit. Past there the Ringgit–Penggerang road wound through dense jungle in what was considered point blank ambush country. Security regulations required that no-one from the mine should venture further west than Ringgit unless they were in a minimum convoy of three vehicles. The safest access to Ramunia was over the Johore Strait from Singapore, and the company kept its own launch.

Barbara was less than pleased with the new arrangement. She had recently been asked to work at the Special Branch Holding Centre, one of the most secret and top-security places in KL, a place where Communists of the highest level were interrogated, a place of covert devices and clandestine, fascinating activity. She'd jumped at the opportunity and when VB announced the impending move, the date of her induction had already been set. Her first thought was to stay on in KL until the CT situation in Johore improved, but VB wouldn't have it. She was his wife, and if she couldn't be with him for the moment then she should be as close as possible to him. He insisted she come south to live in Singapore. Suddenly their roles had been reversed again. Now she was to be unemployed and bored.

VB saw Barbara settled in Singapore at the Queen's Hotel at Mt Elizabeth, and introduced her to some friends on the island with instructions to them to look after her. They did so admirably, but Barbara didn't like being separated and communication was difficult. VB couldn't get away from the mine often and the Singapore office proved unreliable at passing on messages. Occasionally she arrived back at the hotel after a day wandering the town, devastated to find a note on her pillow: 'Hi Charlie, missed you—see you next time. Love, P.' She applied to Special Branch Singapore for a job, but the government was having discussions about Malayanisation policy and she was told that she'd have to wait until the outcome of those talks was known. In the meantime no more Europeans were to be employed. For a while she took on a relief office job with an import–export business, but after the excitement of Special Branch it was very dreary.

Ten years had passed since the Japanese had gone from Singapore. The physical scars they left behind had mostly been removed but the memories and grief were still close to the surface in the hearts of the residents. People still talked of the war and on one occasion, at a cocktail party without VB, Barbara met a British Army general, whose name she didn't catch. Upon Barbara's being introduced as 'Mrs Barbara Perkins', the general inquired of her, 'And to whom are you married, VB or RB?'

Aware that the RB to whom the general referred was Ronald Bertie, she replied, 'To VB.'

His reaction came as a surprise to her. 'Well good for you and let me shake you by the hand. Bruce Perkins is a very brave man. He really did an excellent job after the war, excellent. And no doubt you know that he was terribly shabbily treated. He really should have been given a gong for what he did.'

Barbara made some appropriate noises, but had absolutely no idea what he was talking about. VB had always been reluctant to talk about his war experiences, and the little she did know about what had happened she had gleaned by prompting others, such as Hugo Hughes in KL. Later she asked VB about it, but he brushed off her questions. It was a chapter of his life which he had no wish to relive. He'd closed the door firmly on the memories and preferred not to discuss the war with anyone who hadn't been there with him. That time in his life was dead and gone. It was many years before she heard more.

Two months passed and VB kept a close eye on the progress of the Emergency, which now had a very direct effect on their happiness. He knew they couldn't go on living apart indefinitely and began to think that unless something broke soon, he might have to reconsider his position.

The amnesty was a failure; the Communists would not completely surrender their cause. It was to be a fight to the last man. Some politicians had begun to moot that the British were trying to delay the end of the war to avoid being bound by their promise to give Malaya Independence when the Communists had been beaten. As a direct result the British government made a momentous declaration, announcing it no longer considered that Malaya need wait until the end of the Emergency for Independence.

Then a blitz began in Johore.

As the new year got under way the assault slowly began to take effect. The soldiers stationed at Ramunia Mine thrashed the jungle day and night. While the MRLA platoons were hunted down, the MCP branches and the Min Yuen proved far more difficult to eliminate. Near Ramunia a whole battalion scoured the jungle and rubber plantations in search of a band of five CTs who were led by an old woman. They kept at it for six months solid but the old woman, disguised as a rubber tapper, eluded them time and time again. She had four hundred active supporters in the area and was able to bring enough pressure to bear so that the others kept their mouths shut. The experienced old Communist had a piece of string attached to her rifle and pulled it along behind her so that it could not be seen. When warned by the tappers of the approach of soldiers she would simply drop the string, whip out her tapping knife from her pocket and head for the nearest rubber tree. She was not eliminated until 1959.

Despite such pockets of resistance the hard-core Communists in Johore were gradually being cleared, and by early 1956 the security forces at Ramunia were optimistic that VB could soon bring his wife to live with him. VB had visions of one day relaxing on the verandah of a promised new house on a small promontory away from the mine complex, looking out over the water to the craggy little islands. But for now the reality was that sometimes three weeks went by before he could get away for a weekend. It was apparently going to be at least another few months before he could be with Barbara, and he decided it was a good time for her to go home to Australia to visit her parents, 'to get it over with'.

In his time-honoured style he produced a sea ticket one morning for a ship sailing the next day. 'While you are in Melbourne,' he said, 'have a look around for a dining room suite for our new house.' It was a rush for Barbara to pack and leave and, as when she'd left England, there was no time to say goodbye to friends. 'I'll tell everyone you've gone and you'll be back in Singapore within eight weeks', he said.

The goodbyes were never to be said. A fortnight before leaving Melbourne to return to Singapore a telegram arrived for her:

CANCEL DINING ROOM SUITE STOP ARRIVING AUSTRALIA

She presumed it was from VB.

VB trotted up the steps of the manager's house, opened the front door and walked into the muzzle of a rifle. At the other end of it was his superior. 'I've packed your things,' he said. 'You can get right back on the launch.'

VB had first noticed something odd about the cash transactions for the sale of timber cleared for new work a couple of months earlier. He wasn't comfortable with the thought that someone was apparently fiddling the company, and that day he had visited head office in Singapore and mentioned it to one of the directors. He was surprised that it drew only mild interest. And now this.

He was in no position to argue. In the morning he went straight back to head office to break the news that their senior fellow had gone off the rails. But head office did not seem to be perturbed. Something was mentioned about his staying on and perhaps coming to an arrangement whereby he might benefit. But he said, 'Forget it.' He was not going to be a party to that sort of thing. So that was that.

He was out of a job again.

When VB left Malaya the country was on the verge of Independence. *Merdeka* day had been set for 31 August 1957. By mid 1956 the final steps were being taken to ensure the transfer of government with the minimum of disturbance. In the two years before Independence an urgent education program had been put in place to upgrade training for Malayans, particularly in administrative matters. Gradually British government personnel were withdrawn until the new Malayan government was handed responsibility for the final portfolios: finance, internal defence and security.

Many of the people VB knew stayed on in Malaya for years. With Independence the Chief Minister, Tungku Abdul Rahman, requested that every Malayan minister have at least one senior British civil servant on his staff. Most of the senior army and police officers, lawyers, bankers, engineers, scientists and economists were British; and British capital still flowed into the country. While some civil servants were told they had three years in which to train a Malayan for their position, others, such as Harry Wharton of the Institute for Medical Research, were given as long as eight years.

Patrick Bolshaw stayed on until 1960. Of the coming of Independence, he said:

> I suppose the greatest change was getting used to working with elected ministers as opposed to Heads of Departments. You did hear more about politics and getting rid of the British and so forth, but they were small voices. The average politician, at least in KL, knew they could get rid of us whenever they wanted to. Some of us they kept on while others were encouraged to leave. I felt there was no great pressure to go at first, but later there were a lot of up and coming Malays who felt it was time they got into the jobs. The Malays were always very good to me, and very courteous.

By Independence Ken Belton was No. 2 to the Senior Assistant Police Commissioner in Headquarters in KL. Of the handover, he commented:

> It didn't happen immediately . . . rather when one came back from leave next time, one found oneself appointed to a Malay or Chinese or Indian officer. It was all very amicable and I didn't have any trouble at all. I felt I was being loyal by staying for a while, showing them the ropes and so forth. I thought it was a marvellous handover. The British didn't stay on in Africa the same way because the Africans were different types; they were all for booting the white man out as soon as possible and taking

over his house and motor car and so forth. But in Malaya it was a different thing altogether.

As surely as the new nation was being born, the threat of Communism in Malaya was dying. When Independence was granted Chin Peng could no longer claim to be fighting the 'Imperialists'. Now the guerillas were outlaws in a country ruled by its own people, with the support of its own people. It was only a matter of time before the last few top-ranking Communists were mopped up and the remaining rank and file surrendered. The security forces pressed on to this end with undiminished vigour, but the end of the Emergency was still three years away. Johore was one of the last areas to be declared white.

In July 1960, twelve years after it started, the Emergency was officially declared at an end. In the years to come, all the combined military might of America and its allies could not defeat the Communist guerillas in Vietnam or Korea. But in Malaya, in a war run largely by British administrators and police, the Communists were finally defeated.

Some of VB's friends remained with their companies in Malaya until they retired, then returned to the UK. Others never went home. The Windsors and Perky Perkins were among those who considered themselves more Malayan than British. Malaya, later Malaysia, was their home, and there they remained, through retirement and old age, until the day they died.

FIFTEEN
Little Bit Long Way

I t had never even remotely occurred to VB that Australia, the so-called land of sun and wide open spaces, could have a climate cold enough for a bowler hat. In his suitcase a stack of pressed Aertex cotton shirts reposed, but it seemed that instead a greatcoat and muffler were required. Regrettably he hadn't brought a greatcoat and muffler.

The sprawling city of Melbourne was not quite what VB had imagined of Australia. The weather in early spring 1956 was so atrocious that he complained for years of the winds straight off the Antarctic and miserable, incessant, drizzling rain. Despite this the welcome he received from Arthur and Nancy Smith was warm. They were charmed to at last meet their only child's husband, and it seemed he was everything she had promised he would be in her letters. They'd been intrigued to read of their adventures in Malaya, and VB fitted the picture they'd built up in their minds perfectly. But later, as they prepared to leave, Barbara's mother said to her privately, 'Do keep up the correspondence, dear. Much as I can see exactly why you have fallen in love with Bruce, I can't help feeling that if something happened to you he might forget to tell me.'

'Mother, don't be ridiculous,' she replied, but all the same had to wonder herself. He certainly didn't keep much in contact with his own parents in Cornwall. In fact so few and brief were his letters that Barbara felt guilty for him and though she'd never met them she corresponded with Alfred and Edith Amelia herself and sent them copies of her diaries. They were, by now, getting well on in years and the arrival of each weighty episode of the adventures of their son and daughter-in-law was a highlight in their quiet village lives. When the diary instalments began to arrive from Australia instead of Malaya, it seemed they were equally fascinating.

Within weeks of arriving in Melbourne, Alcan, the Canadian company which bought Ramunia's bauxite, tracked down VB with an offer of a two-year contract position in their exploration division, Alulabs. The work, prospecting for bauxite, was based in the remote far north of Australia. A quick check of the latitude of his first destination, Cape York Peninsula, was enough to convince VB. He'd come to terms with the fact that, with Malayan Independence looming, prospects there were few. He wasn't interested in returning to England and the southern climes of Australia were, he was convinced, uninhabitable. The north of the country was closer to Asia, warmer, and from what he could gather held far more appeal for him personally. It was a far cry from dockyards and slipways, but a job in exploration offered a paid opportunity to see what the north had to offer.

The exploration trips, one to the remote and sparsely populated Cape York Peninsula in 1956 and another to Arnhem Land in 1957, were highlights in VB's and Barbara's lives. Though for the most part it was rough country, there was something about being in the bush so far removed from the cares of the world, with nothing to concern themselves about except the clouds and what had to be done that day. It was hard work, but the physical tiredness was somehow very satisfying. They were exploring for bauxite at a time when there were no accurate maps and no aerial photographs of the areas of interest. Helicopters were not yet in general use in exploration, and just getting to where they needed to be could take weeks. These were initial reconnaissance expeditions; and since bauxite is usually formed at the surface, the work consisted largely of looking over the country for signs of it.

The work for Alcan was to sow the seeds of a deep affection for the rugged, isolated and often inhospitable region which VB eventually made his life. So different to Malaya and Singapore, it was the remoteness of the north of Australia that attracted him. There was so much to be done. It was pioneering stuff and he was excited by it. He didn't consider that the climate would fetter the development of northern Australia. He thrived in the heat and the wet, and did not fully appreciate the fact that most people didn't.

The Northern Territory of Australia. How VB had liked the sound of it. Just the name of the place had that sort of frontier feel about it. This was going to be quite an adventure; six months exploring the eastern region of probably the most remote part of Australia, Arnhem Land, and an excursion through the lonely Barkly Tableland to the south. He couldn't help but smile at the thought of how naive he had been about the north of Australia before the trip to Cape York last year. Even the sheer vastness of the distances involved had astounded him. The isolation of the people and the conditions under which they lived and worked had left a real impression on him.

They were laughing one night about outback hotels in the north. VB had his initiation the previous year on their first night out of a real town. They'd travelled one hundred and fifty miles that day, on a sandy, melon-hole pitted track north of Cairns, on the east coast of Queensland. When they reached a place called Laura the two dusty Landrovers rolled up to the door of a long, low tin shack that was the local hotel. All had been still except for the glow of a cigarette in one corner of the wide verandah, where he'd found three cattlemen squatting over the dregs of several bottles of beer. Before the conversation had got far one of them disappeared around the corner to be noisily sick. VB, mildly concerned, was mollified by another who, in a broad Queensland drawl, said, 'Doan worry aboud 'im. Snow's got spewin' down to a fine art. The landlord'll be in the end room. Y'd bedder goan knock 'im up.'

In Malaya VB had often stayed in the equivalent accommodation known there as 'halting bungalows', in very small, remote places. But they'd never been quite as rustic as this. The entire length of the Laura Hotel was divided into 'rooms' by means of corrugated iron partitions up to the seven-foot level. Each room was barely screened from the inside passage by a thin, faded curtain. Ablution facilities were an old pitcher and basin on a rickety table, and a chamber pot stowed modestly under the bed. The mattress was of straw and sagged like a hammock, and one slept to a loud night-time chorus of snores, coughs and farts from the other guests. Breakfast in the morning was steak, eggs and strong tea at a table covered in very serviceable brown leatherette.

Since then he'd discovered this was fairly standard in outback north Australia, including the Northern Territory, where down-to-earth accommodation met the needs of down-to-earth customers. Those customers were largely cattlemen, and from what he'd seen their needs were pretty basic. VB was no pastoralist but the land on which they eked a living did not look like prime cattle-grazing country to him, and the image of the first cattle-station homestead he'd seen at Cape York was still vivid in his mind. It was not what he'd imagined of the residence of the landlord of a property of some few thousand square miles. York Downs Station, on the track from the telegraph line to Weipa, was established in 1884 and in 1956 its owners still lived in a 1905 vintage pitsawn timber homestead. They'd been out mustering for a few weeks, according to an Aboriginal lady who wandered in from a nearby camp, and it seemed perhaps they lived better in the bush. The homestead was almost derelict, with rotting floorboards, a holed tin roof, rickety chairs—one three-legged and tied to the verandah railing with wire—steps tilting at a crazy angle and water tanks fallen off their platforms and rusting on the ground. Cooking facilities consisted of an open fire, and the only water was the rainwater caught in three rusted 44-gallon drums standing open under the remnants of the roof guttering. The lavatory was the best he'd seen yet; it stood facing the house twenty yards away, its door had fallen off and the timbers of the walls had rotted. The seat had been quite unsittable.

The signs that the cattlemen of the north lived a tough, hard life were around for anyone to see. He'd passed them on the track from Cairns, driving mobs of up to a thousand cattle to market over possibly the roughest stock route in the country. At best the cattle lost condition on the way, and had to be rested and fattened somewhere around Mareeba before they were fit to sell. There was never any guarantee that at the end of it all the price would cover the costs of mustering, droving, sale fees and commissions. It was the last of the droving days, days which had, over the years, broken many a man and beast.

The characters one came across in these places were extraordinary. People who lived in almost complete isolation, people who, on meeting a new face, could hardly contain their intrigue. And as far as VB and Barbara were concerned, the feeling was mutual. In the great expanse of the northern Cape York Peninsula the only white people inland of the missions, other than a bare handful of cattlemen, had been the two linesmen at Moreton Telegraph Station, Harry Barden and George Hall. One day they had stopped in at a moment when Harry and George found themselves with more people than they'd ever seen at once at Moreton. As well as the three in the Alcan team, there'd been Jack Brown, the relief telegraph station operator, Slim, the mailman, who'd stopped in for the night with his Aboriginal off-sider, and Rod Heinemann from Bramwell Station, who rode in late on his horse. The presence of a lady had thrown everyone; but later, when they'd relaxed, Barbara spent an evening to remember sitting on the only comfy chair on the verandah, surrounded by bush characters and listening to the sort of tales she'd read about in Ion Idriess's books. In her diary she could only lament her literary skills.

> How I wish I could write—I mean really write. Maugham or Steinbeck would have loved these people. There are more characters per head of population in this part of the world than I could ever have imagined. Every one of them ooze that definable yet indefinable something to which only a literary master can do justice. There's Harry, small, brown, sixty-one and fond of the rum bottle in a gentle manner, mild hazel eyes peering short-sightedly through a pair of antique spectacles, a pipe, never

alight, either clenched in his teeth or protruding from the pocket of his dusty shorts; Jack Brown, an old mate of Harry's of the same vintage, as lean and brown but with short, white, cropped hair and stubble, his pale blue eyes deep hooded like a bird; and Roddy Heinemann—oh, songs without words—he's just like his homestead; and George, oh, all of them. If only I had a ready pen for characterisation I could surely profit handsomely from spending time in these parts, for the place abounds with living stories.

There was no doubt they had been lucky with these expeditions. Last year in Cape York there had just been the three of them: young English geologist Bryan Summers, VB, and Barbara, an unofficial and unpaid member of the team. They had been delighted with Bryan, and the friendship they forged in the bush was to last a lifetime. He was well educated in that round sort of English way and had a penchant for literature and classical music. He'd packed a small library of books for the trip and carried another in his head. His company was glorious, except before breakfast when he was prone to quick temper and surly countenance. Once fed however, good conversation was guaranteed.

This time there were four of them. Geologist John Staargaard hailed from Holland and had just joined Alcan after working in Brazil. They first met in Sydney and were delighted with each other. John and his wife, Pop, were both good humoured, he erudite, interesting and serious minded, she tiny, vivacious and full of energy and enthusiasm. Barbara noted in her diary her feeling that the trip was going to be a lot of fun, and she was right. Years later John Staargaard judged it as the best he'd had in a long career in exploration. 'The four of us spent about half a year together in the bush without any quarrels; just a lot of good discussion and a lot of laughter. We had the time of our lives on that trip,' he said.

Moonlight bathed the dried grass along the Roper River, and it glistened in soft silver. Under two gnarled ghost gums on the banks of a shallow waterhole, four mosquito nets rippled gently in the cooling breeze and a billion stars winked from above. Two bats flew into the branches overhead and chattered to each other. A sleepy bird chirped once, indignant at being woken. Small brown frogs flip flipped along in the slight damp and a curlew called eerily in the distance.

Breakfast took a long time that morning. VB had never cooked, but last year in Cape York he'd learned to knock up a good batch of bacon and eggs. There was something about a fried breakfast in the bush. The bacon smelled good in the dawn air, as the shadows, long and cool, advanced over the water. A flock of finches flitted round the water's edge, drinking and darting here and there. A crowd of noisy cockatoos broke the tranquillity and two stately jabirus, standing some 5 feet tall in their clerical black and white suits, stood by disapprovingly.

The four of them had already had a few weeks to get to know each other, preparing for the trip, leaving Adelaide in the winter of 1957, driving north along a track traversing the driest part of the driest state of the driest continent in the world, where the silence was immense and the bones of kangaroos bleached by the relentless sun lay starkly on the gibber plains, where the parched salt lakes stretched white and glistening against the red earth; through the centre of Australia where the colours of Albert Nama-tjira's paintings unwound before them in soft purples, reds, oranges and ochres, stark and beautiful against the clean, white peeling bark of ghost gums and the clear blue of the sky; north to the Top End, where there were a few signs of green, eucalypts, rocky outcrops, pandanus and Carpentaria palms fringing the dry creek beds, where the weather had become warmer and VB began to feel more at home, where he'd slept without a blanket for the first time since leaving Adelaide, where he'd looked up at the mosquito net suspended over the rickety iron bed at the Adelaide River Hotel, and it had seemed almost like old times in Malaya. Things were looking up.

It was an unfortunate set of circumstances that led to VB being part of this expedition. He should have been back out with the drillers at Cape York, a far less exciting prospect. Had Barbara not fallen pregnant and miscarried at twelve weeks at a time when he had been back out there with the drillers, the sympathy of Alcan's Exploration Manager, Pat Patience, might never have been aroused; he might never have arranged for them to be together on this trip.

At last they were off the bitumen. It seemed they'd come so far and yet hadn't even got started. The fine powder Territorians call bulldust sprayed up over the trucks each time they hit a patch, settling yet another layer on everything, a slightly different shade from the last, pink to cream to fawn with a mottled brown overlay, to cinnamon to red to pink with a purple overlay. They were driving two brand-new Dodge Power Wagons this time, the design based on American World War II plans. Magnificent machines, they were significantly larger than a Landrover, with more clearance and, most importantly, power winches instead of the crank-handle winches with which they had struggled in Cape York. VB had modified the trucks with tropical cab roofs and extra fuel and water tanks. Now he felt they were just about ready for anything.

VB's spirits were high at lunch on the sandy bank of a creek, for they were well on their way. The billy boiled as a cockatoo screeched in the distance, and brightly coloured finches hopped from Carpentaria palm to melaleuca, from pandanus to white-barked river gum. Their last stop before entering the trackless expanse of Arnhem Land was Roper River Mission. It wasn't the first mission they'd visited on this trip. During a preliminary reconnaissance by air with John Staargaard they'd stopped by at Mornington Island. VB laughed out loud at the *faux pas* they'd made in church. He would be better prepared this time.

It had been a Sunday morning and they were due to leave Mornington. The settlement seemed a neat, well-run place and when the reverend reminded them about the morning's service they'd felt they couldn't refuse. There were few enough white visitors to the island and it wouldn't have done for the Aborigines to see that they didn't attend. It had been a long time since VB had been to a church service for anything other than the usual affairs of hatches, matches and dispatches. But for the next half hour he'd sat piously alongside John, listening to the service, in a rear pew of the little mission church. When it was over he got up to leave, then sat down abruptly when he realised, with alarm, that a collection plate was heading in their direction. A young, serious looking Aborigine moved along the aisle towards them, and proffered the plate first to John. While John searched feverishly in his pockets the Aborigine waited expectantly, to see what the white man would give. But all John could find was one penny. Chagrined and red-faced, he placed the meagre offering into the plate. The young man looked at the penny, crestfallen, then held the plate out to a fumbling VB. He had fished into every pocket of his shorts and shirt, to find their entire contents to be one empty toffee wrapper. There was nothing for it. He looked up at the disappointed young man, then at the plate, and wearing his best choir-boy expression, he said of John's offering, 'That was from me too.'

The sound of the approaching trucks brought a bevy of young Aboriginal children wearing lolly pink *nagas*, a type of wrap worn between the legs and knotted on the hip, running down the slight hill from Roper River Mission. Old, dilapidated houses stood here and there amid dry, poor-looking gardens. On the sand slopes of the hill Aboriginal men and women—the men in shirts and shorts, the women in mission-made 'Mother Hubbard' dresses like sacks with holes at the corners—sat in the shade of bark shanties. Around the corner of the main mission house, a couple of white faces peered, then disappeared. The prospectors' arrival had been expected, but no-one came out for some time. VB got out of the truck and waited a minute or two, putting the slowness of the mission superintendent, in inviting them in out of the sun, to vagueness of manner rather than inhospitality, doubtless engendered by his 'call'.

The purpose of the visit was to get information about the state of the country to the north. If they could get through to Rose River Mission 100 miles away on the east coast, they'd establish a base camp there for exploring the surrounding countryside. But the Roper River missionaries were not encouraging. The only time a vehicle had been through from Roper to Rose River was three years before when someone had got a tractor through. It had been slow, hard going and there'd been a lot of trouble. It was probable that any signs of the route used would long since have disappeared and general opinion was that the Power Wagons would never make it. VB's spirits sagged. It was his job to ensure that they did make it, that was what he was employed for and he cursed the fact that he'd been unable to arrange any transport for the vehicles by sea. Apparently only a very few small mission luggers plied the coast of the Northern Territory, serving only the Aboriginal communities. There was nothing available that could land vehicles or equipment, and there was no choice but to go overland.

The only positive outcome of the meeting were two Aborigines with mission names of Sam and Don, who had walked the route between the missions. Over a jug of lukewarm water and six wheat-meal biscuits, VB spread out the very sketchy maps of the region on the floor of the mission house. Sam and Don pondered over them at length, utterly bewildered, but VB dismissed their confusion. Taking an educated punt that their natural sense of bush navigation would prove far more useful than their map-reading skills, he invited them along, and they agreed to come.

Glad when the business at the mission was over, the party slipped quietly away to camp on the river bank nearby. Later, in the short tropical twilight, three delightful small boys materialised out of the bush, eyes wide with curiosity, and introduced themselves as Harry, Leon and Joseph. Well mannered and eager to be of help, they chatted non-stop, imparting a great deal of information in a short space of time. Seizing an opportunity in a short lull VB asked them if they knew any songs. They didn't know any corroboree yet as they weren't old enough, but they knew some hymns and island songs, which they sang with enthusiasm. 'Do you know any songs?' asked Leon eventually, and watched captivated as the strangers launched into a few Dutch, Malay and English songs. Then VB suggested 'Clementine' and they found they all knew it. As he beat time on the table with a couple of sticks, a rousing chorus of 'Oh my darling' echoed along the flats of the Roper River, through the melaleucas and up towards the quiet mission station.

At the top of a rugged, flat-topped escarpment, up which the Power Wagons had laboured mightily, Arnhem Land opened out before them in a panorama of boundless green plain. There on the first day, the four white fellers just stood and gazed, profoundly moved by the silence, vastness and solitary grandeur of the miles of virgin country. This was the moment they had been waiting for, the moment when the last vestiges of civilisation as they knew it were left behind and they entered Arnhem Land, harsh but beautiful, inviolate and aloof from the rest of Australia.

In the remote, north-east corner of the Northern Territory, Arnhem Land covers an area of almost ninety-six thousand square kilometres, bounded by the Gulf of Carpentaria to the east, the Arafura Sea to the north, the Alligator River to the west and the Roper River to the south. The interior is home to monsoon forests and savannah woodland, the west to ancient and majestic escarpments lying detached and timeless through every changing season. But it was the lonely, sandy east coast they were to explore, difficult to reach and where little had changed for millions of years.

Arnhem Land had been an Aboriginal Reserve since 1931 when the government, in an effort to provide more protection for the Aborigines, declared it so. Uncontrolled by the government, whites who'd attempted to settle the area had brought detriment to the people of Arnhem Land: exploitation of the women, death from disease and armed clashes, ill health and a breakdown in their society through alcohol and tobacco, for they had no inherited tolerance to the drugs. The only hope for their protection came from the few missionaries who had established themselves around the coast doing what they could for the indigenous people. It had not been enough. Since then the government had not allowed white people to enter Arnhem Land without good reason, a thorough screening and a permit. The Alcan party had been through the screening process to find it very thorough indeed. As far as John Staargaard was concerned, it went just a little too far.

It was the syphilis test that narked him. Part of the policy of protecting Aborigines was the control of the spread of disease and sexual relations between white and black. When John heard at the Native Affairs Department that he'd have to undergo a spinal puncture, the Wasserman Test for syphilis, he was outraged and flatly refused. 'Imagine,' he spluttered later, 'with both of us taking our own wives with us! There are some things I don't do for any company—career or no career.' On that matter he could not be budged and VB was thus pressed to do some persuasive talking. Returning to the department alone and with chaste countenance, he'd presented his case to the health official that both he and Dr Staargaard were men of high rectitude, offering as evidence to arrange a letter from their wives testifying to their virtue. The decision, by no means immediate, was to let them go.

Now here they were. It was comforting to have Sam and Don along, sitting with VB in the lead truck and making optimistic comments throughout the journey about how far there was to go and how long it would take. 'Two, maybe three days' they had estimated it would take to cover the one hundred or so miles through to the coast. Their reckoning was a little out, for it was to take seven days, not three, to cover the distance, and the daily mileage record best tells the story: 34 . . . 30 . . . 20 . . . 7 . . . 5 . . . 5 . . . 14. Bumping and grinding down off the escarpment, the country became more forgiving; open dry grasslands, slim stringy-barks and six-foot ant hills of warm, golden brown clay, rounded like African *kraals*, with 'chimney pots' finished in white bird droppings. It was still Alawa country, Sam and Don's country, and the route they navigated was via the billabongs, just as they would have walked it. The creeks were dry now, and birds gathered around the waterholes in their thousands. Black-billed spoonbills waded the shallows; sober-looking pelicans and frivolous black ducks paddled the deeper pools where fish jumped in silver flashes against the blue of water lilies; ibis and long-legged cranes waded the shallows and proud grey brolgas stalked through the trees along the banks. The billabongs appeared like havens for weary travellers and if the time was right VB inevitably suggested a cup of tea could be in order, for he relished the ritual of lighting a fire, boiling up the blackened billy, tossing in the tea leaves and, when it was 'a good colour', swinging the billy to subdue the bits. Tea, he found, never tasted so good as in the bush.

The first bogging was in a patch of saltpan. Later the ti-tree scrub closed up around them until progress slowed to walking pace, through a tangled screen of branches. Worse lay ahead in the dense lancewood country, where three days passed in a blur of punctures. The fire-hardened stakes of the straggly acacias drove deep into the tyres and changing and repairing them, up to seven per day, became routine. The bodies of the trucks suffered as tree branches caught in everything over, under and around them. A small sapling swung up from under the wing of John's truck and shattered a window, showering Barbara with glass. Later the same day an ant hill built around the hidden stump of a tree ripped into the bottom of VB's vehicle, tearing one fuel tank off completely and holing the other. VB cursed and got to work. Close by Sam and Barbara lay underneath the truck surveying the progress. Don, a man of few words, disappeared into the bush; and John and Pop oscillated between the vehicles, finding tools and handing out cut oranges and toffees. VB just got dirtier and oilier, swallowed several gulps of petrol in the siphoning process and lost the contents of his pocket in the grass. For the umpteenth time on this trip he thought about how much easier exploration would be if vehicles and equipment could be landed on the coast by sea. There just had to be some opportunities there. Surely the north would begin to open up soon.

Temporary repairs made, he continued on, reeking of petrol in the front seat with Sam and Don. The news from Sam was that Rose River was 'close up now' and at the river there was a big highway where they could 'go plenty fast'. Sure enough, that afternoon the trucks pulled up at the top of a steep bank. Pandanus palms and tall eucalypts fringed the water of the Rose, and here and there sturdy cypress pines stood out amongst the heather-like purple hue of turpentine bushes. Crossing the river proved tedious, and thick soupy mud on the opposite bank claimed the shear-pins of both winches. After several hours slipping, sliding and airing of expletives in at least three languages, the vehicles were on the other side.

Midday the following day and Sam was once more being encouraging. 'Now we pinish come over Rose River we join big road bilonga Mission—go plenty fast'.

'How far to the road, Sam, long way?' asked VB.

'Bin little way,' said Sam, and VB set off optimistically.

Ahead was the saltpan country of the river mouth, where each wet the plains were flooded by fresh water, turning the whole area into a vast, waterlogged mass. It was a long way around for the vehicles, following the palm-leaf-like meanderings of the edges of the saltpans, and keeping to the ridges where scrubby ti-tree held the sand together and kept it firm. VB made a bold dive with his vehicle across the centre of a drier-looking patch, and dropped through a veneer of sand into soft wet clay. Bogged to the chassis and with not a tree in sight, he joined the winches of the two trucks. Three hours later, by the light of two pressure lamps, the whole party covered in mud and sweat and in an agony of mosquitoes, the vehicle finally squelched out, bringing with it about a quarter of a ton of clay.

'How far's this road of yours, Sam—a little way more?' asked VB, who had displayed more faith in Sam than the others, but was beginning to wonder. Sam only grunted. 'A long way more?' VB asked again.

Sam pondered this for a moment, then with a jerk of his head indicating the general direction he said decisively, 'Little bit long way.'

Sam's estimate translated to eleven miles of bogging and winching, running across high patches or pushing through the dry, white ti-tree belts, bogging and winching, winching and winching. Suddenly the sand turned deep gold in colour, smooth and clean. A cooling breeze from the sea, still several miles to the east, brought with it a tang of salt. At sundown a red, dusty track appeared out of nowhere and Sam and Don whooped. VB breathed a huge sigh of relief and all three leaped out of the truck, dancing as though they had a shirt full of green ants. When John drew up alongside he too tumbled out, while Barbara and Pop looked on at the sight of four grown men jumping up and down, cheering and waving, slapping each other on the back.

A mile up Sam's road a white windsock waved a welcome at one end of a broad airstrip. Further along was the blue of the sea, dark in the gathering dusk; bark huts on the sand dunes; a sprinkling of children, long legged and black, running beside them in the sand, laughing; a garden neatly fenced; a small wooden house, and another, and another; a shellgrit road bordered in sandstone leading up to the biggest of the painted houses; a man, a woman and a small boy, hands outstretched; introductions; a crowd of black faces . . .

'Bruce,' said Barbara, 'You've got a puncture.' And so he had.

SIXTEEN

The Good Lord's Works

V B stood in the grounds of the main mission house and looked around. Under his feet the sand was a soft, fawn colour amply mixed with charcoal left behind after the corroborees that were once held on that patch of ground. Here and there low stake fences bordered flourishing vegetable patches and sandstone blocks marked paths and other gardens. It seemed at first glance that the missionaries had done well with a less than ideal site. And yet facing the beach three small, unfinished wooden buildings sat empty and abandoned as though someone had lost interest a long time ago. And for an Aboriginal mission there were very few Aborigines about. The place was almost deserted. Something, it seemed, was not quite right.

Touring the mission with the superintendent, VB asked, 'What's the hold up with the new school and hospital?' John Mercer gave an exasperated gesture, explaining that it had been a battle to get even this far with construction. Work had stopped last wet season since they'd been unable to get the paint, Masonite and water pipes needed to finish them. The trouble was supply, for the mission received nothing direct by sea. *Cora*, the 'big boat' from Brisbane, occasionally ventured upriver to Roper River Mission, where it left Rose River's supplies. The idea was that supplies would be delivered by Roper's workboat, but that had been out of action for seven months and since then they'd had nothing but what the mail plane carried. The mission normally fed any Aborigines who chose to live at the mission, but there had been no bulk supplies of staple food. They had run short months ago and most of the normal complement of around one hundred and fifty Aborigines had gone back out into the bush on a more or less enforced walkabout, to live traditionally, to hunt and gather their own tucker. VB was surprised at this state of affairs. There really was a dire lack of a shipping service on this Northern Territory coast.

On the beach a few young boys with wire-pronged spears practised their throws in the shallow, tidal water. VB could see the difficulties inherent in landing cargo here from a conventional vessel. Even the mission luggers would have to be beached and unloaded lying cockeyed on their sides in the mud, and it was little wonder the vessel from Brisbane didn't call in at Rose River. Conditions were very similar to the east coast of Malaya, and he wondered whether the rest of the Northern Territory coast was as flat. If so he knew exactly what was required.

Later the fishermen returned in their canoes with the day's catch, upon which the thirty or so Aborigines remaining at the mission largely relied. Some had been hunting for dugong, a large mammal prolific in the local waters, but they'd had no luck today. On the beach the small girls dug for turtle eggs in the sand and for cockles in the mud at low tide while their mothers were out gathering wild berries and sugarbag and fossicking for root foods in the freshwater billabongs. All was well. They would not starve.

Rose River Mission (later renamed Numbulwar) had been established only five years before VB's party arrived, and had a staff of five Europeans. The Aborigines were from the Nunggubuyu tribe and some had 'come out of the bush' very recently. Their language was one of over eighty different dialects in Arnhem Land and their country extended from the mouth of the Roper River, fifty miles north to the southern point of Blue Mud Bay. The few of their number still at the mission chose to live on the beach, in small semi-circular windbreaks of stringy-bark, branches and sand. The four-walled bark huts built within the mission grounds now lay empty. Despite the supply situation, the people seemed healthy, cheerful enough and, with few exceptions, gentle and easy to get along with.

Apart from the fishermen and a few 'garden boys', most of the men who wanted to work were employed on timber cutting and carpentry, working independently at the trade taught to them by John Mercer. While the mission normally fed everyone whether they worked or not, in addition for their labours, 8am to noon and 2pm to 4.30pm five days a week, they received an average of fifteen shillings per week, enough to buy extra bits and pieces from the trade store if there was anything to buy, which, for the moment, there wasn't. John Mercer's success in motivating them didn't go unnoticed by VB. Like most people they showed willingness to work if dealt with in a firm, no-nonsense manner, unlike that employed by the mild-mannered reverend, a kindly fellow, but in VB's eyes not particularly practical. It seemed his idea of teaching the locals good Christian behaviour was to speak sweetly at all times, almost going down on to his knees to ask someone to do something. It was a bit embarrassing and quite obvious to VB that the Aborigines were laughing up their sleeves when the reverend asked for volunteers. Under John Mercer's approach of 'You and you and you—do this,' the Aborigines jumped to it, and very willingly in most cases. After all, they were there at the mission by their own choice.

VB glanced dubiously over the side of the dinghy, then caught John Staargaard's expression. They were both beginning to have doubts about the merits of this plan. VB had intended to hire a launch from Darwin in which to travel north to explore the coastal country. But the reverend had also been planning an expedition north in the mission's outboard dinghy and intended to land at Trial Bay, where he hoped to make contact with a group of myalls, Aborigines still living in the bush in the traditional way. Having planned the trip alone but for an Aboriginal escort he was quick to promote the idea that the two parties combine for the journey, and in view of the immediacy of his departure, VB and John had agreed. Now they were beginning to wonder.

Three Aborigines had left a day earlier in a canoe, carrying reserve petrol supplies to be dumped up the coast. The rest of the gear was down to a minimum but both the mission dinghy and the canoe to be towed behind were packed high with equipment, food, swags, a radio and a change of clothes each. It seemed to amuse the Aborigines no end to see the amount of stuff the white men needed to travel. As VB, John, the reverend and one of the Aborigines, Joalla, climbed into the dinghy the freeboard had disappeared alarmingly. Then Ed Grieg got in. Alcan's assistant chief geologist had unexpectedly flown in on the mail plane to spend a week with them, and he too was fast losing his enthusiasm. The only person still looking cheerful was the reverend, who had said a prayer on the shore before boarding and was displaying unswerving faith. VB and John exchanged glances again, each feeling that since this sort of transport apparently suited the mission fraternity one ought not to pass comment. Chugging out from the beach in the late afternoon, an admiring band of onlookers and two anxious wives waved goodbye.

The latest charts of the Arnhem Land coast were principally based upon those made by the explorer Matthew Flinders in 1803, and VB recalled Flinders' notes on the north-east coast of the Territory that it was 'a poor dried up land, afflicted by fever and musketos which admitted no moment of repose'. Flinders had not been very encouraging. Heading north, the small convoy hugged the shore all the way, travelling in the early mornings and late afternoons to avoid the wind and rougher seas. In the heat of the day, while the others rested, John, Ed and VB explored inland as far as they could.

For two days the weather was kind, but then it deteriorated. As the waves slopped into the dinghy, saturating everyone and everything, VB's spirits sagged. There was no choice but to go ashore at Cape Barrow on the southern-most point of Blue Mud Bay some fifty miles north of the mission, and wait until the weather calmed. He could sense Ed Grieg was beginning to sweat about missing the mail plane. VB suggested he and Ed return to the mission in the dinghy with Joalla, and leave the rest of the party to continue in the canoe when the weather abated.

Thirty-six hours later, well after dark, two exhausted, dirty and sunburned men walked back into Rose River Mission. Divested of much of its load, the dinghy had battered its way valiantly down the coast until, on the second afternoon, the outboard engine stopped dead. The wind died with it and VB left the dinghy with Joalla to be sailed back the following day, while he and Ed Grieg trudged the last sixteen miles back to the mission through sand, mud and crocodile-ridden mangroves. Later Joalla returned with the dinghy under sail and VB dismantled the outboard to find it irreparable. Now VB had John and the reverend stuck fifty miles up the coast with a few paddles and a couple of canoes. It was not an ideal situation.

But as VB's luck always seemed to have it, fortune smiled. The word was that the workboat from Roper River Mission was at last repaired and would soon deliver the long overdue food and supplies. VB got onto the radio and with a little persuasion and a fair degree of remuneration, arranged for the vessel to continue on up the coast and take over where the dinghy left off. In the meantime he had some more permanent repairs to make on the petrol tank of his truck.

VB had never seen an Aboriginal corroboree. He'd heard Barbara speak of them, for she had seen moving pictures of corroborees and heard recordings of their music whilst working for Professor Elkin. But he had no idea of what Aboriginal music sounded like. The missionaries did not approve of corroborees and so the Aborigines held them a long way down the beach. At night, if he strained his ears he could just hear the faint drone of the didgeridoo, rising and falling, rising and falling on the wind. It was intriguing, and while he waited for the workboat he asked one of the old men if they could go down to the beach that evening to listen to the corroboree in the single men's camp. Permission was given.

The moon had risen when he, Barbara and Pop stole down the

path to the beach. Before them, spread out every few hundred yards along the sand for perhaps half a mile, small mounds or windbreaks stood beside fires burning brightly, and dark figures moved against the flames. As they walked the sound of a didgeridoo became louder; he could hear the regular rhythm of tapping sticks, shouting and stamping. They waited, standing full in the moonlight, until a tall figure rose from beside a fire and walked towards them.

It was Ken, little Larumbu's father, a man who, in his daytime shorts and shirt, smiled shyly when he passed. Now he wore only a *naga* and greeted them courteously and with a new-found dignity—he was on his home ground—and walked beside them along the beach as their host. In the half light he looked different, bigger somehow, strange, and Barbara and Pop felt they were aliens in a foreign camp. They felt like intruders and it was a touch unnerving, passing the row of campfires, different heads popping up from behind the windbreaks to look, a dog snarling but from where they could not see. VB did not have the same awkwardness and walked boldly on until he came to the single men's camp. As they approached the strange music stopped. Pop had dropped a little way behind, and as they came up to the campfire with Ken, although it was known they were coming, VB asked again, 'May we watch your dancing?' A circle of heads nodded a welcome and the visitors sank down, out of the limelight, Barbara and Pop digging their toes into the sand as if to make themselves less conspicuous.

VB looked around at the twelve or so single men dancing that night, some not much more than boys, ranging perhaps from fifteen to thirty years of age. One young man was tapping the sticks for rhythm and another, playing the didgeridoo, he recognised as Mr Colin. He was wearing a *naga* and, like Ken, was almost unrecognisable divested of shirts and shorts, somehow more proud and confident. He sat in the firelight, one leg outstretched, playing this extraordinary instrument that looked to VB something like a *sakai* blowpipe. The long hollow wooden tube was balanced on the gap between his outstretched big toe and second toe, and he droned into it making a noise a little like that made by blowing into an empty bottle but magnified a hundred times, with a wide range of notes, a continuous noise as he kept the wood vibrating, distending and emptying and refilling his cheeks, not seeming to stop for breath. VB watched with interest, feeling somehow privileged to be sitting on the beach on this night, watching a celebration he'd never seen the likes of before, so utterly different to the *ronggengs* he'd seen in Malaya. Close by him Barbara watched, captivated, entranced, as reflected in that night's diary entry.

As Mr Colin played the rest of the boys, led by the tireless Melayu, stamped and danced and chanted their strange songs, on and on, keeping time to the rising and falling beat of the tapping sticks, laughing and yelling, their voices rising to a shrill pitch with the quick insistent tempo of 'mosquito'; to a long drawn out slower deeper tone as 'the sea' rolled in, wave upon wave, to the shore, rose in a furious tempest, then quietened; 'spearing fish'—wading through the shallows or paddling a canoe quietly, then stamp, stamp as the three pronged spears found their mark; 'dugong' feeding on the sea weeds, quietly, the approach of a canoe, stamp, stamp, the harpoon drives home and they are off on a wild chase dragging behind the dugong until finally it tires, they hold it under the water until it slowly drowns, to be towed home in triumph; 'wallaby', and here the twelve year olds, who up until now have been stamping and hopping in the background in a side-splitting imitation of their older brothers, come into their own and do 'wallaby', jumping in tiny hops, knees bent, hands tucked limply under their chins, bending and stretching their skinny shanks until all the onlookers are so overcome with laughter that they too finally roll over in the sand in paroxysms of mirth.

There were a lot of songs and dances that didn't seem to represent anything and I asked Ken what these were. 'Oh anyhow,' he says, and anyhow they were. We couldn't understand the words and for all we knew they could have been caricatures of ourselves, for they caused much amusement. There were also many dances from other parts of the Territory, Katherine, Darwin, Oenpelli, Groote Eylandt, Yirrkala which were 'anyhow', and then after 'mosquito' again, the men lay panting on the sand.

Then Melayu stepped forward and a single black eagle wheeled in flight, rising and falling on the wind, diving down and rising again, effortless, weightless, magnificent, until he too was brought to earth, fluttering and dying as Melayu sank to his knees on the sand. It was a wonderful performance; this slim black youth, firelight reflecting back from his lithe limbs, the silent ring of onlookers sitting cross-legged in the sand, the moon silver-edging the clouds that hid it, the strange vibration of the didgeridoo shutting out all other sound, the glowing embers of other camp fires along the beach, cold sand between the toes, the movement of the sea as a backdrop. It will be a long time before I forget 'black eagle'.

VB had never seen anything quite so disgusting. The workboat from Roper was filthy, with sacks of flour and rice, kitbags, boots, dirty clothes and dirty dishes all thrown in the bottom of the boat. It was the first day out and VB had tried to get the boat a bit shipshape but no-one else showed any enthusiasm for keeping it that way and he'd just about given it up as a lost cause. He'd had enough of the company already. The crew of seven from the other mission included one white, a particularly repulsive fellow who'd boasted of having got drunk somewhere, of smoking when he was away from the mission and who had little conversation other than to run down the superintendent. VB shrank at the thought of refilling his waterbottle, but it was getting low. The only water was stored in an old 44-gallon drum, the bung of which was missing so that each time the boat rolled the sea water and dirt on top of the drum ran into the fresh water. He'd watched with distaste as crew members sucked on the end of a short length of hosepipe protruding through the hole in the top, then left it hanging unwashed, from where it dropped with monotonous regularity into the bilge water sloshing about underneath. Now he'd have to suck it himself. There was no chart or map of any kind aboard, the compass was highly in-accurate and he was not particularly happy.

At Cape Barrow there was no sign of John, the reverend, in fact anyone. To the north lay the shallow and reef-ridden Blue Mud Bay, in an area to date uncharted, a fact of little consequence considering their situation. The bay offered few safe anchorages and the southern and northern-most coastlines were lined with thick mangroves. As they reached a small cape in the centre of the bay, VB became concerned. Knowing that the reverend and John had only two overloaded canoes with no keel or outrigger in which to travel, it seemed strange they could have come so far. But then a wisp of smoke floated on the air about ten miles to the north.

The weather had almost immediately cleared after VB left Cape Barrow to return to the mission. Cursing the fact that the boat had gone just when he needed it, John had pressed on, he cross-legged in the bottom of one canoe, the reverend, smiling, in the other. At Point Grindall the two parted company, John to venture out each day, by foot or canoe, to look at the surrounding country, the reverend, keen to find the tribe he wanted to contact, off up the Koolatong River. It was a successful trip, and at sunset one evening the shadowy outlines of five canoes made their way across Jalma Bay to Point Grindall. In one of them was the reverend and the three mission Aborigines he'd taken with him. In the other four were six serious-looking myall elders who had come with the white man to see what he could offer.

The next day had been a Sunday. The reverend didn't approve of travelling on Sundays and asked John not to set a bad example to the Aborigines. Out of politeness, John attended the reverend's beach service, the first white man's corroboree the myall elders had ever witnessed. They sat cross-legged in the warm sand with John, who listened in bewilderment to the story of how Noah got a signal from God who said he was going to drown everyone; and Noah got a lot of chaps to help him build a big canoe, and when God sent the rain to drown everyone because they had been wicked, Noah got into his big canoe and sailed away and presumably every-one else was drowned. John's confusion as to the moral of this story must surely have matched that of the mission Aborigines. The only people who weren't confused were the myalls who, fortunately, didn't understand a word of it.

VB was relieved to have the party together again, albeit crowded onto the filthy craft. The reverend had done his work for now, and made contact with the myalls. He would return again soon. With a bit of luck there would be no more holdups. The next destination was Yirrkala Mission, in the north-east corner of Arnhem Land. It was a tiresome journey. Further north the mud and mangroves became sandy dunes rolling lazily between patches of thick, dry jungle, and the dull yellow of the sea around Blue Mud Bay washed into a fresh, sparkling turquoise. In a sheltered anchorage in the deep water of Trial Bay they made camp ashore. VB was particularly glad to get off the squalid vessel and onto the clean, fine sand of the beach. Later, as the moon rose, a huge turtle dragged herself up the beach nearby and he watched as, with monumental effort, she began to swish, swish at the sand, ponderously scraping out a nest with her flippers. The next morning the Aborigines dug up some of her eggs to supplement the rations. Though he and John had started out well provisioned, their food had gone into the depressingly small general pool and the tinned stocks had soon been consumed. Their staple diet was now rice, cooked to a glutinous, sandy mess by the reverend, and fish baked native-style in the ashes of the fire.

At Caledon Bay the shore swept around in a wide arc before an expanse of sandy hills. The daily exploration trek inland became easier, though there was little of interest for bauxite explorers; old fossile sand dunes, crisscross layering in the sand, over lateritic, mottled clay; red iron laterite near the same stretch and the black of a beach laced with ilmenite and magnetite.

Around the coast near Yirrkala Mission, the cliffs stood out as startling red, and John's eyes lit up. Here was bauxite country. The existence of bauxite in the area was already known, but the government was still sitting on the rights to it. All the same John and VB had a good look around at the excellent stretch of mineral wealth, the development and royalties of which were later to bring enormous changes to the lives of the Aboriginal communities of the area. After a final reconnaissance of nearby Melville Bay, west of Yirrkala, John had seen enough and the old mission boat was turned for the home run. VB had found it uncomfortable on the way north, but now he realised that the weather had been kind on the outward trip. The moon was full and the sea rough. The crowded boat rolled violently and VB, green around the gills himself, leaned over to John, who was not looking particularly happy. 'It won't be long now,' he said soothingly. 'With the reverend's being on good terms with the Almighty and our combined sacrifices to Neptune, nothing can possibly go wrong.'

At 7am, two long days later, a boatload of tired and seasick men trudged wearily up the beach to Rose River Mission.

The mission once again hummed with life. Stocks of bagged rice, flour, tea and sugar had been replenished since the visit of the workboat, and those fending for themselves in the bush had returned. Living among the Aborigines of Rose River had proved an experience enjoyed and always treasured by Barbara and Pop. With the men away there had been more time to get to know the locals; to make friends, to laugh and to have fun with the people who gave Barbara inspiration to sit down and write dozens of pages in her diary.

There had been the trip out to Umudpa, a five-mile string of billabongs twelve miles inland from the mission. A sprinkling of Aboriginal girls had just discovered that truck-riding was not a prerogative of males and had excitedly packed into the back of the Power Wagon with a dozen or more boys. The waterhole, when they came to it, was beautiful, the water clear and clean and covered in water lilies in lilac flower:

> This was the first time we had seen any of the older girls without their 'dirty rags' and the transformation is incredible. Once rid of their frocks and clothed only in their own beautiful colour, they seem to assume different personalities, shrieking with laughter as they splash one another, twisting and gleaming in the

water like eels, completely free of restraint and cares. One girl in particular who has always struck me as rather hoydenish, completely changed in our eyes when, divest of her all-covering Mother Hubbard and with a spontaneous gaiety and full-blooded vitality, appeared as an Aboriginal Carmen, leading the others into the odd water dance of the Aboriginal women that makes such a deep booming and is so impossible to learn; and the little ones changed from rather grubby little urchins that one feels a little sorry for, to soft, black-velvet sweetnesses with gleaming teeth and enormous eyes peering roguishly from under their auburn-bleached curls, who play games in the water, sneaking up under the cover of huge lily leaves to pounce on each other and pull each other under water. The day passed all too quickly!

And gathering pipis on the beach, the task of the younger girls on afternoons when the tide was well out, leaving a large expanse of sand and sea grass to work over:

Occasionally we join them, walking barefoot and squirming our toes down into the soft grey mud beneath the sand to feel for the hard shells, or digging in deep with both hands, squelching the mud between our fingers to bring up a big one for the tin that serves as a basket, or a little one that is looked at with scorn and tossed away. We all get muddy and a bit damp, but nobody minds, and after the tins and their skirts, clutched up tightly to form another receptacle, are full, we sit on the dry sand and play. They love to look through our binoculars (with one eye tightly closed), or my sunglasses which are passed from hand to hand and perched on small blunt noses not large enough to hold them up, or the light meter of my camera is the centre of attraction, and they hold it up to the sun, then pop a small brown hand behind it to shut out the light and marvel at the consequences.

And the new baby, according to the nurse the first to be born at the mission. They had first seen it when it was thirty minutes old, and had returned two hours later:

The transformation is incredible. When first born, Aboriginal children are a bright greyish-bluish pink, and with their mop of thick, black hair they look much more finished than European babies. But in no time their colour begins to change and within a few hours they are black and beautiful, with the only pink still visible on their palms and soles. This one is quite fat—a six pounder—and a sweet little soul. Her mother, about sixteen years old, appears quite pleased with her, though seems to think it very comical the way the sister bathed her and wrapped her up. Ruth [the nursing sister] says that the ones born off the mission are just carried naked or wrapped in a piece of paper bark, or a half cylinder of bark. If it is healthy it survives and if it is not strong it dies, which is probably a good thing as a sickly member of the tribe would have a difficult life indeed. The babies are not washed at all until they are quite old, and Ruth says she has seen babies so encrusted with sand that it is almost impossible to recognise them at all.

And walks along the beach, this one alone, some distance from the mission. Around a slight headland Barbara had seen a tall, naked Aboriginal man walking up the beach towards her. He was carrying a spear in one hand and something in a bundle in the other.

I was a bit wary as I knew he was not from the mission, but there was nothing I could do so I just kept walking towards him. As it happened we may as well have been passing in George Street in the city, for he just walked straight past without glancing sideways. When I returned to the mission I found that he'd been carrying a tiny baby in a coolamon. The poor little thing was desperately ill and he had carried it all the way from Blue Mud Bay, some fifty miles, in the hope that the nurse could do something about it. Unfortunately it was too far gone and it soon died. Instead of giving the body back to the father it was then taken from him to be sent up to Darwin for an autopsy. Of course he didn't understand and was very upset. I suppose in this instance it was some idiot requirement of law—our law— but I thought it was terribly wrong to do that. There are some

things that happen on the missions that really concern me.
Though everyone is kind and well intentioned the missionaries
do not seem to be able to see outside of their own religious beliefs
or have any understanding or appreciation of Aboriginal culture,
which is seen only as something to be discouraged.

Over the following thirty years or so VB saw the role of the missions
in Aboriginal life much maligned. He believed there was ample
truth in the criticisms, but that it should not be overlooked that
in most cases the Aborigines went to the missions voluntarily. He
saw the life of the Aborigine living the traditional way as hard; just
finding enough food to survive was often a daily struggle. When
the missions opened it didn't take the Aborigines long to discover
the benefits on offer. At the missions the Aborigines knew they
would never starve, and the healing powers of the missionaries,
with their fast-acting medicines and injections, impressed them.
Such benefits brought the Aborigines to the missions, and more
often than not, kept them there.

In VB's eyes the missions also brought confusion. Suddenly the
indigenous people were told that their own culture, which had
been handed down the generations for over forty thousand years,
was all wrong. How could they reconcile the Christian sermons
they heard with their own Dreamtime stories? VB had listened in
bewilderment to some of the services held under the big eucalypt
tree at Rose River, wondering how on earth the Aborigines could
relate to what they heard. What did the story about how Joseph
went to a big corroboree and everyone who came to the big corroboree was wearing their best clothes except one man, who got
thrown out, have to do with the kangaroos and the crocodiles and
the storms and the sea that the Aborigines knew? What did they
understand of the symbolism of drinking the blood of Christ and
eating his flesh? Was it some form of cannibalism?

At the end of his stay at Rose River he felt he understood more
about how this particular group of Aborigines came to terms with
their predicament. The Aborigines appreciated the benefits to be

had from the mission, and if taking advantage of them meant listening to the sermons, then so be it. But one day the reverend tried to explain to them how bad smoking was, and that he didn't want to give them any more tobacco. One Aborigine answered, 'What? No baccy! No singsong! No Jesus!' A chorus of agreement from the others followed. That was that.

VB had seen the reverend sweating under heavy boxes and sacks moving stores. He had looked on in dismay at the response of the Aborigines to the reverend's polite invitations to help. The Aborigines were not stupid. Barbara had remarked that the Rose River people showed the classic indications of what Professor Elkin called 'intelligent parasitism'. They had begun to accept and then to demand many of the benefits of white civilisation, but at the same time they were determined to remain Aborigines.

VB saw the missions as being only as good as the people who ran them. The small friendly Rose River Mission was run on very different lines to the larger Mapoon Mission on Cape York, which was different again to the organisation and discipline prevailing at Yirrkala Mission, the rather dishevelled Roper River Mission or the orderly settlement at Mornington Island. He'd seen the confusion of the Aborigines when they listened to the laws of God, and the hurt caused by unthinking interference in a culture that runs deeper than a European could ever then imagine. Over the years to come he would see the missionaries and the organisations that presided over them make many mistakes, errors of judgement by the people on the spot, and errors of policy by the Church and the government. But looking back he viewed those people and policy makers as children of their own era, just as today's policy makers are children of ours. And he appreciated the fact that the missionaries took the trouble to do something about the appalling plight of Australian Aborigines, protecting them from disintegration and perhaps even extinction, at a time when few others were interested.

SEVENTEEN

Hermits and Hard Country

A deep drift of talcum-fine bulldust lay across the track, splashing up the sides of the truck like water and dispersing into a cloud to engulf the vehicle if it slowed too much. It was as if these tracks were superhighways after bashing back through Arnhem Land, and the dirt stretched long and straight ahead. It was early October, 1957, and VB was mindful of what he learned in Cape York the previous year: that everything in north Australia revolved around 'the Wet'. Long before it began, with not a cloud in the sky, plans were being made on gut feelings as to whether the Wet would be early or late, dry or heavy. It was hard to imagine that in possibly only a few weeks the brown, tinder-dry country would become deluged and turn to a sea of vivid green, that meandering, dry watercourses would turn to rivers, flat country into swamps, tracks into creeks, open, cracked depressions into living, breathing billabongs and green tree frogs would sing rapturous odes to the joys of life.

Several thousand square miles in the south of the Gulf country waited to be looked over before the Wet set in, and today their destination was Borroloola. Alongside the main camp of a road gang VB pulled up his truck and got out for a chat with an elderly gent cooking up a damper in a three-legged camp oven. Though beautifully sited on a billabong the camp was a shambles: torn, grey mosquito nets draped half-heartedly over iron bedsteads, blankets trailed in the dirt, pots and pans, knives, pannikins and tins of food dumped unceremoniously around the kitchen tables, and empty cans lay where they had been chucked. In the nearby trees a dozen kite hawks waited, a sure sign of disorder in a camp. The old cook noticed VB look up at the birds, and gave a disgusted grimace. 'Don't know what's wrong with the young blokes these days,' he said. 'Told one of 'em to bury that meat this morning when the fridge had gone orf, but he'd rather chuck it over there. Well I'm not going to do his job for him—let it stink 'em out.' Not fifty yards away lay the remains of a quarter of bullock, black and putrid and seething with flies.

Ahead the drive was hot and uninspiring, through unchanging scrubby bush and ant-hill country. An hour up the dirt road VB again found some diversion over a chat with the other three men of the road gang, and a cup of their brew: a teaspoon of coffee essence, two of milk powder, a tablespoon of sugar, stirred vigorously in a pannikin of lukewarm water—no questions asked.

Forty miles from the settlement three rugged hills marked the turn-off for McArthur River Homestead. Bushfires nibbled the fringes of a billabong and licked at the edge of the track. As the sun began to settle for the night the trucks turned off at a dusty airstrip, and followed it up across a flat plain. Then, suddenly, they were at Borroloola.

On the banks of the McArthur River about thirty miles inland of the south-west corner of the Gulf of Carpentaria, Borroloola was a frontier post well past its heyday. Its *raison d'être* was the river, for although the McArthur was tidal, the water was fresh enough for cattle and there was plenty of it. Borroloola was settled as a staging post when the cattlemen first drove their animals through the unexplored Barkly Tableland in the late 1800s. The McArthur River was navigable as far as the township and stores were shipped by small boat. All around it cattle stations as big as English counties were established and supplied through Borroloola. With the talk of gold in the Kimberley came a rush of hopeful prospectors, many of whom followed the stock routes west through Borroloola, and the settlement thrived. At one stage it boasted a police station and gaol, two hotels, five stores and its European population snowballed to fifty.

In the history of the Northern Territory few white settlements had survived to become anything more than dusty roadhouses, with a couple of rooms out the back to accommodate weary travellers. It seemed Borroloola hadn't even retained that much of its former glory. With the boring of artesian wells it lost its importance as a watering hole. With the advent of the motorcar and the development of the Stuart and Barkly highways, it lost its role as a supply depot. The great cattle drives were no longer and the gold rush fizzled. Suddenly Borroloola was not on the way to anywhere and the life force of the little town died.

Now, the evidence of what once was could still be found here and there, derelict in the dust. To the careful observer, flickers of life were still apparent.

VB had thought he'd met a few characters in his life, but by the time he left the area he'd concluded that on a pure percentage of population basis there'd have to be few regions in the country to touch this one. Setting up a base camp on the sandy banks of the McArthur River, first impressions were that this was going to be a very quiet time, for Borroloola in 1957 did not appear a hive of industry. Indeed the only person in town with an occupation was the Native Affairs officer who looked after the local Aborigines camped further down the river and whose house was the only structure of substance. The old hotel still stood, after a fashion, its loose and rusted corrugated-iron roof creaking in the slightest breeze and its verandah, precariously extending its full length, loose and buckled. Inside nothing remained but a few vestiges of squatters who'd taken up temporary accommodation on the white-ant-eaten floor; two old chairs—one with no back—a rusted bed and a doubtful-looking mattress. Scattered around, both inside and out, was the rubbish left by its incumbents: empty bottles of rum and methylated spirits and an assortment of rusted tin cans. The other building was a sagging corrugated-iron affair on stumps, which served as the local post office. Inside, undelivered mail and unread newspapers and magazines were packed to the ceiling.

Undoubtedly the highlight of Borroloola living was the fortnightly visit of the mail plane. The whole of the population turned out to greet it, appearing at the airstrip as if from nowhere. Mail day proved the best time to meet the locals—a few dozen Aborigines and five whites. It was here that VB met Borroloola's oldest inhabitant.

Roger Jose shuffled up the airstrip looking as though he'd stepped out of the pages of the Bible. (Perhaps his biblical aura had something to do with rumours that he was the brother of the once Dean of Adelaide.) His homemade striped shirt was of a fabric something like mattress ticking and he wore a matching piece draped over his head. A long grey beard adorned the worn but noble features of his weather-beaten face and his feet were shrouded in sacking tied around his ankles and up his legs. His opening gambit, as he eyed the knife strapped to John's belt, was, 'Is this a dagger I see before me?' followed by something about blood on this little hand, delivered in a manner which would have done justice to Olivier. He immediately captured VB's interest.

This was the sort of thing that fascinated VB about people. This was why he preferred not to judge people on their class, race, nationality, sex, occupation or philosophical bent. You just never could tell. Before him he saw a dilapidated old tramp, but there was a lot more to Roger Jose than met the eye. He introduced himself as Mayor and Official Welcomer of Visitors. Later, sitting with VB on the verandah of the old post office, he admitted that these were honorary and self-appointed positions, neither of which put great demands on his time. His life story was not complicated. He'd lived in Borroloola since 1916 and left it only rarely and for short periods. In 1938, when a cyclone blew away his shack, he and his Aboriginal wife moved into a converted 5,000-gallon rainwater tank about a mile away from the hotel. The conversion process had been simple, involving only the cutting of a hole in one side for a door. Though admitting it was a little warm inside, Roger didn't bother with windows, but insulated the tank a little by growing a purple-flowering vine over it. Against one side stood an upturned wheelbarrow in which he carried his wife when her legs were giving her trouble.

What really fascinated VB was Roger's penchant for literature. His main claim to fame was that he was the last custodian of Borroloola's renowned library, which in its heyday had a collection of some three thousand books, some of which, according to Roger, came from a grant from the Carnegie Corporation in New York. The last of the books were now stashed in his tank and over the period of their stay he proved more than generous in lending the dusty, moth-eaten volumes to the visitors camped by the river. Having no desire for money, Roger had never worked very much. In his younger days he had taken occasional jobs repairing roads or fences, but when it looked like his remuneration was getting close to an order that would require the filling out of a tax form, he stopped. Thus he had always had plenty of time to read and over his lifetime he claimed to have read and reread almost every book in the library. A self-taught man, he had a photographic memory and there were pages and pages of the classics imprinted indelibly on his mind. Fond of quoting Bernard Shaw, Shakespeare, Omar Khayyam and the Bible, words were his passion. He savoured them like others would a perfect red wine, closing his eyes blissfully as he drank of them. He was also a philosopher in his way and had spent a lifetime pondering the meaning of it all. Roger Jose claimed that the measure of a man's riches was the fewness of his wants, and as such he was wealthy indeed.

Jack Mulholland was another permanent. Ex Royal Navy, ex Barkly grader driver, he'd come to Borroloola after World War II because he'd heard it was a good place. The first five months of his stay he spent reading library books and when a job came up running the hotel he took it. This suited Jack fine as he rarely had any custom and it gave him plenty of time to sit and think. Jack also had a sideline in radio repair. He had a collection of 'how to' books on the subject and was known in the district for his talent, although not recommended for a quick fix. The deal was that his customers left their busted radio with him and he'd store it in the dust at the back of the pub until another came in bearing the part he wanted. Then he'd take it out of that one, repair the first one, and wait again for the parts for the next one.

When the hotel closed Jack had even more time to think. Like all the residents of Borroloola, he and Roger Jose kept their distance as a general rule, though they did occasionally meet to debate a pre-arranged topic or discuss philosophy. Another of Jack's sources of amusement was his pride and joy, an old 1928 Pontiac car which he kept going using a similar technique to that he used with his radios. The car had so many cannibalised parts in it that it was probably less Pontiac than everything else. VB noticed its tyres were all flat and discovered Jack had lost the crank handle. Despite this, however, Jack assured him she'd go and was fiercely defensive about it. 'And if you won't take my word for it ask a fella called David Attenborough,' he told VB one day.

David Attenborough had visited Borroloola in 1956, just the year before, to make a film entitled *The Hermits of Borroloola* and, amongst other things, had filmed Jack starting up the old girl by putting the rear axle on blocks, putting her in gear, grasping the spokes of the rear wheels, heaving them around until the engine spluttered into life then dashing forward to knock her out of gear.

Jack Mulholland also acted as honorary postmaster and took charge of any mail not collected at the airstrip, tossing it onto the huge stacks of uncollected mail that had accumulated over the years. Taken in by Jack's grandiose title, John asked Jack one day for a stamp, and was told to give the letter to the pilot, since he hadn't a clue how much the postage was. 'That fellow would be too lazy to shiver if he was cold,' VB muttered as they left. Behind him Jack, too, was muttering.

Weeks later, as they were leaving Borroloola, they called into the post office to check for late mail, and Jack made his feelings clear. 'Thank God you lot are going,' he said with relief. 'I've never been so bloody busy in my whole bloody career as postmaster.'

In the midst of cattle-station country, the Borroloola region was easy to explore. VB was relieved to find that the natural vegetation was more open than in Arnhem Land and cattle tracks radiated in all directions. In this terrain there was no need to take two vehicles on local expeditions and he and John usually went by themselves, sometimes for five or six days, leaving Barbara and Pop in camp alone. With Roger Jose's supply of books, the daily chores, diary writing and a snooze in the afternoon, the days passed quickly for them. Borroloola didn't have many visitors, but the few that did pass through mostly found their way down to the camp by the river for a cup of tea, or at the very least, a chat. There were some rugged types.

The ringer was a rough-looking fellow, dirty and unshaven, his hat tilted back, riding in bare feet with his little toe outside the stirrup iron to help keep his feet in the stirrups. He pulled his horse up one morning in the middle of the camp kitchen. 'G'day,' he said, not bothering to introduce himself. 'That coffee smells good.'

He accepted a cup, but stayed put in the saddle, so Barbara went over to chat. Noticing a piece of rag tied around his other foot, she said in general conversation, 'You seem to have done something to yourself.'

'Oh bloody thing!' he said. 'Hit a tree. You can have a look at it if you like, and see what you reckon.'

Carefully, she unwrapped the filthy, bloody rag, to find the ringer's little toe literally hanging by a thread, the bone totally disconnected. 'I'm afraid it doesn't look very good,' she said. 'I think you'd better go up to the hospital in Katherine and have it properly seen to.'

'Don't like goin' to town,' the ringer replied. 'Do you reckon it'll grow back on again?'

Barbara peered once more through the dirt at the almost severed toe and said, 'No I'm afraid it won't grow back on again.'

'Oh well,' he said, 's'pose we'd better cut it off then. You got any scissors?'

Barbara rummaged in the medical kit, found the scissors, cleaned his foot and then neatly cut off his little toe. She dabbed a little antiseptic on the wound, wrapped it in a clean bandage and the job was done. 'Would you like to keep the toe?' she asked, jokingly.

Doffing his sweat-stained hat and handing back his empty cup he said, 'Nah, she'll be right. Gotta be off. Thank you ma'am,' and rode on his way.

Then there was Harry Blumenthal. When VB and John were around, Harry was a regular visitor to the camp, and over many a dinner and/or breakfast they learned something of his life. A crocodile shooter with no fixed abode, Harry worked his way around the Gulf country living off the land and his croc skins. An immigrant from Latvia, he'd had a hard time in World War II and had come to outback Australia to escape the memories and people in general. He had a few makeshift shacks scattered around the region but largely lived in the open, occasionally spending time around Borroloola shooting in the McArthur River and finding a bit of company among the residents of 'The 'Loo'.

Harry Blumenthal was all man: shaggy, sunbleached hair, tanned face, thick, dark beard, a bullet wound in his left arm, tough and a little wild looking. Usually dressed only in a pair of tattered shorts, his body rippled with muscles like sprung steel that left the ladies of the camp a little in awe. He'd promised John a crocodile skin to take back to Holland and he kept his promise. The night Harry turned up in a canoe to pick him up, John was a little taken aback. He was only too aware that the man-eating salties came upriver this far, for there was a big one taking cattle at the crossing not too far away. But he climbed into the canoe and they slipped quietly downriver, phosphorus illuminating the water with tiny submerged sparks, occasionally stopping so that Harry could shine the torch, searching in the light for the cold, red glint of the eyes that gave the skulking reptiles away. John could imagine the crocodiles lurking beneath the water, listening to the strange slurping and sucking noises of the tide running through the maze of tree roots and fallen debris, to the splashing of fish, to the plop of a pandanus nut falling into the water, to the quiet plip, plip of the paddles.

'There,' Harry whispered. He'd spotted a freshwater croc which looked, from the distance between its eyes, a good size. The paddling stopped and the canoe drifted silently towards it, until the soft crunch of the hull scraping the river bed betrayed them. With a lash of its tail the crocodile whipped around and in a flash, Harry had leapt, harpoon in hand, out of the canoe into the blackness. Seconds later he emerged, his hair and beard dripping wet. He had missed it.

Harry liked to harpoon first, shoot later. By shooting first the animals would all too often sink quickly, to be lost in the depths of the water. When securely harpooned, he'd pull the thrashing croc close to his canoe before shooting it in the tiny target, half an inch below centre between the eyes, or directly in the eye if shooting from the side. The bullet had to shatter the small brain so cleanly that the crocodile would not move again, otherwise the whirling, furious animal could smash his canoe. Later that night Harry was successful, and John got the skin he wanted.

Over breakfast the next morning John recounted his adventure. 'He actually dived in on top of the crocodile?' asked Pop in disbelief. Privately VB and Barbara, too, wondered whether John did not like to spoil a good story for a mere matter of veracity. It wasn't long before they had a chance to see for themselves.

It was a warm night and the canvas sides of VB's tent were rolled up, leaving only the mosquito netting gently moving with the faintest of breezes. They were by now accustomed to the noises of the bush at night, but Barbara woke to a sound she couldn't identify, and sat up. Fumbling for a torch, she turned it on, and jumped as the beam shone straight out through the mosquito net and into the eyes of a crocodile about ten feet away. Wildly she shook VB, gasping, 'Bruce wake up, quickly—there's a crocodile right outside our tent!'

'Come off it, Charlie,' was his first response, but the urgency in her voice had him leaping off the air mattress. Hurriedly doing up his sarong he grabbed the rifle from beside him and cocked it. 'We'll have to go out. You shine the light so that I can see what I'm doing,' he said, retrieving his sarong which had fallen off again.

Gingerly they stepped out, VB with the rifle already aimed at the brute's head. The crocodile had not moved a muscle and for a split second VB hesitated, enough time to notice a stout rope tied around the animal's snout. Slightly mollified, he investigated further and found that its legs, too, were bound and that it was tied to the tree under which they were camped. 'Well that's bloody handy!' he said, for it was a reasonable-sized croc, around eight feet in length and not the most ideal company at such close quarters, tied or not. But there was nothing they could do about it and they went back to bed, sleeping fitfully until sunrise.

Breakfast was earlier than usual that morning, and as it was cooking Harry Blumenthal strolled into camp. 'Sorry I had to tie the croc so close to your tent but it was the only tree that was handy by. Got an order for stuffing so couldn't put a bullet in it, and didn't want to have to lug it right up the bank. I'll move it this morning.' Apologies over he sat down to breakfast under the dining tent fly, a small distance up the river bank.

Halfway through his bacon and eggs, something caught VB's eye. Turning, he saw the croc had loosened the rope tying its feet and jaws, and was wriggling free. 'Oh, Harry . . . I think your croc's off,' he said casually.

Harry's head whipped around to see the crocodile heading smartly for the water and he took off, knocking his chair, the table and his breakfast flying. Launching himself onto the animal's back at about the time it hit the water, he clung to it like a man possessed as the crocodile rolled over and over, lashing its tail wildly. On one brief surfacing he managed to shout to the onlookers, 'Get the bloody rope!' and disappeared again. VB retrieved the rope and was coiling it when Harry surfaced for a second in time to splutter, 'Bloody chuck it!' VB chucked it.

The four of them stood mesmerised as the struggle continued, until eventually this extraordinary character had the crocodile tied up again and emerged dripping wet and exhausted. VB and John helped haul the animal a few feet up the bank and retied it to the tree, while Harry walked back up to the dining area in search of the rest of his breakfast.

The sun beat down on a ground baked hard by six months without rain and wisps of burnt grass eddied in the hot air. Exploring the region was hot work, very hot. The dry season was coming to a close and the suffocating tropical build-up had begun. Even VB had to admit that this was hard country for Europeans. It seemed to be inhabited only by the eccentric, the type with something to hide or the exceptionally rugged and determined. Every now and then he and John came across the derelict remains of a cattle station at which the owners had lost hope and abandoned their dream to the white ants. Rosie Creek was marked on the map, in the north-west of their concession half way to the Limmen Bight, and VB was looking forward to seeing some new faces. But Rosie Creek Homestead was no more than an empty corrugated-iron shell with a couple of bush beds standing forlornly in the corners. On one of the beds he spied an old book, *The Imitation of Christ* by Thomas à Kempis, and it seemed extraordinary that such a work would be found in such a place. But the literary influences of the Borroloola Library had spread far and wide, and he picked up the mildewed tome to return it, belatedly, to Roger Jose.

To the east of their concession, a dirt track linked up the few cattle stations in the region, a circular route from which to base an expedition. From Borroloola it led east, past the Manangoora turnoff, through a part of the country which seemed to vary with every bumpy, dusty mile. Manangoora Station backed onto the sea and the track through to the homestead provided an easy route from which to look over that piece of country. Towards the coast dense stands of pandanus and ancient-looking palms grew, their trunks crowded with rings, some buckled and stunted and others tapering to a lofty crown. The soil looked richer than further inland, and the low banks of the Wearyan River were as red as the central desert. Looking at the map it seemed that this station, sitting alone in saltpan country on the Gulf, must have been the loneliest place on earth and VB wondered who on earth they'd find there. Eventually they came upon a tumble-down shack made of what looked like paperbark. By now he knew enough of cattle station homesteads in the north to realise that this was probably it.

At the sound of the vehicle engine, a smallish, weather-beaten man of around seventy emerged from the shack, looking out from a beard which seemed to engulf his face. As the visitors stepped forward, smiling and with hands extended, Andy Anderson gave a shy and completely toothless grin. It wasn't often that Andy had visitors, and since he went into Borroloola only about once a year to collect stores delivered by lugger, he wasn't a great socialite. But he was hospitable enough and invited them into his humble, one-room abode to sit on a chair strung with sacking. The rest of the furniture was of similar construction: bush timber, greenhide and old hessian, simple and serviceable. There were few amenities besides a woodstove, a receiving only radio and a few books scattered around, but it appeared that Andy had found what he wanted in life.

VB and John set up their camp on the Foelsche River opposite Andy's place. They were not aware that the man they'd just met was more famous than either he or they realised. For this was 'Andy', mate of bushman, poet, talker and author Bill Harney, whom Barbara's father, being in the publishing game, knew well.

Bill and Andy went back a long way, to 1911, when they were both droving cattle on Korobulka Station. Later they joined up as army recruits together in Burketown, then after World War I the two of them operated the pack-horse mail route from Wollogorang on the border of Queensland, to Borroloola, until Bill won some money in a lottery. The proceeds went towards Seven Emus Station, a few hundred square miles of ground to the south-east, and then later the country that was to become Manangoora Station. Bill let Andy in on the properties from the beginning, giving him a half share. Later he signed both stations over to Andy asking nothing in return, for he had itchy feet and wanted to move on. Manangoora was now a grazing property of six hundred square miles. At one time Andy did a stretch in the Borroloola Gaol for cattle duffing, and whilst serving his stretch he finished off his education by virtue of some of the literary works housed in the Borroloola Library. Some of what he learned rubbed off later when he came to name his two half-caste sons Trotsky and Lenin.

Andy Anderson had lived out there since the early 1920s and obviously had no desire to live any other way. When VB first met him he couldn't help but wonder how the owner of two cattle properties, on which the staple diet must surely be steak, could get by without teeth. Before saying goodbye his curiosity got the better of his manners, and at the risk of sounding presumptuous he popped the question. He got his answer. 'When I went into the big city to get m'teeth pulled out they wanted to make me a set of falsies. But out in the bush falsies are more trouble than they're worth, and just end up kicking around in the dirt. Anyway it would've meant I would've had to stay longer in town and I don't like the bright lights. So I got a mincer and I do all right.'

The main track began to change course to the south-east, towards Wollogorang, close to the Queensland border. At Seven Emus Station VB and John stopped to camp the night. The homestead was deserted and they guessed that Trotsky, Lenin and the rest of the comrades were out mustering. Thirty miles or so further along they called into Pungalina Station, near Calvert River. If the size of the mango trees engulfing the paperbark and iron homestead was anything to go by, the homestead had been there since the days of ox and cart. Once again it was deserted, the only sign of recent habitation a rifle still slung on the wall, and a half-empty gin bottle on the table. Later they heard that the old man had recently died, and it seemed a lonely way to go.

From Pungalina, there was nothing for sixty-five miles. The map showed they'd briefly crossed the Queensland border before turning south-west for Wollogorang Station. John was eager to get to a place shown on the map as Redbank, and they passed Wollogorang without stopping.

William R Masterson was the proprietor of Redbank Mine, and had been since around 1918. A former bank employee, he'd come out bush to escape the city after his only son had died in World War I, making a new life for himself out of a claim on a bit of low-grade copper in the weathering zone of a mineralised area. His home was a cool, dark cave in a piece of rocky escarpment some twenty miles west of the Queensland border. It was late in the afternoon when VB and John found him, lounging on a bush timber and sacking deck chair at the entrance to his cave. He was smoking a pipe and reading a copy of the *Illustrated London News*, some months old, for which he had a subscription. At eighty-something years old Masterson was no spring chicken, but he leapt out of his chair like a man half his age and welcomed his visitors heartily. Wiry and fit looking, a natty blue scarf tied rakishly around his neck, his singlet was cleanish and his white beard the neatest they'd seen in weeks. 'How do you do,' the old hermit said in a well-modulated, perfect BBC accent. His speaking voice would not have seemed out of place in the best of London society and had been acquired, VB decided, from having spent forty-odd years with little company other than his radio, on which he religiously listened to the BBC World Service.

Masterson was quick to produce a billy full of strong tea. In his cave was a refrigerator box, a contraption with mosquito netting around it over which hung a dripping bucket of water. Out of it he produced what looked to John like a softly furred green rabbit. On closer inspection it proved to be a cake, homemade out of a packet, and very mildewed. 'I hope you don't mind but I added a solid dose of garlic powder to it to give it some taste,' Bill said as he handed them a plate each. They accepted politely, and though VB hardly noticed the fungus, John privately wondered at the things he would do for a company when still hoping for a career. The cave could have been tidier, VB observed, but it was serviceable and, sitting comfortably in a 'Masterson deck chair' they listened to the old man tell his story. From where they sat the view over the lowlands of the north of the Barkly Tablelands was little short of magnificent. Bill Masterson thought he had it made.

John had never seen anything quite like Redbank Mine. Though old Bill had many years experience, John soon spotted that he didn't know a lot about the business. His small shafts ran randomly in every direction, and any time he passed some ore he dug it out and sent it to Mt Isa Mines, the company which sent him his supplies and his *Illustrated London News*. Masterson's team consisted of himself and two Aboriginal women who stood at the top of the incline shafts turning the windlass and emptying the rawhide bags as they were winched up. Holes for the shafts he drilled with a drill rod and hammer in the most primitive way, and when they were deep enough he loaded them with dynamite and put a fuse on it. Materials had to come a long way to Redbank and Masterson didn't like to waste them. In view of this the fuses averaged about one foot in length. VB watched in amazement as the old man lit the fuses with his pipe and then scrambled out as fast as his eighty-odd years would carry him, running for safety and ducking the boulders sent flying by the explosion as he went.

The Redbank area, John assessed, was not going to make either Alcan or Masterson a fortune and, leaving the friendly hermit to his work, they headed north-west. It was now almost the end of November. There'd been a few isolated storms, but the black soil was still dry and almost rock hard. It would turn to a sticky mire after a few inches of rain, completely clogging the wheels of the vehicles.

By early December the strangers at Borroloola had moved on to spend two or three weeks looking over the southern region of the concession from a new base at Robinson River Station, seventy miles south-east of Borroloola. There the camp overlooked a dry river gully, and the four of them shared its one waterhole with a hundred species of birds and a herd of station horses. VB knew that south of Robinson lay the best cattle country in the Northern Territory, the black soil and Mitchell grass plains of the Barkly Tablelands, almost one thousand feet above sea level. He had learned not to expect much, but the vast region of dry, withered grass and hard baked ground had John reaching for his camera to photograph what passed as first-class cattle country in the Northern Territory of Australia. The folks back home in Holland would never believe it.

Three weeks on, the rain storms were becoming more frequent and it was time to move out. Supplies were running low. The last side of bacon from the Borroloola supply boat, *Cora*, and the last of the eggs from the local station-owner, Jack Camp, had gone.

To VB, breakfast was now a grim affair. Only two cartons of tinned food remained and the powdered milk was finished, assisted with enthusiasm by a part-wild cat. The day came to pack up for the last time, a big job from a base camp, and it was done with an air of melancholy, for the four of them had immensely enjoyed their six months in the bush. The often difficult conditions, the heat, the dirt and the dust had been overcome by good humour and companionship and that indefinable sense of wellbeing that comes from being away from the frenzied existence of man-made society.

For VB the whole experience of northern Australia had been positive, and not only because he'd so enjoyed it. He'd been amazed at how undeveloped it all was, at what a lot had to be done. From what he'd seen there were Aboriginal communities existing from hand to mouth with an unreliable line of supply. Mineral exploration would certainly be soon getting under way in force, yet there was little in the way of infrastructure to support it. He wouldn't mind getting back up to Darwin for a good snoop around, to see what he could see.

The camp was packed up, everything except the supporting poles for tarpaulins, which they left for other travellers, and a 'Masterson deck chair' VB had knocked up during their stay. The tea, the billy and the cups had been left out and they sat down for a final nostalgic brew, composing a notice for the amusement of Jack Camp, to be pinned to a box lid nailed to a tree:

TO LET—FURNISHED

This desirable country residence; extensive grounds; private swimming pool; panoramic view; within easy motoring distance famous seaside resort Manangoora; guided tours to such well known beauty spots as Horse Pocket, Kelly's Gap etc; hunting and fishing by arrangement.

Excellent neighbourhood.

APPLY: *J. Camp, Real Estate Agent, Robinson River*

Note: *Prospective tenants must undertake care and maintenance of one respectable, elderly cat (house trained: no followers).*

EIGHTEEN

The Fundamental Orifice

V B had a thing about unusual names. He would almost certainly remember someone called Archibald Snodgrass-Dorkes, no matter how brief his acquaintance. But it was not just that the name Aitken-Quack appealed to him. Hearing it again brought pleasant memories flooding back: memories of Harold, charming and highly respectable, and carefree days at sea *en route* to Singapore in 1937; of Sunday curry tiffin at the Planters Club before the balloon went up; of happy visits to Harold's enchanting, Tudor-style bungalow on the rubber estate outside KL in 1955, of sipping *stengahs* on the verandah as the late afternoon sun cast gangly shadows through the rubber trees.

Cooped up in inclement Melbourne in April of 1958, it all seemed a long time ago. Alcan had cut back its exploration program in the north of Australia and there was nothing on the horizon for VB. The north of Australia had captured his imagination, but he still had his heart set on the Far East and was scouting about for an opportunity to return. But then out of the blue Bryan Summers rang from Darwin. There he'd met the congenial Richard Welford Aitken-Quack, known generally as AQ, who was looking for a manager for his company, Dartim Shipping Pty Ltd. Bryan had told him he knew just the man, and VB jumped at the opportunity.

Barbara was not so enthused. They'd spent a few days in Darwin before the Arnhem Land trip and she hadn't been impressed. It had seemed a shabby little place, and she couldn't help but wonder at the evident lack of civic pride of the residents; no-one seemed to bother very much with gardens and the whole town had an air of nobody really caring. VB on the other hand had been pleasantly surprised. He'd been told by someone that Darwin was generally known as 'the arse-hole of Australia', and was prepared for just that. On the contrary he felt the place had potential. Built on an attractive piece of coast on the shore of the Arafura Sea, it should have been delightful. The dry season climate was pleasant and in the semi-tropical surroundings it could have been beautiful. No, it wasn't beautiful, but VB was inclined to be charitable.

Apparently AQ had arrived in Australia recently from Hong Kong where he'd been 'in shipping' for some years. VB couldn't recall Harold having mentioned a brother, but this person assuredly must be one of the family, and he himself was indeed interested in returning to north Australia. The fact that there was no shipping service to speak of on the coast of the Northern Territory loomed large in his mind. Surely the place must have vast potential. In terms of lifestyle, no, Darwin was not the Far East, but in VB's eyes it had a most agreeable latitude, a latitude which came with a cast-iron guarantee that tomorrow would be hot.

A large, ruddy faced, portly gentleman sporting a handlebar moustache waited at the Darwin airport to meet the plane from Melbourne. RW Aitken-Quack watched as the passengers braved the sun, crossing the steaming tarmac to the terminal where amidst the throng he welcomed VB warmly. At this first meeting under the grinding airport fans VB was in no doubt that here indeed was an Aitken-Quack; charming, eloquent and, it seemed, a gentleman in every sense of the word.

In the cool of the Darwin Club potted palms lay scattered among the cane chairs. Passing VB a large, cold beer AQ settled back to talk about Dartim Shipping Pty Ltd. The company had been around only six months. Its principal business was a small 300-ton general cargo ship, *Melva*, which operated between Darwin and East Timor, a Portuguese colony some four hundred miles north-west of Darwin. As AQ talked VB calculated in the back of his mind that opportunities locally for such a vessel would have to be limited. Being a conventional ship *Melva* required deep water to berth, and there were no wharf facilities other than Darwin on the entire Northern Territory coast. Territory waters were tidal and shallow. The low-lying shore stretched for over a thousand miles and besides the odd makeshift buffalo or crocodile shooters' camp, the only real communities were the few Aboriginal missions and government-run Aboriginal settlements. These were served by luggers which beached to unload, lying cockeyed on their sides at low tide. *Melva* could not do that. But as AQ explained, Dartim also had a few agencies to look after, the main one being Timor Oil Ltd, a company exploring for oil in East Timor. Again VB did some calculations and had to wonder why, with a staff of one lady to do the paperwork and a young fellow to do the legwork, such a modest outfit required another manager.

As if in answer to VB's thoughts, AQ said, 'And of course I'm in and out of town a lot, which is why I need you to manage the place. In fact I'm leaving in ten days. I'll be interested to see how you go with the locals. Territorians are a special breed, you know.'

VB had to agree. From what he'd seen Territorians *were* a special breed. Darwin seemed very much a man's town, where the male residents fostered the image of tough, hard-working, hard-drinking blokes with steel-capped boots, short shorts and blue singlets. The real Territorian displayed rather a grim satisfaction at having endured many a hardship and setback and regarded those who preferred to live in the south as soft. (VB had the opposite view, that the climate in the south was the more difficult to endure.) Even their language exhibited something of their determination and understated pride that they didn't let things grind them down. VB learned over time that in the Territory 'a bit of a blow' was a cyclone or gale-force wind and to be 'light on' was to be penniless or destitute. A 'cheeky feller' was often nasty, a 'cranky feller' angry and bad-tempered and a 'sulky feller' usually downright dangerous. His family in Cornwall would scarcely have believed that the Northern Territory, an area five and a half times the size of Great Britain, had a population of only nineteen thousand whites (including some two thousand part Aborigines)[1] and an estimated sixteen thousand full-blood Aborigines. Darwin itself, the largest town, was home to only ten thousand people.

The fact was that the history of the Northern Territory had served to weed out those who could not cope with privation and asperity, and had left a hard core of great Aussie battlers. Territorians had always been tough. They had to be, for Darwin had been devastated at least twice in its short history. In 1897 the struggling settlement had been almost obliterated by a cyclone, and the fruit of twenty-five years of back-breaking labour in appalling conditions was destroyed in two short hours. Since then Darwin had weathered one or two other 'blows' which had left the town a mess of twisted wreckage, but it had taken World War II to really give the residents another nasty kick in the strides, to devastate the town all over again.

It was another source of pride for Darwinites that they really knew what war felt like, for theirs was the only city in Australia to have been seriously and repeatedly attacked by a hostile power. Four days after the fall of Singapore in 1942, the residents of Darwin, a town alone on the doorstep of an Asia under siege, had but one minute's warning of impending disaster. When the air-raid warning belatedly sounded that February morning, the harbour had been crowded with ships, US and Australian flags hanging limply from their masts in the humidity. The first bombs targeted the wharf area, raining death and destruction on the wharf and naval vessels, clustering like solemn, grey, sitting ducks. The attack was deadly accurate. With little opposition, the Japanese squadron bombed the RAAF base and the main town centre with devastating effect, killing around two hundred and forty people,

---

[1] *In 1957 official government statistics counted part Aborigines as whites.*

and injuring between three hundred and four hundred people.
The post office and telegraph office were annihilated and the
communication with the southern states neatly severed. A procession of people fled Darwin on foot or in heavily loaded vehicles
of every conceivable type. The one road that led south, 'the
Track', was packed with cars, trucks, bicycles, rickshaws, push-
carts and even, as the official Royal Commissioner later reported,
municipal sanitary carts. That first attack was by far the worst,
but on a further sixty-three occasions over the next twenty-one
months, the Japanese attacked the town from bases in Timor,
Ambon and the Celebes in an effort to subdue the Australian
defence from assaulting them in their new territory to the north.

When those residents who had fled south returned after the war
they found Darwin still a shambles. Bomb craters pock-marked the
streets, Chinatown had been razed, twisted steel and debris lay in
heaps, the harbour was scattered with the hulks of sunken ships
and their houses had been looted. But inherent in the character of
the Territorian was a willingness to have another go. The locals
were no strangers to adversity and disappointment, and life in the
postwar years wasn't easy. It was said of Darwin that its economy
was based on the export of empty bottles and full public servants,
not the ideal base on which to rebuild once again. Virtually every
industry that either government or private enterprise had tried to
establish over the years had proved disappointing. A ship from
Singapore visited Darwin for subsidy rather than cargo and other
shipping services were irregular. It was not uncommon for the
town to run out of beer and when a ship carrying beer kegs berthed
at Stokes Hill the wharfies were inevitably moved to unheard of
activity in their haste to provide drought relief to the town, in the
hotels of which the perishing regulars sat dismally sipping at their
'plonk'.

The reconstruction of Darwin had again been a painfully slow
process. In 1958 when VB arrived, Darwin was thirteen years into
its lengthy postwar struggle to lift itself above its unflattering reputation as the country's fundamental orifice. That attempts at beau-
tifying the town had been almost non-existent was not surprising

considering that Darwin had not had a Town Council for some twenty years; it had been disbanded when the military took over. At the end of the war the long-suffering residents endured for a further twelve years the agonising machinations of a Town Management Board before the Darwin Municipality was finally reconstituted. In 1958 the fledgling council was just getting onto its feet and beginning to take an interest.

Though governments had been united in their efforts to increase the quantity of life in Darwin, the quality of life received little consideration, for Territorians had a severe lack of political clout. VB was not impressed, and he wrote to Barbara in Sydney, where she was now staying, 'The Northern Territory is treated like a colony. The people must be the only Australian citizens without a vote or at least without a voice in the government of the country. The one federal representative is only allowed to speak on matters directly connected with the Territory.' He was amazed at this state of affairs, and he had only just arrived. Yet some Territorians had endured forty-seven years of this 'political robbery'. They had heard all the promises from visiting Commonwealth representatives and had seen little change. They still felt themselves exiles in their own country, at least in the eyes of the great south. Understandably they had chips on their sunburned shoulders. And understandably they'd had a gutful of big talkers from out of town.

VB sat down to read the latest edition of the twice-weekly missive from Barbara. He knew AQ was in Sydney, and wondered whether he'd looked her up as he said he would. A glance at the first line gave him his answer.

> *What is this male! I can't make head or tail of him—he's either extraordinarily honest or the biggest poseur I've met in years. At the moment I'm having difficulty even thinking about it because I am suffering from what should be called a hangover, only it's the wrong end of the day. On our first meeting I got his life story with not one grain of modesty in the whole recital— plus future plans as far as they concern himself becoming Mayor*

*of Darwin and Japanese Consul. He has such enormous confidence
in his own rightness it makes me feel almost apologetic for him.
Can he really be so sure of himself or is it a facade to cover
something else? Perhaps you, being male, are more enlightened
as to his true character. If so, please write soon as I am most
puzzled!*

Her extraordinary weekend had begun with an invitation from AQ
for a drink at the Australia Hotel at 5.30pm on the Friday. 'How
will I know you?' she'd asked.

'I'm about six feet tall and built to match,' he replied. 'I've just
shaved off my moustache and I'm generally considered quite good
looking.'

With a description like that she imagined she couldn't have missed
him, but she did, and had to locate him through the head waiter.
Cocktails turned into an expensive dinner at the Caprice Restaurant,
followed on Saturday with a full day at the races and another
extended dinner. By the end of it all Barbara was exhausted, and
a little concerned. An incident over dinner at Sydney's smart
Chelsea Restaurant a few days later did nothing to lessen her dis-
quiet. During the course of the evening AQ's manner and diction
were impeccable and although he quaffed an enormous amount of
alcohol he showed no sign of intoxication, that is until Barbara
unwittingly admired the silver coffee service. 'Would you like it
my dear? I'll buy it for you,' he declared. Acutely embarrassed,
there was nothing she could say to dissuade him and she watched,
mortified, as loud negotiations ensued with the manager over the
price. Finally he wrote out a cheque for three hundred pounds,
whereupon the manager conspicuously packed up the service in a
box and handed it over.

In the stone cold sober light of day AQ must have had second
thoughts about his purchase, for this was the last Barbara heard of
the coffee service and it was never mentioned in conversation again.
She later heard that he took it with him in the box when he travelled,
and had his coffee served out of it wherever he stayed.

When VB heard about all this he was amused. 'Don't worry

about him,' he told Barbara. 'All that proves is that underneath his bluster he's a good-hearted soul.' He'd already learned a little of AQ's generosity around town, although not from AQ, for he hadn't seen him since he left. AQ had promised to return to Darwin within a fortnight. In fact it was to be six months before he reappeared, and in the meantime VB carried on alone, occasionally getting hold of him on the telephone or receiving instructions through the mail. As the weeks went by VB learned more of his boss, that he was known also for the way in which he dealt with recalcitrant wharfies. AQ had agonised over the slowness of the Darwin waterside workers—after all, one couldn't run a ship that way in Hong Kong. When on at least two occasions charm and perfect manners failed to impress, he had produced a pistol from his pocket and brandished it in the general direction of the source of his anguish. Apparently it had the desired effect.

There was much about Darwin that VB found agreeable. The climate had been very well behaved after Melbourne and he was still convinced that this neglected backwater of a place would one day get going. Darwin should have been pleasant, as it was built upon an attractive, narrow peninsula in an enormous harbour. From the main wharf right out to the entrance to the harbour the coast was fringed with mottled cliffs in white, pink, and ochre, burnished-gold beaches and rocky outcrops. The fact that Darwin wasn't pleasant to look at was due to poor administration rather than any inherent flaws in the geography. VB saw the problem as the itinerant nature of the public servants, who came to Darwin for a handsomely paid two-year stint and were more interested in the promotion they'd receive on returning to the south than in improving the aesthetics of the place or the welfare of its permanent population.

But to VB the most pleasing feature of Darwin was its proximity to South East Asia. The island of Timor, which provided Dartim with so much business, was only a short haul to the north. To the west the fascinating islands of Indonesia sprawled across several seas. His beloved Singapore was only five days' steaming away. The people who lived in the southern parts of Australia talked about the isolation of the north. To VB however, they were the ones who were isolated. They were isolated from the rest of the world, while Darwin was on the doorstep of Asia.

> *Whirlies of dust from the red-brown laterite road swirl past the front door, tossing up leaves and dried grass and fallen bougainvillea flowers in a mad fandango. It is the beginning of the most oppressive season of the year, the build-up to the Wet, and the sky is a heat haze of soft grey. The sea opposite is brilliant turquoise patterned with dark indigo. Around the cottage the long grass has dried to a brittle, heat-seared gold. A frangipani peers stiffly around the corner of the front door, the waxy, startling white flowers sitting delicately on the end of elephantine stems. A dun-olive casuarina tree grows on the beach in the sand, and its crown waves wildly above the cliff top at the slightest breeze.*

Barbara gazed out of the window of the tiny, blue-painted, one-bedroomed shack on the Nightcliff seafront as she wrote. It was the first week in October 1958 and the best accommodation VB had been able to find was modest indeed. When the sea was rough the waves crashed on the cliffs, the salt spray forced its way through the louvres, and they slept under an umbrella.

Arriving in Darwin from Sydney Barbara had found VB suntanned and as usual too full of life and enthusiasm. He was working a standard nine-to-five day, the shortest hours he'd worked for years, and the Dartim office was sociably located at the Darwin Club, facing Mitchell Street in town, where no end of people seemed to drop in for a chat.

VB had been befriended by one Group Captain Arthur Harrison of the Royal Australian Air Force, who seemed to be constantly around the Perkins' cottage. 'Stripper' Harrison had got his nickname as an engineer with the RAAF during World War II, commanding an Airfield Construction Squadron responsible for building airstrips in Australia and South East Asia. A few years VB's senior, Stripper was described by Barbara at the time as intelligent, moderate, kind, sophisticated, reasonably good-looking though inclined to bags under the eyes, and a complete gentleman.

It was Stripper Harrison who introduced VB to the 'society' of

Darwin, the pinnacle of which were the bank managers, who lived in the nicest houses and were most sought after for dinner parties. At first VB was regarded with some suspicion as he was considered 'trade'. But Darwin was a little short of good stock and couldn't afford to be too particular, and before long invitations to polite little Sunday morning gatherings began to arrive. Being a small town, the conversation generally included a degree of gossip. The ladies vied with each other in the fashion stakes, for dressing up was a form of escapism for women who were often bored and had little in the way of amenities to make life easier. Darwin was as formal as the southern cities and an invitation to the seven-gabled Government House, perched on the cliff above the wharves, called for hats and elbow-length gloves. Occasionally there was a major function, such as the opening of the new Fannie Bay Hotel, where big wigs and little wigs forgathered, tripping over each other in riotous confusion. VB much preferred the Officers' Mess at the RAAF.

Darwin's formality didn't extend far outside this realm. In the public domain entertainment and culture extended only as far as the Star Picture Theatre in Smith Street, where at interval cockroaches could usually be spotted running down the aisles with the Jaffas. The theatre was a great favourite among the Aborigines who came into town from the settlements and cattle stations, and on Western night it was always packed. The alternatives for dining out were equally limited, as Barbara lamented.

Though the food is poor, the Darwin Hotel is probably the most elegant (although that hardly describes it) because it has white tablecloths. The Don Hotel has a Chinese cafe which turns out very good food in most insalubrious surroundings; the Seabreeze varies, depending upon who is doing the cooking; the Olympia, run by a thin Italian man and a buxom Italian woman, makes superb Italian food, though it sometimes feels like dining in a little Napoli of bare Italian knees and hairy chests to the music of inhaled spaghetti; the Latin has a number of tables set in the back yard where it is pleasantly cool, and is quite agreeable if

one can get a table far enough away and upwind of the gentle-
man's lavatory; and there are one or two absolute impossibilities
with neither food nor surroundings of any merit.

VB's nine-to-five days were not destined to last long, and by the
end of 1958 a thing called the Humpty Doo Rice Development
Scheme had ended them absolutely. The agricultural project had
been launched several years earlier on such a large scale that it had
captured the national interest.

There had been many such agriculture projects in the Territory
and they had almost all failed, thwarted by physical isolation, transport difficulties and the nature of the country. Memories dulled
quickly, however, and the Humpty Doo rice project was hailed as
'the future granary for South East Asia'. Darwin was close to the
overseas markets where ninety per cent of the world's rice was
consumed. Much of this rice was produced in countries under
Communist control and to the backers of the project, headed by
an enthusiastic American, Allen T. Chase, the apparently ideal rice-
producing country on free land in a democratic country had sounded
too good to be true.

Stripper Harrison had got the rice bug when the heavy earth
moving equipment of the RAAF Airfield Construction Squadron
was called in to construct the first dam for irrigation in 1956–57.
The idea was that land would not be leased to private farmers until
the first company, Territory Rice Ltd, had proved the scheme's
viability. But Stripper had pulled a few strings and managed to
secure the five hundred acres used for the original CSIRO pilot
scheme, a plot close to the Adelaide River with independent
irrigation.

Stripper's duties with the RAAF were ever demanding and since
he couldn't manage the plot on his own, he'd asked VB if he was
interested. VB agreed to look at it and they drove the seventeen
miles down the bitumen and twenty-one miles east on the dirt to
the cattle station where it all began, where a flat, black-soil plain
stretched for thousands of acres and water was available from the
permanently flowing Adelaide River. In the wet season the fine

soil turned into a sodden, sticky mire, difficult for cattle but seemingly perfect for rice. To VB it all sounded very promising. Leagues of scientific and agricultural types were involved and they were all making laudatory noises about it. He'd seen it done before—simple country folk in Malaya and Siam grew rice easily. They had no backing from multi-millionaires or Commonwealth scientific bodies, and produced magnificent crops very successfully. It didn't look like a difficult business and he agreed to take it on. A small company was then set up under an agreement whereby the Perkins team would do most of the work involved, in return for a one-third share of the crop, if any. Stripper would fund the first year.

Life in the Perkins camp from then on became dominated by rice, rice and more rice. The cottage was scattered with pans of water and blotting paper, and each day VB and Barbara peered at the germination tests, willing the rice grains to burst heartily forth from their fawny jackets. For the most part the rice obliged and in ninety-eight per cent of cases bright green, healthy shoots emerged.

In the last half of November 1958 the first fifty acres had to be deep ploughed, disced and planted, all out of office hours. Stripper was around to assist but a three-month posting to the south loomed and VB would be on his own for the first crucial wet season. The theory was that the normal wet season rainfall would take care of the first few months, then for the last month before harvest the *padis* would be irrigated.

As luck would have it all did not go well. Far from being able to forget the rice crop for a few months and leave it all to Jupiter Pluvius, the usual black stormclouds appeared only infrequently over Humpty Doo. The 1958–59 wet season was unusually dry and the high evaporation rate sucked the moisture from the black soil nurturing the thirsty shoots. VB installed irrigation pumps from the outset and kept them going twenty-four hours a day. Thus began the daily grind of driving the thirty-five or so miles each way, largely on a dirt track, to refuel, oil and grease the pumps. On a good day the round trip took two and a half hours, with either a 5am start or a 9pm finish. After a few weeks of this VB

hired a fellow named Tom to help out. He was looking forward
to his first day off for months but when Sunday came, Tom turned
up on the doorstep to announce he'd been thrown out of camp at
Humpty Doo.

Tom had not been hired for his manners or tact and on his second
day on the job he'd had a fight in the camp workshop, the lead up
to which Barbara noted in a letter to her parents.

> Tom approaches a fellow bending over his work and says 'Give
> us a light mate.'
> No response.
> 'Can you give us a light mate!'
> Still nothing.
> Tom (very loudly) 'Oi!'
> The fellow looks up questioningly.
> 'I said can you give us a light you deaf bastard!'
> Although the course of the conversation is about average in
> this part of the world, unfortunately this particular gentleman
> was deaf, and somewhat touchy about it. Rumour has it that he
> was also a bastard. So they ups and into it, and eventually Tom
> was run off the place. We are once more attending to the pumps
> ourselves.

While her sense of humour was still intact, Barbara was finding
conditions very trying. Unlike VB the constant heat seemed to sap
her energy and there was little escape from it. A dip in the sea was
now out of the question since it was seawasp season, and swimming
pools were a rare luxury in Darwin. Things were not going well
at Dartim and she'd taken over the paperwork in the office. With
that and the frequent trips to Humpty Doo there seemed no time
for anything but work. She missed being in the bush, when they
were all in their camp-beds by 9pm. She missed the time when
dinner could be as simple as opening a can of corned beef and
heating it over a fire. She missed the fun she and Pop had washing
the clothes in a running stream, in the shade of a river gum with
their toes dug into the clean sand of the McArthur River. She
looked forward to a time when they could afford one of those

agitator things for clothes washing, to reduce the hot hours she spent plunging and scrubbing over the tubs at the cottage. She commented to her mother that she now worked full time and as well did the same work as two *amahs* plus a cook and herself had done in Malaya, in something of the same climate. And she was also worried about AQ.

'Don't worry me with trifles now, dear boy. I shall look into that later.' VB put the phone down, frustrated. The bank account was looking grim, it was the end of the year and AQ had visited Darwin only once, and then only for a day or two. For the first six months VB had been tolerant of his errant nature, and made excuses for him to everyone. AQ *was* finding business for Dartim, but his frequent withdrawals from the company's bank account from places such as Sydney's Double Bay and Queensland's Gold Coast were making life difficult for him. The business was ticking along nicely yet there never seemed to be enough money left over to pay the bills. Fending off creditors was not at all VB's thing.

Worse was to come, and early in the new year everything went to pot. *Melva* returned to Darwin to load a good cargo, but there was not enough money to pay the crew or the stevedoring and wharfage charges.

'I've told you, old bean,' AQ said, 'I'll be there very shortly to sort out the financial problems, in fact I shall book the fare this morning. Just toddle on as you can and do try not to worry.'

Once more VB was placated. When all seemed lost a telephone conversation with AQ inspired renewed faith in him. He trusted AQ, and to keep things moving he used his own money to pay the crew and other clearance charges to get *Melva* out of port and on her way. Unfortunately, that was the last he was ever to see of his savings.

The next bundle of bills hailing from AQ in the south got no further than VB's desk. There was nothing to pay them with and phone calls from creditors were getting desperate. Because there was no money for the office girl, Barbara plugged on alone.

AQ didn't show up again until late in January 1959. By then VB could not mistake the fact that whisky was the chink in the armour of this paragon, and that AQ was a periodic and compulsive drinker. It was within his capacity to dry himself out and not take a drop, but then suddenly he'd have a bottle of champagne for breakfast and it was on again. Physically he showed no sign of intoxication and the only clue VB ever had was that he became more magnanimous and prodigal than ever, liberally dispensing money or favours to anyone, particularly attractive females.

The only thing VB could think of to do was to send AQ to sea to dry out. AQ agreed, insisting he take *Melva* to Singapore where he said he had a cargo for her. A week later there was still no word from the vessel and nothing from AQ. The first they heard was through an ex-crew-member, who'd just had a letter from his mate Bluey aboard *Melva* in Singapore, the details of which Barbara noted.

Taking everything with a grain of salt, everything that could possibly happen has happened. The skipper got lost between Timor and Singapore and steamed for two days without knowing where they were; they arrived in Singapore and off-loaded cargo at Pulau Bukon since when they have been sitting out in the Eastern Roads waiting for a return cargo; AQ has disappeared ashore and no-one has seen him for days; there is no money and no food aboard; the mate has threatened to kill the cook; the cook called the Master a bungling, incompetent b———; the cook went to the police and complained about the mate; the police came aboard but not before the mate had rammed the police launch with Melva's *tender; the police bound over the mate while the cook and the rest of the crew are not allowed ashore. Since AQ has disappeared there does not appear to be a return cargo and the ship's agents are owed five thousand pounds and the ship is now in hock until it is paid. In the meantime AQ is still apparently drawing money through the Hong Kong account and there is nothing with which to run the office in Darwin. Bruce is most disappointed as he wanted to see AQ make a real go of it and confound the critics, but I am afraid he's left it too late to retrieve the situation. Bruce has not paid himself any salary for*

*some time and everyone to whom AQ owes money are panicky
and credit is getting tight.*

VB had always understood that Mr Aitken-Quack *was* Dartim
Shipping, a company registered in Hong Kong. But on 4 March
1959, a letter arrived from a Dartim board member indicating that
in fact AQ was only the company's managing agent. Extracts read:

> *. . . we want nothing further to do with AQ . . . most obvious
> that the situation has been brought about by waste, extravagance
> and almost criminal negligence spending money on outrageous
> high living and pleasure . . . bottomless well of champagne and
> self indulgence . . . save what is left and make a fresh
> start . . . Dartim Hong Kong directors ready to resign . . . would
> like to reorganise along proper lines . . . can personally assure
> you that your stocks are high in the reorganisation and a good
> situation will be offered.*

The revelations shocked VB, but he was immensely relieved that
someone else was taking an interest in the affairs of Dartim. A
fortnight later when a shareholder appeared and promptly assumed
responsibility for many of AQ's debts, he felt even better. On 23
March, Barbara wrote,

> *At the moment everything is in a state of chaos, with legal advice
> being taken left, right, and centre, gentlemen with assorted Powers
> of Attorney rushing hither and yon and peering deeply into affairs,
> and Bruce not knowing whether he's on his head or his heels
> trying to help everyone at once and as usual forgetting himself.
> It's all most amusing, except that we are flat broke.*

In her letters home Barbara put on a brave face for the sake of
her parents. In reality she was not feeling very brave at all. Their
savings were gone, the future was uncertain, she felt low and
disheartened. VB was talking about making a go of it on their own
but she wondered how they could do it with absolutely nothing to
start with. VB had done his dough, but his seemingly irrepressible
optimism remained.

In fact VB was a bit excited. Working for AQ, it would have been difficult for VB to do anything for himself without causing some hurt to AQ. For all his foibles, VB still could not help but like the man and was sad for AQ that he'd made such a hash of it. But now AQ was out of the picture and VB had no ties. When the bank manager suggested they could take the office furniture and typewriter as part of what they were owed it sounded better than he had dared hope for. Together they lugged the desks along the dusty concrete verandah of the Darwin Club and into a vacant office further along the row. Barbara made a makeshift sign out of the lid of a wooden box and banged it up on the door: 'VB Perkins & Co'. 'I'm the "& Co",' she said firmly.

Suddenly they were in business for themselves.

NINETEEN

Bent Khaki Shorts

I f the local newspaper was anything to go by the gentleman of impeccable breeding was still the talk of the town. 'They're all Sore at Achin-Core', read the headline, and another referred to AQ as 'The Get it Done Man'. In the back of his mind VB wondered how his association with AQ would augur as he tried to start a business on his own. It was comforting to hear local businessman Roley Ryan stand up and make a public speech at the bar of the Darwin Club one evening in April 1959. 'I just want you to know, Bruce, that we reckon you've had a pretty raw deal and a rough nine months. I'm right behind you and I'll be glad to see such a good bloke getting onto his feet. In fact if you need a couple of thousand to tide you over then it's all right by me.' There was a chorus of approval from onlookers. It was a difficult time, but such words of support eased any doubts in VB's mind that he really could make a go of it.

VB Perkins & Co, set up as a partnership between VB and Barbara, described itself as 'Shipping, Mining and General Agents', a name designed to cover just about anything that might come up. For a few days absolutely nothing did but then VB landed the Timor Oil agency, the work which became the life support in the first couple of years, and the little enterprise got off the ground. That year Timor Oil began a drilling program in East Timor, generating extra work and a guaranteed steady income. In theory the Timor Oil agency should have been a straightforward business of overseeing the shipping of supplies ordered from Sydney through Darwin to Timor. But in fact it was the 'small' shopping orders from Timor which kept them on the go: Jack Mitchell wants something for stopping radiator leaks; Dunbar needs some spare parts and a couple of awkward-sized spanners; Col Smith needs some drugs for his allergy; we're running short of fresh meat—can you send some airfreight on the *Dili Dove*; is there anything that will get rust out of clothes; Ike dropped his watch in the drink and it needs mending; can you fix up something to use in the drill-rig seals until the proper ones arrive; we forgot to order the drill collars—get them here— quickly! With the rice in the early morning or late evening, the days were becoming very long, but there was always time off at night for sleeping. At least, until Alex Jamieson gave them the agency for his cattle shipments.

The prospect inspired romantic ideas; notions of chuffing down to the wharf to be first up the gangway (apart from the customs officer) with a briefcase tucked under one arm, to be greeted by the ship's captain attired in long whites, a button-up jacket and neat tie, and having produced all the ship's papers out of the briefcase, being free to sit in the deep cool of the captain's cabin, sipping long, tinkling *parfits* or *stengahs*. If only it had really been like that.

At 0630 hours on a cool May morning VB and Barbara watched, relieved, as their first completed cattle shipment slipped away from Fort Hill Wharf. The sun peeped over the top of the East Arm mangroves, the cattle pens and races lay empty on the wharf and a sudden, unreal quiet fell over everything. There had been no tinkling *parfits* before the ship sailed, just the customs clearance and a strong brew of coffee. In the last four days sleep had been a rare thing for VB, and by now any romantic conceptions about the cattle business had dissipated as surely as the manure slick left in the ship's wake.

Cattle carriers are not glamour ships and the *San Miguel* was awkward-looking and malodorous. The captain who greeted them was middle-aged and fat. A pair of bent khaki shorts held up his corporation, his wrinkled shirt was open and he wore his shoes with no socks. He was not what Barbara had in mind, but he was friendly enough and she was consoled a little by the sight of the Chinese first and second officers who looked more the part in long white trousers and white shoes.

VB's mornings had started at 2am for three days running, as he'd met the trains and counted heads as the cattle were unloaded. Loading day was long, yet there were not nearly enough hours in it. Jamieson had assured them that it wouldn't take more than four hours to load twelve hundred head of cattle, but Jamieson was an optimist. While VB co-ordinated topside, Jamieson worked feverishly below decks all day, his eyes glazed with enthusiasm and fatigue. By 5pm Jamieson's overalls were split right down the leg and by 10pm he'd collapsed on the deck and was rushed the few blocks to the Darwin Hospital, where an X-ray showed a fractured patella, courtesy five hours earlier of a large grey bull.

It was 1.30am by the time everything was done, cattle races pulled away from the ship's side, gates closed, final tally completed, and the captain asked VB and Barbara to have a beer with him. By now he'd put away so much he was feeling morbid, that he was too fat and ugly for his age, that no-one loved him and that he was destined for a lonely life at sea with a lot of filthy beasts. When he farted accidentally it was as if his world had fallen in on him. He looked mortified and while Barbara flushed and looked away, VB did his bit towards consoling him. 'Better an empty house,' he said soothingly, 'than an evil tenant.'

The allure of the cattle business had faded, but at least it paid some bills. Not so the enterprise down the track at Humpty Doo. After the dry wet season, the heavens opened up. In the April of 1959, fifteen inches of rain dumped upon the rice *padis* in twenty-four hours. For weeks VB couldn't get a vehicle close to his plot, and waded through deep, black sludge to get in. The pump disappeared in the murk to be rescued only when the flood receded to knee deep. The crop was damaged, the ground was a bog, the harvest was delayed. The rice stems weakened and couldn't support the ripe heads. Many fell to the ground. Then a blanket of black and white descended. The area was the traditional breeding ground for magpie geese and the birds couldn't believe their luck. They'd found the rice grains excellent tucker when sown and the sprouting seedlings the tenderest of morsels. Now the rice was mature and it was a goose's heaven.

The crop was a disaster for Territory Rice. Germination rates were low and cattle broke through the fences. Despite the deluge, Harrison Dam never filled, there was trouble with the pumps, lightning set fire to the power substation and water management was a nightmare. The Harrison–Perkins crop didn't break even, but it had a higher yield than either Territory Rice or the government crops. Since VB had nothing to lose except some sleep and what little spare time he had, he decided with Stripper to give it another go.

VB was quite chuffed with the idea of becoming a father. It was probably about time—after all, he'd be forty-seven—and though he'd never had any interest in children he thought having one of his own might be a good thing, as long as it didn't yell too much. For Barbara, the unplanned pregnancy was a shock. Deep down she was delighted because she really did want children, but how they would fit into their present life she couldn't fathom. She had been married to VB almost six years and had loved every minute of it. But life was more difficult now they were so bogged down with work. It was all she could do to keep up with her husband's pace. VB was in great demand socially and his long working hours didn't deter him from accepting invitations or from inviting people for dinner unexpectedly, and often. His enthusiasm for life was infectious, but there were still the chores to be done.

VB's bush-learned culinary skill with bacon and eggs and ability to knock up a pot of tea (of good colour) ended his domestic pursuits absolutely. Everything else he considered women's work. He had an expression which he delivered with a wink and a grin,

'It's no use keeping a dog and barking yourself.' But even he realised that things were not the same as they were.

In December 1959 his thoughts wandered back to the old days as he wrote to his mother:

> I'd like to get over to Borneo at some juncture. Northern Australia has plenty of prospects but it is a hard place to live, even for a tropical bird like me. I'd trade all the washing machines and cooking gadgets in the world for the services of my old cook and amah. I resent all the time Barbara spends on what I call the mere mechanics of living, when there are so many more important and more pleasant things to do.

For Barbara the heat was trying but she coped with their less than ideal situation. She enjoyed VB's company immensely and all she wanted was to be beside him. He was the centre of her existence and the sunshine of her day and night. She knew that nothing would change as long as she could be freely available to follow him and do whatever he wanted to do, but she wondered how, when the child was born, she would ever be able to do that. And there was one thing she knew for certain. He wouldn't change his ways to accommodate her, or a family.

There were no votes in Darwin. From the south it was seen as a frontier settlement, a man's town, and no-one from the government was concerned about making conditions easier for its residents. The town sewerage system wasn't yet complete and there were still dunny cans and outdoor loos in the city blocks. Few complained. Some even found their outdoor dunny a salvation. VB's friend George bemoaned to him that while he was down the track with his truck trying to make a quid, his wife and her hangers-on sat around for hours in his donga (demountable house) drinking his beer. His dunny, which because of the large consumption of liquid was in great demand, sat on a slight slope facing Daly Street in full view of the traffic on the main road into town. He'd spoken to VB about his idea of chopping the door off, making it unusable to all but the most stout-hearted. Later VB heard of the outcome of the plan. Apparently it had worked like a charm.

In the meantime, unless the forthcoming small Perkins was to live permanently on the dining table at the shack at Nightcliff, they had to find somewhere else to live. Months of looking turned up nothing and Barbara found it wasn't only houses that were hard to come by. Many basic household necessities were simply not available to buy in the shops, and life was difficult for women. Each time a family packed up to move to the south a scramble ensued for anything going. One friend was sent by his wife to a 'moving south sale' with instructions to buy a bedstead to elevate their mattress from the floor. He came home with a pool table instead and his wife caught the next plane out of town, never to return. The heat and the trying conditions in Darwin broke many marriages.

The house that became known as 'Perkinsville' wasn't much, but when it came onto the market at a reasonable price, VB grabbed it. He liked the half-built dwelling in Mitchell Street West because it was close to the office and the wharves, and he had the idea of eventually reverting to one of the ways he'd learned in the East: to come home each day at lunch for a shower, a rest and a change of his cotton shirt, which he always wore with the collar turned up to keep the sun off. The reality was that there was rarely time for a rest and Barbara—now amongst many other things, the *dhobi amah*—objected to VB changing his shirts as often as he used to do in Malaya.

Perkinsville was similar in design to most government houses on stilts, except that it had a large, split-level living area that wasn't yet built. Barbara returned from a short break in Melbourne, eight months pregnant, to find the house VB had bought in her absence had a ladder up one side for stairs, a couple of burners for a stove, no fans and no internal doors. VB's intention was to complete it himself, at some stage, eventually, when he had time. But with VB Perkins & Co and Harrison's all-consuming rice, time was not forthcoming and progress was slow.

In March 1960 Barbara presented a tiny pink bundle to its father in the maternity ward of the old Darwin hospital. VB was a little

*'What's the press saying about it…?' With Special Branch Chief Bill Humble,
Kuantan, 1955.*

The house on the riverbank at Kuantan, 1954.

Breakfast on the track, Simpson Desert, South Australia, 1957.

'Um…there's a crocodile tied up outside our tent.' Inspecting it with Harry Blumenthal the next morning, Borroloola, 1957.

'If it's good enough for the mission fraternity…' Setting out to explore the east coast of Arnhem Land from Rose River Mission, 1957.

Amusing the girls at Rose River Mission, 1957.

Barbara running out the winch cable, Arnhem Land, 1957.

Cooling off in the RAAF Base pool, Darwin, 1963. From left: *Barbara, Antony, Mandy and VB.*

Rolling drums by hand, offloading Hawk *at an Aboriginal settlement.*

'Somebody's sitting on my paper...' With Penelope, 1981.

Warrender *holding on in the surf at Mena, West Timor.*

VB with Joss at a St John's Investiture, 1988.

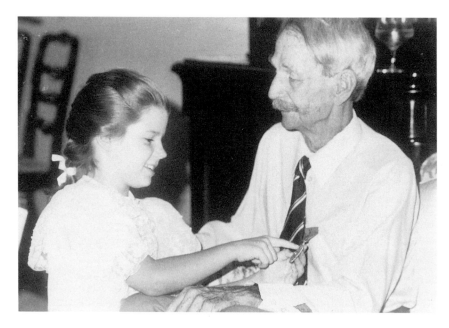

Penelope inspecting Daddy's Order of Australia medal after the ceremony, 1989.

Aboard Frances Bay *in Darwin*. From left: *Antony, VB and Mandy, 1992.*

awed, but pleased and proud and the occasion inspired him to conceive of a name for me which touched on his sentiment for the old days. He came up with 'Mandalay', for it was redolent of Burma and the Far East, yet his heritage suggested something Cornish might be appropriate. He'd lost his virginity in a little Cornish village called Tregony and he rather liked that too. Barbara was a bit horrified by his inventions, and VB suggested 'Mandaley', which to him still had a fragrance of the Old East. Despite her protests he called me Mandy from then on.

After a few days at home and when she'd become a little more confident about the baby business, my mother began popping into the office with me as she could. Before long the little piece of concrete floor under the office fan was second home for my basket, and the sound of the typewriter as comforting as any lullaby.

The suspicion that the Territory was never going to float off to fame and prosperity in a rice *padi* had been sneaking up on VB for some time. Now it pounced. The 1959–60 rice crop was better than the previous year but damage by magpie geese, water management, variable seed quality and weed infestation took their toll. Then there was the Territory's ever-present *bête noire* to contend with: getting the product to market. The North Australian Railway couldn't provide a direct service to the southern states, since it stopped before it got very far. Haulage south by road was difficult in the Wet due to floods. Shipping in bulk over the main wharf was fraught with difficulties; it was expensive to charter a ship for small irregular shipments yet there was no regular shipping service to export markets in South East Asia. There were also enormous problems on Darwin Wharf. In 1960, while in Hong Kong it took twenty-four hours to unload three thousand tonnes of bagged rice, the wharfies in Darwin took twelve days to load it, blowing out the transport costs again. VB was disgusted. The financiers of Territory Rice bailed out and the company went into liquidation. The nationally promoted Humpty Doo Rice Development Scheme, the Territory's biggest ever agricultural project, had failed.

Stripper Harrison, however, was nothing if not game and VB

was an optimist. Their crop had almost broken even that year and they decided to try again—just once more. A few other small-scale farmers did the same. They shouldn't have.

The 1960–61 crop was once again only fair. Just before the harvest, two hundred head of cattle broke through the fences and trampled the crop into the ground. VB was exasperated and the Harrison–Perkins team finally closed the chapter on Humpty Doo bloody rice.

Since the war in the Pacific the tides had ebbed and flowed in Darwin Harbour to reveal glimpses of the rusted hulks of ships that came to a tragic end during the Japanese airborne attacks of 1942. The rights to the roughly twenty thousand tons of scrap steel in the wrecks were owned by local resident and deep-sea diver, Carl Atkinson. In 1960 he sold them to the Tokyo based Fujita Salvage Company and some of Darwin's residents were outraged. The town resounded to cries of protest about the Japanese benefiting from wrecks they had made the graves of so many Australians and Americans.

When the Japanese salvage teams arrived a furore broke out. There were some ugly scenes in the town. The only Australian War Crimes Trials to be held in Australia had taken place in Darwin soon after the war, and Darwinites had long memories. Sentiments ran high in the pubs and after a few beers many a man claimed he was ready to 'slit the throats of the little yellow bastards'. In the interest of the safety of the Japanese workers the administration was forced to confine them to the wharf area.

VB was appalled by this state of affairs. If anyone had a right to hold a grudge against the Japanese he did, but he felt that the war was over, what was done was done and these civilians should not be held responsible. He felt that it behoved everybody to be at least civil towards them. It was his nature to forget unpleasantness and get on with life and he very much wanted other people to feel the same. He had a habit of taking Barbara and me for a drive on a Sunday morning, what he called 'poking about' to see what was going on. One morning he found himself on Fort Hill Wharf, where a few Japanese were sitting around, relaxing as best they could under such confinement. VB took the opportunity to meet the Japanese again, this time on a more equal platform, and he stopped to talk to them. They chatted at length of the salvage operation, then of their personal lives. One of the men had a daughter of my own age at home and the sight of me brought tears to his eyes. After that VB visited the Japanese on the wharf regularly and on several occasions took them a carton of beer and had a drink with them. It was his way of trying to atone for the conduct of some of the locals, which he regarded as disgraceful.

VB viewed Japan at the time of World War II as an ancient culture bound up in mediaeval beliefs, customs and ethics. He'd seen the strict discipline among the Japanese inspired by harsh military codes and that they too had suffered at the hands of their superiors. He saw the Japanese senior officers beat the Japanese junior officers, who would then beat the Korean guards. It was unfortunate that the POWs happened to be at the end of the line. VB forgave the Japanese, but found it far more difficult to forgive the Germans. That the Western-educated Germans, with so much culture and science and 'civilisation' behind them, could be responsible for the slaughter of so many people in such a fashion was beyond his comprehension. In his eyes, their deeds were far more despicable, and he was never swayed from this conviction.

TWENTY

Five-Pound Perkins

'TEAPOT WITH SPOUT ARRIVED STOP'

It was a brief telegram, but VB was confident the family in Cornwall would get the message about the arrival of his son. Once again he was chuffed about it all. That didn't mean, however, that he'd necessarily become any more of a family man. In his eyes that was fine, but it was something that could always be put off until tomorrow. Nevertheless he'd agreed with Barbara that since they had one child, they ought to have another as company for the first, and Antony Bruce was born in January 1962.

Barbara's days were unremittingly long and it was good fortune that Antony, or 'Boy' as VB called him, was a placid baby who spent most of his first year of life doing little other than sleeping, eating and beaming at everyone. By contrast I was an active child who liked stimulation, and as such had become quickly bored with office life, forcing my mother to part with me to a childcare facility earlier than she felt comfortable with. While she worked in the business as she could, VB offered her little support as far as the family were concerned. He was always interested to hear of our progress and immensely proud of his 'sprogs'. But he believed that children were to be seen and not heard. He liked us to be done up and paraded for guests to admire, but then sent to bed with a pat on the head and no fuss.

VB was approaching fifty, and at an age when many people might have been planning their retirement he had thoughts only of what a lot he wanted to do with his life. In the optimistic climate of the early 1960s, hope for the Territory, dampened by so many previous disappointments, once again re-emerged. Mineral exploration around the top end of the Northern Territory was stepping up and VB nurtured his mining contacts, keeping well abreast of developments. There was an evident air of expectation.

VB had thought long and hard about the problems exploration geologists would have once they became serious about testing their leases around the coast. There were no roads and, except on Aboriginal settlements, there were no airstrips. Landing a drilling rig or bulldozer by sea from a conventional vessel would be a difficult and expensive exercise. Navigational challenges were not new to him and his experience in Malaya gave him a respectable background in the business of shipping in shallow, tidal waters. The opportunities on the Territory coast for the versatile little vessel known as the landingcraft were readily apparent to him.

For some time VB's eye had been on *Loellen M*, a small ex-Australian Army landingcraft described as a dilapidated old rust bucket, though never by VB. She had been operating on the coast of Timor, and though she was nothing very startling, she was available. After a little dickering VB arranged to purchase her from Timor Oil for a modest sum, to be worked off against services rendered by VB Perkins & Co. *Loellen M*, an ALC40 landingcraft,[1] had seen her heyday during World War II, when vessels of her ilk were used for amphibious operations, landing troops and equipment

---

[1] *Sixty-seven feet in length, they had a twenty foot beam and a three and a half foot draft. Three hundred and eighty horsepower hung off their blunt stern and they were capable of eight knots. The hull was of thin flat plate and angle iron, and in their original state the decks were open with no permanent shelter or accommodation. Their propulsion system was usually a Cadillac V8 engine with a reduction gearbox, and if they were built for a one-way mission the only gear was forward. Attached to their rudder was a massive tiller, at the end of which two strong men were required to steer them.*

onto open beaches throughout the Pacific region. The Australian Army had one hundred and twenty-two of them at one stage and, because they were built as 'disposable', some did not survive the war and were left to rust away, scattered on the beaches where they landed. Most never lived to see the late 1950s or early 1960s, but here and there a few relics still survived. *Loellen M* was one of these, having been sold by the army, modified to some extent and put into civilian service.

Her arrival in Darwin was inglorious, towed from Timor by VB's rival-to-be, Ever-ready Ted Fitzgerald. She was in very poor condition, but VB had in mind a rebuild and many modifications, and he took his plans to the banking men. On paper it all looked very good, but when they came down to the wharf to inspect her in the flesh, the bankers took one look and went home. No-one was interested, and in the end it was a family tragedy that financed *Loellen M*'s rebuild. Barbara's mother, to whom she was very close, was killed in a traffic accident and left her share portfolio to be equally divided between her husband and daughter. The nine thousand pounds worth of share certificates arrived in the mail and very soon after the reconstruction began. The old landingcraft was hoisted onto the Boom Wharf with the help of VB's friends from the Fujita Salvage Company and their large floating crane. Over several months *Loellen M* was strengthened structurally and her capacity increased from forty tons to eighty tons deadweight. Her bow door was modified, her sides built up from three to eight feet high and she was re-engined with a couple of second-hand Dorment ex-RAAF generator engines, procured with the help of Stripper Harrison. Crew accommodation was refitted, but remained, shall we say, rudimentary.

VB was convinced that Darwin's public wharf was not where he wanted to be. He'd never resorted to AQ's spirited, pistol-wielding tactics, but he'd felt the same frustration. Darwin Wharf had a reputation for congestion, delays and disputes. Part of the problem lay with the wharf's inadequate infrastructure, but the main problem was wharf labour. Burns Philp employed members of the North Australian Workers Union as stevedores, but only on a casual basis.

Wharf work was slow, hard and stinking hot. Containerisation didn't yet exist and the tropical sun beat down relentlessly into the airless holds of the ships. The sweating wharfies had little mechanical assistance. Safety standards were poor and in general shipowners had little concern for such matters. Wharfies were relatively well paid for the work they did, but since their positions were not permanent they became effectively unemployed after each ship had sailed. The fundamental flaw in this system was that the longer the wharfies could keep a vessel in port, the more money they made. The fact that they had no permanent employment also bred a great distrust of employers and wharf work attracted the militant type of man who had an inbred hatred of the boss.

Just around the corner from the wharf, the eastern side of the peninsula that made up the Darwin town area was not one of Darwin's beauty spots. The foreshore land, owned by North Australian Railways, was a tangle of railway lines, shunting yards and railway sheds. VB had a good poke around the muddy, mangrove-lined beach, and found the strip between the high-tide and low-tide mark met his needs. This land was leased by the North Australian Railway to the pearlers, but there were no pristine, white-painted boats attended by white-suited gentlemen in Panama hats to be seen; their haul was not the precious outcome of an irritated oyster, but mother-of-pearl shell, the lining of which was highly fashionable for buttons and other ornament. There was no glamour in this business. The pearling luggers were usually dirty and often unseaworthy. They returned after days rolling at anchor in the south-east winds, to unload their catch at Frances Bay, beaching awkwardly on their sides on the gooey, grey mud.

Just above high-water mark the pearlers squatted for hour after hour, sorting shells in two old sheds. When VB discovered one of the railway leases was held by a deceased and bankrupt estate he bought the shed, paid the back rental owed and a year's lease in advance. *Loellen M* had few requirements: a smooth bottom to rest upon and enough water at high tide to float her on and off. In due course she was brought around from the wharf to the first operational base of the VB Perkins & Co shipping service: an old, tin, ex-pearling shed half entangled in feathery, green, coffee-bush scrub, and a bit of mud upon which VB had built a makeshift ramp of rocks and bush saplings. And there it all began.

Loellen M was no *femme fatale*. VB looked at her through rose-coloured glasses but even he had to admit that. She was boxy and graceless but she could do the job. A low tank landingcraft, her cargo deck was below the waterline so she was very stable, but difficult to operate. She had been fitted with a set of two watertight doors just inside the bow ramp, secured by around eighty nuts and bolts, all of which had to be undone by hand. If the tide came in whilst she was on a beach with the bow door open, the water flooded the hold and engineroom, effectively sinking her. There were no fo'c'sles or above-deck walkways, and the bow ramp was operated using a hand winch situated aft, just behind the wheel-house. The ballasting system was crude. In theory the tanks under the deck were filled and emptied for ballasting with a portable pump from the deck. In practice this was a tedious business and crews found it easier to use 44-gallon drums filled with sea water, emptied simply by tipping them over on deck so that the water drained back into the engineroom to be pumped out. Hatch covers and tarpaulins kept some of the sea spray out, but if the load was high the hatch covers couldn't be fitted. Under certain load conditions water collected up for'ard, to be drained once again by the trusty portable pump. It was a basic sort of system but it worked reasonably well.

Loellen M began her career with VB Perkins & Co by moving stores and equipment for the few mineral exploration companies working the north coast of the Northern Territory and Western Australia. Her schedule was dictated by the tide. Her skipper made landings wherever equipment was required: on white-sand beaches fringed by sparse sand dunes or tangled coastal vine forest; at clearings in the coastal mangrove belts or on the muddy banks of tidal rivers. Landings were at or near high tide, and the bow door couldn't be opened until low tide, when the glorious texture of the mud was exposed, slimy, soft and at times opalescent with the gases from decaying vegetation, but often concealing jagged rocks or gibbers just beneath its surface.

Navigation up the muddy, tortuous byways of the coast is a slow and cautious business. The saltwater, tidal creeks twist their way through stilt rooted mangroves that sit out of the water as though frozen in time, writhing up, snake-like, from the mud. At low tide saltwater crocodiles bask serenely on the banks, while in a big Wet torrents of seething, frothing water whirl down at a speed of up to eighteen knots with the outgoing tide. Territory seas, never the real blue of the oceans to the south, are clearest in the dry and deep turquoise in colour. In the Wet the water transforms from grey to milky jade to aquamarine and the sea is muddy for miles around the mouths of the gushing rivers. In the dry season the South East Trade Wind blows strongly, and at irregular intervals a windspeed of over twenty-five knots for days at a time makes the sea rough for small craft. During the Wet the sea is calmer in fine weather, and in a depression the steady rain keeps the sea flat. But the top end of Australia hosts some of the most intense and unpredictable electrical storms in the world that still 'frighten the hell' out of even the oldest hands at sea.

Working through heavy surf to beach on unsurveyed shores was difficult and dangerous. The only navigational aids outside Darwin were a slightly updated version of Matthew Flinders' magnificent general chart of the north coast of Australia, a sextant, a leadline and a very sketchy knowledge of tidal patterns. There were no depth sounders and no radars. In rough weather the surf breaking on the beach gave some indication as to where the shallow areas were, but running up onto uncharted reefs, rocks and sandbars was in the nature of the work. The stresses on VB's landingcraft were great and, to his profound regret, maintenance costs were horrific.

It wasn't uncommon. *Loellen M* was loaded and ready to leave for Groote Eylandt but for an engine problem. The cashflow was down to critical and the fact that BHP paid promptly—fifteen hundred pounds when *Loellen M* left port and the balance on her return— was crucial to keep the business afloat. The creditors had been on the phone that day and if there was one thing VB preferred to avoid, it was creditors. The engineroom was a flurry of oily activity and VB, popping in for the third time in the hour finally said, 'That will do for now. We'll just nip out on one engine and pull up around the corner on Mindil Beach to finish the job.' Shortly afterwards *Loellen M* limped out past the main wharf, while VB sent someone up to town to pick up the cheque.

Loellen M had landed the first prospecting team for BHP at Groote Eylandt and now she was supplying the operation throughout the exploration-and-drilling period. Often she returned from Groote with water seeping into her tanks where they were holed on hidden pinnacles of rock at the landing. For the next two or three days in Darwin VB had his work cut out, laying her up on blocks at Frances Bay, repairing the punctures and replacing plates. His cargo was always delivered, but he didn't bother publishing a timetable.

Around the Gove Peninsula the low bauxite cliffs of startling red stood out among the grey-green and white palette so characteristic of the coast. Since VB had first visited Gove by mission lugger several years before, a space tracking station known as ELDO had been established, providing *Loellen M* with further work. Her first delivery for the possible future bauxite mine involved the transport of two Landrovers and equipment to the beach at Melville Bay, for Messrs Gutteridge, Haskins and Davey, the consulting engineers making an appreciation of the project. The engineers had a typical bush-bashing job, the vehicles being driven slowly and tediously through the thick scrub. In the late afternoon they were to meet at the potholed wartime airstrip, the only clearing in the vicinity. At the designated time and unbeknown to each other, both drivers chose to give their vehicles a burst on the strip. Approaching via two different taxi-ways alongside of which the spear grass was eight feet high, neither bothered to slow down or look when the two runways crossed. Their rendezvous was more spectacular than planned. Though the men crawled unscathed from the wreckage, the Landrovers were write-offs which *Loellen M* dutifully collected on her next trip. The vehicle population within a thousand or so square miles of Gove

Peninsula totalled exactly three, the third being the truck belonging to Yirrkala Mission. In view of this, the odds against a collision in the north of Arnhem Land would have to have been high, and VB wondered how they explained it to the boss.

Missions in the north of Australia were settled largely along the tropical coast and on the shores of the larger islands, where they were assured of an adequate rainfall and pleasant sea breezes. There they were easily accessible by sea, the mission luggers providing a source of supply and communication. As the service provided by *Loellen M* became more established, some of the missionaries saw an easier means of supply and a few of the old luggers were phased out.

The arrival of *Loellen M* became something of an event at the missions. Work disciplines varied under different churches and missionaries, but for the most part the Aborigines not engaged in other activities would come down to the beach to help. Mission cargo was delivered in bulk and provided the vital needs of the communities. Sacks of flour, rice, tea, sugar, milk powder, sago and tobacco were staples. Soap was shipped in the form of bars forty inches long. There were no packets of laundry detergent, cans of insect spray or other luxuries; and soft drink, cordial and biscuits didn't exist on the missions. Alcohol was strictly forbidden. Unloading was all done by hand, often with each man, woman and child pitching in and doing what they could; the men, one each end of a sack or drum, and the women and children tossing boxes to each other, giggling when they dropped them in the sand.

Along the entire coast, Yirrkala Mission was the only settlement to have a real landing ramp. It was a rough stone and concrete affair some four to six feet above the seabed at its seaward end. *Loellen M* had used it only once or twice before; in the earliest hours of one morning, it let her down. With the tide out, the full weight of the vessel, her stern overhanging the end, rested upon the ramp. A loud crash shattered the night as the ramp crumpled, toppling *Loellen M* backwards into the water. She came to rest in an unusual and expensive attitude, her bow pointed to the stars and the engine-room, galley and part of the after hold thoroughly flooded. VB took it on the chin, and scrambled to get *Loellen M* going again. Costs of maintenance were always high, but an event like this put VB Perkins & Co on the brink of ruin, teetering.

It was Friday and there was nothing in the kitty. Skipper Tom Conroy spotted VB in the yard and took the opportunity to mention to him that it was payday. VB tugged at his moustache for a moment, and felt in his top pocket. Whisking out a five-pound note that he carried in his shirt for such occasions, he asked seriously, 'Will this see you through until Monday?'

'Yes, okay,' Tom said, obligingly.

VB always owed Tom, but as Tom saw it, 'It was all very friendly and you knew Bruce would always come good in the end.'

Getting by for another few days by means of a fiver earned VB the nickname 'Five-Pound Perkins'. For the first few years the company scraped along and everyone involved had to make do. There was no choice. VB's ability to always come good on his debts was in no small way due to the efforts of Barbara, for VB had a real aversion to the day-to-day management of money. In fact he found it so distasteful that throughout his whole business career he left the task to someone else.

Finding the money to pay the crew became a nightmare for Barbara, as she was left to do the rounds of everyone who owed them each week. Often she had no choice but to front up in person to collect, a task she absolutely dreaded. It wasn't always as easy as handing over five pounds until next week—*Loellen M*'s other skipper, Mick Keenan, a part Aborigine with a growing family to feed, couldn't afford to wait. Through the agency side of the business Barbara took every chance she could to make a penny, and when she discovered that her nickname in some circles was 'Mrs Two Percent', it really upset her. The boys in the yard called her 'The Duchess', because she 'spoke proper', but she didn't feel at all like a Duchess—she felt like Mrs Two Percent. VB's avoidance of the money side of things meant that the financial worries were left to her, and life in Darwin did not seem to be getting any easier.

As a businessman VB was a visionary. He could see the potential of things and if it was something that interested him he wasn't afraid to have a go or take a risk. The challenge of moving a difficult piece of cargo to a difficult place was something he loved, and he tackled the challenges with optimism. The optimism didn't always pay off. He was fondest of the marine-engineering side of the business, and picking up junk from auctions was a favourite pastime of his. His memory for what he had was tremendous and he prided himself on his ability to meet mechanical challenges out of the stock of stuff that he kept, in the early days, in the garage at Perkinsville. Aspects of the business that he found disagreeable he would pass on to someone else to deal with or else ignore altogether. If the bank manager rang VB with a concern over the bank account he would say, 'Speak to Mrs P—that's her department.' He didn't like listening to gripers and even employees who had a gripe which five pounds couldn't fix would be sent along to see Barbara with a comment to the effect that 'Mrs P will sort you out!'

In 1964 Freda Brown, known as Mrs B, began work in the office and Barbara was released from some of the day-to-day aspects. With her bright smile and cheerful voice Mrs B was perfect to cope with VB's ways. In her words, she revelled in making his peace for him on the phone and in the office, in reminding him of all the things he had promised to do, of people he had to phone back, and calming the ones that he forgot to tell her about. Mrs B loved her job. Of this period she said:

> Going to work for Mr P didn't really feel like going to work. The office was like a second home to me and he was so easy to work for—too easy really. He was never in the office much but he did write beautiful, clever letters to people and I think that kept us out of a lot of trouble. I have to say Mr P was the kindest and most pleasant boss that I have ever known and I couldn't say a bad word about him as a person. But I'm afraid money didn't worry him. He let others worry about that.

Apart from Barbara, the other person who worried about finances was Russ Gole. The company's accountant lived interstate and visited his clients in Darwin about once a month. The beans having been counted, Russ Gole regularly tried to persuade VB to sit down and review the financial affairs, but most of the time VB found something more important to do. He was a 'big picture' man and if handed the trading results he would invariably ask 'What does the bottom line say? Are we in the black?' and then hand them back. As long as he was kept generally informed he was happy.

Money or lack of it never concerned him. Having lived in the East for years, where signed chits were accepted for everything from a whisky soda to a new motorcar, he considered cash was a nuisance and bagged out the pockets. Thus, besides his top-pocket fiver, he rarely had any money on him and preferred to frequent shops such as 'Hairy-toes' (Haritos) in Daly Street where he was known and they'd send a bill. His years of antique trading in London had also left their mark. VB had an incredible talent for making do in most respects, but if something took his fancy he'd occasionally revert to his antipodean habits and buy it on the spot. On one of the first occasions there was enough money in the bank account to pay the crew without a scramble, VB went along to an auction of Persian rugs. It was the first such event of its kind in furniture-starved Darwin, and he bought a utility load of rugs with the crew's pay. Barbara was furious but he insisted that they were a good investment and that he could probably get a good price for them later on. That was no consolation to Barbara, who was forced to spend another two days frantically knocking on doors. And most of the rugs he never did part with.

TWENTY-ONE

No Silk Gloves

Things were happening. There was no doubt about it. VB knew he had to find more shipping tonnage and this was his big chance. His beloved *Loellen M*, despite her facelift, was not going to last forever. She was doing the job but she was slow, difficult to work and, he had to face it, a donkey's breakfast of a landingcraft. She'd carried out the first manganese samples mined for GEMCO, a new BHP subsidiary formed to work the deposits proven at Groote Eylandt. Now, in 1964, they were talking about feasibility studies on the development of a bauxite and alumina industry at Gove. He had to move. He knew what he wanted. But since he had nothing but a mortgaged house and a none too impressive vessel with which to seduce the bankers, he wasn't going to get it. They just wouldn't finance him to the tune of a new vessel, so a second ALC40 would have to suffice. He had a hull in mind, but the modifications would be expensive.

Things had gone well at the meeting in Sydney with the Commonwealth Development Bank. Now he phoned Barbara in Darwin to tell her all about it. VB was animated, for this was the way he liked to do business: 'Delightful chaps . . . had an excellent lunch with them in the directors' dining room . . . well-stocked bar fridge . . . very interested in the project . . . no problems with finance so no point delaying . . . off to Newcastle tomorrow to get started . . . will keep you posted.'

Barbara inferred that all had been settled.

Several weeks later a pile of bills from Newcastle lay on Barbara's desk, but there was still no sign of the money in the bank account. In the manager's office of the Commonwealth Bank in Darwin, Barbara waited as Hedley Caine contacted the Development Bank in Sydney to inquire as to what had happened. She watched across the desk, concerned, for though fairly non-committal on the phone the bank manager's face was grave. Gently, he put the phone down and turned to her. 'I'm afraid that although the loan has been approved in principle,' he said, 'no formal application has been submitted, so there is no money forthcoming at this time.'

VB had once again let the paperwork slip his notice. They'd had a meeting over lunch and he'd assumed that a gentleman's chat was enough and all would be taken care of. Barbara was stunned. Hedley, too, appeared a little unsettled and calling for two strong cups of tea, he pushed aside the pile of dubious cheques he'd been considering and bent his mind to the problem. A lengthy discussion later he sent Barbara off with a pile of documents through which she worked overnight, delivering them to the bank in the morning to be approved and sent off post-haste in the bank's bag with a covering letter. Within a blessedly short time the money came through.

Friday night of a long weekend in Newcastle and VB's new landingcraft, *Hawk*, was in the water ready for a final inspection by the marine surveyors the following week. The work was complete. VB was in high spirits. The refit and modification had gone well and to celebrate he had put on a party. With him was the other Territory landingcraft operator, 'Ever-ready' Ted Fitzgerald. Ted had also seen opportunities and set out to meet them using modified ex-army landingcraft hulls. Like VB, Ted was not keen on paperwork and his company, Marine Contractors, worked on a straight charter basis, 'so much a day and that's it', mostly overseas around Timor and West Irian. It happened that his landingcraft, *Porpoise*, had just been refitted and she too was back in the water ready for the survey required under New South Wales law before being officially allowed out of port.

VB looked at his watch. It was 1am. 'It's time we were sailing,' he said. Ted, too, rounded up his crew. They would do a runner together. The vessels were already fuelled and provisioned. They were ready. The engines were started and quietly *Hawk* and *Porpoise* eased away from their berths and disappeared into the night, renegade landingcraft, fugitives from the law.

On Tuesday morning the surveyors found them gone. Somebody mentioned they'd gone on a trial up the river to prepare for survey the next day, and by the time it was discovered the landingcraft really had gone they were already in Territory waters, where nothing really mattered.

The Northern Territory had always been a maverick sort of place. In the small-ships industry an 'anything goes' attitude prevailed, since there was so little in the way of government control. The Port Authority, created only in 1963, had no authority outside the limits of declared ports. With no local legislation the Navigation Act, administered by the Commonwealth Department of Shipping and Transport, was applicable. However very little interest in the Territory was ever demonstrated by the departmental officers and in practice the Navigation Act was not applied. There were no survey requirements at all for small craft operating in Territory waters. As such, outside of the port it was every man for himself.

Crews on small ships required no qualifications. In any case, since there were so few aids to navigation in the Territory it was generally accepted in the industry that a little local knowledge was worth a lot more to a skipper than any fancy piece of paper showing a mariner's certificate of competency. Professional mariners were not interested in working on luggers or small landingcraft. Conditions were crude. Life-jackets were usually left on the floor or under a bunk somewhere, dirty and covered in oil and grease after they had been used as pillows on the deck. It was too hot to sleep in the cabins. If the weather wasn't too rough everyone slept outside. The work attracted rough types, often young men who were a little on the wild side and didn't mind a drink. Safety procedures were a bit lacking but no-one was too concerned. There was always the dinghy.

VB was on his way home from a dinner engagement. High tide was around 8pm and *Hawk* should already have sailed. On the spur of the moment he turned into Frances Bay Drive; he'd just pop into the yard to see she'd got off all right. There was a bit of a wharf now, built of fill supported by concrete slabs. As he got closer he saw the shadowy outline of *Hawk* at her berth. There were no lights on and everything was uncannily quiet. Something was wrong. He was about to step across onto the deck when he heard it. 'Help,' said a voice. 'Och mon, help me!' It was coming from the water. He looked down and there was his skipper, clinging to the side of *Hawk* with one hand, and to an apparently lifeless body with the other.

'Good Lord,' he said, shocked. 'What on earth are you doing in there?' Swiftly he found a rope and threw them a line. Peering down into the dark he could hear the sounds of a skirmish. Getting them both out was a struggle; the first was just a deadweight, but eventually VB had them back on deck, and heard the full story.

The crew had been up to the pub and the only one to return at sailing time was the deckhand. He promptly fell off the wharf and hit his head on a rail. The waiting skipper, who saw it happen, jumped in to rescue him. But the skipper was not much of a swimmer himself. Each time he let go of the unconscious deckie to try to clamber back aboard, the outgoing tide whisked the deckie away and he had to make another lunge to haul him back. They had been in the water for almost an hour before VB came along.

The incident came as no surprise to VB. Drinking was so much a part of the lifestyle in the Territory of the 1960s, that finding and keeping reliable crew was a nightmare. He'd had a few reliable skippers, but keeping the other three crew members was a different matter. Though crews might be arranged days or weeks in advance there was never any guarantee they would actually turn up to sail. A useful place to find an extra hand or two in an emergency was the Darwin Workers Club. Deckhands were not so difficult to get and if VB couldn't find anybody with experience, there were almost always a couple of willing ringers at the bar, in town on leave from a cattle station. They couldn't usually tell one end of a boat from another, but they were generally young and fit and used to hard work. VB often returned from a crisis mission with a couple of raw recruits in tow, cowboy hats, high-heeled boots, dusty swags over their shoulders.

Keeping engineers was the biggest headache, since the job required a bit of knowledge. But one still could not afford to be fussy. The story goes that Ever-ready Ted once needed an engineer badly and tried his luck at the Workers Club. Walking along the public bar he asked, 'Anybody a marine engineer around here?' There was no response. He walked a bit further. 'Looking for engineers—any engineers here?' Still nothing. When he'd done one round he began to get desperate and yelled, 'Well can anybody push a bloody lawnmower?'

One voice responded, 'Yeah I can do that.'

'Come with me then,' said Ted. 'You're on as engineer.'

The Northern Territory was traditionally renowned for its large population of persons variously described as derelicts, dropouts, long-grassers, no-hopers or hippies. In Darwin in the 1960s it was easy to live out of a swag on a beach or in a park, and the climate, easy-going atmosphere and slow pace of the town made it a Mecca for those who favoured this lifestyle, or had simply fallen on hard times. Frances Bay had its own little community who resided principally at Black Joe's doss-house, not far along the foreshore from VB Perkins & Co. Black Joe was an alcoholic Swiss who'd acquired his nickname because of his lack of instinct for washing. Joe's other claim to fame was a perfect, hexagonal, bolt-shaped dent in his head which marked the occasion he had fallen head-first into *Loellen M*'s hold. On good days Joe could be found, usually with a can of beer in one hand, tinkering in the workshop at VB Perkins & Co. The value of Joe's services was doubtful, but VB kept him on anyway, on account of his services in better days.

Joe's doss-house was a broken-down old place with several rooms and a large veranda. A couple of dilapidated caravans lay

entangled in a jungle of coffee bush in the yard. For two pounds
per week his clients rented rooms complete with a bed, a chair
and part use of an old kero fridge. Hot showers were available by
means of a homemade copper pipe coil pinched from VB Perkins
& Co, as was the oil with which it was fired. Those of more modest
means rolled out swags on the verandah for two bob per week.
Outside, the thunderbox was connected to a septic tank, the centre
of the proprietor's attention on the day it overflowed. The stench
was simply too much, even for Joe. When he finally decided a
clean out was in order he enlisted the help of a well-known character named Tracey. Having got the lid off the tank and begun
work the enormity of the task overwhelmed them, and they realised some fortification was required to tackle the job. It took a full
bottle of rum to prime them into resuming the task of emptying
some of the putrid brew into a couple of 44-gallon drums. Several
more of Joe's clients were then pressed into service and the drums
were loaded onto the back of his little ute. But in the course of
the loading operation Joe fell fast asleep. It was late and Tracey,
unable to wake his landlord for instructions, drove off into the
twilight in a rum-induced haze, wondering what on earth to do
with his evil load. He drove round the block a couple of times
and, passing Government House, an idea struck him. With the
help of an offsider he tipped the whole lot on the lawn outside.
The following day news of the event was all around VB's yard.
Joe had driven past the residence to check on progress and later
reported, 'There's a hell of a stink up at the Gov'nor's and they're
still cleaning up the lawn.'

VB had to be desperate to resort to finding crew at Black Joe's,
but it did happen. Skipper Snowy Roberts had all hands but an
engineer one morning. He phoned VB and together they jumped
into the old green truck and headed for Black Joe's. There VB
peered at the prostrate bodies lying around, still unconscious from
the night's drinking binge. He had a good look at one fellow lying
spreadeagled on the floor and, recognising him, gave him a couple
of prods with the toe of his boot. 'Oh yes,' he said with a twirl
of his moustache. 'I believe this chap has sailed with us before. He

can go along as engineer. We'll get him aboard and by the time you get to the Vernon Islands he should have sobered up.'

VB Perkins & Co got the job done, but it was no silk-glove service. VB had to be at crisis point to resort to a drunk. He had a reputation for giving people a go and of helping them out when they needed it, and preferred to employ young, fit men. He could turn a blind eye to some things, but he did not approve of drinking on the job and tried to keep his vessels dry. His success in this respect was limited. Many a tall story was told to him by employees attempting to cover themselves, for he was known for giving people the benefit of the doubt.

Each employer had his own way of dealing with the alcohol problem. Next door at Marine Contractors it was standard practice for everyone, including the boss, to get into work in the morning and have a few beers. Then throughout the day, while they were loading, they'd have a few more beers. Close to sailing time Ted had a surefire method of ensuring his crew wouldn't go off to the pub and fail to return. He'd bring a couple of cartons aboard and stay with them, having a few more beers until it was time to leave. Often the skipper got under way with a drunk and inexperienced crew and found himself skipper, engineer, mate and deckhand all at once. But when this happened to skipper John Conway, he was smart enough not to keep going. He'd just leave to keep the boss happy, and stop around the corner somewhere, usually the other side of Emery Point where he'd drop anchor until the next morning. 'It was the safest way. I knew my capabilities. Once it got that bad that I was starting to flake out like the rest of them it was time to take heed.'

Ever-ready Ted didn't muck about and patience was not one of his virtues. His favourite expression was 'Bog it up 'er!' and he would either use it or act upon it whenever he wanted to hurry things along. His D6 Caterpillar bulldozer gave him more than a little capacity to push things around and he used it to this end frequently. One morning he found a truck blocking his access at Frances Bay and got into his dozer and pushed the truck off the road, rolling it three times in the process and writing it off. When the owner later walked into his office, before he had time to say anything, Ted said, 'How much?' and wrote out a cheque on the spot. The transaction was completed with a gruff, 'Don't park there again.' Ted's bulldozer also came in handy for pushing the landingcraft off the mud when they were sticking a little, and he had been known to push a hole right through the vessel's side.

On another occasion a semi-trailer was hopelessly bogged in his yard and Ted told one of his boys to get in his truck and push it out. 'Bog it up 'er, bog it up 'er,' shouted Ted. So the lad duly bogged it up 'er. As he pushed the fan through the radiator with the bull bar, Ted was still shouting 'Keep it goin'!'

It was Port Keats on the radio. VB picked up the receiver and through the static he thought he heard something about a sinking. It was 19 November 1965, and the weather had been bad. 'Can you repeat, over,' he said. The reception was terrible.

'Crew here . . . don't know whether . . . abandoned ship . . . *Loellen M* . . .'

He put the words together in his mind. 'My God,' he thought. 'Could it be true?' It hit him like a steam train. Urgently he asked for more information and across the stormy airways from Port Keats he put the pieces of the story together.

Loellen M was making a delivery for an exploration team. Beached near Port Keats, west of Darwin, fuel was being pumped ashore as heavy, black cathedral clouds gathered overhead. The storm hit fast along a broad front, lashing the coast with rain and fierce, squally wind. The timing was the worst. The murky tide had just lifted *Loellen M* from the bottom and she was caught off guard and swept sideways along the beach. Jagged rocks ripped at her bottom plating. She was badly damaged but skipper Mick Keenan was not aware of this and got her off quickly and out into deep water. The sea had whipped up into a frenzy. As he headed for shelter behind Cape Hay, water seeped into the engineroom. Only one of the 6,000-gallon tanks of cargo fuel had been emptied and *Loellen M* was already heeling from her lopsided load. The crew manned the pumps, desperately trying to contain the flood. The engineer bent over to unblock a choked pump inlet as a huge, green wave smashed against the stern. It threw him off his feet and onto the port engine throttle. The engine stopped dead and wouldn't restart. The pumps were losing the battle. Slowly, *Loellen M* began to yield, heeling further and further, until she was almost on her side. The crew were now on the gunnel, contemplating the fact that the lifeboat was underwater.

Among the dismal party was a ringer, seconded to the crew at the last minute, who was to prove VB's belief that a little cattle craft could indeed come in handy at sea. As the empty 6,000-gallon diesel tank was forced free of the lugs securing it to the deck, it floated freely and begun to drift away from the stricken vessel. The cowboy saw his opportunity. Perched on the gunnel he coiled a rope and lassoed the walking-stick-shaped breather pipe on the top of the tank. The sea had calmed a little and the tide was on its way in. The crew abandoned ship, clinging to the rope which was by now rigged around the tank such that they could all get hold of it. The unlikely lifebuoy towed them all safely to shore, where they walked into Port Keats.

Loellen M was faithful to VB's conviction that the ALC40s did not sink easily. The tanks built into her hull kept her afloat for hours after the crew had given her up, but by daylight the following morning her twenty-five-year career had come to an end. She did not go down alone. To the north the ketch *Margaret Mary*, which had served the Catholic missions since 1951, sank in the same storm.

VB was in a spot of difficulty. Losing *Loellen M* couldn't have happened at a worse time. With work burgeoning he had contracts that he now could not possibly fulfil. He had to do something fast. Within weeks he found another ALC40, this time an ex-army landingcraft which had only ever been in service for the government. While VB organised her modification, extension and re-engining, Barbara took care of the paperwork towards an insurance payout of thirty thousand pounds. With that and a loan of four thousand pounds from one of VB's skippers, the finance was arranged.

Continuing the ornithological theme, VB named his new acquisition *Kestrel*. She was pressed into service in 1966, while the demand for shipping on the coast was booming. VB's shipping facility had made exploration that would otherwise have been difficult, if not impossible, suddenly feasible. One task he undertook for an exploration company was to land helicopter fuel, and clear and mark landing sites at fifty-mile intervals along the 2,400-mile stretch of coast from Broome in Western Australia, to the Roper River in the Gulf of Carpentaria. The job was done in shallow, uncharted waters, navigating by trial and error, using an anchor hanging below keel level to feel for the bottom. For exploration geologists things had got a lot easier in the few short years since he and John Staargaard set off from the Rose River Mission in the tiny mission dinghy with a couple of canoes. BHP was mining the huge deposit of manganese at Groote Eylandt, and with the mine a town had to be built and supplied. By May of 1966 Nabalco's mine feasibility study had begun at Gove. In the latter part of the year, along with the normal workload, room had to be found for the many demountable buildings and enormous amount of equipment necessary to keep a large camp supplied. It was a strip of coast where nothing very much had ever happened. Now, in those two isolated pockets, there was real development.

1966 was a fateful year for VB, in more ways than one.

For a long time Barbara had succeeded in putting it out of her mind. But gradually, as she became more unhappy with her life in Darwin, she began to dwell on such things, the more hurtful things. It wasn't so much what VB had done, but more what he had not done that hurt her, things that were typical of the way he lived his life. There had been the time when she'd lost her mother. She was an only child and she and her mother had been very close. Barbara and VB had been playing cards with friends at Perkinsville that night. The phone rang and he'd answered it. He had been very quiet and instantly Barbara had sensed it was bad news, the worst kind of news. He had turned around and gravely told her what was too awful to contemplate, that her mother had been killed and her father critically injured in a car accident. She had been utterly devastated. Doug and Jinx Moir had made moves to leave, but VB insisted they stay and play a few more rounds. His feeling was that it was no good going to pieces. It wasn't until after several more subdued rounds that the Moirs went home.

The next day there was a vessel in port and Barbara had to be in the office all day. In between work that had to be done she was on the phone, first to the hospital in Melbourne. Her father was as well as could be expected. Then to the airline office. 'No plane for two days. It's full but we'll try and find you a seat.'

Then to her father's friends. 'Don't come yet. He'll need you later. Your mother's funeral is on Friday.' There was no way she could be there. The sense of being totally cut off was just another hardship of living in the Territory.

It had been a hot, busy, terrible day. She was looking forward to getting home, to having some time to think about what had happened, to talk about it to VB, to be comforted. But when she walked into the house carrying the baby basket she found him preparing to go out in his full mess bib and tucker. 'You're not going out tonight are you?' she said. 'I was hoping we could have a quiet night.'

'Have you forgotten?' VB replied. 'It's dining-in night at the mess. I always go to dining-in night, you know that.' He put his arm around her shoulder. 'I'm very sorry about your mother, but there's nothing we can do for the poor old girl now.' He was very kindly about it, but it was not enough. Dining-in night was a men only affair and Barbara couldn't go with him. He left her alone at this time when, above all else, she really needed him.

She tried being alone that evening, but could not bear it. She picked up her three-month-old baby and walked blindly out of the house in tears. For an hour or so she walked and walked, along Mitchell Street, down Gardens Hill and along the moonlit Mindil Beach, cradling me to her chest. Finally she turned back.

At Myilly Point where the Moirs lived in a CSIRO house, the lights were still on and she found herself knocking on the front door. Doug opened the door and welcomed her warmly, then, looking over her shoulder asked, 'Where's Bruce?'

'He's gone to the RAAF Mess,' she said. 'Can I stay until he comes home?'

At about 11.30pm, there was the sound of a car on the gravel outside. Doug shot down the stairs. VB was standing there at the door, still in his mess clothes. Doug looked him straight in the eye, and said, 'You bastard!' and punched his friend hard on the jaw.

VB reeled backwards. 'What the hell was that for?' he spluttered. He really had no idea.

To VB, death was something that happened as a part of life. Once a person was dead there was nothing you could do to bring them back. He expected those left behind to think about the happy times, and have the strength to keep going. His own parents had died in the last couple of years, and he was very sorry at their passing. But they had had a good innings. Death was an unpleasant but natural thing and there was nothing surer than that it would come to everyone eventually. On the Burma–Siam Railway one couldn't be fazed by death. If one's willpower broke or one didn't have the mental strength to put it to the back of the mind, then one died. It was as simple as that. One had to get on with the business of life.

VB had acquired a wealth of experience of what life could be. He had learned that it could be lived to the maximum and enjoyed to the fullest, both socially and at work. He had also learned that life could be very short and very depriving. He had experienced hardship and horrors such as most men could not begin to imagine, and because of this he looked at life from a different perspective. Disasters or major mishaps did not faze him and if there was something of a practical nature to be done he would tackle them head on, picking up the pieces and starting again. Other things, although they mattered greatly to him, he preferred to ignore in the hope that they might go away. He had a very strong sense of inner calm and happiness, and he didn't like it to be upset by anyone else. For this reason he refused to let things worry him.

VB was forty-one years old by the time he married Barbara and he had been a bachelor for a long time. He was an independent man, but marriage suited him. He looked upon it as something where the person he loved was around the place most of the time, to accompany him socially and look after him at home, but when something interesting came up he simply went off and did it by himself, leaving his wife to do her own thing. Unfortunately Barbara was not as independent and had different expectations. To her marriage was something where one shared everything, and in that regard they were mismatched.

Life did change when Antony and I came along. Barbara was no longer free to follow VB and he altered little to accommodate the family situation. Socially and at work he brimmed with enthusiasm and drive, but he did not see much outside his own circle of radiance. He spoke proudly of his children to his friends, but he didn't like noise and the day-to-day domestics of child-rearing didn't interest him. If he came home and Antony or I were making a fuss he would go right out again, returning only after he knew we were in bed. If Barbara suggested that we all go down to the beach after work he'd say, 'Good idea! You three go off and I'll be right down.' But then he would be sidetracked. Invariably he would have found someone else to talk to and would leave Barbara disappointed. If they were at a party and Barbara was tired and VB was not, he would say, 'But the night is young. Hang on and I'll cast around and see if I can find someone to drive you home.' He expected his wife to be just as independent as he was.

In more than one way VB was British, through and through. He was not inclined to show his emotions, either publicly or in his home. He loved Barbara and presumed that she knew it. She, on the other hand, needed to be shown affection and a little bit of appreciation, but the most she could hope for, when she was exhausted and dispirited by the work and the heat, was a pat on the bottom and a congenial 'Cheer up, Charlie'. VB's work and social commitments kept him so busy that they began to see less and less of each other, meeting at breakfast and occasionally in the office when he came in long enough to sit down. While *Hawk* and *Kestral* were being rebuilt he was away interstate for extended periods of time. It was work that he enjoyed.

Barbara missed more and more the quality time she used to spend with him, for to be with him was to be constantly amused. She found him erudite in his way, he kept amusing company and his conversation was always interesting. She was intrigued by the way he could change the course of conversation at a dinner party, if he found it lacking. His usual diversion was to break into song, usually Gilbert & Sullivan, something to the effect of 'The flowers that bloom in the spring, tra-la, have nothing to do with the case . . .' The fact was that VB was ideal company. An honorary member of the RAAF and Army messes, he was socially very much in demand. As such he was not at home very much.

Because of his gregarious nature he was, on occasion, insensitive to his friends who had young families and needed a quiet time at the end of an exhausting day. The process of feeding and bathing children was something that existed on a different plane to his own. At six o'clock the sun was over the yardarm and it was time for a 'glass of sherbet' with somebody. He loved to be surrounded by people and assumed that everyone was like that.

Since they had been in Darwin he had lived exactly as he had in Malaya. Barbara found herself the cook, the *amah*, the *nonyah* (baby *amah*) and the *kebun*, while VB lived as though all those people were not one and the same. She was also the one with, as Russ Gole put it, 'the business ability' and had put a lot of overtime into the company over the years, further adding to the strain. But still VB thought nothing of inviting people home for dinner at 9 o'clock at night and was quite oblivious to the fact that Barbara might have spent the day juggling two demanding children with various letters to Port Authorities or financiers, that the night before she had been up intermittently attending to a child who had been heartily throwing up in the bed, in the bathroom, on the rug. These things never entered his mind. But he noticed if his socks weren't rolled up exactly the same way as his *amah* used to do it, with the toes turned inwards so that you could just slip them over the end of your foot and pull them on.

Barbara found it impossible to discuss seriously with him what she felt was their deteriorating relationship. She tried but he didn't like unpleasantness and brushed off anything disagreeable. If she tried to pin him down he would usually say 'Don't rock the boat, Charlie. It'll be all right,' then disappear. But it wasn't all right. Barbara was no doormat and knew what she wanted from life. This was not it. VB was still one of the most amusing, interesting people she had ever met, but she knew that things could not go on as they were.

In early 1965 Barbara took Antony and me to Sydney. She rang Russ Gole, told him she wasn't going back to Darwin, and asked him to send her some money. It was a desperate plea to try and get through to VB that something was wrong, that this was not something to be brushed off lightly. Russ, as she knew he would, immediately got on to VB and told him to come south and fetch her.

VB was shocked and bewildered, and immediately flew to Sydney. He couldn't understand what the problem was. He was very happy. 'We've never even had an argument!' he said. And they probably hadn't, because he didn't like arguing. Arguing was an unpleasant business. If it looked like trouble was brewing he would simply walk off, leaving Barbara furious and frustrated.

Barbara returned to Darwin, but eighteen months later nothing had changed.

VB was in his element when surrounded by interesting men. From the time of their marriage their various abodes had always been full of men who dropped in, and Barbara had never felt any attraction towards them other than their company and conversation. In mid 1965 Michel came along. French, dark, emotional, he was in many ways the antithesis of VB. He had lived for years in Indochina, where his father was a colonel in the French Army. He and his young family were forced to flee the country by Ho Chi Minh and his Communist terrorists, and had come to Australia to make a new start. An engineer, Michel was sent to handle the Darwin end of Forasol's oil-drilling operation at Port Keats, serviced by VB Perkins & Co. Barbara's first impression was of an arrogant Frenchman, but as their friendship developed there was an untimely attraction.

When Barbara realised how much she was beginning to depend

upon Michel's friendship she was horrified. She was tired, unhappy and, like many other Territory wives in this male bastion, finally decided she'd had enough and that it was time she removed herself from the scene for a while. The business was at last in good shape, Russ Gole was in financial control and in late 1966 she left for an extended holiday in the south, taking only the children and the few of her mother's share certificates which remained. She wasn't sure if she was coming back. She really wanted to be happy with VB, and to return if only he would change. But he wouldn't change. He was what he was. She found it impossible to dislike her husband and deep down she still loved him. But she desperately didn't want to hate him.

I was six and Antony four when we boarded the passenger ship *Centaur*, bound for Perth. To us it was all a huge adventure. With the excitement of the ship leaving, the streamers and the flags, we had no conception of the gravity of the moment. We did not realise that this time our father might not come for us. We did not realise that as we waved our father goodbye on the wharf, we were saying goodbye to our family as we knew it.

Friends say VB missed us all terribly after we'd gone. Friends say it was the closest they'd ever seen to depression in VB. But this time he did not come. This time it was a matter of pride.

In Perth we moved in with Bryan Summers, the geologist with whom Barbara and VB had been on the Cape York trip. He and his wife, Lila, now had three daughters. It was a big household for a few months, and we children had a lot of fun. With childish naivety we had no idea that our family had broken up. If our playmates at school asked us where our Daddy was we'd tell them that he had to work in Darwin, but that he would come and see us when he had time. There were never any tears or histrionics. Neither ever spoke ill of the other to us. The integrity of our parents was such that the break up of the marriage was very easy on Antony and me. We didn't even realise it was happening.

Despite their separation they always remained good friends. Barbara still maintains that in many ways VB was one of the finest men she has ever known. VB once told me that when my mother left it was the worst thing that had ever happened to him. Those were strong words considering his history. For myself it was many years later that I really even thought about it, or realised what a tragedy it was that they did not remain together. Not because we suffered in any way from trauma or lack of love in our new situation, but because, in our eyes, they were both such marvellous people.

TWENTY-TWO

Romancing the Schooner

'You stupid clot!' VB shouted. 'You're coming in too fast. Watch it!' VB couldn't believe his eyes. This was the newest addition to his fleet. He knew he'd thrown to the wind all his practical experience of shipping on the Northern Territory coast. He knew the old auxiliary schooner *Coringle* was not what he needed to expand, but he'd been desperate for more shipping tonnage and his love of sailing ships had got the better of him. Now as he watched her careering towards Stokes Hill Wharf with Mayday Morgan at the wheel, he felt helpless. For a split second he closed his eyes to the sight of her magnificent eighteen-foot bowsprit splintering on the wharf into a thousand pieces.

Not since that time long ago in Tregony had he had an older woman. This time he'd fallen for her completely. *Coringle* was built four years before VB was born, in 1909, by Woodleys Ltd in Sydney, makers of fine trading schooners and small wooden ships. In her heyday she'd been a three-masted fore and aft schooner, resplendent in fidded top masts and three gaff topsails, foresail, mainsail and mizzen. She'd carried three headsails and her history was nothing if not romantic.[1] She wasn't the unspoilt beauty she once was, but she'd still beguiled VB. Now, stripped of her beautiful bowsprit, she looked bare, naked. VB was not happy. Neither was Mayday Morgan. It was the crunch that did it for him; he had the wind up and told VB in no uncertain terms where he could stick his ship.

The moment VB came across John Sime was blessed. It was another of those desperate situations. *Hawk* and her crew were abandoned up the difficult Roper River, the skipper having flown off on the mail plane from Roper River Mission after being offered another job over the radio. He had to find another skipper, and luck was with him when he saw John Sime, a gentle character with a soft Scottish brogue, sitting on a well-heeled fishing boat on the main wharf. In John Middleton Sime, VB saw a fisherman in need of a dollar. That the weathered figure in a pair of tattered khaki shorts had grown up as a member of one of the wealthiest families in all Malaya seemed unlikely. Though VB knew the name Sime well, the mention of it did not twig in his mind any association with WM Sime, OBE, co-founder and owner of the firm Sime Darby which, when VB was in prewar Singapore, owned half of all the rubber plantations and tin mines in Malaya. Nevertheless, the man who was to become *Coringle*'s skipper was the son of the founder and himself a one-time co-owner of the famous Sime Darby Inc., which grew into the biggest multi-national corporation in Malaya and Singapore. Since then John had lost the inheritance he received when his father died, by entrusting his shares to another to look after. But of what could have been, he was philosophical.

---

[1] *Her career began in the coastal trade and in the 1930s she lightered bagged wheat from the last of the classic, square-rigged sailing ships, grand old ladies of the sea waiting at anchor in the blue waters of Spencer's Gulf, South Australia. In World War II she was conscripted into the US Army from Sydney and fitted out as a radio relay vessel. She was attached to General MacArthur's headquarters and sailed the Pacific war zones, following the American and Allied landings. Her last owner, a hydrographic surveying company, removed her fidded top masts and mizzen and fitted a wheelhouse to her aft section.*

'It doesn't matter to me. It's all dead and gone now and I'm having a good life fossicking and sailing. I probably would have died of alcoholism if I'd been a wealthy man.'

John Sime was a little more understanding than Mayday Morgan of VB's affection for the old schooner. 'She was a nice old thing, for a sailing ship. With a prevailing wind she would have got you to Arabia or Africa all right, but for what we were doing she was *awful.*' *Coringle* was underpowered, unwieldy and difficult to manoeuvre in a tight corner. Over the years her back had broken and standing aft at the big, wooden, spindled wheel the skipper couldn't see over the bow. To see where he was going, John had to climb onto a chair on his war-damaged, none too steady legs, and stick his head out of a hole specially cut in the wheelhouse roof. It was a little tricky making port. At best *Coringle* managed four and three-quarter knots speed. But when the wind and currents were all wrong she made no headway at all, or worse. When she was pushed backwards through her own wash by wind and water, her huge, central, sailing rudder counteracted the two smaller motoring rudders behind the propellers, and she was unsteerable. She was nothing if not a challenge.

Crew watches at sea were necessarily short—two hours on the wheel and eight hours off—except in bad weather when the pumps had to be manned. In a big beam sea the mild-mannered *Coringle* turned cranky, recklessly flicking her great steering wheel as the waves hit the sailing rudder each time the bow dipped, scorning the efforts of the exhausted helmsman. The crew of *Coringle* were often green, both in experience and colour, for she rolled alarmingly especially in a heavy head sea. It was in such a sea that John walked out of the wheelhouse with a handful of battered life jackets he intended to use as fenders to stop vehicles, on deck as cargo, crashing up against the rigging. A pale-faced deckie eyed the life jackets John was carrying and was convinced that his time had come. 'So this is it then?' he said.

'No, mon!' replied John, amused. 'You won't be needing these just yet,' and continued on his way.

Once or twice, when the spirit moved him, John dragged out

the weather-beaten old sailing rig, in the mainsail of which was a large hole judged good humouredly by the crew to be the result of a stray cannonball. Rigging her was a performance, but John thrilled to the change in *Coringle* under sail, when the old schooner found herself again, her awkwardness under power turning to sheer grace as the breeze filled her sagging sails, the rigging creaking and straining as she heeled and slipped through the water in elegant abandon.

The only wharf outside of Darwin was a small, none too robust structure at Gove. Elsewhere cargo was off-loaded in the same manner as the old mission luggers. Where the bottom was muddy but kind, *Coringle* beached and the cargo was derricked over the side and carried off with the help of the local Aborigines. As John Sime saw it, 'It was a bit of a struggle to off-load the old thing. But in those days the Aborigines were wonderful the way they'd come and help. They'd get one on each end of every drum of fuel, and it was heavy work. They always seemed cheerful enough about working and were very friendly. At Snake Bay they'd even come aboard in their lunch break to teach me to play the didgeridoo. We couldn't have done it without them and, in those days, neither could the landingcraft.'

VB sat at the wheel of the crane with the boom just touching *Hawk*'s bow door. Then, ever so gently, he gave her a little nudge. The tide was just high enough to sail and he wanted to give her a little hurry on. He'd done it often before. This had been VB's first ever real piece of stevedoring equipment, a very, very second-hand Cranvel Crane, useful for all sorts of things. The gluey, grey mud sucked and gurgled at the bottom of *Hawk*'s hull then, with a liquid squelch, relinquished it. *Hawk* floated and began to drift backwards and VB, satisfied, turned around in his seat to reverse off the ramp. The skipper, Snowy Roberts, also turned around and, engines half astern, backed *Hawk* out into the channel. *Hawk* slipped out into deeper water, Snowy blissfully unaware that the hook at the end of the crane's boom had caught onto the angle iron of *Hawk*'s bow door, that he was towing the crane, and his

boss, out to sea. Onlookers ashore were treated to the spectacle
of VB standing on the cab roof of the crane, shouting expletives
in the direction of *Hawk*'s wheelhouse. But the first thing Snowy
noticed was a cross-looking figure with a bedraggled moustache
swimming in the muddy, churned up water, shaking his fist in
his general direction.

The crane, still firmly attached to the bow of the landingcraft,
was eventually unhooked and salvaged at low tide. But as VB admitted, it was not a particularly useful exercise.

In the early days VB had done much of the stevedoring work
himself with the help of a few casual labourers; now he was able
to employ some permanent hands in the yard. Mechanical assistance
was still minimal and most cargo was loaded by hand, a task taking
between two and five days. There was no demarcation of jobs.
Employees oscillated between working ashore and going to sea.
When no vessel was in port, those on shore worked maintaining
machinery, building or developing and reclaiming the land. VB
became adept at finding fill from building sites and other works,
and every year the shoreline was pushed a little further out and he
had a little more land to work with.

Improvisation was a founding philosophy at VB Perkins & Co.
For a few years the only equipment in the yard was an old Blitz
crane hired from somebody else. But VB had always had a bent for
adapting and making do, and his first endloader was a classic example
of his propensity to see a use for something that no-one else could.
The endloader was dubbed by VB the 'helicopter' because it went
about everything arse about face. It started as a standard tray-backed
Landrover. VB reversed and repositioned the cab so that the steering
column and steering wheel angled back across the bonnet. He
mounted an old tractor seat on the front bumper bar facing backwards and by using reverse gear as the forward gear, and forward
as reverse, the driver could load it up with cargo and drive aboard
with the cargo up front. The result was enormously satisfying to
VB, for he loved to innovate and adapt what he had, and by his
accounts it worked very well.

Nothing in the way of capital works ever happened in a hurry at VB Perkins & Co. Time was only spent on projects such as sheds and seawalls when there was nothing more important to do or if VB had come by some free or cheap material. The land that he was reclaiming and developing was not his and there was by no means any certainty that it ever would be.

Though *Coringle* quickly became VB's sentimental favourite, she was a financial disaster and made a loss almost from the outset. She was slow and impractical and eventually her wooden hull began to show signs of needing recaulking. On the landingcraft the cost of repairing propellers and bottom plating was a constant drain on resources. When *Hawk* and *Kestrel* suffered from small holes in their hull, the crew when need be carried out makeshift repairs by plugging them with tapered matches which swelled when wet, proving a useful temporary measure. Though *Hawk* had two good engines, *Kestrel* was at times unreliable. Using his rare talent for scrounging engines and parts, VB accumulated five main engines for her. Two drove the ship, one was always hanging on a chain block ready to be bolted in if needed and another sat in a box on the floor of the engineroom. The fifth was usually in the yard workshop being overhauled.

For most of the time the company struggled financially and employees had to make do. But in 1967 Snowy Roberts decided he wanted a radar for *Hawk*. The company could not afford such an extravagance and VB had to inform Snowy that the answer was no. Snowy would not be dissuaded and VB eventually agreed that Snowy buy the radar himself at a cost of one thousand pounds, to be repaid by VB over a period of six years. When Snowy finally got his fancy new toy he was the butt of many a joke among the crews. But VB Perkins and Co now had its first piece of professional navigational equipment. It was a sign of things to come.

TWENTY-THREE

The Time Comes

There was no lunch this time. The room didn't even sport a bar fridge. They'd been at it for three hours, he, Russ Gole and the Sydney bankers, going over and over the proposal to build a new landingcraft, in every minute detail. They were talking big dollars, $300,000 to be exact, and the atmosphere in the room was formal. VB was confident he'd got his message across: that the cargo was there, that the Northern Territory desperately needed a better class of shipping service and that the time to build was right. The lack of collateral to secure the loan was the major issue. Again and again the lenders ran their fingers down the list of assets put up before them: three elderly vessels the values of which were largely already spoken for, an oddball assortment of machinery, and a few improvements on a piece of waterfront land belonging to the Commonwealth Railways Department. It was a gruelling session. All around VB the faces were grave. The meeting was winding up and he was asked for a short summary as to why the bank should fund the proposal. He had said it all already. What more was there to say except what was so patently obvious to him. He stood up and looked around the room at the banking men. 'Gentlemen,' he said, 'the time has come for me to shit or get off the pot.'

There was merit in VB's less than eloquent words; the time was right. But his application was refused. Without title to the land at Frances Bay the improvements were worthless and the collateral to secure the loan simply wasn't enough.

VB was frustrated and bitterly disappointed. GEMCO was talking about doubling the mine capacity at Groote Eylandt. Nabalco had signed a contract to build an alumina refinery and there was a township and a mine to be developed in Gove over the next few years. The shipping capacity in the Territory to support these new towns just wasn't there. Previously he had approached Nabalco about them financing the new landingcraft and chartering it to him, to buy it back over a period of years. But Nabalco was a big company and had the big company mentality of sourcing everything through Sydney. Tin-pot towns like Darwin and seat-of-the-pants landing-craft operators like VB Perkins & Co were not part of the grand scheme as they saw it. His proposal was tossed back at him.

Skipper John Sime was also disappointed to hear the outcome of the application. He had already lent VB $15,000, a small start towards the landingcraft to be. Quietly, he took himself in to see the local man at the Commonwealth Bank. He still had a few shares in a subsidiary of Sime Darby and asked whether it would sway the bank's decision if he lodged them with the bank as security against the Perkins loan. The answer was probably. Within eight days the certificates had arrived from overseas and the loan was granted.

Between them *Hawk* and *Loellen M* had been green, black, even pink. Pink hadn't been VB's preferred colour but he'd come by the paint awfully cheap. Up until the new landingcraft was com-missioned it was the cost of the paint that dictated his policy on colour. Now things were different, but he still maintained he wasn't fussy. 'You can paint my vessels any colour you like,' he'd say, 'as long as it's red.'

VB had had the designs for the new 250 deadweight ton/500 cubic ton capacity landingcraft in hand for some time. She'd have twice the speed and three and a half times the capacity of his old landingcraft. He had spent hours at his desk sketching and redrawing the bow and bow ramp, the design of which was all important for efficient beach landings of heavy equipment.[1] Watching his ideas finally come to life at Carrington Slipway in Newcastle was an exhilarating experience. He had poured his heart and soul into the new landingcraft at a time when his life was, in other aspects, bleak. As the project unfolded, the excitement of seeing it through helped to ease him through the loneliness and loss he felt after his family left him.

VB changed tack when he named *Fourcroy* after a Cape on nearby Bathurst Island, instead of a bird. It was as though the new geographical theme marked a turning point for the company; when *Fourcroy* began plying the warm waters of the Arafura and Timor Seas in July 1968, she set a new standard for shipping on the coast of the Northern Territory. She was the first Northern Territory owned vessel built to the requirements of Lloyds Register of Shipping, and it gave VB a real sense of pride to see her surveyed to the top classification, 100 A1. Her design was innovative and incredibly successful, so successful that while others came and went over the years, *Fourcroy* is still with the company thirty years later.

The move away from the old ex-army landingcraft was timely, for things were about to change for the owners of the motley assortment of small, completely unsurveyed ships operating in Territory waters. Local operators had looked on with suspicion at a team including the Principal Nautical and Ship Surveyor when they visited Darwin in 1967. And well they might have. Their worst fears were realised when they received a circular shortly after reading: '. . . any Australian or limited coast-trade vessel operating within the waters of the Northern Territory will be subject to certain provisions of the Navigation Act as soon as possible after

---

[1] *Unlike the ALC40s the design was for a high tank landingcraft, with the level of the deck above the waterline. Freeing ports down the sides drained the water off the deck and into the sea so that hatch covers were not necessary. The internal water-tight door behind the bow ramp was unnecessary and she wasn't constrained by waiting for low tide to load and off-load. The ballasting system was designed to improve her ability to hold onto a beach in rough weather.*

January 1st, 1968. This means that all vessels trading will have to be slipped and surveyed some time in the New Year.'

It struck the fear of God into many. The economics of bringing their vessels into survey just didn't stack up and several well-insured old rust buckets were brought to a watery grave. On good authority one local mariner sank seven over his career, usually by putting a jack onto a beam under the engine bearers, and pumping until something gave way; usually the bottom of the boat.

Being the owner of a new landingcraft with a swag of fancy certificates from Lloyd's did not mean that the new survey requirements didn't concern VB. *Hawk* and *Kestrel*, like all ALC40s of their era, had problems with the tanks in their hull. Great faith was put into the fact that they were built to withstand shelling in battle, and that a few holed tanks among forty-six was nothing to worry about. Chicanery got him out of a few scrapes, but VB knew that the old landingcraft could not survive on ruse forever.

Dawn cast a soft light over *Hawk* as she headed backwards for Black Point. In the forward hold two of the crew were knee deep in water. One man stood on a 44-gallon drum, the others passed buckets of water up to be tipped over the side. The sea was rough, white caps swallowed by the deep swell. Now they were going full astern the waves had stopped pounding up for'ard and she wasn't taking as much water over the bow. The skipper, John Sime, wasn't happy. He'd argued with the yard foreman about the stowing of that four-ton bundle of fibro, and lost. They'd sailed badly trimmed, down by the bow. A few hours out he'd manned the pumps and overnight the inlets had clogged with wet cardboard.

He was heading to the ranger's beach at Black Point when the wheelhouse radio crackled into life. It was Darwin, calling *Hawk* to go to the aid of the wooden cargo lighter *Jensah*. The timing was disastrous and John cursed. 'Nay,' he said in answer, 'ye'll have to tell Tony Carl I canna help him. I'm sinking meself!'

Back in Darwin word got around. Hearing of the incident the new Government Surveyor took a renewed interest in *Hawk*. Later John tried to explain. 'Everything was under control,' he said.

'Well yes, I was sinking at the time, but you just called me at a bad moment.' He'd passed on the distress signal from *Jensah* to a fishing boat anchored nearby, restarted the pumps on the beach and when the sea calmed, set out to rendezvous with another vessel with a derrick, to move the offending bundle of fibro aft. The rest of the journey had passed without further incident. Nothing untoward about that.

John's explanation did not impress, and *Hawk* was banned from further open water journeys. Her loss was a real blow to VB, and he was pretty terse about the way it had happened. Of all the bad luck . . . Of all the bad timing . . .

Just as VB feared, *Coringle* was not a hit with the surveyors either. But although she'd been a financial disaster, she had been there when he needed her and had got him out of a tight spot. He could not help but have an affection for her and hated seeing her stranded on the beach. For some time he kept her on a mooring in the Frances Bay channel, turning aimlessly with the tide and slowly but surely deteriorating. In 1969 the Sailing Club hosted the first national Catamaran Week. It was the biggest event the club had staged and VB was enthused when it was suggested *Coringle* should feature. He had her polished up and partly recaulked for the occasion, and tenderly took her around the harbour to Fannie Bay. It was to be the proud old lady's last voyage. Her final charter was as one end of the race finishing line, accommodating the race officials and spectators in fine style. On the last night of Cat Week she hosted the grand finale, a pirate party. VB was there as a dashing Captain Hook, and while the guests revelled and cavorted, laughter floated out across the water. The last of the cooling sea breeze sent the festoons in *Coringle*'s rigging fluttering gently. The ugly scars of age and lack of attention were lost in the darkness, and the moon and coloured party lights flattered her gracious lines. It was a fitting end to a career of some sixty years.

Later VB salvaged bits and pieces from her, and treasured them. Her wooden wheel became a permanent part of a balustrade at Perkinsville, her winch a part of a table and her ship's bell was hung in the Sailing Club Bar. He was not in town the day she was deliberately set alight to clear more space in the yard, and returned to find only the skeletal remains of his old schooner on the beach, black and charred. He was absolutely furious, and never quite forgave those responsible.

Coringle and *Hawk* saw the end of their days, but miraculously *Kestrel* passed all the new survey requirements. In 1969 VB changed her name to *Keats*, after the Aboriginal settlement of Port Keats, and kept her for a further three years. By then the era of the old ALC40s had well and truly passed.

VB had begun to think launching day would never happen. Over the last few months he had frequently paced the dock, frustrated and tugging at his moustache over the delays. This was his second new vessel, a slightly bigger, three-hundred ton deadweight landingcraft, *Warrender*. He'd had to settle for a smaller outfit in Brisbane to build her. She was the largest building the shipyard had undertaken and there'd been problems from the outset.

Warrender was to be launched sideways, in the traditional fashion. VB hovered over the preparations, arguing with the yard management about ballast. The engines were heavy in the stern and he wanted her ballasted forward for the launch. The yard management, however, knew better, and VB did not get his way.

The champagne bottle crashed on the gleaming red hull. A small crowd clapped and cheered as *Warrender* began her descent towards the muddy water of the Brisbane River. Halfway down the slipway, the cheering faltered. Then it stopped abruptly. VB's smile vanished and he watched, horrified, as his prediction came true. *Warrender* slewed sideways. Her weighty stern overtook her bow and instead of hitting the water beam on, her aft section careered in first, tipping her ingloriously off the slipway. She landed with her stern embedded into the river bottom and her bow sticking up in the air in no dignified fashion.

The launch had been a disaster. *Warrender* would have to be salvaged, the inevitable damage to her rudders, propellers and stern tubes repaired, another launch arranged and more precious time would be lost. The commotion died down and the crowd dispersed.

VB stalked up a set of stairs to the shipyard manager's office. At his heels were his engineer, Keith Lang, and skipper, Oskar Bachmann. They had never seen VB so angry. They wouldn't miss this for anything. In the office the manager and chief engineer waited uneasily for the onslaught. When it came it was short, and to the point. VB stood up very straight, his blue eyes piercing. 'Gentlemen,' he said. 'I think it's high time that the parents of both of you gave some serious consideration to the idea of getting married.' With that he turned on his heel and walked out.

VB was now fifty-seven years old and since he had begun the business he had thrown himself into his work with the enthusiasm and energy of a man thirty years younger. He was rarely in the office, preferring to be outside driving the crane or supervising loading or capital improvements. The company had ticked along nicely while he was away in Brisbane, with a skeleton team holding the fort. Mrs Brown ran the office and Chris Rooney, a young Englishman, acted as assistant manager, yard foreman and general factotum. Russ Gole still watched over the finances and kept VB informed as to the 'big picture', which was, in short, that the company was highly undercapitalised and desperately in need of new stevedoring machinery. But VB avoided debt where possible and still preferred to buy old bits of machinery from auctions. They often broke down and the yard became a repository for what were known as 'Mr P's follies'. The year 1971 was not a good one. As well as the payments on *Fourcroy* there were progress payments to be made on *Warrender*, and the delay in her launching until mid-year created a cashflow crisis. A major refinancing strategy had to be undertaken.

To Russ Gole it was now clear that VB simply did not have the desire to manage the company financially nor take care of the day-to-day operational problems on an ongoing basis. If things were going along smoothly he lost interest, tending to run the business on a program of crisis management, for at that he was good. Small things that people did wrongly could annoy him. If someone tied a granny knot where a bowline should have been he'd give them a gruff dressing down. Yet major disasters not obviously caused by stupidity, such as the fire aboard *Fourcroy*, didn't upset him. The net result of the fire was the loss of *Fourcroy*'s entire accommodation block. Inspecting the damage with Chris Rooney, VB showed no sign of grief. He was already planning in his mind how to rebuild it. In front of him was a challenge: to do the whole job in his own yard, using his own workshop crew. He knew he had the resources and he set out to make it happen. He revelled in getting the show back on the road.

The effects of VB's war experiences manifested themselves in many ways. His exuberance was natural but his ability not to worry about things was the result of having seen the very bottom of what life could dish out. Having once struggled against the odds just to live to see another day, problems in a business seemed superficial. His character had proven excellent for seeing the opportunities, having the confidence to get the business started with nothing and for coping with risk and trauma. But the company could not survive forever on crisis management.

VB could see the merits of Russ Gole's suggestion that he employ a manager. Chris Rooney was still young and inexperienced but his older brother Roger, who had worked aboard *Loellen M* in 1962, had an extra ten years experience in various occupations since VB had last employed him. VB had always liked the Rooney boys. They had a privileged, English public-school education but they were no-nonsense, straight from the shoulder lads who were not afraid of hard work. They could have stayed in England and followed their well-to-do father into the Rooney Brush Company, but they chose adventure and both had a game, entrepreneurial spirit about them. Roger Rooney took the position, and not long after VB took himself off for a month or two to poke about the world, on what was to be his first real holiday ever.

Since Barbara had left him VB's domestic requirements were taken care of by a housekeeper. He taught her to fold his socks just the way his *amah* used to do it, and there was always a hot meal waiting for him when he came home for lunch at noon. He was well enough provided for in these respects, but this was a lonely period of his life. He hated being by himself. He had enjoyed the company and attendant trappings of marriage and he missed Barbara, speaking fondly of her to his friends.

Barbara's resentment of VB had long since dissipated since they parted, and though his lack of action on various family matters still infuriated her, she found it impossible to dislike her ex-husband. She rarely allowed herself to dwell upon how things could have been under different circumstances, had they not come to Darwin, for the memories of what they once had were too fresh. With Michel she had found real happiness, but her admiration and fondness for VB always remained.

To counter his loneliness VB had thrown himself into his work and social life, rarely spending an evening alone. He relied on his good friends for companionship and they got used to him popping around for dinner unannounced. Often he would telephone 'The Nunnery', a house at Fannie Bay in which several single ladies resided and where he was nicknamed 'Five o'clock Perkins' for his habit of ringing to say, 'What are you lot up to this evening? I've got steam on main engines around here,' by which he meant the housekeeper had put something in the pot for dinner and they were all invited. Or on a Saturday evening VB would go to the Sailing Club, round up six or eight people (ensuring that at least two females were among them) and invite them to Perkinsville for dinner. Having poured a round of drinks his proven form was to settle the gentlemen at the bar, while the ladies were given a cook's tour of the contents of the refrigerator and handed a packet of rice.

As children, Antony and I regularly made the long, rough trip to Darwin in the old Fokker Friendships, hopping up the Western Australian coast on the 'milk run' from Perth to Port Hedland, to Broome, to Derby, and to Kununurra. Antony was always thoroughly and noisily sick at every landing, and VB learned to expect to be presented with the sick bag he always saved for his father.

Life for VB went on pretty much as normal when we were around. The very first time we went home to Perkinsville without our mother, I was seven years old. It was our first separation from her and, because she had taken nothing with her when she left, the house had not changed at all. Yet Perkinsville seemed empty and strange without her. When the housekeeper served sloppy scrambled eggs for dinner I burst into tears. Mummy never did sloppy scrambled eggs and I knew only too well my father's philosophy on food meant that I would have to eat it.

'What are you laughing about?' VB said, gruffly, of my unhappiness. 'You're going to have to buck up, Charlie. We're going out as soon as you've eaten.' And so we were. We spent our first evening back in Darwin without our mother at a party at Admiralty House. I accidentally broke a glass and burst into tears again, much to VB's chagrin. It wasn't the broken glass but the tears that he didn't like. He wasn't very good with tears.

The insecurity didn't last long. Being towed around to our father's various social engagements became the norm, of which my general memory is of Antony and me amusing ourselves to the background of chortles from VB and great hilarity from everyone else. Apart from the regulars at Perkinsville, the house always seemed to be full of submarine-commander types and nabobs and all manner of people who were passing through Darwin and had heard they should look up VB Perkins. As children, having people constantly around was stimulating, and for a short time before bed each night, we were employed to ensure that the peanut and olive bowls were not empty and, when we were old enough, to pour drinks and 'make sure the tide wasn't out' on anyone's glass.

The nitty-gritty of looking after children was not VB's forte. When Antony was young, he once wet his sheets and VB dealt with it by means of a couple of copies of the *Bulletin* placed strategically underneath the offending bottom, preferring to leave changing the bed to the housekeeper when she came on duty the next day. I was most amused to note the newsprint tattooing Antony's backside the next morning. The idea of changing the sheets himself would not even have occurred to VB. Despite this he proved he could rise to the occasion when it was really called for. The night the tooth fairy failed to deposit the customary twenty cents under Antony's pillow, VB was quick to save the situation. Confronted by a tearful small boy he spluttered, 'What! Surely not!'

and marched into the bedroom with an air of high dudgeon. Determined to get to the bottom of the outrage he engaged Antony in an examination of the sheets and, whipping twenty cents from his pocket, reached down behind the bed. 'Hey, Boy, look here I've found it,' he said. 'It must have fallen down behind the bed.' Antony was immediately and utterly delighted. Looking on, as I was, and with the benefit of two years additional worldly wisdom, I began to have some doubts about the habits of tooth fairies.

VB's absolute horror of wasting food meant that the worst sin his children could commit was to leave something on their plates. This caused several standoffs. We learned early in life that when he said, 'If you don't eat it for dinner you will eat it for breakfast,' he meant it. He was also strict about matters of politeness and social niceties. From a very young age Antony was drilled into standing when a lady entered the room, and at meals we were both taught that saying 'No thank you, I'm full,' was impolite. 'If you must say something,' he counselled, say 'No thank you, I'm replete.' The first time Antony tried this one in the company of ten adults, he muffed it by boldly declaring 'No thank you, I'm perspired.'

Such startling success with our social deportment did not come about through VB raising either his voice or his hand. I can remember no incidents of either. When discipline was required it was enough for him to employ his disapproving look, inherited no doubt from his mother, when his eyes narrowed and his lips, barely discernible under his moustache, became thin and drawn. The result was terrifying and usually produced the desired effect.

On Saturday afternoons at around 3pm the East Point (Gentlemen's) Tennis Club convened on the court behind the Trippes' house on East Point Road. As a founding member and patron, VB was a regular. The club became an institution of Darwin society. It was only because of the excellent company to be found at the EPGTC that he had given up sailing, which clashed on Saturday afternoons. Only a disaster of catastrophic proportions would prevent him from turning up for a hit, a cold beer and the conversation of his fellows, and on the one occasion our flight back to

Perth left at this hallowed time of the week, someone else was detailed to airport fatigues.

As youngsters we spent a great deal of time in the office, where the kindly Mrs Brown kept us well supplied with biscuits and orange cordial, and endlessly drew pussy cats for us. Failing that, amusement could be guaranteed in the staff lavatory, where several bright green frogs habitually clung to the rim of the loo, just underneath the seat. When we were a bit older VB would give us pocket money for tidying up the store cupboard, for pulling out infernal coffee bushes or rolling empty drums about the yard.

At home he commissioned a friend to build us a cubby house in the garden, out of the bridge deck of an old lugger. The cubby saw good service, but VB's real saviours were his friends with children of similar ages. The Watt family had three. 'Uncle Don' was the manager of the local brewery, a position to which he had no doubt risen through his untiring efforts to be super-efficient at whatever he did. His repertoire included entertaining children and he, having no doubt consulted his manual on the subject, did an excellent job. His endearing and enduring wife Blanche, who coped well with her husband's efficiency, also coped well with having Antony and me around an awful lot. So did VB's very good friends Lucille and Wilfred Arthur, who lent their youngest son, Peter, to the cause, and we three spent a great deal of time haunting the jungle behind their house on the Nightcliff foreshore, or scavenging around the World War II army dump on the beach across the road, looking for ammunition.

As children we regarded our father with great affection, though he never did many fatherly things with us. I don't recall him playing anything other than mahjong, backgammon or Scrabble with us, but somehow we never expected it of him. Neither did the fact that he rarely remembered our birthdays seem of much consequence. Perhaps it was because on the odd occasion that he did remember (or our mother had rung to remind him) what arrived in the mail did not inspire us to great anticipation. Antony once received a pair of BOAC socks (though several sizes too large they were at least unopened and still wrapped in the plastic in which they were issued) and a rather loudly coloured cravat, both of which VB had found in his wardrobe. At ten years old Antony was not overly thrilled by his new apparel but, as we both well knew, our father didn't much like birthdays.

VB was not a demonstrative person; a kiss on the forehead and a pat on the back was more his way. We never saw any obvious displays of emotion on his part but his closest friends insist he adored us and I guess we knew that. We realised he was not the average Dad and did not compare him with the doting young fathers of some of our contemporaries. In the ranks of fatherhood, it cannot be denied that VB did not distinguish himself. But for our part, we loved him all the same.

TWENTY-FOUR

Situation Normal, All Fouled Up

N ine million dollars. It was no small biscuits in a little place like Darwin, but that was the sort of money Freeport Indonesia was pumping into the local economy. It was good work for Darwin landingcraft. Freeport's copper and gold mine in the western part of New Guinea lay at an altitude of 3,700 metres, on the vast pinnacle of Carstensz Top mountain in Irian Jaya, 5,030 metres high at its glacial peak. Since the mine's inception in 1967 the landingcraft had been supplying it, landing cargo as far up the river as possible. It was adventurous stuff. The crews came back with amazing stories: stories of native pilots taken aboard from canoes in mid river, adorned in nothing but a bone through the nose and penis gourds; of being grounded high upriver where the tide does not reach, waiting for rain on the glacier to bring them water; of being alone in a strange and remote part of the world with a reputation for cannibalism, and being terrified when curious tribesmen appeared out of the jungle with teeth filed to horrifyingly sharp points to board the stranded vessel.

In 1973 *Fourcroy* was doing much of the Irian Jaya work. That which Freeport could not purchase in Darwin was brought by sea from the south and transhipped from the main wharf to VB's yard. Now it was all at risk. The events unfolding from April were to bring VB's company to its knees, to the brink of disaster.

VB had watched the goings on at the wharf over the last thirteen years from afar. He didn't like what he saw. The Darwin wharfies had been members of the belligerent watersiders' branch of the North Australian Workers Union (NAWU), and their main claim to fame was that they had turned Darwin into the most militant port in Australia. Statistics of man-hours lost through unauthorised stoppages in 1970–71 were exactly double those of its closest rival in the country. The wharfies didn't confine their industrial action to issues relating to their own conditions and industry, and strikes over unrelated and sometimes trivial 'sympathy issues' were especially frustrating to those who depended upon wharf labour.

When the Darwin Branch of the Waterside Workers Federation (WWF) was formed out of the NAWU, VB had reason to feel uneasy; the wharfies regarded his outfit as a lucrative target. Australian watersiders had a tradition of electing leaders who were members of the Communist Party. They, in turn, had a tradition of disruption.[1] Darwin had been known in the 1960s as 'Little Moscow' and prominent Darwin watersiders still regarded a visit to the Soviet capital as an essential part of their education. VB had been staggered to learn of this. Having once worked under the threat of being shot up by Communists, that element within the organisation did not appeal at all. In Malaya Communists were executed for their troubles. Now they wanted to take over his business.

---

[1] Communism on the Waterfront *was a booklet published from within the WWF in 1961 for distribution to members. It amounted to a desperate plea to members to censure the practices of the Communist leadership of the WWF. Its thirty pages were crammed full of detailed cases of Communist 'conspiracy, lies, standover and smears' within both the WWF and the Seamen's Union and was summed up with the assertion that, 'The bitter truth is that . . . [the Communist Party] has no firmly held policy for the benefit of the Federation members. It is a day to day policy of deception, obstruction and destruction to further the current political plans of the Communist Party—with the overall plan of making Australia an easy prey for International Communism.'*

Goofy, Storky, Boots, Rodent, Fat Pat and the others settled into their drinking possie—a few empty milk crates and an old car seat next to the cargo shed—enjoying their just deserts. The company always laid on a carton or two after they'd finished loading. It was a tradition, a kind of thank you for a job well done. Their leader had a stack of common sense and it rubbed off on all of them. They had a real pride in what they did. Somehow the performance of the waterside workers only made them feel better about themselves, more determined to be different.

For years VB's employees had joined no union. They had permanent jobs, there was no demarcation and everybody pitched in and worked at whatever had to be done. They took turns at going to sea and working ashore. By and large they were happy with what they were paid and, partly because they didn't do the same thing every day, they had real job satisfaction. Unlike the wharfies, they didn't mind working in the rain, and were paid a bit extra for doing so. There was a good spirit among them. VB had their utmost support in the fight against the wharfies. Still they knew they could not fight alone, and they joined the NAWU.

At the same time the WWF took over the work of the small lugger operators working from the main wharf. VB watched as one by one, businesses folded. George Haritos put a freezer into his *Betty Joan*, and went fishing. Sid Hawkes ran a lugger, *Larrpan*, and confided, 'It's just not economic any more. You never know what the wharfies are going to do next. A bloke can't run his own business on his own terms. I'm getting out.'

Then it began. In April 1973 the wharfies black-banned two containers of frozen and perishable food that had arrived from the south, bound for Freeport Indonesia. The result was predictable. Freeport moved their supply base from Darwin to Singapore. Australia lost a large source of export earnings, the Darwin economy lost nine million dollars a year, VB Perkins & Co lost the Irian Jaya work and the WWF lost the transhipment work.

VB was furious. His mind was made up. This shipping industry was not all that Mr Onassis would have cracked it up to be. As a matter of principle VB was against handouts from the government, and was not interested in owning a business which could not stand on its own feet. He was sure that if the wharfies took over his work VB Perkins & Co would be consigned to the same welfare queue as its contemporaries around the nation that could not operate without government subsidy. He was not interested in being dictated to by the WWF. He'd rather close down the whole operation and do something else than give in—and he'd fight to the bitter end.

The May Day Parade on the May Day public holiday had always been a bit of fun in Darwin. Men, women and children braved the sun to line the hot city streets and watch the oom, pah, pah and revelry pass them by. The year 1973 was no different and the thirteen floats, including one urging people to protest at the French atomic tests in the Pacific, wound their way through the streets to the Esplanade Oval. It was a good parade and when the last float passed and the last of the children's icecream had melted down their fronts the crowds began to shuffle off. But then they stopped and looked again, for a parade postscript was making its way, with great commotion, along the street. It was the ruffians from Frances Bay, banned by the organisers for not having officially entered.

A large red landingcraft float headed the contingent. As it passed the crowds looked with interest at the group of fellows sitting on the deck wearing WWF T-shirts. They had pillows under their shirts for bellies. They lay back with their feet up, drinking beer from an esky beside them. At the business end of the vessel the team of fit looking blokes wore 'Save Darwin's Small Ships' T-shirts, boldly emblazoned with 'SNAFU'. (I was told by VB as I was presented with mine that it stood for 'Situation Normal, All Fouled Up'. I have since heard less polite variations on that theme.) They were tossing boxes about, looking industrious. The popular song 'You Can't Get Me—I'm Part of the Union' blared from loudspeakers. The next float was a black coffin on the side of which was painted 'RIP Freeport Indonesia'. Then came a mobile crane and a container garlanded with a banner proclaiming 'We're having

Manning problems!', a reference to WWF Secretary, Brian Manning. Bringing up the rear of the procession was a black Ford motorcar. In it sat VB Perkins, himself. He was wearing a halo.

Barely a day had passed over the previous month that the *Northern Territory News* did not carry a headline about the small-ships issue: 'Darwin Supply Work Lost by Black Ban', 'Waterside Dispute Flares into Pub Brawling', 'Agreement on Barge Cargo Handling Ruinous', 'Watersiders Would Ruin Companies Barge-loaders Say', 'Barge Dispute—A Nail in Port Coffin'. WWF picket lines appeared outside VB's yard. Tempers became frayed.

It seemed that everything was against VB. The NAWU changed tune and the new secretary advised the yard crew to join the WWF. (The yard crew promptly resigned from the NAWU and joined the Transport Workers Union.) The Australian Stevedoring Industry Authority found against VB in a special hearing. Their job was to interpret the law, they said, and the law was clear in that all cargo within a port area must be handled by registered waterside labour. The Federal Minister for Labour refused to amend the Stevedoring Industry Act. VB and every one of his employees wrote to him, only to be told to negotiate with the WWF. The Prime Minister showed no sympathy. In all the vastness of government, there was no-one to help save the small-ships industry. VB saw it as a matter of vital importance to the Northern Territory, but no-one was interested.

VB's only hope was a small loophole in the law. Section 7N of the Stevedoring Industry Act provided exceptions to compulsory membership of the WWF, one of which was, 'Persons in the regular employment of a person engaged in an Industrial Undertaking, being persons whose duties include the performance of stevedoring operations in connection with that undertaking.'

Only thirty per cent of the work carried out by VB's yard crew was stevedoring work. The rest of the time they worked on capital improvements such as reclaiming land and wharf building, repairing and maintaining vessels and machinery, delivering cargo around the town and whatever else came up. It seemed the only way out was to get the company classified as an Industrial Undertaking. By now both VB and Roger had lost faith in the government's desire to see private enterprise work. They were desperate times calling for desperate measures, so they drew a leaf from the WWF's book.

Over the next few weeks Roger was less efficient than usual about reminding the Aboriginal communities to order fuel. The yard crew was less efficient about loading all the cargo, and the occasional pallet was left sitting in the yard. *Fourcroy* was working in Timor, and in mid September 1973 *Warrender* too was sent to Timor. Roger made a formal announcement on the radio, television and in the national press. VB sent a personal telegram to the Prime Minister, one to Clyde Cameron, the Attorney General and several other Cabinet ministers. The message was straightforward: VB Perkins's vessels were overseas and would not be brought back into the country until the company was classified as an Industrial Undertaking, exempt from using WWF labour.

Still nobody listened. The Aboriginal communities ran short of food and the RAAF was put on standby for an airlift. Still nothing happened. Then the Aboriginal communities began to send tele-grams to Canberra supporting the small-ships issue. Suddenly the Federal Labor government listened. Within seven days the land-ingcraft operators, VB Perkins & Co, Barge Express (begun in 1966 when Ted Fitzgerald's brother-in-law came to Darwin) and Marine Contractors, were each classified as an Industrial Undertaking. The battle had been won.

In July 1973, three hundred nautical miles north of Darwin, Barge Express's *Green Seal* gurgled to the bottom of a pale emerald sea. She was one hand short at the time, with a crew of only three. The fourth had failed to return from the pub before they left Darwin, and the skipper had sailed for Irian Jaya anyway. All hands were rescued but the national maritime unions began sniffing around and discovered that, in a backwater of a place called Darwin, landingcraft had been putting to sea with unqualified masters, unqualified engi-neers and short of deckhands. They pounced.

By the end of the year the seagoing unions had joined the fray. The Seamen's Union signed up a couple of employees, and when they had some coverage they threatened stoppages unless the company agreed to substantial rises in pay and leave. The battle with the wharfies had cost VB Perkins & Co dearly, and it was in no position to withstand any stoppages. The company had got as far as it had largely because of the loyalty of its employees. The relationship had always been good and they wanted it to stay that way. At the time it seemed inevitable that the seagoing unions would eventually take over the work. By the first week of 1974 the old system of permanent employees swapping between working ashore and going to sea, a regime under which they and their families had been happy, was gone. Suddenly they were either seamen or yard crew. Suddenly, the old days were over.

The Seamen's Union black-banned VB's dumb-barge, *Timor Trader*, that was towed behind *Fourcroy*, in the otherwise marginal drummed fuel trade to East Timor. The Seamen's Union claimed she cost jobs, and all of a sudden *Timor Trader* was stranded in Darwin, fully loaded with drummed kerosene, aviation fuel and petrol bound for Dili. VB avoided union high-flyers, and Roger flew to Sydney to try and reason with the Federal Secretary of the Seamen's Union, EV Elliot. Mr Elliot was a member of the Central Committee of the Communist Party of Australia, and did not appreciate the concept of economics in business. The meeting was a complete failure. *Timor Trader* was refused even one last voyage to Dili to deliver the cargo with which she was already loaded.

Four hundred nautical miles to the north, East Timor was short of fuel. As the Harbour Master slept peacefully in Darwin one night, a Portuguese tug moved stealthily into Darwin Harbour. A dinghy loaded with officials from non-union customs and quarantine waited to meet her. The tug entered Frances Bay piloted by the light of Roger Rooney's torch. The clandestine operation continued in VB's yard and by daylight the black-banned dumb-barge was well out to sea. The Seamen's Union were furious at this 'snatching'. In seventeen years of business VB had never been confronted with a strike. Now, for the first time, he had one.

In the meantime the WWF had not been idle. Government had not listened to VB's lobbying to have the Stevedoring Industry Act

concerning waterside labour in a port area amended. But it listened
to the WWF when it wanted to bring the Act before Parliament to
change the section concerning Industrial Undertakings. In November
1974 VB and Roger were forced into another round of desperate
lobbying. Despite many visits to Canberra their voices once more
fell on deaf ears. It wasn't until they enlisted the support of the
Transport Workers Union and four other unions, by pointing out
that the change to the legislation would prevent their members from
working on wharves all over Australia, that there was cause for hope.

The unions protested to the government. Suddenly the brick
wall facing VB crumbled. The Labor government immediately listened to the unions and the amendments were dropped. By the
end of it all VB was left with a distinct lack of respect for politicians.
It seemed to him that the government was not at all interested in
seeing private enterprise work; he began to wonder whether there
was any hope for Australia at all.

VB still had a dream. It was a dream of running a shipping service
to his old stamping ground, Singapore. Yet he still wanted to have
the capacity to land difficult cargo in difficult, out of the way places,
and for that he needed a purpose-built, foreign-going vessel. The
fact was that he would never be able to finance such a vessel while
he had no title to the land he had built at Frances Bay to use as
collateral. And the knowledge that it could be taken from under
him at short notice ate away at him.

The first approach from the Commonwealth Department of
Aboriginal Affairs had come the previous year. The government,
concerned for the security of the supply line to the Aboriginal
settlements during the WWF dispute, had offered to buy equity
in the company. It all sounded good. Government equity would
solve the problems over title to the land; there'd be ample funds
from the Aboriginal Loans Commission at five per cent per annum
for vessel finance and yard improvements; and where new services
were provided, direct grants would be considered.

VB had done it once before. In 1971 he sold a share of his business
to a large organisation with a view to gaining access to finance.

The finance had not been forthcoming and he'd bought the shares back promptly. Now the promises from Aboriginal Affairs sounded like a way forward when there was no other. He decided to go with the offer, and in November 1974 the Aboriginal Loans Commission, through a company called Arnhem Transport Pty Ltd, acquired seventy per cent of the issued shares in VB Perkins & Co. Six months later they acquired a further five per cent.

It wasn't one of VB's better decisions.

TWENTY-FIVE

The Girl Next Door

R eluctantly VB sat in his pseudo-timber-lined office, in the ATCO demountable that was the hub of VB Perkins & Co. He had some paperwork on that day in September of 1973, but he was thinking about what he wanted to do outside. The phone rang and he picked it up.

'Hello. It's Jocelyn Strickland here,' said a voice on the other end of the line.

He thought for a moment. An image of Tom Strickland's long-haired thirteen-year-old daughter flitted across his memory. Tom had been posted back to Perth some seven years ago and he hadn't seen him since. Casting his mind back he couldn't remember having seen Jocelyn for two or three years before Tom left; perhaps it was ten years ago.

'I'm here in Darwin for a holiday and Barbara suggested I look you up.'

Tom Strickland and VB Perkins had always had a love in common. Tom's passion for sailing equalled that of VB's in his younger days, and when Tom became founding Commodore of the Darwin Sailing Club in 1963, VB was there as a founding member. The club began with around six boats sailing the waters of the harbour off a graceful arc of sand at Fannie Bay. At the day's end the sailors gathered at a small rotunda on the beach to watch the sun set the sky blazing crimson over the water. Tom found VB very willing to lend his resources to the cause of sailing, and when a more permanent base was mooted, VB got involved in the building of the first 'club house', a modest cabana of steel pipe, cyclone mesh and coconut-palm thatch. From there the club went from strength to strength. VB later became Patron, a position he held for the rest of his life, and through the Sailing Club there was always an association between the two men. But Tom Strickland never dreamed just how that association would continue.

The likeable Tom, Darwin manager of McRobertson Miller Airlines (later manager of Ansett), had lived with his wife, Judy, next door to Perkinsville for three years in the early 1960s. Judy Strickland was friendly with Barbara and had always felt a little sorry for her neighbour, knowing how she suffered from the heat, had little in the way of conveniences and spent long hours working. Judy often heard the typewriter banging away at all hours of the night, and wondered at how Barbara coped with it all. The Stricklands' three children, Tony, Jocelyn and Ann, were usually away at school in Perth, but in the school holidays Judy was pleased to see her eldest daughter take an interest in the goings on at Perkinsville and become a blessing to her neighbour. Jocelyn had taken quite a shine to me as a child and enjoyed keeping me generally amused and babysitting for Barbara.

Now, in 1973, Jocelyn was a young woman, fresh from an overseas trip during which she had seen some of the world and fallen in and out of love. Her experiences had matured her, perhaps beyond her years, and when VB met her again he recognised her immediately.

Having known VB when she was a child, Jocelyn had no notions of romance, just a real curiosity. The attraction she felt when they met again was unexpected. VB was now sixty years old and she twenty-three, yet his conversation amused and interested her and the twinkle in his eye held a magnetic appeal. It seemed VB was quite different from any other man she had met. His charm was disarming. His dignity and maturity made the younger men she had known seem somehow unfledged.

They saw a lot of each other in the two weeks Jocelyn was in Darwin, and it was a thrill to hear from VB that he'd hold a dinner party in her honour. But when he explained that she was also to be the cook she was horrified, and came up with an excuse. 'I'm returning to Perth earlier than planned,' she said, and VB cancelled the dinner party.

On the evening in question he called in at the Sailing Club, and there among the throng he spotted her. Approaching from behind he said in her ear in a low, unmistakable voice, 'Caught!'

Indeed Jocelyn was caught. VB had taken to calling her Joss, saying that she was his good luck (*joss* meaning 'luck' in Chinese). VB also had no visions of long term romance, but he soon found Joss to be a lot of fun and, with youth on her side she was certainly a good stayer at a party. She was well travelled, well educated, well mannered; quick off the mark (he was impressed when he asked her how, if he gave her $500, she would invest it so that he would get the best return, and she said 'On myself, of course!') and altogether presentable. One could always ignore the odd raised eyebrow at their age difference. Age, he thought, was only in the mind and he was not of a mind to feel old.

Weeks later, back in her home in Perth, the thought of VB haunted Joss, the distance between them left her empty. But it wasn't long before he turned up on her doorstep. VB, in the fashion of the time, wore his hair longer than usual and his curls, Joss thought, were a little unruly. She was aware that the new man in her life was highly unconventional and in Perth was terrified her straitlaced friends from school might see them together so she walked a little apart from him in the street. After the first time he visited again, and then again. When at last he rang her from Darwin to deliver the simple message 'Come be my love', she had already made up her mind.

Stepping off the plane in Darwin in March 1974 she searched for her flamboyant man in the crowd, but he was nowhere to be found. In his stead was a respectable-looking character who had come straight from the barber. VB was itching to introduce her, to claim her as his own, and that night he took her out to dinner with his crowd; the first time of many that Joss saw him burst into song in public. A few days later she was dining with his friends at their lovely home in Nightcliff. So impressed was she by the culinary skill and elegance of their hostess that her nerves got the better of her. How would she measure up if Bruce was used to this sort of thing? She excused herself from the table and walked out through the garden and onto the foreshore. Then she threw up.

Perkinsville was still seen as something of an open house by VB's friends when Joss moved in.[1] His well-entrenched habit of inviting large parties of people for dinner at short notice did nothing to ease her into her new situation. With very little cooking experience she was truly thrown in at the deep end, but found the strength to carry on in VB's ever-present calm in the face of her panic. When she dropped the roast on the kitchen floor five minutes before twelve guests arrived she fled to the bedroom in floods of tears. VB was ever cool, despite the fact that whilst picking up the roast he split his trousers. Sitting on the edge of the bed administering a comforting pat on the bottom, he said, 'Here, Charlie, I've brought you a brandy, collected up the spuds and dusted off the lamb. We've got steam on main engines again and we'll need you to show the flag.' The ravaged seam soon had Joss laughing and the evening was saved. Fortunately, as long as the plates were warm, VB rarely had any complaints about what he was served.

As VB's new love, Joss was the subject of a good deal of speculation and gossip around town. Some thought she was one of my friends for she looked so young. 'Bruce has got a schoolgirl living with

---

[1] *A recipe for Jellied Gazpacho appeared in the 1974 edition of a fund-raising cookbook for the Royal Prince Alfred Hospital. It was submitted by Roger Rooney's gregarious mother Rachel, visiting from England, and was prefaced by the following: 'One of Darwin's greatest hosts is Mr Bruce Perkins. He keeps an almost open house day or night and I had the good fortune to stay with him last year. I happened to mention that it was my birthday and at once he said we must have a small "Hooley"; this turned into forty good friends for dinner and I was to be the cook. The date was 21st March 1973 "in the wet", 95 plus 95 humidity and not much to choose from in the shops. This dish can be prepared the day before and can be served cold.'*

him!' one of VB's older friends commented, and there was some conjecture that it would not last. But for Joss it was easy to forget the thirty-six-year age difference, for VB had friends from all walks of life. His older group of friends he saw often, and the fellows from the Officers' Mess at the RAAF and the Army were of varying age. There was also a younger group of very fun people in their twenties and thirties whose company VB thoroughly enjoyed. With such a wide spectrum of friends age didn't seem to matter. Joss never felt awkward about the relationship because VB made it easy. It was a perfectly natural thing to him and his confidence gave her confidence. Besides, she was having a wonderful time.

Living with VB there was always something happening and Joss found he attracted a fascinating assortment of people. Like bees to the honey pot they came to Perkinsville, and she never quite knew who would turn up next. She met the sort of people she never dreamed she would meet—war heroes, English aristocracy, NASA engineers—yet as far as his friends were concerned, he did not discriminate. Be they from any background, profession, colour, race or creed, they were welcome if he liked them. The back door was never locked, and often the first thing they knew about a guest having spent the night was the smell of bacon and eggs frying in the early morning.

Fitting into VB's scene had not been difficult, but at the back of her mind Joss wondered how her family would react to the new arrangement. Then there were the inevitable complications from VB's past. Barbara still spoke to VB regularly on the phone, for he often rang to sound her out about various matters, and she followed his life from a distance. Barbara knew of his need to have someone around and she'd felt sorry that he lived alone. When she heard that Joss had moved in she was surprised, but pleased for him.

Antony and I arrived in Darwin in the next school holidays armed only with the knowledge that the girl we remembered as 'Jossy', who used to babysit us when we were little, was living at Perkinsville. VB did not prepare us, and at the ripe old age of twelve and fourteen the idea that Joss was living anywhere other than downstairs where the housekeeper lived didn't occur to us, for it seemed she was barely older than we were. On the first night Joss walked through our bedroom to VB's room, and I assumed she wanted to get a book, or something . . . As I lay wide awake waiting for her to re-emerge my imagination churned as to why she could be taking so long. The minutes mounted and my theories began to seem less likely. As the truth dawned it all began to take on a dreamlike unreality.

But the shock did not last long. Though he never sat down to discuss it, the fact that VB showed not one iota of coyness about the situation soon dissipated any conception we had that this was something out of the ordinary. There was inevitably some initial teenage resentment from us about the new rules presiding over Perkinsville since Joss's arrival, and no doubt our presence on school holidays did nothing to make Joss feel more secure, but overall we all settled as well as could be expected into the new arrangement.

Perhaps the last people to find out about Joss's new situation were her parents. Judy's first reaction was to declare that she would never speak to Jocelyn again. But as she later put it, 'one has to get over these things, and get on'. It was during the business of 'getting on' that they became more concerned for their daughter's life than for her morals. A telephone call was the last communication between the Stricklands and their eldest daughter before Christmas 1974. Joss had talked excitedly of her forthcoming trip to Portuguese Timor with VB; of the drilling rig to be moved from a remote location on the rough southern coast; of having to find a new landing site on the open beach for *Fourcroy*. They were due to fly to Baukau on the north-eastern coast on Monday, 23 December, but as Christmas approached a loitering tropical cyclone dumped inches of rain on the island. The day before Christmas an MMA (MacRobertson Miller Airlines) pilot assured Tom Strickland that all flights to Timor had been grounded for a couple of days, and he assumed they hadn't gone. But they had.

TWENTY-SIX

All Pinish

The night had been abominable. They were damp, chilled, muddy and exhausted. They'd been driving for almost twenty-four hours now, bouncing, bumping and sliding across the highlands of East Timor. It hadn't stopped raining since he and Joss arrived, but VB had a job to do and he wasn't going to let a little bad weather put him off. He should have. They had made it from Dili, across the innumerable washouts and gullies of the mountains, stopping frequently to repair washaways with stones and pebbles, to the lowlands on the southern side of the country. At the surging Betano River, just nine miles short of where VB wanted to inspect a landing site for *Fourcroy*, they'd had to give up. It had been a rotten Christmas Day.

On Boxing Day morning they drove back into Dili. The town seemed unusually flat after the tortuous mountains, and the white-washed buildings held a fresh appeal against the mud of Dili's mostly dirt roads. The driver swerved to avoid a wandering pig and at last they pulled up outside the Hotel Dili. VB had been a little testy, but was now resigned to the fact that the trip had been a waste of effort. It had stopped raining but it didn't look as though the weather would really clear for days. He didn't notice a face appear quickly at the window of the hotel. Then the front door was flung open. A man rushed out to greet them and before he had even reached them he spluttered, 'It's all gone! Everything is all gone.' VB looked at Joss. What on earth was the fellow talking about?

'Darwin,' he said. 'A cyclone has blown it all away and there is nothing left. The Bank of New South Wales is gone. The Post Office is gone. The Vic Hotel has been wrecked. It's all been wiped out.'

Momentarily VB was lost for words. The enormity of what he had just heard took a few seconds to register. When he'd gathered his thoughts enough to speak, the inevitable tirade of questions began. But there were few answers. The Hotel Dili was half full of people from Darwin. Telephone communications were out. Everyone was desperate for information. None were more desperate than VB. Had his vessels all been sunk? Was there anything left in the yard? Had anyone been killed? How had Perkinsville fared? Godammit! How could this have happened without him?

Thoughts of breakfast were forgotten in his haste to get hold of a short-wave radio. He hurried over to one of the dusty Chinese shops and bought one without so much as a haggle. Back in his room huddled over his purchase he twiddled the dial urgently. He picked up Radio Australia, and through the static got enough information to confirm what had been said. It had happened again. For the third time in its short life, Darwin had been devastated. This was the worst ever. Darwin airport was closed to all except emergency traffic and there was little chance of his getting back in a hurry.

VB cursed roundly. He had never been so frustrated. For the next day or two his mind spun with thoughts of how much would have to be done, and he desperately wanted to get back and be doing it. There seemed no chance of that for days, maybe weeks.

On the second day VB's ears pricked up at the sound of a DC3 cargo aircraft descending over Dili. Timor Oil was exploring again and the plane had a load of the company's equipment, bound for Sydney. There was space enough in the cold cargo hold for two people to return to Australia; probable landing place, Gove. Many hands went up but it was decided that VB should go, along with the top-ranking public servant.

At Dili airport VB almost jogged across the runway to the aeroplane.

In the shade of the tin shed that was Gove airport VB didn't have long to wait. It was only twenty minutes before the first light aircraft carrying evacuees from Darwin landed. Some twenty Aborigines filed off the aircraft and across the tarmac, carrying nothing but the clothes they were wearing. As they passed VB asked one of them how things were in Darwin.

'All buggered up,' said the man. Then more decisively, 'All buggered up, pinish!'

VB knew the drill only too well. Cyclone warnings came and went every wet season in Darwin and most people were pretty blasé about them. Perhaps newcomers might still batten things down and rush around to the supermarket to stock up on canned foods and batteries at every warning, but most had been through the rigmarole so many times unnecessarily that they had lost interest. Only weeks ago there had been another warning of a cyclone approaching on a similar track, and it had turned abruptly before reaching Darwin. Christmas Eve would have been the last time anybody wanted to concern themselves with cyclone warnings, particularly the boys at VB's yard, who would have had serious drinking on their minds.

Over the last few days VB had been over it in his mind time and time again. It was likely that preparation in the yard would have been minimal. Christmas tradition came in the form of a slap-up party in the yard on Christmas Eve. He could just visualise it. At around 6pm all would be ready, grog laid on and chilled, eskies bulging promisingly. Cheese and biscuits, a secondary considera-tion, would be carelessly arranged on an old trestle table and a rough assortment of chairs scattered in readiness. Cyclones would not have featured on the program of the evening's festivities.

But VB should have known he could count on Keith Lang. In an outfit in which almost everyone was young except the boss, Keith Lang stood out as a bit of an oldie. Something of the same vintage as VB, 'Klang' was an engineering type, currently working in the

office. He had seen a lot of things in his time, and on Christmas
Eve he had been uneasy. When he suddenly locked up the booze
and announced that there would be no party, his popularity nose-
dived. For the last three days he had been keeping abreast of the
radio warnings and that afternoon, from the point at Larrakeyah,
Keith had looked up at the unsettled sky. He hadn't liked the look
of it.

On Christmas Eve he and a couple of others had quietly gone
about the task of battening down in the yard. They tied down what
they could, stored any loose material which could turn into lethal
missiles and put extra lines on *Fourcroy*, in port for the night. The
big problem was VB's recent purchase from Nabalco: twenty-seven
demountable houses, the remnants of the original base camp at
Wallaby Beach, lying stacked at the end of the fill waiting to be
sold. Keith surveyed them doubtfully and concluded that there was
nothing much that could be done. There were too many of them
and the way in which they were stacked made it impossible to tie
them down.

As the cyclone approached the coast the authorities were ready
and waiting. They had been tracking it for days by satellite and
radar, watching it growing in intensity, and had issued fifteen warnings. But even they had never imagined just what was in store for
the town. At around midnight a vicious, screaming gale roared
across the shores of Darwin and tore into the city with a fury so
intense that no recording devices could withstand it. With the
windspeed still rising, the last measurement of its strength was two
hundred and seventeen kilometres per hour.

With utter contempt for mankind and his endeavour, Tracy
ripped through the suburbs where terrified men, women and children sheltered as they could while their houses were torn apart
around them and their worldly possessions disappeared into a
howling, inky blackness. For around five long hours they clung to
toilet bowls or floorboards, hid under laundry troughs and cowered
in the driving rain on the lee side of cyclone fences. The wind flung
lethal debris at incredible speed, twisting steel poles into tortuous
shapes, flattening brick walls, uprooting century-old rain trees, and

lifting refrigerators and cars into the air before dropping them with careless disregard. At the airport thirty-eight aircraft were battered and at the RAAF Base a Dakota broke its moorings, became airborne and landed unceremoniously in Group Captain Hitchins' garden, several hundred metres away.

Dawn broke over Christmas morning and shocked residents stared about them in disbelief. As they stumbled about, wet, cold and barely clad or wearing pyjamas, the dazed population searched for loved ones and neighbours trapped under the wreckage, or for treasured possessions such as photographs which could never be replaced. Among the ruins a few bits of tinsel and the odd soggy Christmas present which had somehow retained its wrapping served to remind some that it was actually Christmas morning. Occasionally a wry 'Merry Christmas' echoed in the eerie quiet.

VB looked out from the plane's window and saw devastation. He was a master of understatement, but for perhaps the first time in his life he found his usual term to describe a disastrous mess utterly inadequate. What he saw as the aircraft flew in was no donkey's breakfast. It was something worse, far worse. In the newer northern suburbs, lightly built in the dynamism and confidence of the last ten years, the scene was of decimation. Thousands of homes lay strewn about, crushed by the force of the wind, leaving nothing but 'dance floors': the floorboards and toilets on stilts. In other residential areas the loss of roofs, ceilings and internal walls was almost general. The only buildings to fare reasonably well were the newer concrete and steel structures in the city. Later he found the historic stone buildings such as the Town Hall and the Church of England reduced to a heap of rubble. All around the harbour the wrecks of vessels lay washed up on the shores. Many more had sunk after being smashed against or forced under the wharf. Small vessel owners who had made for the open water too late in an attempt to escape the cyclone had perished in the furious seas. Sixteen were drowned. In Darwin there was not a leaf to be seen, and every tree that had not been flattened was a skeleton, barren and stark. And there did not seem to be any birds, anywhere.

It was not difficult to catch up with people, to see how they had fared, for most of his employees were now dossing down in the twisted mess of his yard. His twenty-seven bargain demountables were scattered as far away as the other side of Frances Bay. Some torn in half, most crumpled, several with miraculously few dents, they had been lifted and flown like cardboard boxes to be dumped wherever. The office was now but a door frame, the store and smoko room just a few sheets of bent and buckled corrugated iron clinging tenaciously to some wall struts. The cargo shed and workshop roofs had gone with the wind, but the walls remained and were now swathed with tarpaulins. Inside VB found a refugee camp.

Most of his employees had lost their homes and all their possessions, but that had not stopped all but one of them from turning up at the yard by 9.30am on Christmas morning. Keith Lang had walked in to work that morning, for most of the roads were impassable. (Besides that, his car was missing. It wasn't found until clean-up operations were well under way; a house had landed on it and it was parked fair in the middle of the kitchen.) He had called in to the police station en route and a tired-looking desk sergeant said to him, 'You're from Perkins? We need a road cleared from Casuarina to Darwin Hospital, fast. Can you help?'

Later, in the yard, Operations Manager John Butler called a meeting. 'We have no office, and no money,' he told the men. 'There is no bank and no guarantee when you will be paid, if ever. If anyone would like to walk out the gate, that's fine. On the other hand if you want to help there is one hell of a lot to be done.'

Every one of them stayed, and by mid morning they were out on the streets with two front-end loaders, two forklifts and a mobile crane. Many steel power poles were bent double and ninety per cent of the power lines were down. Using the machines and armed with a pair of wire cutters each, they set to work unblocking the vital arteries of the town, pushing the power poles and debris off the streets and clearing the wires. Initially there was no co-ordination of the work because the roads were blocked, there were no telephones and no means of communication. Keith Lang and his team worked long hours in the next few days, with several building companies that brought out their backhoes to clear the ditches. All over Darwin a spirit of co-operation and goodwill prevailed. Men and women in essential services worked hard to assist those in need. There were no questions asked, just heads counted.

VB was immensely relieved that *Fourcroy* had fared well. Because the tide was out when the cyclone hit she had sat it out low on the mud, safe and secure against the concrete wharf wall. When John Butler arrived at 7am on Christmas morning the crew were still snug in their bunks, fast asleep and blissfully unaware of the devastation around them. They had staggered back to their cabins after a night 'on the turps' and slept through the whole of the cyclone. The look on their faces as they emerged, bleary eyed, to look around them, he would never forget.

Warrender had returned to port in the early hours of 27 December, doubling the number of hot meals and showers available, and boosting the morale of those who were exhausted, shocked and dispirited in the first few days. Meal rosters were tight, and Pedro and the other cooks worked harder than they ever had. Nobody went hungry. VB could not help but feel a little proud of his employees. They were good performers, and he was pleased with the progress they had made by the time he arrived. A petrol station had been set up in the yard, for VB Perkins & Co was one of the few immediate sources of fuel in the town: two thousand drums of fuel originally bound for Dili. A procession of government vehicles flowed through the yard, for there was no electricity and so the petrol stations around town could not pump fuel. The gravity-fed emergency tanks belonging to BP and Shell were punctured. VB Perkins & Co Pty Ltd was declared an essential service facility by the National Disasters Organisation.

Evacuation was a priority and as soon as the runways were cleared the massive airlift of some twenty-six thousand people began. Men, women and children, many carrying only the pathetically small bundle of belongings they had been able to salvage, queued in the heat on the tarmac of the airport. The airport terminal was still a mess of twisted wreckage, and when they had finished with the roads, volunteers from VB's yard took the tipper and two front-end loaders and, supervised by Qantas engineers, began the task of clearing the debris from what was left of the building.

A large Navy Taskforce of some ten ships was on its way by sea, but Darwin Wharf was still a wreck. *Fourcroy* and *Warrender* would be needed to lighter the heavier cargo ashore. HMAS *Melbourne* began discharging emergency supplies on 2 January. As Wessex helicopters ferried the lightest cargo ashore, VB's landingcraft waited for cranes to move the cargo from the flight deck of the aircraft carrier. They landed the supplies in the yard and on the return runs ferried out enormous amounts of damaged military and air-force equipment, to be taken south for repair. Throughout it all VB was rushing hither and yon, organising. This was the sort of stuff he enjoyed. There was nothing like a good disaster to get him fired up and enthusing. This was when VB Perkins was at his best.

In Dili, Joss waited, frustrated, wondering what was going on and even where VB was. Now at least someone had rigged up some sort of communication with the RAAF in Darwin. When a chance came to get a message to Group Captain David Hitchins, Joss said, imploringly, 'Ask David if I can come home.'

'Tell her she can bloody well stay where she is!' was the reply. 'I'm trying to get rid of the women, not bring them in!'

'Ask him whether he's seen Bruce,' she urged.

'Yes, I've seen Bruce and he's fine,' Hitchins relayed, and she had to be satisfied with that.

New Year had come and gone before the Australian government commissioned two Fokker Friendships to fly to Timor to pick up the stranded passengers and repatriate them to Australia. Their destination was Broome, in Western Australia, but during the flight permission was given for the aircraft to land in Darwin and passengers were advised that those who lived in Darwin and wished to disembark could do so. Joss did so without hesitation and counted herself as fortunate to be on the first plane load of absent residents to be allowed back into Darwin. It was 2 January 1975.

Mitchell Street was almost unrecognisable. Perkinsville, she was relieved to find, appeared largely intact. Outside a large piece of corrugated iron, boldly emblazoned 'This house is alive and kicking!' stood against the stone wall. There was a sign of life up in the rafters where a builder was nailing on a makeshift roof. Stunned at the devastation she picked her way through the branches of an enormous beauty leaf tree over a hundred years old, now naked across the driveway. The brick garage cum lifeboat servicing workshop was just a heap of rubble. Under the house she flicked a switch. Nothing happened. There was no power, and doubts about returning flooded over her. She tried a tap. Water gushed and she breathed a sigh of relief. As long as there was water she knew she could cope.

With the roof had gone all the ceilings except the one in the main bedroom. An internal wall had caved in, furniture and paintings were strewn everywhere. Some of VB's precious rugs had blown away and flooding rain had damaged almost everything. But they had been lucky. All the external walls had held except part of one, and VB later described the house as being a bit like the curate's egg—good, in parts. With the house still open to the weather, VB had found himself a doss inside the Reserve Bank in town, and spent the first few nights on a mattress, packed in like a sardine among many. Now he was obviously back, for a pile of dirty socks and assorted *dhobi* lay next to the bed. Joss hopped in a car parked in the street and drove down to the yard to find him. When he saw her turn up out of the blue, the first thing he said was, 'Oh good. You can cook my dinner.'

'Oh yes?' said Joss. 'On what, may I ask?'

VB had forgotten that he'd given away his gas cooker to some of his boys camping down at the Tipperary Yard, another piece of land he leased along the foreshore.

When dinner time arrived that evening, Joss suggested they join a group of friends driving out to the Darwin High School, where emergency workers were serving meals.

'Certainly not,' VB said. 'I vowed many years ago that I would never again line up for food. Besides that I am not interested in any handouts from the bloody government.'

There was nothing to eat in the house, but seeing no point in arguing with him Joss joined the entourage and left him at home.

At the high school the queues were very long. After a time Joss noticed among the throng that VB had arrived. When she caught up with him she said, 'What happened? Were you getting hungry?'

'It wasn't that,' he said gruffly. 'You know I never dine alone.'

TWENTY-SEVEN

Trouble in Timor

S aturday afternoon was sacred to VB. Anybody who knew him at all knew not to arrange anything at that time, because that was when the East Point (Gentlemen's) Tennis Club convened. Wives had to go along with the fact that this was a men-only affair, and a certain protocol applied. Interruptions were simply not welcome. Joss knew this well, but under the circumstances . . .

She dialled the number. 'I know it's forbidden to make phone calls,' she said apologetically, but would you mind informing VB that there is a dead man in the bottom of the garden.' With news like that she expected him to come rushing to her aid, but she was disappointed. Dead men had long since ceased to move VB; not even the twenty metres from the tennis court to the telephone.

The reply came back via someone else. 'There is no point getting your arse in an uproar about it. If he's dead he won't present a problem. He'll be home after the next set.' He wasn't.

The ship's cabin that was the cubby house lay among the tangled cyclone refuse in the last corner of the garden to be cleaned up. It was there that Joss came across the prostrate figure that had given her such a fright. When she had recovered she spoke to the still form, and then prodded it with a stick. There was no sign of life. She threw a few stones onto the roof of the cubby. Still nothing. Since then she had remained inside the house, haunted by the idea

348

of a dead body in the garden. It was almost dark when VB came home, and when they went to look the body had disappeared. On further inspection he found a suitcase neatly stowed. With that he concluded that the fellow was not, in fact, dead, but had simply moved in. Later he discovered he'd been living there for weeks. It was happening all over Darwin.

In the aftermath of Cyclone Tracy, accommodation was a problem not only for businesses and returning evacuees, but also for those enterprising builders and tradespeople who made their way up to Darwin to cash in on the rebuilding effort. People had to make do with what they could find and one could not afford to be particular. Joss found herself living alone for three months while VB took himself off to Guyana, South America, consulting on river transport for the World Bank. Without lights, in a house with no roof or ceilings, her only company was an assortment of possums and frogs. Later, in what VB dubbed the 'Joss House' (the hastily erected structure where the garage once was), she had to have a truck driven up from the yard each night, to be parked for privacy against the void where the huge double doors should have been.

It was a difficult time. Yet Darwin was a town filled with that rare human spirit which it seems only a disaster of massive proportions can bring about. Throughout 1975 a steady stream of evacuees returned. The fondness for the Territory of many of the old timers had been reinforced by the stay in the south, and they overcame the heartbreak of having lost everything they owned to return and start all over again.

The eleven thousand or so people who remained behind in the biggest evacuation in Australia's history were resolved to prove the sceptics wrong. Those who said Darwin was a lost cause had not figured on the guts and determination of its long-time residents. Very soon a new Darwin began to emerge, yet again, out of the wreckage of the old.

VB's association with the island of Timor was now in its fourteenth year. It was an association distinctly divided, as distinctly as history had divided the eastern and western regions of the island itself.[1] Portuguese Timor had always seemed a sleepy sort of place to VB. He had noticed that no-one seemed to rush about, not even the young Portuguese military men doing their national service, their 'tropical training'. They lounged about Dili and Baukau, cigarettes dangling from their bottom lips, waiting out their time, restless and bored by their forced exile to this far-flung and undeveloped colony in the backblocks of the world. The Portuguese administrators, many of whom also appeared to be counting the days to the end of their posting, went about their business with a casual indifference VB noticed early in his relationship with the country. (In 1959 he had been left to feed a shipload of cattle he had purchased for the Portuguese government for four months while waiting for the promised ship to turn up. He had put the losses down to experience.)

While the Portuguese never seemed in a hurry, the same could be said of their subjects, a mixed population of Proto-Malay and frizzy haired Melanesians, with a sprinkling of more recent Chinese and Arab immigrants. Here and there black-faced African descendants of slaves or conscript soldiers of the Portuguese added further spice to the racial hot-pot that was East Timor. To VB the Timorese people appeared a gentle and friendly folk. It was hard to imagine them getting excited about anything very much, and he had been surprised on that occasion in 1959 when Timor Oil's people on the ground in the south found themselves caught in a trouble spot. He was even more surprised that, though it was the first uprising in Timor since the Japanese occupation, it hadn't turned a hair in Australia or the international community. He hadn't seen any reports of it in the papers, though his own office was abuzz with the news, since it was there that the exploration

---

[1] *The eastern portion of Timor was ruled by the Portuguese who, in the 1520s, were the first Europeans to stake a claim there. For several centuries West Timor had been ruled by the Dutch but when, in 1949, the Netherlands East Indies became independent Indonesia, the Dutch moved out and it became incorporated into Indonesia. East Timor remained a Portuguese colony.*

geologists, having escaped Timor, sought refuge to write reports.[2]

Certainly it seemed that the 1959 uprising had been thoroughly quelled by the Portuguese, for the 1960s were a time of peace in East Timor and the link with Darwin remained strong. Landingcraft regularly plied across the Timor Sea to deliver supplies, and since 1972 *Fourcroy* had been doing the 'milk run' to Dili, with three thousand drums of fuel each month. But it was the wilds of Timor that most enthused VB. Small communities, isolated from Dili by the poor state of the roads, had to be supplied by sea, and their crops of maize and coffee transported to the capital. Landing cargo on exposed, unsheltered and remote coasts was the stuff of which his business was made. The risks were there and landings in the monsoon were rarely uneventful. It was after one such landing that VB, impressed by the resourcefulness of his crew, delivered to them what was his highest accolade.

They had just returned from a trip to a small village on the south coast of West Timor, having delivered a cargo of Australian Aid. On landing *Warrender* had been swept high up onto the beach, stranded hard and fast, broadside on to the frenzied, beating shore. Far from help of any kind the crew were left to their own devices. But they managed to resurrect two rusted and neglected bulldozers extracted from the long grass nearby, previous gifts from Australian Aid, and used them to dig a massive channel alongside the stricken vessel. When the moment was right they had the two dozers pushing

---

[2] *Camped near Uatolari on the central southern coast of East Timor, the geologists had had their breakfast interrupted one morning, when a group of armed and hostile Indonesians wearing red ribbons burst into camp. Some were carrying Communist flags. The geologists were forced at gun-point to hand over their own rifles and the keys to their vehicles, and then the group drove off leaving them shaken but unharmed. It was the beginning of a short but bloody would-be revolution in which, according to the geologists' accounts, many native Timorese, also wearing red ribbons and obviously well prepared, took up arms, attacked Portuguese posts and burned houses as they took Uatolari. For a short time they also took Viqueque, to the west, until the Portuguese army moved in to violently quash the rebellion. In its wake some several hundred people were killed and around one thousand injured.*

with engines screaming until *Warrender* toppled awkwardly into the hole to float at last. On hearing of their efforts VB was very pleased. 'One day,' he told them, 'you will all get a gold watch as big as a frying pan.'

It was obvious by the early 1970s that there was more than a sniff of independence in the air for East Timor. Portugal, under threat of being financially broken by its colonies, had begun to decolonise. East Timor was on the brink of change, but VB would never have imagined just how dramatic that change was to be. All seemed to be progressing reasonably well. In mid 1975 the Portuguese government announced an election scheduled for October 1976 and complete independence a year or two later. In fact it was not to be. In fact it was the beginning of the end of East Timor's dream of independence, of VB's service to East Timor and that country's long-held and close ties with the nearby city of Darwin.

As *Warrender* steamed out of Dili harbour in July 1975 the master, Colin Buhl, looked back at the lazy little port that he and VB and so many others had fallen in love with. It looked quiet and tranquil, just as it always looked. Naked children splashed about on the beach and here and there fishermen stood knee deep in the water casting throw nets at small schools of darting fish. Squatting figures sorted nets on outrigger canoes coasting across the bay under colourful sails. West of the wharf the whitewashed belltower and red roof of the old Catholic church stood out against a backdrop of tousled green, and to the east the many arches of the government offices lent a formality to Dili which seemed at odds with its way of life. Along the Esplanade the embedded Portuguese cannons faced out to sea as they had done for centuries, and up in the mountains behind Dili the war memorial lay as another solemn reminder of Timor's troubled history.

Colin had served in the region during World War II and had visited the memorial to pay his respects, not only to the Australians who had died there, but also to the Timorese people who had suffered so terribly during the war, after the Australians evacuated the island. The fate of the East Timorese people during that time has been labelled one of the greatest catastrophes of World War II, in terms of relative loss of life. Out of a population of around 470,000, at least 40,000 East Timorese people died from starvation and Japanese brutality. It occurred in a country which, under Portugal's Fascist regime, could have remained neutral.

Standing by the war memorial it had crossed Colin Buhl's mind how often he had heard those who had served in Timor remark at the way the Australian government had given so little recognition to the efforts of the Timorese during that time. Had it not been for the Australians' uninvited presence on the island the hapless Timorese people may have escaped, if not an invasion by the Japanese, certainly the cruel and devastating reprisals that were the result of helping the Australians. He and his contemporaries had been left with the uncomfortable feeling that Timor had been abandoned by its neighbour. Now, as Colin headed *Warrender* to the opening in the reef across the harbour, the sultry haze already shimmering over Dili behind him, he could not have known that this was not to be the last time Australia would be accused of just that.

Except that Timorese money suddenly didn't seem to be worth very much, the crews reported little sign of trouble on those last few visits. Later VB commented that Dili was so pleasant and the people so gentle that, immersed in the bucolic tranquillity of the place, it was probably easy to overlook a few rumblings of dissent. When he learned, in August 1975, that there had been a coup in Dili, it came as a shock. It was a bloody little civil war between two rival political factions, UDT and Fretilin. Though it lasted only a fortnight before Fretilin took control, it destabilised the country and Indonesia did not waste the opportunity to launch an assault.

The Australian government's policy in dealing with Indonesia, the sprawling country to the north-west, was to be friendly and work towards its development and stability, and on the matter of East Timor, to pursue a 'do nothing' policy of non involvement. But the government did get involved, when it placed an unofficial embargo on the fuel *Fourcroy* normally carried to Dili. The view was that continued supply could be seen as a form of military aid to Fretilin. The much-needed fuel remained in the yard in Darwin, yet VB well knew that it was no more than had been required for years for the normal civil functioning of East Timor.

The Australian government maintained the fuel embargo throughout September and October 1975. In Dili there was no petrol to allow the distribution of aid to the rural areas, where most of the fighting had been and where it was most needed. It wasn't until early November that, under pressure from lobby groups, the embargo was lifted, but only enough to allow distribution of a shipment of aid to the regional centres of East Timor. Australian government officials flew to Darwin to personally monitor the shipment.

VB was uneasy about East Timor. The country had been an integral part of his business for most of the seventeen years he had been in Darwin, and he didn't like the look of things. There had been an exodus from Timor to Darwin since the trouble began, and the reports that came with the fleeing residents were worrying. He knew well the meagre resources of this small undeveloped country. When Indonesia began making its first moves it was difficult to imagine East Timor having a hope of standing up for itself. Then George Haritos paid him a visit to tell him about that last aid shipment with the previously embargoed fuel. He'd been aboard Barge Express's *Alanna Fay*.

George had been a bit edgy entering the port of Dili. When the lights of the town suddenly blacked out ahead they almost turned around and went home. Then the radio crackled with a message from the Fretilin administration that all was well, and they'd continued on to the wharf. Dili was now home to thousands of refugees from the mountains, and the fuel, food and medical supplies *Alanna Fay* delivered were desperately needed. The crew were treated well, and dined at the Turismo Hotel with Fretilin leader Xavier do Amaral and spokesman Jose Ramos Horta. Do Amaral was not quite what they had expected of a rebel Fretilin leader. He was small, intelligent, gentle, sincere. In an almost humble way, he spoke of his wishes to see the people of East Timor finally have a go at governing their own country. He admitted they didn't have much to fight with, and gave the impression he didn't have a lot of optimism either. But they were going to give it their best. George had come away impressed and sympathetic.

The wharf had thronged with people the next night as *Alanna Fay* prepared to leave. Among them a group of mostly Chinese people stood with their bags packed, imploring the crew to take them to Darwin. But *Alanna Fay* couldn't take them. When she eased away from her berth leaving the fearful would-be refugees behind, a small wooden launch with a 75-millimetre gun lashed to the top of the cabin was the only other vessel tied up at the wharf. Someone had asked Xavier do Amaral what it was. He'd grinned and said, 'That's our Navy.' Now, as they steamed out of the harbour into the moonlight, Indonesian destroyers turned their guns toward the plateau town of Atabae, inland on the north coast.

On 7 December 1975 the Indonesian Navy steamed quietly towards the north-east coast in the early hours of the morning, to land troops at Dili. At the same time Indonesian transport planes droned overhead to disgorge their cargo of commando paratroopers onto the population centres. It was the end of East Timor's hopes for independence. That, save for two further aid shipments, was also the end of the established landingcraft trade to East Timor, for the Indonesian government threw an information cordon around it, blockading it to the outside world. The blockade included not only journalists, but the International Red Cross and all foreign aid workers. Over the next few years many thousands of Timorese died of starvation, some estimates being as much as one-sixth of the total population.

Fourcroy and *Warrender* each made one further journey during the period, this time for the Indonesian Red Cross. The cargo was made up of staples for survival: milk powder, flour, rice, high-protein biscuits and medical supplies. When *Fourcroy* tied up in Dili harbour for the last time, the usual casual, smiling faces were not there to greet her. In their stead fully armed Sumatran paratroopers patrolled the dock. The master, John Dangerfield, was informed that no-one was allowed off the wharf. The days of wandering ashore to roam the gardens around the government buildings, to fossick around the local markets or wander through the back streets where the goats and pigs roamed freely and sarong-clad women carried their produce on their heads, were gone. Suddenly, Dili was not the delight it had been. Through his binoculars John could see that the town had taken a battering. Evidence of small-arms fire and broken windows was general. To the north of the wharf VB's bulk-fuel-storage dumb-barge, once used to store fuel for the power station, lay high and dry on the beach, a casualty of war.

During *Warrender*'s visit, crew members came back with reports of seeing an Indonesian cameraman filming what looked from the camera's angle to be military trucks fully loaded with the aid they had just delivered. The crew could plainly see that the trucks were loaded up one side only, giving the impression that there was twice as much cargo as there actually was. The trucks were last seen heading towards the military barracks. As he listened to the reports, VB imagined what the report accompanying the footage would say. And he could not help but feel sad for East Timor.

TWENTY-EIGHT

Winds of Change

V B loved his old, green EJ Holden. It didn't have a second gear but he could get by without that, and though the floor had rusted through in several places, he didn't need a key to start it. This convenience, he felt, more than made up for its deficiencies, despite the fact that it was often nicked. (So well known to the police was it that any green EJ Holden found abandoned was assumed to be VB's, even one discovered at Ayers Rock.) When the police finally put it off the road permanently, he was not pleased. He brought it down to the yard and gave it pride of place next to the office, where the wet season spear grass quickly engulfed it. It was a bit of a nuisance and there was talk in the yard of someone pushing it over the end of the wharf as fill. But no-one was quite game enough to do it.

VB was never one to splash money about. The fact was, however, that having sold a major equity share in VB Perkins & Co to the Aboriginal Loans Commission, he found himself with a modestly large pile of the stuff, a bit of an embarrassment really. For the first time in his life he was very much in funds, and conceded to buying himself a new 'truck'. The dent this uncharacteristic splurge made in his stack was appreciably small and left him pondering what on earth to do with the rest of it. When the notion of going into the cattle business was first mooted by a friend and business associate, he rather liked the sound of it. The idea of a place in the country appealed to him and, significantly, he could put the old EJ on the back of a truck and send it down the track where, unregistered, it would have a new lease of life. So it was that he joined two associates to purchase three adjacent cattle stations in the Katherine region, three hundred and thirty kilometres south of Darwin.

Between them Manbulloo, Gorrie and Dry River stations covered an area of three thousand four hundred square miles. There was not a single cattle man among the new owners and a manager was quickly installed. Gorrie and Dry River were little more than vast, undeveloped blocks of land in the style of those VB had visited around the Barkly region in 1957. But Manbulloo, at 1.2 million acres, had once been part of Lord Vestey's huge, sprawling cattle empire. The old homestead lay on the high side of the Katherine River nestled among shady trees. An overgrown tennis court to one side was testament to the station's better days. Tucked in behind a line of giant mango trees were the kitchen and staff quarters, and the dining room stood shaded and alone in an open style, catching the breeze through huge fly-screened windows.

Manbulloo straddled some fifty kilometres of the Victoria Highway on the way to Western Australia. Somebody had once done a bit of a helicopter survey and when VB and his cohorts bought the station it was estimated it carried around five thousand head. But nobody really knew. For VB and Joss, Manbulloo Station was a pleasant diversion; a place where VB could tinker in the workshop and try to get bits of obsolete machinery going again on very little. He enjoyed taking relatives from provincial Cornwall down the track, astounding them with the stuff of the Northern Territory: the vastness of the country, the first sight of a Territory road train thundering along the road towing up to three articulated trailers, the impersonal vision of dead beasts, bloated and forsaken on the fenceless highway or, in the harsh dry season country, the oasis-like tranquillity and beauty of the watercourses. For visitors there were always horses about and those disinclined to ride could, in the season, find amusement on the stockyard fence dodging sprays of sand and manure, as the big-boned, drought resistant Brahman-cross cattle were drafted, branded and castrated in none too gentle fashion. Or there was the bore run: an early start with the bore mechanic, almost a full day of bumping about on the front seat of a Landrover along hell-rough tracks and dry creek beds, a stop every hour or so to check a bore pump and water trough, returning in the late afternoon, hot and tired and overwhelmed by the scale of it all. Revival, close at hand, came in the form of a large, tin pannikin of strong, sweet tea and a cold beef sandwich; the delicious cool of the Katherine River, soaking off the dust and the heat of the day amid a fine tropical display of pandanus, palms and ferns; a battered chair in the long shadows of a spreading poinciana, a beer, whisky soda or, if one was inclined to the local tipple, a Bundy rum and Coke, to the accompaniment of the mellow voice of Kris Kristofferson, drifting across from the ringers' quarters. Then it was dinner time—beef, again.

With the purchase of Manbulloo VB couldn't help but notice how things had changed since he had first visited cattle stations in the far north of Australia in the 1950s. The dark figures in bright checked shirts and cowboy hats, high-heeled boots jammed firmly into the stirrups, working cattle competently on horseback, had seemed an integral part of station life twenty years earlier. Now they seemed to have disappeared. A group of Aborigines had a permanent camp by the river on Manbulloo, but not one of its residents worked on the station. Manbulloo was not alone in that it no longer employed Aborigines.

VB had stood back and watched the politics of Aboriginal affairs from a distance since he had been in Australia. The coastal Aboriginal settlements of the Territory were staples of his business, and now his company was seventy-five per cent owned by the Department of Aboriginal Affairs. In the years since 1957 when he had first come into contact with the Aborigines of Arnhem Land, he had seen enormous changes. But from where he stood it seemed that although a lot of money was being splashed about, things weren't getting any better for the Aborigines. Indeed, despite all the granting of rights and increases in expenditure on welfare, things appeared to be getting considerably worse.

VB had seen the positive effects of the change in the late 1950s and 1960s in the government's long-standing policy of 'protection and segregation' to one of 'assimilation'. The Commonwealth government had poured an unprecedented amount of money into the cause. They used missions and government-run Aboriginal settlements to implement their policy of 'planned interference' which would serve to prepare Aborigines for their inevitable encounter with white society. Missions no longer struggled along by themselves as VB had seen at Rose River. Now they were being injected with money, the primary aim being to improve health, housing and education in Aboriginal communities. VB saw the effects of the policy in the nature of the cargoes he shipped: from predominantly staple foodstuffs, more and more vehicles, machinery, building and construction material was moved out to the communities. Old settlements received injections of capital, and occasionally his landingcraft carried Aborigines to one of the new settlements which suddenly began to spring up around the coast of the Northern Territory.

The 1960s also saw the Aboriginal population begin to increase and a new social welfare bill introduced whereby the old legal restrictions on all Aborigines now applied only to those people, be they black or white, declared wards of the state. Amongst other things the Aborigines gained the right to vote, the right to equal pay and conditions on pastoral properties, and the right to drink alcohol. The new legislation was seen by its authors as opening the door to Aborigines to shape their own lives. But the policy of assimilation, implemented only in 1957 and designed to run over a period of several generations so that Australia's tribal Aborigines would be gently guided towards finding a place in white society over a reasonable amount of time, lasted no more than fifteen years.

The Labor Party had become a champion of the cause of Aborigines, and the wave of promises on which it surfed into power in December 1972 included the emotionally charged issue of 'self-determination'. A new Department of Aboriginal Affairs was created and the Whitlam government careered headlong into a package of new reforms for Aborigines, with the objective of self-determination in economic, social and political affairs. The policy of 'assimilation' was abandoned; evolution in Aboriginal affairs suddenly became revolution. Within a very short time, the effects of this revolution on the coastal settlements he served became all too evident to VB.

Alcohol became a real problem. VB was against alcohol for the Aborigines of Arnhem Land from the beginning. Soon after the laws changed, pallets of beer and wine began to arrive in his yard for shipment to the government-run settlements. VB did not like it and refused to ship it. The missions still did not allow alcohol, and for as long as he could he stood by his principles. But with self-determination, the missionaries who had spent their life's work in these places were suddenly told by the Aborigines, 'We're the bosses now.' All the communities began ordering large stocks of alcohol and the effect on the society of the Aborigines was devastating. Organisation began to break down. The arrival of one of VB's vessels at an Aboriginal community had always been greeted with enthusiasm and the work parties detailed to carry out the unloading had been willing enough. Now enthusiasm for work waned quickly and after a while the crew began to have difficulty finding anyone willing to help with anything. Someone had to be sent ashore into the community to round up a person just to receive the cargo, and there were often problems in getting the cargo up to the store before the cartons had been opened.

That the Aborigines seemed to have lost the enthusiasm for work did not surprise VB, for the people from the government had come to the communities promising money for nothing. The Aborigines were told that all they had to do was put their mark at the bottom of a piece of paper, and money would appear in their accounts.

With the change in attitude to work during the 1970s, the small industries that had been built up over the years with the help of the missionaries and welfare officers began to close down. VB saw his interport trade in Arnhem Land dwindle to next to nothing.

The once good backloadings of cargo to Darwin from the settlements disappeared. The meat industry at Croker Island, which supplied the other islands, stopped production. The timber that came out of Lake Evella was no more. The oyster industry at Goulburn Island closed down. The fruit and vegetable garden at Cadell River and the cashew-nut orchard at Garden Point dried up and died from lack of attention. The timber industry and the fishing project at Maningrida folded. Some of these projects had been funded by direct grants from mining royalties which flowed through the Aboriginal Benefits Trust Fund. There was little incentive to make a success of them, since when the projects folded, there was no requirement to repay the loans.

For full-blood Aborigines the problems of the breakdowns in organisation went deeper, to the nature and culture and traditions of the people themselves. On many of the communities there was an unnatural gathering of people from different clans who were suddenly expected to run the industries themselves, albeit with advisers. If the Aborigine in authority was not someone with 'tribal' authority, the others took no notice and the system failed. Aborigines were traditionally hunters and gatherers and they had carried out this work on an immediate-needs basis. When they were hungry they went out to find food. There was no agriculture and they had no concept of working for future benefit. They were not materialistic and their custom was to share everything with their families and friends. When, for example, the Fishing Project at Maningrida eventually failed, it was not because of lack of funding but because, when the fishermen went out to catch fish, if a dugong or a turtle happened by, the day's work would be abandoned for the thrill of the chase and the delicacy of the reward. Often work would be abandoned so that boats could be used to run family and friends around from place to place, for the fishermen found it difficult to say no. When they did have a good haul of fish they'd stop off on the way home and share it with others, and only what was left was brought back to be sold to pay the costs of fuel and maintenance of the boats.

At this time the full-blood Aborigines of remote communities in the Territory had little concept of money or where it came from, and no concept of the value of the buildings and equipment shipped to the communities. Some buildings were destroyed because fires were lit inside on the floorboards, on a cold night. Others were destroyed through sheer boredom-induced vandalism. Sometimes they were destroyed because it just happened. On one occasion *Fourcroy* waited to sail with the tide at Raminginning, her load of three large, prefabricated houses unloaded and waiting to be collected on the shore. As the master watched, a goanna wandered underneath one of them. Two locals, seeing an easy feed, decided to smoke it out, but in the process set fire to the houses. All three were destroyed before they even left the landing. At the same port of call a large load of bagged cement on pallets was delivered, but nobody wanted to do the work of moving it. Next time *Fourcroy* called it was still sitting there, and the next time and the next. Months later the wet season arrived and ruined all the cement, and it was eventually bulldozed to make a concrete landing. Frequently equipment sent out to the communities came back to Darwin a few months later as backloading, beyond repair.

To VB the colour of your skin or where you hailed from mattered not. What mattered was that you knew how to work, and he had employed some hard-working Aborigines in the earliest days. But more recently Aborigines willing to work had been fewer and farther between. With the involvement of the Department of Aboriginal Affairs in his business, VB again took on a number of Aboriginal and part-Aboriginal apprentices. Several part Aborigines did very well. One in particular became the most faithful, trusted and long-standing member of the yard crew, and a personal favourite of VB. The employment of full bloods, however, was less successful. Often they did not turn up for work, or if they did they frequently left after a couple of hours, for they did not have the same sense of need or urgency as whites or their part-Aboriginal brothers.

For all this, VB admired the delightful ability of the Aborigines to be themselves, despite the disintegration of their life and culture around them. It seemed to him they wanted the goods and services the white man could give but they didn't want the white man's interference. They wanted to be helped but they didn't want to be judged, and they resented being looked at through 'white man's eyes'.

VB was not a great orator about Aboriginal affairs, but he had lived through the changes in the Aboriginal communities on the coast of the Northern Territory since the late 1950s. He could be moved to say his piece when he saw reports by what he called 'do-good trendy lefty reporters from the south' who had no appreciation of the difficulties of Aboriginal welfare in the Northern Territory. They would come with their cameras and film the trashed houses and the beer cans littering the beaches, the poor old drunks lying under the trees at the communities, the children who were sick from the squalor and malnourished through living off Coke and crisps, and then report that what was needed was more rights and more money. They would fail to point out that the reason that juvenile health had deteriorated was the breakdown in parental care due to the grog and the lack of discipline of a people stuck inexorably between the old way and the new. They would visit the outstations and observe that there were very few amenities and that people were living in humpies and that there was no school teacher. They would fail to point out that the teacher had left because nobody was turning up for lessons. They would fail to point out that the reason these outstations were set up in the first place was because the elders wanted to turn their back on the money and the houses and the 'social advances' such as alcohol that were further destroying their culture. These Aborigines wanted to return to their traditional land and something of their old ways to try and save what vestiges of pride and tradition they had left, to salvage their nobility, innocence, and true spirituality from the greed and materialism of the white man's ways.

It annoyed VB that these journalists from the southern states—many of whom either hardly realised they had any Aborigines in their own communities or, if they did, very probably ignored their problems—would stand back and loftily denounce the Northern Territory. It seemed an irony that the cities from which these

reporters hailed were embroiled in their own race-related problems, while those who lived in Darwin lived in certainly the least
racially prejudiced town in the country, where people of all colours
lived together amicably, tolerantly and mutually beneficially. But
then it was no secret that the blackfellers, the grog, the Stubbie
shorts and the thongs were all part of what made the Territory
good copy.

In VB's eyes something had gone wrong in the late 1960s,
early 1970s, when the tribal Aborigines of the Northern Territory had been propelled into the white man's world too
quickly by politicians who perhaps put more thought into how
their policies would appear to the sympathetic white voters than
into the effect on the society of the Aborigines themselves. The
policies were blanket policies. But what might have suited a
third generation family of fringe-dwelling part Aborigines in
Sydney was not what was required for the full bloods of Arnhem
Land or Central Australia, where the Aborigines had come in
from the bush more recently. To VB, dignity was all important
in a man. He would say of the government's policy of giving
all and requiring nothing, 'You emasculate any man when you
take away his work.'

When VB spoke of Aborigines he spoke not of part Aborigines
but of the full bloods, the laughing, gentle people he fondly remembered from Arnhem Land: the women sitting cross-legged on the
beach chopping pandanus nuts for breakfast; the dignified old men
sitting nearby, perhaps with one leg tucked up underneath in the
warm sand, the other stretched out in front; the children splashing
about in the shallows, their white teeth flashing happy grins and
their dark skins shining with dull copper overtones. Living in the
Territory VB heard the subject of Aboriginal affairs argued and
debated *ad nauseam*. Political correctness had never featured in his
agenda, and his own view of the problems that had befallen these
people he would sum up succinctly, 'It took my ancestors, and
yours, thousands of years to get to where we are now. Anyone
who thinks the Australian Aborigine can do it in fifty is asking a
great deal too much.'

It was under the umbrella of 'self-determination' that the Aboriginal Loans Commission bought in to VB's business, but it didn't take long for VB to decide that the new arrangement was 'all paperwork, no performance'. The government shareholder employed an endless stream of consultants from the south, but none of the promises made to VB came true. The funds for a new foreign-going vessel, the designs for which had been approved and put out to tender, did not materialise. He realised he had made a mistake. By 1977– 78 the Aboriginal Loans Commission's source of funds was drying up and VB gave up hope. At the same time the agonisingly slow decision-making processes took their toll, and VB Perkins & Co was going nowhere. When he could stand it no longer, VB asked if he could buy his business back. The answer was yes. To finance it he sold his interest in the cattle stations, and by October 1978 it was done. He was more than happy to have it to himself again.

VB's dream of running a liner service to his old haunt of Singapore seemed further away than ever. Since the trouble in East Timor there had been little opportunity for work overseas. It was clear that a liner service to Singapore was not just going to happen; it had to be made to happen. With this in mind general manager Roger Rooney took a chequebook to Singapore and bought drilling mud, timber, cement and anything else he thought he could resell in Darwin to fill a southbound leg. There were no exports from the Territory to speak of and VB put up some money to buy cattle and enlisted the help of a couple of ex-cattle shippers who had fallen on hard times to find markets in Asia for the cattle. In 1978, largely on the strength of that cargo, *Fourcroy* began a two-monthly service to Singapore, via Brunei. It was never going to make any money, since *Fourcroy* was too small and all wrong for the job, but VB was willing to cop the losses in pursuit of his dream.

Suddenly there were more union problems. The Seamen's Union (now part of the Maritime Union of Australia) demanded more pay and everyone wanted 'cattle money' for the northbound leg. The WWF (also now the MUA) objected on principle to a scheduled international service being run from anywhere other than their wharf and confirmed their long-standing blackban on any Perkins cargo transhipped over the main wharf. The blackban was to remain in force until the mid 1980s, serving only to lose the wharf yet more business.

Since the Seamen's Union had taken over his vessels, VB felt that many of the crew were no longer his employees. The Seamen's Union dictated whom the company should employ and if and when someone should be dismissed. Seamen were chosen by the union from the local roster and their loyalty was to their union. VB Perkins & Co was little more than a posting for them. There were problems on the vessels as frustrated officers had to contend with difficult and antisocial behaviour from people whom it was almost impossible to fire. When a habitually drunken cook threw all the pots and pans from *Fourcroy*'s galley over the side, the union said give him another chance. When he did the same thing again, the union said the cook needs alcoholic rehabilitation and the company must pay for it. George Haritos had packed up his own boat because of the WWF, and worked for VB for a short time. But he couldn't control the crew and objected to being called 'Comrade', and soon left to join Barge Express where, on the smaller landingcraft, he would have to contend with only one seaman instead of five. Colin Buhl left to buy himself a fishing trawler. His income would be less secure but at least he'd have command over his crew.

VB found the whole union bit highly unpleasant and did what he could to avoid involvement. He disliked and actively evaded the branch leader of the Seamen's Union in his long whites and gold chains, and always tried to dodge even a fleeting contact. (I once saw him duck down behind the bar at the Sailing Club, and it wasn't until I assured him that the coast was clear that he came up again.) He was not anti-union on principle. He believed in a fair day's pay for a fair day's work. But he also strongly believed that the unions had gone too far; that though this island nation should have had a shipping industry to be proud of, the maritime unions had all but destroyed it. He thought it was a tragedy for Australia.

VB was not a vociferous character, but there were a few matters about which he could be moved to take to the podium. One was his view that Australia had started from the wrong end, that it should have started in the north and worked down. The way in which the Northern Territory was administered from the south also inspired passion in VB. When on 1 July 1978 the Northern Territory got what it so badly wanted—real self government without losing the trappings of the Commonwealth—there was good cause to celebrate. That was not to say that his view of politicians had changed. Although his place on the government's official-function invitation list always remained, he considered the Cabinet to be young pups doing their own thing and was of the firm opinion that they would be well served by listening to those of an earlier vintage when such folk had something to say.

He was the first to admit, however, that self government marked a change in his fortunes, for the matter of the Frances Bay land quickly made it onto the agenda of the new Cabinet. Twelve years had passed since VB first applied to the government for a long-term lease over the land he had built. Throughout that period he had battled long and hard with the Port Authority over their requirement that he pay wharfage on his own facilities. The day the Cabinet excised all Frances Bay land above low-water mark from Port Authority control was a happy one indeed. At last he was truly outside Port Authority control. At last he was free of the wharfies. In due course Darwin Town Area Leases were granted. Later these were converted to freehold title and now, at last, VB had some collateral on which to borrow. Work on financing his dream started straight away.

TWENTY-NINE

Vision Accomplished

V B made a point of staying in the office this morning. He was waiting for a phone call, and he was a bit pleased with himself. This should settle the matter of whether or not he was romantic. He'd show Joss that he'd learned a thing or two since the first time round, that he knew a bit about feminine sensibilities. He'd purchased the ring all right, emerald and diamonds; that was the easy part. But the notion of presenting it over a candlelit dinner made him feel a little squeamish, and he'd come up with a better idea. The ring was now in place on the tea-towel hook in the kitchen, under the towel.

At around 9.30am his phone rang. It was Joss. He listened with satisfaction, and then said, 'Ah, well you see I've always wanted to know how long it took you to get around to drying the dishes.'

Flushed with success, VB privately resolved to do it again one day, not too soon of course. The next time he walked into a jewellery store was in Bangkok, accompanied by all six fellow members of a delegation from the Australian Trade Development Council. With the support and advice of his entourage he bought a large sapphire and diamond ring. With the ideal of a candlelit dinner still in the back of his mind, the moment he chose to give it to her was as close as he could imagine: at a dinner in Singapore for the entire delegation, with everyone making loud laudatory noises. Then there was the natural pearl he'd bought. He'd had it in the drawer of his bedside table for a while, waiting for the perfect moment. One night at Perkinsville, over coffee with guests, the ladies were instructed to conceal it in the cake and make sure Joss got the right piece. The plan worked: Joss didn't swallow the pearl and VB retired that night satisfied that he had shown these youngsters something of the business of romance.

When at last he proposed they'd been together six years. There was no to-do about it. He simply said, 'It's about time we got married, Charlie.' The wedding, in November 1979, was a simple, low-key affair under the coconut palms in the garden at Perkinsville, with twenty-five invited guests. Fifteen minutes before it began the neighbour started to mow his lawn, and Joss got into a state. VB, as ever calm and diplomatic, wandered next door to ask the neighbour whether he and his wife would like to attend their wedding, scheduled to begin in fifteen minutes. The lawn was left uncut and the neighbours came along.

The ceremony began and VB stood proudly beside his young bride, she in a pale, softly draping dress, orchids nestled in her long hair, her hands at a loose end. 'Bruce,' she burst out suddenly, 'my flowers!' VB had promised to arrange a bouquet but had forgotten. He ducked around to the front of the house and returned with a handful of pale purple vincas. The guests regained their composure and, very soon, they were married.

Six months later and to the delight of both of them, Joss fell pregnant. From day one the child-to-be was known as 'Penelope', and when it arrived at last, Penelope it was. VB rushed up to the hospital and entered the delivery room in surgical cap and gown, bearing another handful of Perkinsville's best vincas.

A few days later he left for Singapore to launch a ship.

Ploughing north-west through five emerald seas to Singapore was a far cry from what *Fourcroy* was designed for. Using such a small ship on such a long haul was never going to be economic, and designs for a new vessel had been kicking around in VB's office for years. In his heart he knew that a big landingcraft would push a great deal of water in front of it, and in terms of fuel efficiency was not suitable for a straight Darwin–Singapore service. But the ability to deliver to remote places in South East Asia, to send his ship to land on beaches in the wilds of the South China Sea where no ship had been before, was important to him. The Shell Oil Company was at that time planning major exploration work in remote areas of Sulawesi, and looked like needing landings of heavy equipment. That was the nature of his business. Goddammit, he likes to be able to do it.

The vessel to be called *Frances Bay* was built in Singapore, and VB spent a lot of time there over the construction period. Singapore was changing rapidly. Before his eyes whole blocks of the city's inimitable character were being torn down and replaced by modern edifices of concrete and glass which blotted out the skyline that he had known so well. Still VB behaved as if nothing had changed in forty years. He was often without money in his pocket and had little appreciation of what day-to-day things cost. He wanted to sign for everything and when he couldn't he frequently found himself in a spot of bother and had to call on his employees to fish him out of awkward situations. The modernisation of Singapore was taking place at a cracking pace. The modernisation of VB Perkins was proceeding somewhat more slowly.

Occasionally VB took time out to look up old friends. Joss, Antony and I were with him on one of his jaunts around the Peninsula in search of the old Malaya. He wanted to drive the white sand beaches of Pahang just like he used to, but the Avis Rent-a-Car was not the same as the old Windsor jeep, and we got bogged. In the cool highlands of Fraser's Hill, where the buildings were so English that in the fog one could have sworn one really was back in England, he found Bill Bangs, from the prewar days, and spent an evening sitting around his fireplace sipping port and talking of times past.

In KL new hotels were rising like phoenix from the ashes of the old town, and we moved on quickly, for VB was keen to get to where he knew nothing would ever change: Perky's place. Ronald Bertie Perkins still lived very much the life of the colonial planter at his magnificent house, *Bukit Tersenyum*, some fifteen kilometres south of Port Dickson. Joss had done this jaunt before, and they laughed about the last time, when VB had stepped on a stone fish at the beach. It was agony and, while the servants ran a bath and called the doctor, Joss poured whisky on the wound. VB had grabbed the bottle and taking a large mouthful said in exasperation, 'Inside, Charlie, not out!'

For myself, a visit to Perky's was like stepping back into the colonial past, to a life at odds with the change and development in Singapore and KL. My own memories are vivid: the book-lined walls of his beautiful house; the winding stairs to the observation turret overlooking the Straits of Malacca; the many-sided dining room looking out onto the manicured gardens; the attentions of Perky's faithful boy, getting on himself now; Whisky and Soda, his German Shepherd companions, lying expectantly on the rug under the dining room table; the vast, leather-lined back seat of the Jaguar; but most of all, two of a slightly eccentric kind, from another era, animated, laughing, bonded as only two people who have been together in hell and come out the other side could bond.

The new ship came down the slipway in Singapore as if in slow motion. She really was one hell of a big landingcraft, a touch under eighty metres long. VB watched as what had started as doodlings on his desk hit the water, and it was a very proud moment. His only regret was that he saw it with no member of his family there beside him, for his wife and three children were all in hospital. Having just given birth to Penelope, Joss was the only bright spot on the domestic front. The 'sprogs' had given him little cause for joy in recent months. Antony had cancer. I had a broken neck.

Antony, all of eighteen years old, was jackarooing on a Territory cattle station when the trouble began. A Ewings tumour had developed on his upper arm, apparently after he had been kicked by his horse. (Not wishing to impugn the character of the horse and purely incidentally, the animal was known on the station as 'Shit'ead'.) At the same time, I was recovering from three fractured vertebrae as a result of coming to grief against a tree while breaking in a young horse on my mother and Michel's farm near Perth. I was twenty years old and had just begun the last semester of my Bachelor's degree. It had happened at a time when life was busy and full of fun. The break was high in the neck and the doctors said it was a miracle that I wasn't dead.

VB flew down to Perth to visit me, and found me lying in hospital with my hair shaved off, callipers screwed into my skull and two kilograms of lead hanging off the back of my head. From the reaction of friends, one of whom passed out in a heap on my bed, I cannot imagine that I was a pretty sight. But if VB was shocked at the sight of me he didn't show it. Nor did he offer sympathy. What he did do was speak to me about things which I had never heard him speak of before. I had at that stage some vague notion that he had been a POW, but had no idea where or how or what. He filled me in for the first time and I felt privileged. He told me about it to help give me strength. He saw my present adversity as a potential character-building exercise not to be wasted.

'Life is not always good, Charlie,' he said. 'Sometimes terrible, unexpected things happen and if there is nothing practical to be done to improve the situation, it must be accepted and the best made of it. It is the only sensible thing to do, for if you can't manage that you will hurt not only yourself but also those around you. There is absolutely nothing to be gained by crying over it.'

I pointed out that to date I had not shed a tear. He said he was proud of me.

It was six o' clock on a chilly dry season morning in August 1981. The eastern sky glowed soft pink over Frances Bay. The yard crew waited, standing around near the new bollards of the not quite completed Number Five berth. Other employees, not as used to early mornings, sat sleepy eyed on the bonnets of cars parked haphazardly on the wharf. It was months after the launch in Singapore. The fitting out had been completed, the sea trials were over, most of the problems had been sorted out and the day had come at last. The new landingcraft, bedecked in signal flags for her arrival, appeared quietly around the corner of the Power House point and everybody stirred. Clusters of people walked over to the edge of the wharf. It was a full tide and *Frances Bay* sat high in the water. As she approached she looked, to me, enormous.

Noticing the blue and gold 'VBP' on the funnel and the company flag flying from the mast, I glanced at VB. He was not saying much, just watching, savouring the moment, occasionally tugging at his moustache. He looked incredibly happy. Next to him stood Joss, with baby Penelope bright eyed in her arms. The landingcraft eased closer and the two big Deutz engines engaged to slow astern, changing pitch from deep in the engineroom. Tears blurred my sight of her for a moment and I felt foolish that the note of those engines could bring such a lump to my throat. VB thumped me on the back and grinned.

It had happened at last. This was the vessel that was going to ply the waters to his beloved Singapore, and make a success of it. It was a momentous occasion, not only for VB, but for the employees who had played a part in making it happen. That morning they saw Mr P's dream come true.

That it happened at all was against the odds. The shipping industry in Australia was a macho business shackled by militant unionism. The waterfront was a belligerent and unfriendly place for ship-owners and succeeded in sinking many a worthy enterprise. Most of those which managed to stay afloat did so only through government subsidy. That VB made a success of his shipping business without such handouts was due, not to his business acumen, but to his vision, independence and determination. There were other reasons too: his likeable character helped keep the loyalty of his employees, particularly throughout the turbulent early 1970s during the battle with the wharfies when everything could have so easily turned; that he employed young people who were keen and had no preconceived notions about waterside work; that he was interested not so much in a piece of paper which said what a man could do, but in seeing for himself what a man could do; that he was willing to give people a go. If a man said he couldn't do something, VB would say, 'Have you tried?' His employees learned on the job and attitude was all important.

VB Perkins & Co was not some monolithic and impersonal enterprise. There were no glittering offices and everybody pulled together. VB himself was never flashy and he'd say of the modest nature of the office building, 'We can't make people too comfy or they might never want to go home.' He was heavily involved and almost universally described as a great bloke to work for. He was also respected. When he saw something he didn't like he would huff and puff and grumph about it, but people knew that once he'd got it off his chest it was over. General Manager Roger Rooney never expected anybody to do anything he wouldn't do. Physically he was a very hard worker and set an example for others in that respect.

VB was chuffed when members of the US Defence Department heard of *Frances Bay* and came to look at her, taking a copy of her plans back home with them. But to VB's disappointment the heavy equipment exploration work around remote South East Asian beaches failed to eventuate. As a landingcraft she was a success, but her landing capacity was wasted on the modern facilities of Singapore. However, *Frances Bay*'s liner service to Singapore and Borneo created a new link between Darwin and her near neighbours and as the trade built up, gradually less and less cargo had to be bought to fill the ship. By 1984 the trade pioneered by the landingcraft had increased to the extent that cattle were no longer vital on the northbound leg to keep it viable. *Frances Bay* was moved back to the coast, for the requirements of the thriving mining towns of Gove and Groote were now so large that all of her 2,200-tonne capacity was required. For the Singapore service the company began chartering conventional ships.

Suddenly VB and his potty little business, now called Perkins Shipping Pty Ltd, began to attract some interest in government circles. These 'pointy-bowed' ships were the sort of vessels they liked to see tied up at their wharf. Conventional ships did not excite VB to anywhere near the same degree as his landingcraft, but to the bureaucrats the sight of them flying VBP flags and steaming past the main wharf to Perkins's yard made VB and his band of renegades a little less easy to ignore.

Pretending VB's overseas service did not exist had been something of an art form among the men of influence in the sphere of Northern Territory ports and shipping. Every few years during the late 1970s and 1980s there had been a big splash in the media about the government push to attract a big international shipping line to Darwin to create a 'land-bridge to Singapore'. Rarely was there a mention of Perkins Shipping in any government literature about ports and shipping services from Darwin. Though VB could never really understand why this attitude prevailed for so long, he had some theories. It could have been because these people did not like the fact that he had always done his own thing his own way and had refused to have anything to do with the main wharf. It could have been because while they were attempting to attract flashy overseas shipping lines to come and use their multi-million-dollar container crane, the less than flashy place around the corner with the piles of fill still sitting about at the end of the wharf was already moving much of the cargo. It could have been because they had in mind only how their own wharf looked and did not stop to consider the larger picture of their country's balance of payments. It could have been that the enormous deficits which Australia incurred through its reliance on foreign-owned shipping lines did not mean much to them. Right on their city's doorstep a fully Northern Territory owned shipping company was getting the job done with no assistance or subsidy from anyone. It could have been that they had never stopped to consider or appreciate what a rare thing that was in Australia.

As the 1980s moved on VB kept no more than a paternal eye on the day-to-day operations of Perkins Shipping. He had other feathers in his cap now, and he was finding life in his seventies very full and very agreeable. He loved going down to the yard and rarely failed to go to work and 'show the flag'—then he'd duck out of the office to attend to other business.

The modern marvel of television had come to Darwin later than to other Australian cities. It got off the ground in black and white in 1971 and VB, having seen its potential, had become a founding director and shareholder of Territory Television Pty Ltd. After the cyclone the television station got going again in colour and by 1980 VB sat as deputy chairman, much to the puzzlement of his family. His interest in the television station had always been an enigma to us, since he rarely watched TV. At home he had never even bothered to learn which button to push to turn the thing on or off. Besides the news (usually ABC—'one has to know what the opposition are doing') and an episode of the ABC's *A Big Country* program, entitled 'Perkins Navy' and featuring himself, the only program I can recall him taking any interest in was the shipping saga *The Onedin Line*, and then only if someone else had it on. But as the chairman of the time assured me, VB did not have to know about television programs; others knew all about that. 'Bruce had vision and ideas and in matters of money nobody was more honest than he was. You knew when he said something it was straight down the line.'

VB had been involved in St John Ambulance since 1977. One of the roles of St John executives was to target local businessmen to donate to the St John Endowment Trust. Although VB was very good at lending people money, he had a great weakness when it came to asking others for it and would visibly shrink into the background when the matter was brought up at meetings. But on the understanding that this sort of thing inspired horror in VB, he was not hard pressed in this, and eventually became President of the St John Council in the Northern Territory in 1988. A year later he was invested as a Commander Brother in the Order of St John.

The Minister for Arts wrote to VB in 1988 to ask him to be Chairman of the Northern Territory Museum and Art Gallery. VB replied in writing, asking the question, 'Am I to be an exhibit?' This small point was soon clarified and he accepted the position, serving until 1991.

As one of Darwin's more presentable citizens VB was sought after for many and varied engagements, particularly when there was someone of importance in town. Though he could be a little distracted—even, dare I say it, offhand with people who bored him (particularly women with no conversation)—when he turned on the charm it was something to behold. So it was one evening at dinner at Admiralty House in honour of a visiting Japanese Admiral. VB was seated directly opposite and there were more than one at the table interested to see how they got along.

The Admiral was obviously unbriefed on the background of fellow guests and during the course of their conversation somehow the unlikely subject of where VB was during the war came up. Suddenly the room went quiet, as people waited for his answer. VB smiled and with perfect charm said, 'I was a guest of your Imperial Army for three and a half years.'

The Admiral, visibly moved, replied, 'I'm very sorry to hear that.'

Onlookers watched, glued, as VB smoothed with great charisma through the awkward situation, with an assurance born of genuinely bearing no grudges.

Having a new baby at the age of sixty-nine and a child around the house throughout his seventies was not quite what VB had imagined of his twilight years. He coped remarkably well, better than any of us thought he would. The years had mellowed him and although he still didn't like noise, he was more tolerant of the family situation and the 'children are to be seen and not heard' rule was relaxed. That is not to say that he curtailed his social activities at all or changed very much about his life. Joss still had to manage getting Penelope bathed, fed and to bed around the regular six o'clock traffic through Perkinsville. But things were easier now. He was comfortable financially and babysitters were easier to come by. Antony had recovered from his cancer and I from my horse accident, and we had been seduced by our father into joining the firm and were usually around to help at cocktail hour. VB was very fond of his children, and his youngest kept him younger, better, longer.

VB's old-fashioned views about the role of a wife always remained. He never discussed with Joss what was happening in the business, nor anything at all to do with money. He had established with Joss early in their relationship that household chores were not his department. Conveniently he still had no idea of how to operate any of the appliances in the house. Even the stereo he avoided, for all he needed was his radio, a simple affair with little more than two large knobs, one for tuning and one for volume, on which he would listen to the news in the morning and to the stock exchange report before his lunchtime 'camp'.

Perkinsville operated pretty smoothly these days, for Joss was excellent at keeping a house shipshape. The culinary department had long since sorted itself out and somehow everyone was fed, even under the most difficult of circumstances. The night the whole rump of roast beef caught fire in the electric oven just as Singapore's Trade Commissioner, his wife and several other invited guests were due to arrive for dinner was probably the first time young Antony P proved he had inherited his father's ability to stay calm in emergencies. Flying down the stairs, he scooped a bucket of dirt from the garden and threw the lot in on top of the dinner. The fire was extinguished and VB was very proud of him. And if, later, the Trade Commissioner noticed the crunchy bits, he didn't mention it.

VB's preferred corner of Perkinsville was the bar, although 'at' rather than behind it. If his family were not around to pour, a guest would inevitably be shown the ropes. In view of this Joss was surprised when VB accepted an invitation to a charity 'VIP Cocktail Making Competition' at the Sheraton Hotel. He was known to pour a fine whisky and soda, brandy and dry or gin and tonic, but VB had never shown a flair for anything more exotic. His claim that he could pour an excellent Singapore Sling was news to his wife.

VB stood in his place among the other competitors at the long table. Before him lay the ingredients for his brew and some cocktail-making accoutrements. The go-ahead was given, and immediately his confidence was thrown. Everyone else was putting things into a blender. His was a simple concoction and a blender was a piece of equipment completely foreign to him. He inspected the control panel. There were four buttons: 1, 2, 3 and stop. His confidence returned. Of course he could drive the thing and since it appeared to be what was required, he would give it a go. Very carefully he poured the gin, tonic, and one or two other ingredients into the machine. As an afterthought he tossed in some ice as well. The numbers on the machine, he surmised, were an indication of speed.

He calculated that the ice would require the machine to be fired on all cylinders, and he hit 3. The resulting blast of cold ice and tonic that hit him in the face, wet his shirt and sprayed his neighbouring cocktail makers, was not what he had in mind.

Joss had been frantically gesturing to him from the second row to put the lid on the blender. Now she could only cover her eyes. When she removed her hands, mortified, the tablecloth in front of him was no longer pristine and a sheepish looking VB with a piece of lemon attached to his moustache was being fussed over by a concerned attendant with a towel. Needless to say, he didn't win.

VB was seen as something of the eccentric Englishman around town. His visual trademarks were his curled moustache, cap and turned-up collar. With a seemingly endless repertoire of amusing sayings, VB's fondness for quoting Shakespeare and Kipling always remained. He simply loved words and his conversation was liberally salted with nautical expressions and peppered with Malay and old Cornish adages. He was rarely embarrassed and enjoyed the unexpected. If the wine bottle was empty he'd bring it to the attention of the waiter by sitting the empty bottle on his head. He loved to sing and was wont to break into song at the most unexpected of moments. He delighted the Indonesian dignitaries at a formal Trade Delegation dinner by standing up and delivering a full-bodied 'Clementine' in Indonesian. He knew well how to win the hearts of the women around him at work, even that of the nose-pierced, tattoo-breasted yard smoko lady, who confided her fondness for Mr P to me one day. 'D'ya know he's the only bloke wots ever opened a car door for me in me whole life. What a gen'lman.'

Darwin is a young place and the climate isn't pleasant for retirees. There are few elderly people in the town, even fewer elderly people with a child at heel. In that endearing innocence of youth the fact that her Daddy was so much older than everyone else's, that he didn't show up for P&C meetings and that he wasn't much good for piano recitals or swimming pool basketball, never concerned Penelope. He showed up to her ballet concerts and besides, he'd always assured her that he was only forty-six. That wasn't all that old. Though he'd mellowed with age, as he got older it was not always easy for him to cope with having a child around. There were times when he was hard on his youngest daughter; when perfectly normal childhood behaviour annoyed him and he would snap unreasonably at her. But Penelope was blessed with a loving nature, and she took him just as he came and her love for him was unreserved.

Joss coped, juggling the demands of motherhood with the social demands of being the wife of VB Perkins. There were difficult times. As with Barbara, she found infuriating his unwillingness to discuss things that might prove unpleasant. He simply would not be upset. Once she became so enraged that she threw a whole shelf of books from the bedroom bookcase at him, and stormed out of the room. An hour later she returned to find him sitting up in bed reading the newspaper, all the books neatly rearranged on the shelf. He looked over the top of his spectacles at her but nothing was ever mentioned about it again.

VB had always avoided babysitting fatigues, but on this occasion there was no escape. They were in Perth for the America's Cup, staying in a motel, when one afternoon Joss retired to bed with a migraine, leaving VB in charge of toddler Penelope. He took her off to play on the swings for half an hour before returning to the motel, where one unit looked much like another. Young Penelope spotted an open door and wandered in. VB faithfully followed.

A very nice couple were sitting on the sofa, and VB assumed they were Joss's guests and were waiting for her. He exchanged pleasantries and made himself comfortable while Penelope played with their children. He was pleased to have company. He chatted for a while and, noting that the sun was over the yardarm, offered the couple a drink. They accepted. He poured three whiskies from the bar fridge and sat down again. After a second round of drinks and almost an hour later he got up to visit the bathroom. The unfamiliarity took him aback. The pots of axle-grease on the sink didn't look like Joss's and the toolkit on the shelf very definitely wasn't his. Then it dawned on him. This wasn't his room at all.

Through the 1980s and into the 1990s Perkins Shipping never looked back. It had its good years and its not so good years but over time it built up a more solid capital base from which it was able to better withstand the downturns in trade when they came, as in shipping they inevitably do. There were a few more minor scuffles with the sea-going unions, but the days of out and out brawling were over. The battles of the early 1970s over stevedoring labour served the company well, and the pride of the yard crew in being able to turn a ship around faster than probably any other in the country always remained. The men in the workshop and welders' shop, who had never joined a union, worked long hours when need be to meet seemingly impossible deadlines, and played a vital role in providing the business with a solid keel on which to rest. Changes in management and board structure brought an end to the days of the 'beer with the boys' style of management which served the company well through the difficult years. Perkins Shipping transformed gradually into a thoroughly professional outfit and the new incumbents adopted a more formal approach to management. When computers were introduced, VB saw the 'Jesus boxes' as one more reason to steer clear of operational affairs.

'Old Jack' Markham was at this time superintendent engineer. The grumpy, cursing, good-hearted, outstandingly efficient ex-naval commander with oil rags permanently protruding from every pocket, was a great favourite of VB, and when Jack died unexpectedly, in honour of him VB called the first long-term bareboat charter of a brand-new ship, *Markham Bay*. Four years later in 1991 *Markham Bay* was replaced by another new, bigger ship of four thousand tonnes. VB named her after another old favourite, and she was christened *Coringle Bay*.

In June 1989 VB was admitted as a member of the Order of Australia for his services to transport, particularly shipping. His friends commented that it was not before time and that the award should have been higher, and put the slowness of the government in recognising his achievements down to the fact that he did not always see eye to eye with politicians. All the same, VB was very pleased to receive his gong.

At work the door of VB's office was always open to anyone who wanted a chat rather than a gripe. I knew he had arrived each morning when I heard the cheerful 'Good morning, Mrs Speckled Hen', as he greeted his secretary at the top of the stairs, then to me, 'Hi, Charlie', often accompanied by a tweak on the ear. When it was time for a cup of tea he'd remark casually to someone in passing, 'I'd give anybody a cup of tea if I had one.' His ability to get what he wanted without necessarily asking for it and in the most pleasant of ways always served him well. He amused his staff with his regular rounds of the offices, offering them the remains of his lunch. He simply could not bear to see food wasted. For those who worked near him, he was a delight.

From his desk VB had a commanding view of the yard and he kept a watchful eye out of the window. When he saw something he disapproved of he'd leap out of his chair and bang furiously on the window to attract the attention of the offender. Failing that he'd pick up the phone and dial 'Young Mr P's' number and, much to Antony's annoyance, instruct him to drop what he was doing and go off in pursuit of the errant forklift driver.

His natural faith and trust in his fellow man meant that VB was always vulnerable in business. When this trust in others was questioned he would say simply, 'Well, look at Steve Brodie. He took a chance. He jumped off the Brooklyn Bridge.' Inevitably the uninitiated would ask what happened to Steve Brodie, and he'd reply, 'Oh, he drowned.' He had a relaxed approach to business deals and had once tossed for a house he jointly owned with a friend. VB won. He was from the school of hard knocks and wanted his children to be brought up similarly, yet he was very generous with others outside of the family who came to him with their troubles. He'd never been a particularly good judge of character and there were one or two business ventures outside of shipping in which he came an awful—no, a formidable cropper, losing a lot of money through betrayed trust. But these incidents did not loom large in his mind. He was a forgiving man and did not dwell on misfortune. He had learned many years earlier what really mattered in life, and money, though it was nice to have, was not something he could ever become aggrieved about.

VB had encouraged his children to follow him into the shipping business. He succeeded in this for a time and Antony and I learned quickly not to expect any favours. My pay was always set by my father, and for what seemed an awfully long time and despite my degree, it was less than that of the cleaning lady. (The day I matched her paypacket was a real milestone for me.) His family, quite rightly, were expected to do it the hard way. He had a real terror that his children would turn out to be wimps if indulged in any manner whatsoever.

Perhaps because he liked having me around, VB managed to overcome his inherent male chauvinism as far as my career was concerned. There were times, however, when he lapsed and if he wanted somebody to nip up to Woolies to buy him 'a packet of lollipops' (sweets), I was usually it. I didn't mind. Since I had been working with him my attachment to him had grown enormously. Now I felt that if anything happened to him the void in my life would be so enormous it would engulf me completely.

The idea of slowing down or of having a day off occasionally would have been, to VB, tantamount to admitting the end was nigh. His shipping business gave him a good life and, along with the youth of his wife and child, kept him young in spirit. But there were very definite signs of change. He started talking more about the old days; reminiscing about his family, about Singapore, even about the war. He spent a lot of time at his desk, for his body was not what it once was and, in a major change of habits, took up writing letters to his old friends now and again. Occasionally he'd pick up the telephone and ring people like Weary, just to see what he was up to. He and Weary Dunlop had become friends since the war years, and always looked each other up when they were in the same town. They were something of the same vintage, and both had a little more time on their hands these days.

When age began to take its toll on his health he would not bow to it and continued to do everything that he always did, including driving himself everywhere in his 'truck'. He still did not like the word 'can't', and though his dislike of it had served him in good stead over the years, in many ways it had been frustrating to others, particularly in business, since he could promise the impossible in the firm belief that it could somehow be done. This spirit seemed to particularly assert itself when he was behind the wheel of a vehicle. Nothing would fire his determination more than being told by a passenger, particularly a family member, that something could not be done. We learned the art of diplomacy early, for we'd all experienced boggings and scrunched gate-posts as a result of careless language such as 'can't'.

VB had learned to drive in Cornwall in the late 1920s, when there was no such thing as a driver's licence. When they did come in, those who already had a vehicle were issued a licence with no questions asked, no tests required. This inauspicious beginning to his driving career did not instil in him any great respect for the rules of the road. VB swore that if Darwin ever got traffic lights it would be time for him to leave town. When in the early seventies Darwin did get its first traffic lights VB didn't leave. By that time he was well ensconced and decided that perhaps he and the traffic lights could learn to live together . . . but if parking meters were ever introduced that really would be it. Fortunately the parking meters never came.

VB was not a badly behaved person and despite his private feeling that rules were made for the blind obedience of fools, he did not like to transgress them unless he felt it absolutely necessary. In sixty years of driving he had never had an accident, if one doesn't count gate-posts, and he objected to new-fangled devices dictating to him how to avoid a collision. He learned to respect the decision of some traffic lights, those which were not part of his daily routine, but he resented having his life disrupted on his twice-daily journey to and from the yard, and found great satisfaction in bucking them by travelling a highly circuitous route through the city in order to avoid even one.

Darwin had changed much in the thirty-odd years since VB had arrived. It was no longer a crass and ugly frontier town, but rapidly becoming a modern and beautiful garden city, just as he had always expected it to. But to VB there were downsides to the changes. Over the years Darwin became busier and the route he had to take to work became more and more convoluted. At a time when he really should not have been driving at all, he was crossing four lanes of peak-hour Cavenagh Street traffic each morning, to get to the only one-way back alley that would get him successfully through town with no lights. By this time none of the family were keen to travel with him. When finally lights were installed at the bottom of Bennet Street on the way to Frances Bay there seemed no way of avoiding them, and I wondered how he would cope.

I discovered how one day when he drove me to work. He and the Bennet Street lights had come to terms with each other. If the light was red and there was a lot of traffic he would stop in good grace. If the light was red and there was no-one coming, he would go. If, as on this occasion, the light was red and there was someone coming but if he hurried he could just make it through, he would hurry and just make it through.

For all his transgressions VB was only ever pulled up twice by the law for driving through a red light in Darwin. The first time he was caught out, the policeman followed him home to tell him he could expect a summons to court over the incident. With his usual charm VB complimented the officer on his diligence and invited him in for a drink. The policeman politely declined and the summons never arrived. The other occasion was at 1 o'clock in the morning, when VB, with his best choir-boy expression, said, 'Oh! I didn't think it would matter at this time of day.'

The policeman pulled himself up to his full height, and, puffing out his chest, said, 'Sir, it *always* matters.'

Once again, no ticket was issued.

Maybe I never really believed VB would get old. Maybe the idea of it appalled me and I had refused to think about it. When age finally began to take its toll I found watching it more difficult than I could ever have imagined. VB detested even the smallest indignities of age and vehemently cursed them in private. Joss bore the brunt of the change in VB stoically and did her best to conceal his failing health to others as he became frustrated, irritable and acerbic at home.

To the rest of the world he presented a brave face. If asked how he was he'd confide that, 'We people who don't drink and don't smoke and go to bed early are almost bound to be well.' If questioned about how things went at the doctors he'd reply, 'The quack has been a bit off-colour recently so I just called in to see how he was.' He had to be very low indeed to admit that he was firing on about two out of six.

His sense of humour provided good cover for his failing short-term memory because people were accustomed to his amusing, nonsense comments. Remembering people's names was not a problem either because he could simply address people as 'Charlie'. And he still had that talent of being able to get away with things. When he forgot about a Territory Television board meeting until he was chased up, the board members were startled when his Greek fisherman's cap suddenly flew in onto the table through the slightly open door. There was no sign of him, until a voice from outside said, 'Can I still come?'

In the world political climate of the time the birthmark on the top of VB's head had become known as his 'Gorbachev'. Except during his time as a guest of the Japanese Emperor he had always worn a cap or hat out of doors, but the searing tropical sun had already taken its toll. When Gorbachev turned nasty VB was advised to have it permanently removed.

He was almost eighty years old and had not been well for months when he was admitted to hospital, but the operation was a complete success. For five days his head healed beautifully and he was due to be discharged on the Monday.

At around 2am on Saturday VB had a stroke. His condition was stable for twenty-four hours but by Sunday he was deteriorating quickly. His surgeon came to look at the dressing on his head that morning, to see that the skin graft had taken perfectly. Joss couldn't help but notice that VB's doctor, as he gently retaped the sticking plaster, struggled with his own tears. Everything had been going so well.

VB began to fade away on that Sunday. Among the many thoughts which crossed Joss's mind was, she being Catholic, the irony of

VB going on 1 November, All Saints Day. It was just the sort of thing he would do. Through the dreadful hours that followed, Joss, Antony, Penelope and I sat with VB, never leaving his bedside. Nurses and doctors hovered and all the signs were bad. The hours blurred into one another, but somewhere around the middle of the night a nurse whispered to us that he was dying, and from that moment it seemed VB did not dare close his eyes. The longest night we would ever know wore on, and I couldn't help but feel that if he could just hold on until the first rays of the sun filtered through the curtains, everything would be all right. People didn't die in the daytime. His dear daughter Penelope, all of eleven years old, stayed bravely with us all night, never once leaving her father to rest on the wheelie bed provided for her.

In the early hours of 2 November 1992, VB's remaining kidney began to fail. In the dim light we heard a nurse whisper that something called 'shutdown' had begun. Every so often VB's eyes closed a little and his breathing stopped. In unison the four of us jumped, terrified, desperately urging him to hang on, promising that he would be better soon. The old fighting spirit that had saved him when he lay on his death-bed in 1943 was still very much with him, and he responded to our pleas with every ounce of willpower he had left.

The duty nurse shook her head at our panic. 'You must let him go,' she said quietly. 'You're not doing him any favours in asking him to fight on, just prolonging his agony.' She asked us to go outside and talk about it while she sat with him.

Half blinded by tears we walked a little way down the dark corridor. Each of us knew that what she said was right, but Antony, Penelope and I could never have found the strength to do what had to be done. We walked, absolutely devastated, back into the room. We took our places by him once again and a little time went by. Then, ever so gently, Joss leaned over and whispered in his ear, 'It's all right to let go now, Bruce. I'll be with you all the way.' A flicker of recognition passed across his eyes. I felt him squeeze my hand with the one hand of his that still worked. We kissed him goodbye. Only then did the desperate labouring of our very determined father and husband begin to quieten.

Perkinsville was festooned with flowers and alive with people the week after VB died. Joss, Penelope, Antony and I spent the week walking around in a daze, with all the fuss and attention barely able to find a moment to be alone with our grief. Our grief was not so much for VB, for he had lived a very long, very happy and very full life. His time had come and he had gone as he wanted to go, without ever having had the indignity of needing a nurse maid, with no ado and no scenes. Our grief was more for ourselves, for the overwhelming sense of loss that we felt, for the sense that a big part of our life had been taken from us and that it was the end of an era.

The house seemed crowded that week. Crowded yet empty. All around lay reminders of VB: the line of pewter-mug sailing trophies rescued from besieged Singapore; *Coringle*'s majestic wooden wheel of which he was so fond; the 'Perkins Circus defeats Wharfie Clowns' plaque; the old ship's compass on which he used to hang his cap each evening; the painting of *Warrender* in a stormy sea; the miniature firing cannon made as a gift by his workshop staff and myriad nautical paraphernalia he had collected over the years.

In between planning the necessary formalities, laughter floated out to the street on the sultry November air, for it was difficult to talk about VB without thinking of something funny. On occasions a particularly raucous bout of hilarity caused Joss to look askance at her guests and to wonder what on earth the neighbours were thinking, yet she well knew that VB would never have condoned her being concerned about that. He never liked death to be a morbid affair.

VB had a splendid sendoff, one of which he would have approved. In the dusty corrugated-iron grandeur of the international cargo shed local dignitaries assembled alongside VB's family, friends and employees for what was, more than the mourning of his death, a celebration of his life. Darwin's Bishop Collins had known VB since the early days of shipping to the mission stations and, though VB was not one of his flock, he had asked to perform the funeral

service. Before the service Joss had mentioned her willing VB not
to go on All Saints Day, and he said to her, 'Turn around and look
at all these people. And you say he was not a saint?' She laughed.
No, he was far from a saint.

The sun began to set over the harbour for the final farewell. The
crowd took their places on the deck as *Frances Bay* steamed slowly,
with its bow door lowered to just above water level, past the moored
yachts and fishing boats of its namesake. In a clear place in the
harbour the engines quietened. From above the winches creaked
and ground as the bow door was lowered a little further. Joss bent
down close to the water, scattering her husband's ashes into the
warm sea that had been so much a part of his life. VB's favourite
Greek fisherman's cap followed and as the door dipped into the
warm water of Darwin Harbour, hundreds of flowers floated off
the door and onto the water.

There were more speeches later, when the dignitaries had left,
and an assortment of people ventured up onto the dais in the cargo
shed. The speeches moved easily between the eloquent, beautifully
crafted oration of a theatrical friend to the moving, straight from
the heart effort of VB's head truckie, Wombat. It was later that
night when it really hit me how the business VB had loved would
never be quite the same again. The yard was quiet, most people
had left and my husband and I were honoured with an invitation
to have a beer in the 'Twilight Tavern', the old VB Perkins & Co
office demountable that was now the yard crew's watering hole.

Sitting on a dirty, blue plastic chair I looked around, remembering
the days when this modest donga was the hub of the Perkins empire.
The serviceable woodette walls had not changed, but the maps and
shipping schedules that once adorned them had been replaced by
naked pin-up girls with larger than life bosoms. Dave the welder
and Pod the truckie, beer cans in hand and with a wistful look in
their eyes, leant back on their chairs and looked around them.

'Mr P used to sit here . . .' said Pod.

'Yeah,' said Dave. 'Just think. Mr P used to actually sit
here . . . Right bloody here.'

Index

THE HORSES TOO ARE GONE

Michael Keenan

The drought had reached crisis point. Cattle farmer Mike Keenan decided there was only one solution: he would have to get his starving cattle—and his beloved horses—to greener pastures north of the border. But when he finally got there he found his troubles had only just begun. South-west Queensland seemed like a modern-day Wild West, and as Keenan moved his cattle along the traditional droving routes in search of long-term pasture, he had to match wits with a host of characters—as well as Nature herself.

The Horses Too Are Gone is the true story of Keenan's struggle to survive against mounting odds, and it's an action-packed adventure that rivals any fiction. A fresh voice from the Bush, Mike Keenan writes with a deep passion and knowledge of Australian life on the land, tinged with a sadness and nostalgia for a way of life that is under threat. *The Horses Too Are Gone* will strike a chord with all Australians.

MIKE KEENAN is a fifth generation cattle farmer from New South Wales.

Bantam paperback   ISBN 0 73380 167 6

IN THE MIDDLE OF NOWHERE

Terry Underwood

One woman's powerful story of love and life on a remote cattle station

A city girl with dreams of the country, 18-year-old Terry Augustus was training to be a nurse at St Vincents Hospital when she met John Underwood, a young, born-and-bred cattleman. Flat on his back in Ward 3, nursing a serious spinal injury sustained while mustering cattle, John was itching to get home. And home he finally went, to his family's cattle station, Inverway, up in the Northern Territory. He promised Terry he'd write. A postcard arrived a week later.

After five long years of writing letters, John and Terry married and moved to their new home—a tent and a newly drilled bore in the middle of nowhere. Their love for each other was only matched by their love for this 'last frontier' in the heart of the Territory. Modern-day pioneers, John and Terry built their station from scratch and raised and educated a new generation of Underwoods there. Times were tough and there was heartbreak, danger and struggle, but the power of love and strength of family ties helped them overcome every obstacle.

In the Middle of Nowhere is their story. It's a story of beating the odds, told with warmth and a genuine knowledge of the Outback and its people, and the issues they face today. It's a real story of the Territory, and is as vast, dramatic and inspiring as the land that lies at the heart of this unforgettable book.

TERRY UNDERWOOD—wife, mother, cattlewoman, nurse, bookkeeper, cook, gardener, photographer and counsellor—was the winner of the Northern Territory Telstra Business Women's Business Owner of the Year in 1997, and was previously a Northern Territory Rural Woman of the Year finalist.

Bantam hardcover

ISBN 0 73380 130 7

GREG NORMAN: THE BIOGRAPHY

Lauren St John

Greg Norman has been the best golfer in the world for almost a decade. He is an electrifying performer—as ruthless on the golf course as he is in the board-room—and a magnetic personality, yet his career record is rather less than the sum of these parts. Famous victories, such as the 1986 and 1993 Opens, are interspersed with inexplicable failings and outrageous strokes of misfortune, most notoriously at Augusta, where he lost a six-stroke lead to Nick Faldo in the 1996 Masters.

Norman's bold, do-or-die approach to the game is the key to his popularity as well as his phenomenal financial success. He lives at 100mph, scuba-diving with sharks, racing Ferraris with Nigel Mansell and taking joy-rides in F-16 jets. In between he plays golf with Bill Clinton and negotiates multi-million-dollar deals, then he flies in to tournaments by helicopter and wins by five or ten strokes.

In charting Greg Norman's tempestuous career, Lauren St John has journeyed from his roots in Queensland to Great White Shark Enterprises on the other side of the world in West Palm Beach, Florida, interviewing his wife, his caddies, coaches, managers, friends and foes, and, of course, Greg Norman himself. The result is a comprehensive and dramatic portrait of one of the most gifted and charismatic golfers ever.

LAUREN ST JOHN has worked for the *Sunday Times* for the past six years. She has also written for *Golf World, Today's Golfer* and *Golf Weekly*. Her other books include *Shooting at Clouds: Inside the PGA European Tour* and *Seve*, the acclaimed biography of the Spanish genius Seve Ballesteros. Her last book, *Out of Bounds*, was shortlisted for the 1995 William Hill Sports Book of the Year.

Bantam paperback   ISBN 0 73380 098 X

Everybody has a Packer story. This is the real one . . .

THE RISE AND RISE OF KERRY PACKER

Paul Barry

A warts-and-all account of a man who despises social niceties, doesn't expect to like people or be liked by them, and is powerful and bloody-minded enough not to give a damn what anyone thinks.

Canberra Times

Reporter Paul Barry comes to this book with no mean reputation. He pulled no punches in a biography of Alan Bond, nor does he hold any in this account of Packer . . . His thorough account of an enduring dynasty paints a picture of how individuals can have the levers of power pulled to suit their interests.

The Courier Mail, *Brisbane*

Two years of intensive research and hundreds of interviews make *The Rise and Rise of Kerry Packer* a compelling biography of Australia's least understood tycoon.

The Rise and Rise of Kerry Packer was shortlised for the 1994 CUB Banjo Award for Non-Fiction and has sold more than 90,000 copies in hardcover. PAUL BARRY's first book was the highly acclaimed *The Rise and Fall of Alan Bond*. Born and educated in England, Paul was a journalist with BBC TV before coming to Australia in 1987 to work for the ABC TV's *Four Corners*. His films have won numerous awards and commendations.

Bantam paperback   ISBN 1 86359 338 1